Augsburg College
George Sverdrup Library
Minneapolis, Minnesota 55404

WITHDRAWN

PADUA IN THE AGE OF DANTE

Author and Publishers are
indebted to the trustees
of
THE LITTLE FUND
for a contribution towards
the cost of publication

TO
MY MOTHER

Fresco, S. Antonio, Padua

Giusto de' Menabuoi: a view of Padua, with S. Antonio and B. Luca Belludi in the foreground

PADUA
in the
AGE of DANTE

by

J. K. HYDE

MANCHESTER UNIVERSITY PRESS
BARNES & NOBLE, INC., NEW YORK

© 1966 J. K. HYDE

All rights reserved
MANCHESTER UNIVERSITY PRESS
316-324 OXFORD ROAD,
MANCHESTER 13, ENGLAND

First published
in the United States
1966
BARNES & NOBLE, INC.
105 Fifth Avenue, New York 3

Printed in Great Britain by Thomas Nelson (Printers) Ltd, London and Edinburgh

Contents

	page
Preface	vii
Abbreviations	x
Note on Terms	xii
I Introduction	1

PART ONE
THE GOVERNING CLASS

II City and Contado	29
III Nobles and Magnates	57
IV Knights and Podestà	91
V Judges and Doctors of Law	121
VI The Guildsmen	154
The Notaries	154
Doctors and Physicians	175
Other Guildsmen	178
Moneylenders and Usurers	181

PART TWO
THE GOVERNING CLASS IN ACTION

VII The Commune and the *Pars Marchionis*	193
VIII The Expansion of the Paduan Commune	220
IX The Crisis of the Paduan Commune	252
X Padua and the Dawn of the Renaissance	283
Appendices	
The Paduan Guilds in 1287	311
The Statute of April 1278	312
The Matricula of the Paduan College of Doctors of Law	315
List of Sources for the History of the Paduan Commune	318
Bibliography	326
Index	336

GENEALOGICAL TABLES

1	The Estensi	70
2	The Da Castelnovo	74
3	The Da Lozzo	75
4	The Camposanpiero	81
5	The Carrara	83
6	The Papafava	84
7	The Enghelfredi	117
8	The Maccaruffi	120
9	The Campanati	137
10	The Da Prato	142
11	The Tadi or Da Rossano	149
12	The Buzzaccarini	152
13	The D'Andrea	164
14	The Mainardini	165
15	The Dalesmanini	186
16	The Scrovegni	189

PLATES

Giusto de' Menabuoi: a view of Padua, with S. Antonio and B. Luca Belludi in the foreground — *frontispiece*
reproduced by courtesy of the Museo Civico, Padua

I The Seal of the Paduan Commune — *facing page* 32
reproduced by courtesy of the Museo Civico, Padua

II Giotto: Enrico Scrovegni presenting the Arena Chapel to the Virgin — *facing page* 190
reproduced by courtesy of the Museo Civico, Padua

MAPS

I	The City of Padua in 1320	36
II	North-East Italy	232
III	The Paduan Contado 1276-8	*end of book*

Preface

Padua in the Age of Dante is an attempt to give a broad picture of the governing class of an Italian city-state in the years usually characterised as the culminating period of mediaeval culture, but sometimes described in Italy as the very early Renaissance. This double terminology is a reflection of the fact that it was in the late thirteenth and early fourteenth century that the distinctive urban civilisation of northern Italy, which had been growing in obscurity for some two centuries, came of age and was set upon the course which was to lead to the greater Renaissance of the fifteenth century. The age of Dante may be regarded as a time of relative prosperity and early maturity which was brought to an end by the economic and political troubles of the mid-fourteenth century.

The approach adopted has been that of the social historian; as, however, social history has become a fashionable phrase to which a number of different meanings have been attached, it may be useful to make clear at the outset the sense in which it will be used here. In the first place, I understand by social history a history which is primarily concerned with social facts, that is, the ideas which people have about society and the way they divide it into groups. In most societies, this means chiefly two things, the concept and role of the family, and class structure. Part One is chiefly concerned with social history in this narrow sense. The first two chapters set the topographical and economic background for the whole study: Chapters III to VI consider various economic and occupational categories within the governing class with reference to the basic ideas of the family and nobility which have been explored in the first part of Chapter III.

Social historians have rarely confined themselves to the rather narrow territory which is exclusively theirs; commonly they have used it as a vantage point for studying the structure of a society as a whole, so that social history has come to mean a type of history in which the inter-relations between social, economic, political and intellectual aspects play an important part. It is with social history in this broader sense that Part Two is concerned. Chapters VII to IX consider the action of the governing class in the political sphere, or the relations between the social and political structures; Chapter X deals with the intellectual tradition found in the Paduan writers of the period, regarded as the reflections by an articulate minority upon the life and experience of the governing class as a whole.

The attempt to write history in depth inevitably involves the writer in a number of difficulties. The social history of even a relatively small society like that of mediaeval Padua is in fact incredibly complex and can only be conveyed to the reader by carefully selected examples. On the whole, I have concentrated on a relatively small number of representative families and individuals who consequently reappear in several different parts of the book. I have tried to minimise the disadvantages of this piecemeal treatment by the liberal use of cross references; in places it has been hard to find the narrow path between superfluous repetition and the crediting of the reader with excessive feats of memory. Another problem raised by the broad approach is that the writer is bound to trespass upon many specialised fields where he can hardly avoid making statements unacceptable to at least some of the experts. I can only express the hope that the mistakes which I have made will prove to be of the kind that will provoke fruitful discussion and further investigation.

Almost every problem encountered in the preparation and writing of this book has had some effect on the references and bibliography. In principle, I have tried to give the ultimate source of the facts and opinions put forward in the text, and as this book is mainly based on unpublished archive material, this has meant that most of the references are to documentary sources. In the interests of simplicity, the citation of secondary authorities has been restricted to works with a close bearing on the argument or helpful for the general orientation of the reader; in particular, no attempt has been made to cover certain controversies over matters of detail. The final bibliography includes only those books and articles cited in the text or notes, and no attempt has been made to give a comprehensive guide to the literature on any part of the subject. It is preceded by a list of the chief primary sources for the history of the Paduan commune from 1256 to 1328 which indicates, where appropriate, where they may be found in print. This list is intended to provide both the credentials of the present study and a guide to those wishing to undertake further research.

During the preliminary research and the writing of this book I have received help from so many people that it would be impossible to name them all; all that I can do here is mention a few to whom I feel a special debt. The original idea of undertaking such a study was given to me by Professor R. W. Southern. The guidance and encouragement I owe to Mr D. M. Bueno de Mesquita has extended from my initiation into Italian studies right up to the last stages of the preparation of this book, when he was kind enough to read through the penultimate draft of the introduction. The draft of Chapter X was read by Dr R. W. Hunt and his comments enabled me to avoid a number of pitfalls. At different times Professor R. Weiss, Dr N. Rubenstein and Dr P. J. Jones have given me the benefit of their expert advice.

In Italy, my first debt is to Professor P. Sambin who was my protector and guide from first to last. I am grateful to Professor E. Ruffini who instituted the Luca Ruffini Scholarship from which I benefited during my first year in Padua. One of the incidental pleasures of my research has been the courtesy and co-operation I have received from the librarians and archivists of the various libraries and archives in which I have worked. I wish to record my gratitude to Count Novello Papafava, whose liberality in allowing me to consult his private archives was in accordance with the tradition of encouragement to scholars for which his family has long been noted. Also, my thanks are due to Dr Guido Billanovich, whose unrivalled knowledge of the documents relating to the Paduan pre-humanists saved me from some disastrous omissions.

My greatest debt is to my wife for her help and encouragement during the preparation of this book, and particularly for her helpful criticism at every stage in its composition.

J. K. HYDE

Abbreviations

AAP	Atti e Memorie dell'Accademia di scienze, lettere ed arti, Padua.
AAV	Atti dell'Accademia di agricoltura, scienze e lettere di Verona.
AD	Archivio Diplomatico, Archivio di Stato, Padua.
AIV	Atti dell'Istituto Veneto di scienze, lettere ed arti.
ALKM	Archiv für Literatur und Kirchengeschichte des Mittelalters.
AMS	Archivio Marchionale Segreto, Archivio di Stato, Modena.
ARAP	Atti e Memorie della R.Accademia di scienze, lettere ed arti, Padua.
ARIV	Atti del R. Istituto Veneto di scienze, lettere ed arti.
AS	Archivio di Stato.
ASI	Archivio Storico Italiano.
ASL	Archivio Storico Lombardo.
AV	Archivio Veneto.
BISI	Bollettino dell Istituto Storico Italiano.
BJRL	Bulletin of the John Rylands Library.
BMCB	Bollettino del Museo Civico di Bassano.
BMCP	Bollettino del Museo Civico di Padova.
BP	Biblioteca Piazza or Padovana, the local history collection in the Biblioteca Civica, Padua.
BRDSPU	Bollettino della R. Deputazione di Storia Patria per l'Umbria.
BSC	Bollettino Storico Cremonese.
CDP	Codice Diplomatico Padovano.
DSSCDCI	Documenti e Studi per la Storia del Commercio e del Diritto Commerciale Italiano.
FSI	Fonti per la Storia d'Italia.
GSLI	Giornale Storico della Letteratura Italiana.
JEH	Journal of Economic History.
MGH.SS	Monumenta Germaniae Historica, Scriptores.
Misc.RDVSP	Miscellanea di Storia Veneta, R. Deputazione Veneta di Storia Patria.
Mon.RDVSP	Monumenti della R. Deputazione Veneta di Storia Patria.

MRIV	Memorie del R. Istituto Veneto di scienze, lettere ed arti.
NAV	Nuovo Archivio Veneto.
RDSPR(M)	R. Deputazione di Storia Patria per l'Emilia e la Romagna, Sezione di Modena, Studi e Documenti.
RIS	Rerum Italicarum Scriptores.
RSDI	Rivista di Storia del Diritto Italiano.
RSI	Rivista Storica Italiana.
Stat.Coll.Iud.	Statuta et Matricula Collegii Iudicum, Archivio Antico dell'Università, Padua, MS n.123.
Stat.Com.	Statuti del comune di Padova sec.XII all'anno 1285, ed. A. Gloria (1873).
Stat.Not.	Statuti della Fraglia dei Notai c.1260–1341, Archivio Notarile, Padua.

Note on Terms

Currency

All sums of money given in £ s. d. in the text and notes refer to Venetian deniers petty unless otherwise stated. Venetian deniers gross (gr.), worth about 32 deniers petty, were sometimes used. The gold florin was quoted at 22d. gr. in 1300 (A. S. Vicenza, Torre 34, n. 27) or £3: 9s. od. petty in 1323 (Arch. Vescovile, Padua, Diversorum f. 2v.).

Measure of Land

Measures of land in the Paduan documents of the period are given in *campi* or occasionally in *mansi*. The *campo padovano* is thought to have been the equivalent of 3,862 square metres, or rather less than an English acre. The meaning of *mansus* is not clear, but it seems to have denoted an area of about 20 *campi*.

Genealogical Tables

The tables given in the text are intended only to illustrate the argument and are not necessarily a complete record of the families in question.

CHAPTER I

Introduction

EARLY in the year 1300, the Paduan annals record that the incoming *podestà* ordered a period of public festivities, with jousting and other amusements, to celebrate the great freedom enjoyed by the city (*propter maximam Paduae libertatem*). The central square was cleared of the stalls of the tradesmen which generally filled it, and the lists were set up under the walls of the great Palazzo Comunale where the judges of the commune normally sat. In the crowd which occupied the stands around the margin of the square, the nobles and knights, judges and guildsmen who constituted the city's governing class, stood out in the special robes which they wore for the occasion. The immediate pretext for the celebrations is obscure, but whatever it may have been, there is no doubt that the Paduan commune was near the height of its prosperity, influence and power. Among the older spectators of the brilliant scene, many must have recalled the very different state of the city some forty years before when it was emerging with its resources pillaged and its upper classes decimated from the tyranny of Ezzelino III da Romano. Ezzelino had gained control of Padua in 1237 largely through the support of the Emperor Frederick II whose prestige he skilfully exploited to serve his own ends. In his heyday he ruled a substantial part of north-eastern Italy, from Verona to the fringes of the Venetian lagoon, ostensibly as an Imperial agent but in fact as an independent despot. His state represented one of the earliest attempts to bring a number of major Italian cities under the *signoria* of a single individual, and at first his firm government must have brought considerable benefits to some classes of the population. But in Padua, Ezzelino never succeeded in winning over the majority of the nobility and the leading citizens, and his control of the city was maintained only by force. The last years of his rule were marked by a reign of terror, which came to an end in June 1256 with the capture of the city by a crusading army of Paduan exiles and Guelph partisans from neighbouring cities. It was a rare occurrence for a major city to be taken by assault, and the comparative ease with which the capture of the city was accomplished is a measure both of the incompetence of Ezzelino's lieutenant and of the lack of support for the regime among the citizens.

The capture of the city in 1256 opened a new chapter in the history of the Paduan commune. Unlike later despots, Ezzelino seems to have made little or no changes in the formal constitutions of the cities he controlled, but his personal government emptied their institutions of all real power. The returning exiles and their friends restored the constitution to something like what it had been in 1237; they repealed all Ezzelino's legislation and destroyed the records. Carried through in the aftermath of a great victory, the revolution which this represented was remarkably successful. For the next fifty years, while most of the cities of Italy were shaken from time to time by civil wars and revolutions, and many communes succumbed to various forms of personal rule, the Paduan state enjoyed a period of stability and orderly development, during which the franchise was widened and the guilds were given a greater voice in the government without any breach in the continuity of the essentials of the constitution. The disputes which developed with the magnates and the clergy, though they sometimes led to violence, never constituted a serious threat to the stability of the state. From the final extermination of the Da Romano family in 1260, Padua enjoyed more than forty years' freedom from major external threats, and wars were few, of short duration and on the whole successful. Favourable circumstances enabled the commune to more than double the territory under its control, first, in 1266, by extending a protectorate over the neighbouring city of Vicenza and its contado, and then by the annexation of the county of Rovigo in 1308. These conditions brought wealth not only to established families but to many individuals of the professional and guildsman class, while the prosperity of the state can be judged from its public works, like the reconstruction of the Palazzo Comunale and the building of the basilica of S. Antonio.

Within less than a generation, the fifty years ending in the first decade of the fourteenth century had come to be seen by Paduan writers as something of a golden age. The deterioration in the position of the Paduan commune first became apparent with the arrival in Italy of the Emperor-elect Henry of

Luxemburg in 1310. A revolt in the subject city of Vicenza was given Veronese support and there soon developed a life and death struggle between Padua and Verona for the domination of the Venetian hinterland. In their basic resources, the two cities were probably not unequal, but the Veronese had the decisive advantage of a unified command, Cangrande della Scala being both the virtual head of state and a general of considerable ability. Under the hammer blows of successive military defeats, the Paduan state disintegrated from within. The various parties and factions within the ruling class which had co-operated well enough in better times, were divided as to what should be done in the increasingly desperate situation and turned on one another. From 1314 onwards, the state was shaken by riots and threatened by civil war so that in July 1318, those parties which wished to preserve the independence of the city agreed to elect Giacomo da Carrara *defensor, protector* and *gubernator* of the commune as a means of securing the unity they desired; eighteen months later, the same interests arranged the transfer of the *signoria* to Frederick of Hapsburg, one of the contenders for the Imperial title, in return for a promise of help against Cangrande. Neither of these manoeuvres represented a fundamental and irrevocable change in the constitution, and neither led to victory or an acceptable peace.

The death agony of the Paduan commune lasted until 1328, when Marsiglio da Carrara seized control of the city and opened the gates to the Veronese. The installation of Marsiglio as *signore* brought to an end the communal period in the city's political development; for the next seventy-five years, the Carrara dynasty was the focus of Paduan political life. Beginning as creatures of the Della Scala, the Carraresi came to represent Paduan independence and to them the citizens seem to have been willing enough to surrender the much-abused self-government of the communal era. Admiration for the brilliance of their court and their sometimes heroic struggles against powerful external enemies should not be allowed to obscure the fact that under the Carrara, Padua was little more than a buffer-state between the Della Scala of Verona and the Visconti of Milan on the one hand, and the Venetians on the other. The balance finally descended in 1405 on the side of Venice, and Padua's independent history came to an end with the absorption of the Paduan state by the Venetian republic.

The years 1256 to 1328 form a clearly defined period in Paduan history which may be conveniently described as the communal period. Politically, it was characterised by the sovereignty of the Consiglio Maggiore which from 1277 numbered a thousand members out of an adult male population of not more than eleven thousand. This distinctive polity was only the most visible manifestation of certain underlying economic and social patterns; although they are much more difficult to discover and describe, the Paduan social structure and the economy which supported it were an integral part of the physiognomy of the city in this particular period. This is no doubt true of all societies in all periods; what makes the Paduan example particularly interesting is that the constitution, by spreading political rights relatively widely, made possible the expression of the interests of the citizen body in political life more directly and immediately than would have been the case under a less representative form of government. The political leaders were dependent on the votes of the Consiglio Maggiore, they had also to respect the ideal of government in the common interest, *ad communem* and not *per partem*. In the eyes of a small intellectual *élite*, Padua was a *respublica*. The characteristic writers of the communal period were both citizens and intellectuals, and in their works can be traced the thread of a local tradition which can at times add a further dimension to the description of the period, that of representatives of the governing class reflecting upon their experience.

The subject of this study is what can be known of the ruling class of the Paduan commune. Inevitably, the sources go a long way to defining the limits of the picture which can be drawn. The records before 1256 are so sparse that the early history of the commune will always be obscure.[1] Even for the period after 1256, the sources for a detailed study of the workings of the communal government no longer exist, for the revolutions of the fourteenth century took a heavy toll of the public records of the commune and others were lost at a later date. For

---

[1] See A. Bonardi, 'Le origini del comune di Padova', *ARAP* XIV (1897–8), pp. 209–54, and XV (1898–9), pp. 1–38; M. Roberti, 'Nuove ricerche sopra l'antica costituzione del comune di Padova', *NAV* ns. III (1902), pp. 77–97. For the documents relating to Padua up to 1183, see A. Gloria, *Codice Diplomatico Padovano* [*CDP*], Mon.RDVSP ser. I, vols. II, IV & VI (1877–81).

example, of the great spate of legislation passed by the Consiglio Maggiore, very little which was not incorporated into the communal code of 1276–85 or the Carrara code of 1362, has survived. The private documents of the communal period are fairly numerous, but they give only a partial picture of the private transactions of the time. The bulk of them were preserved until the nineteenth century in the archives of religious houses, and, in general, they throw light only on those secular estates which passed sooner or later into religious hands. Few family archives go back to the fourteenth century, and the notarial records which in other cities illuminate the business life of the period, are in Padua disappointingly meagre. If it were dependent on documentary material alone, the political history of the Paduan commune would be sketchy and its social history almost non-existent.[1]

Inadequate in themselves, the documentary sources have an important role as a check and support for the literary sources. The Paduan commune was outstanding in the production of historical writings. Apart from a number of annals which together give a continuous outline narrative from 1174, literary activity in Padua was concentrated into two short periods which coincide with the rise and fall of the commune. The events of the first half of the thirteenth century leading up to the restoration of the commune are covered by Rolandino's history, which appeared in 1262; at a more popular level, the *Chronicon Marchiae Tarvisinae et Lombardie* contains much material relating to Padua, and continues up to 1270. The dissolution of the Paduan commune is described in the historical works of Albertino Mussato, a Paduan citizen who played a leading part in many of the events which he records. Henry of Luxemburg's Italian expedition and its repercussions in Padua are the subject matter of his *Historia Augusta*; a continuation known as the *De Gestis Italicorum post Henricum VII* carries the story of the commune, with some lacunae, down to the last months of 1320, while the *De Traditione Patavii ad Canem Grandem* is a monograph on the establishment of the *signoria* of Marsiglio da Carrara between 1325 and 1328. Finally, the unpretentious chronicle of Guglielmo Cortusi which is a primary source from 1311 to 1368, is especially valuable for its picture of the whole transition from

[1] See List of Sources for the History of the Paduan Commune 1256–1328, below, pp. 318–25.

the commune to the *signoria*. One consequence of this distribution of the sources is that the composition of the Paduan ruling class becomes most clear during the process of disintegration.

The works of Giovanni da Nono which belong to an entirely different non-narrative tradition, were also compiled during the last years of the commune round about the year 1318. The *De Generatione aliquorum civium urbis Padue*, which is the most important of the trilogy, is one of the earliest and best examples of the Italian municpal social chronicles, a genre which became very popular during the Renaissance. It is the indispensable foundation for the social history of the commune. Other insights into the Paduan ethos can be gained from the miscellaneous writings of the Paduan pre-humanist group, especially the masterpiece of the movement, Mussato's tragedy *Ecerinide*, which represents a re-working of the Ezzelino legend in classical dress, intended to teach the lesson of Rolandino to the generation of Henry of Luxemburg and Cangrande della Scala. The parallel between the Emperors Frederick II and Henry VII, and their Veronese allies Ezzelino da Romano and Cangrande della Scala was one which occurred also to Da Nono and was apparently widely accepted by Paduan citizens. The idea of the communal period as a distinct era in the city's development had been formulated almost before the republican regime had been brought to an end.

Although this study is concerned with two or three generations of the ruling class of only one city among many, and one moreover which never exerted its influence beyond a small region and did not become the nucleus of a Renaissance state, it is not an essay in local history in the sense in which that term is generally understood. The English historian is accustomed to regard national history as the dominant and determinant, and local history as subsidiary and contingent. In Italian history up to the nineteenth century, these roles are reversed; Italian history is essentially local history. This is especially true of the period from 1250 to 1494 when it is quite apparent that the centralising forces are conservative and anachronistic and the growing points are clearly in the localities and mainly in the city-states. It is this point rather than mere size, intellectual distinction or political autonomy which gives the history of Padua a radically different significance from that of say York or Toulouse at the same period. The latter were both politically and culturally subordinate parts of a larger entity; the major Italian cities, on the other hand, were the autonomous components of a distinctive culture, and one which was, moreover, in many ways the most advanced in Europe.

Italian society from the thirteenth century, predominantly urban, lay, post-manorial and post-feudal, is an outstanding exception to almost all the historians' generalisations about the high Middle Ages, yet it was not a fringe area like Scandinavia or eastern Europe but the centre of Christendom. Even in the best modern studies of mediaeval Europe, the Italian element tends to be under-represented mainly because the national histories are so few and present such a confusing picture. This state of affairs is not new. Before the nineteenth century there were histories of Italian literature and art, and accounts of foreign invasions, but beyond these, political histories of Italy scarcely existed.[1] Historical writing was in the hands of men whose first loyalty was to their local city, whether this was still politically independent or not; at their best, these local historians present a loving picture of the city as a social organism, drawing its nourishment from the soil and with the branches of its civil constitution supporting fruits in the shape of public buildings, works of art and illustrious citizens.[2] Some of the most attractive examples of this genre belong to the sixteenth and seventeenth centuries; the most worthwhile embody the fruits of eighteenth-century erudition. The best general history of the Paduan region, Verci's *Storia della Marca Trivigiana*, was published from 1786 to 1791, and the last history of the Paduan church, Dondi dall'Orologio's *Dissertazione sopra l'Istoria Ecclesiastica Padovana*, appeared between 1802 and 1815.

During the nineteenth century, the character of Italian historiography was transformed. On the one hand, history became the concern of professional historians and academic specialisation split up the unity instinctively grasped by the

[1] For a stimulating introduction to the special problems of Italian historiography, see D. Hay, *The Italian Renaissance in its Historical Background* (1961), pp. 26-57.
[2] Two notable Paduan examples are B. Scardeoni, *De Antiquitate Urbis Patavii et Claris Civibus Patavinis* (1560), and A. Portenari, *La Felicità di Padova* (1623), both continuing the tradition established in the fifteenth century by M. Savonarola, *Libellus de Magnificis Ornamentis Regiae Civitatis Padue*, the best edition of which is by A. Segarizzi, RIS XXIV, xv (1901).

writers of the old school; at the same time, the ethos of the Risorgimento inhibited Italians from recognising frankly the radical disunity of their past. As a result, syntheses at the local level were discouraged, and the way left open for a number of short cuts to national history. The most obvious of these was to concentrate on the major cities, especially those which provided the nucleus for one of the larger states of the Renaissance. Another tendency, often almost unconscious, was to take a single city as the norm by which all others must be measured; Davidsohn's monumental *Geschichte von Florenz* (1896–1927) in which every aspect of Florentine history was considered, even if the various elements were not very satisfactorily related to one another, probably did a lot to encourage historians to regard Florence as the Italian commune *par excellence*. Yet heterogeneity was the essence of the Italian scene; the development of so many centres of contrasting types—trading towns and industrial towns, bankers' towns and agrarian backwaters—cannot be reduced to a single scheme. Each type made some contribution to the complexion of the whole.

In the last forty years or so, there has been an increased appreciation of the economic side of Italian history, closely related to the opening up of notarial archives by historical research.[1] The leading position occupied by Italian merchants and financiers in the business life of western Europe has been underlined, though the tendency to regard the Italian international merchant-banker in isolation from his native city is not without its dangers.[2] At the same time, much more of the economic diversity of the various regions of Italy has been revealed; though many details remain to be filled in, it is already clear that territories which might be geographically contiguous could present the sharpest contrasts in terms of their economic development. But, most important of all, there has in recent years been a largely unheralded reaffirmation of the primacy of local studies, and some pioneer economico-social or socio-political histories of individual cities have begun to create

---

[1] The most recent general survey is G. Luzzatto, *An Economic History of Italy from the Fall of the Roman Empire to the beginning of the Sixteenth Century*, trans. P. J. Jones (1961), with a useful bibliography, pp. 168–74.

[2] Y. Renouard, *Les Hommes d'Affaires Italiens au Moyen Age* (1949); A. Sapori, *Le Marchand Italien au Moyen Age* (1952), with a very full bibliography.

the essential materials from which a general picture of mediaeval Italy and her place in Europe may some day be built up.¹

It is hardly possible to write a local study without at least some working hypotheses as to its relationship with a wider world, so much does the assessment of local manifestations depend on the way in which the general and normal development is envisaged. It is better that these hypotheses should be stated rather than allowed to remain implicit; even if the lines of the Italian and European setting have later to be modified, it will be better to present the story of the Paduan commune in a context which is tentative rather than in no context at all.

To trace the main lines of Italian development through the central period of the Middle Ages, the most convenient point of departure is the Carolingian age. In the first place, it was in this period that the fundamental division of Italy, which has persisted in some respects down to the present day, reached its definitive form. Earlier invasions and settlements had long before destroyed the unity imposed by Rome; nevertheless, it happens that those parts of Italy which were effectively linked to the empire of Charlemagne through innumerable local variations follow a single pattern, while those parts which remained outside—the South, the islands and Venice—follow a course which is radically different. Again, the institutions which form the background to the Italy of the communes—the Empire, the counts and the temporal power of the bishops—cannot easily be understood without reference to the Carolingian period. Finally, in the early ninth century, the differences between Carolingian Italy and the rest of western Europe were probably less than at any other time in the Middle Ages; for Italy and Europe, the tenth century marked the parting of the ways which were to lead to the striking contrasts of the early Renaissance.²

Nineteenth-century historians tended to be preoccupied with the phenomenon of Italian disunity in the Middle Ages,

---

[1] E.g. D. Herlihy, *Pisa in the Early Renaissance* (1958); E. Fiumi, *Storia economica e sociale di San Gimignano* (1961); E. Cristiani, *Nobiltà e popolo nel comune di Pisa* (1962).

[2] For early mediaeval Italy, see G. Romano and A. Solmi, *Le dominazioni barbariche in Italia* (1940–5), and G. C. Mor, *L'età feudale* (1952), both in the series Storia Politica d'Italia, ed. F. Vallardi.

which they variously ascribed to national character, the influence of the popes or the German-Imperial connection. Seen from the standpoint of the mid-ninth century, the breakdown of the Regnum Italiae does not seem to require any special explanation. Everywhere in the former Carolingian state, the central power collapsed, and only in France did the subsequent revivals lead eventually to the emergence of a strong kingdom. It may be doubted whether Italian affairs would have taken a radically different course even without the strains imposed by the Imperial claims of the Italian kings and the intervention of outside powers in the peninsula. The Carolingian order was already largely in ruins when, in the mid-tenth century, Otto I established the link between the German and Imperial crowns which was to persist for the rest of the Middle Ages. Though, in the long run, the German connection may have made the attainment of an effective Italian kingdom impossible, it is also arguable that through its agency, the kingdom was kept in being for much longer than if it had been dependent on Italian resources alone. By a gradual decline, the German Emperors in Italy passed from being effective though intermittent rulers to become the leaders of a faction until, in the end, they were merely the tools of the factions. At what point the Imperial cause in Italy was irretrievably lost will always remain a matter of opinion. The obvious landmarks are the Investiture Contest of the late eleventh century, the stand of the Lombard League against Frederick Barbarossa in the late twelfth century and the failure of Frederick II to build a new state in the North and Centre on the basis of his Sicilian kingdom. With the extinction of the Hohenstaufen in 1266, it is clear enough in retrospect that the Empire could never be rebuilt, yet intelligent Italians continued to look for an Imperial saviour until well on into the fourteenth century.

The moral effects of the continued existence of the Empire in the wings, as it were, of the Italian scene, far outweighed the material results of the later Imperial expeditions. In a period of the greatest political fragmentation, the Emperor personified a wider loyalty than that provided by civic patriotism. For the Italians of the Middle Ages, the Empire was a part of the unchangeable order of things; if the Emperor himself was seldom seen, they were reminded of his existence by the laws of Justinian which were daily cited in their courts. Naturally, these ideas had a stronger hold on the literate minority than on the population at large, but they could affect political behaviour; it is noticeable that it required considerable provocation to induce the communes into a direct revolt against the Emperor; whenever possible, resistance was directed only against his lieutenants. Another result of this mentality was that for generations the cities made peace and war, legislated and raised taxes without reference to any higher power, without ever asserting the sovereignty which they were exercising in theoretical terms. Nominal subjection to a universal Empire remained the foundation of their political thought long after it had ceased to have any real meaning. The other great check on local self-sufficiency was, of course, the Church; even the highly developed cult of local saints could not entirely obscure the fact that Christianity was a universal religion, and great as were the powers of the later mediaeval Italian state over the clergy, the claims of the papacy could not be completely ignored. Together the Empire and the Church point towards the great gulf dividing the mediaeval city-state from its ancient predecessor. The citizens of the communes valued their local independence but they lacked the Aristotelian conviction of the ultimate value of the life of the *polis*.

The multitude of states which makes the political map of twelfth-century Italy resemble a patchwork quilt, was a special instance of the breakdown which at some stage affected all the former territories of the Carolingian state. In part, this condition was the result of centuries of relative anarchy brought on by invasions and the impoverishment of the crown, and accentuated in Italy by the absence of the Emperor for long periods. But it was not only the links between the crown and the local authorities which broke down; local jurisdictions were also subject to a process of fragmentation which was in part the result of the policies of the Emperors themselves.[1] Charlemagne had introduced a potentially disruptive element by his reliance on both the bishop and the count for the administration of the county; succeeding Emperors leaned more and more heavily on

---

[1] See P. Vaccari, *Dall'unità romana al particolarismo giuridico del medio evo* (1936); idem, *La territorialità come base dell'ordinamento giuridico del contado nell'Italia medioevale* (2nd. ed. 1963); F. Niccolai, 'Città e signori', *RSDI* XIV (1941), pp. 168–291.

the Church, at first granting to bishops and abbots immunity from the jurisdiction of the counts and finally transferring full comital powers to them. As a result, by the mid-eleventh century, most of the major Lombard cities were ruled by their bishops, while in the outlying areas and particularly in Tuscany, the lay nobility still retained much of their power. During the eleventh century, the chronicles record a number of obscure revolts by the citizens against the bishops, but it was only in the last quarter of the century that the turmoils associated with the Investiture Contest and the First Crusade shattered the façade of the old order to reveal the institution to which the future was to belong—the commune.

Italy did not become a land of cities in the eleventh century; in a sense it had always been so from classical times. It is true that between the sixth and the tenth centuries, the cities, in common with the rest of the country, had passed through periods of impoverishment and depopulation; many were destroyed and lay derelict for a time; a few, like Aquileia, were never rebuilt. Yet there can be little doubt that in some places, the continuity of urban life from Roman times was never broken, and offices for the regulation of highways and drainage, trades, markets and local defence—the basic functions without which any but the most rudimentary urban life is impossible—may have continued without a break. Intermittent evidence shows the citizens gathered into assemblies representing either the urban parishes (*pievi* or *populi*) or the gates of the Roman city, for the administration of affairs of common interest. The city as a whole, acting through the assembly before the cathedral (*conventus ante ecclesiam*) retained the elements of a corporate personality, including the power to hold common property. More important than the survival of individual cities, was the fact that northern Italy, apart from a few mountainous or frontier regions, remained a country governed and administered from urban centres. Even the Lombards, the least urban of Italy's invaders, based their rule on a series of royal cities under the direct control of the king's *gastaldi*, while, in Pavia, they had a true capital city of a kind unknown in the barbarian states north of the Alps. Paradoxically, the jurisdiction of town-based officials was probably never more restricted than in the eleventh and twelfth centuries, the heyday of the castle-dwelling nobility whose connection with the town might be slight or non-existent;

yet it is precisely at this time that the signs of an urban revival become unmistakable.[1]

Though the Italian cities did not, like many of their counterparts in northern Europe, owe their existence to the mediaeval economic revival, they were nevertheless completely transformed by it. Much attention has been given by historians in recent years to the economic history of the Middle Ages and, although the nature of the sources means that many aspects will always remain obscure, the general outline of an economic revival beginning about the tenth century and proceeding, with only temporary and local setbacks, until the early fourteenth century, has become clear. The first aspects of this economic movement to attract attention were the growth of towns and industry in Flanders and Italy, and the development of commercial relations linking these centres with the eastern Mediterranean; in the last forty years, the dominant role played by Italian merchants and bankers along the whole length of the London-Levant trade axis has been extensively illustrated by Italian and American scholars.[2] It is obvious, however, that this so-called commercial revolution cannot have stood alone, but must have been accompanied by something of the nature of an agricultural revolution which made it possible to feed the great towns of the thirteenth- and early-fourteenth-century boom. Indeed, of the two, the agricultural revolution was in a sense the more fundamental, since it appears to lie nearer to the root of the change in the economic climate of western Europe which first becomes apparent towards the end of the tenth century. Behind the rise of the towns and of commerce, and the great works of land reclamation and colonisation for which there is some evidence from almost every part of western Europe, there would seem to be the common factor of an increasing population, and the most likely cause for such a persistent and decisive

[1] For a serviceable study of the origins of the Italian communes from the Lombard period to the early twelfth century, see L. Chiappelli, 'L. formazione storica del comune cittadino in Italia', *ASI* ser. VII, vola LXXXIV–LXXXVIII (1926–30); for further bibliography, see Saporis *Le Marchand Italien*, pp. 77–92.

[2] A good introduction to this subject is provided by the chapter by R. S. Lopez in the *Cambridge Economic History of Europe* II (1952), pp. 257–354, and R. S. Lopez and I. W. Raymond, *Mediaeval Trade in the Mediterranean World* (1955); for further details, see the works of Lopez, Reynolds, de Roover and Vitale in the bibliography to the above.

change would be some improvement in agricultural technique, possibly the gradual introduction of triennial rotation of crops.[1] If, as must be admitted, there is not and there may never be adequate evidence to prove this theory, it has at least the advantage of putting forward a cause commensurate with the supposed effect; earlier explanations in terms of the ending of wars and invasions, or the opening up of particular trade routes were far too restricted in scope to account for such a widespread phenomenon.

Despite the considerable progress which has been made in the subject in recent years, the materials for a balanced picture of the economic development of northern Italy in the Middle Ages are not yet available. This is because research has in the main been concentrated on long-distance trade and large-scale industry, so that the character and relative importance of local and inter-regional trade is largely an unknown factor; agrarian developments which, in view of the high urban population must have been of great importance, have also been relatively neglected. This is particularly unfortunate because in a complex economic movement of this kind, inter-relations are of crucial importance. The most that can be attempted here is to indicate some of the problems which, in the present state of knowledge, seem to be of outstanding significance.

If the theory of a general rise in population is accepted, then the economic history of Italy may be viewed as a series of responses to the challenge of more mouths to feed. The challenge must have arisen first precisely where our knowledge is most dim, in the agrarian society of the tenth and eleventh centuries. Dr Herlihy, working from the evidence of rural leases, has suggested that during the tenth century there was a crisis characterised by the fragmentation of holdings, indicating over-population and impoverishment, but in the course of the eleventh and twelfth centuries, this pressure was somehow overcome and the sub-division of agricultural holdings arrested.[2] On the second point, at least, there can be little doubt, for the relatively abundant evidence relating to the twelfth and thir-

---

[1] This theory has been put forward by Lynn White, Jr., *Mediaeval Technology and Social Change* (1962), pp. 69–78, with regard to northern Europe only, but may be equally applicable to northern and central Italy.

[2] D. Herlihy, 'The History of the Rural Seigneury in Italy', *Agricultural History*, XXXIII (1959), pp. 18–32.

teenth centuries shows that by that time food production, assisted by imports, was generally able to keep up with the demands of the towns. The profits from the land were high and secure enough to attract the investments of merchants, but though the towns grew considerably, there is nothing to suggest that they were in danger of being swamped by an influx of starving peasants. Only in the early fourteenth century do we find traces of a food crisis coinciding with other signs of strain in the economy, which ushered in the mid-fourteenth-century recession which is the watershed of mediaeval economic development.

How the favourable conditions of the twelfth and thirteenth centuries were established will probably never be known in detail, for the evidence is not adequate to provide the statistics necessary for a satisfactory explanation. But it is self-evident that agricultural development must have played an important part. The agrarian organisation of northern Italy seems to have led the way in Europe in certain important respects; the manor as an effective unit disappeared very early and serfdom died out in the more prosperous areas in the course of the thirteenth century. The cultivation of the land passed into the hands of *livellarii*, the holders of long leases which were in effect hereditary, who paid a fixed rent or a proportion of the produce. These factors, coupled with rising prices, probably encouraged innovations such as the introduction of complex rotations of crops and improvements in fruit growing and viticulture. New land was also brought under cultivation on a large scale, though here the opportunities varied widely from region to region. In some parts of the peninsula such as the Lombard Plain and the valleys of Tuscany, there were vast areas of derelict land awaiting drainage and reclamation, but in the mountainous areas there must have been much less room for expansion. It would be interesting to know how far these inequalities were adjusted by internal migration and how this was affected by political factors.[1]

[1] With regard to agricultural developments, I have made considerable use of the chapter on Italian agriculture in the new edition of the *Cambridge Economic History*, I by P. J. Jones; I am much indebted to Dr Jones for allowing me to read the manuscript of this chapter before publication. Further advances in this subject are most likely to come from intensive local studies; P. Torelli, *Un comune cittadino in territorio ad economia agricola* (1930),

Although agricultural productivity must in the long run have kept pace with demand, modern experience suggests that it is unlikely to have risen quickly enough to resolve the problem of rural over-population unless substantial relief had been obtained by emigration. The opportunities for movement outside Italy were very restricted; the Italians who are met with from England to the Black Sea were nearly all merchants or bankers with their roots still in Italy, not colonists or settlers. The main factor in the absorption of the surplus population was undoubtedly the growth of the towns; in order to survive, Italians had to develop new non-agrarian sources of livelihood. In a phrase of Professor Lopez, commerce became the frontier of the Italians.

A consideration of the results of recent research into Italian commercial activities outside Italy suggests that to some degree, enterprise abroad was a reflection of restricted opportunities nearer home. This is clearest in the case of those international merchants who came from cities which had few resources apart from their situation on an important trade route; the men of Asti, Chieri and Piacenza who specialised in trans-Alpine banking are an example of this. But, in general, it is striking that participation in long-distance trade and finance by the men of the various cities bears no simple relationship to the size and local importance of the cities themselves. The predominance of the Tuscans over the Lombards as merchant-bankers in northern Europe cannot be explained by an advantageous geographical position, except in so far as proximity to the papacy gave the Tuscan moneylenders an important customer and an entrée into many parts of Europe as collectors of papal revenues. If the Florentines travelled more than the Milanese, and the men of a minor Tuscan commune like Pistoia had interests in northern Europe far exceeding those of their Lombard counterparts, the reason probably lies in the relative possibilities for expansion in local trade and agriculture.[1] The fact that even at Pisa, the third seaport of northern Italy, the interests of land and sea were roughly of equal importance suggests that the significance of international trade has been greatly

---

which is concerned with the province of Mantua in the eleventh and twelfth centuries, is an example of the kind of work which is required.

[1] See Renouard, *Hommes d'Affaires*, pp. 62–72; Sapori, *Le Marchand italien*, pp. xlv–lix, and bibliography, ibid., pp. 43–63.

exaggerated.[1] Long-distance trade should not be considered in isolation; it was only a part of a complex economy, whose overall pattern is in many ways still obscure.

Just as the commercial revolution must be seen as no more than the crest of a wave whose base extended deep into the Italian countryside, so the urban industries which developed particularly in the thirteenth century need to be placed in their local setting. In many ways, the hand-industries of the Middle Ages were more at home near the source of their raw materials in villages and small towns rather than the great cities. Industrial development was not a primary factor in Italian urbanisation but was attracted to the towns by the advantages of markets and cheap labour. But in moving to the cities, ties with the countryside were not broken; if most Italian wool was of inferior quality, the same did not apply to Italian leather, linen and dyestuffs. Indeed, the unusual degree to which the Tuscan textile industry was dependent on imported raw materials and foreign markets may have obscured the more typical reliance on local products; with very few exceptions, the chief resource of any Italian city was the wealth of its own contado. Even the growth of Florence into the greatest industrial city of the Middle Ages must be related to the fact that she controlled the largest territory in central Italy.[2]

The growth of the Italian cities in the eleventh and twelfth centuries made it not only possible but imperative that they should seek to reassert their control over the surrounding territory, if only to secure for themselves an area from which they might draw victuals and raw materials. The institution through which this political dominance was achieved was the commune, in essence a sworn association of private individuals coming together as equals to promote their common interests. There was nothing necessarily urban about the commune; indeed, the rural communes of Italy appear almost as early as their counterparts in the city and follow out a similar development on a smaller scale. Again, it follows from the private nature of its

[1] Herlihy, *Pisa in the Early Renaissance*, p. vii; throughout, Dr Herlihy emphasises the ties between the city and its territory.
[2] E. Fiumi, 'Sui rapporti tra città e contado nell'età comunale', *ASI* CXIV (1956), pp. 18–68; the same author's 'Fioritura e decadenza dell'economia fiorentina', ibid. CXV–CXVII (1957–9), offers some reassessments of the accepted views on the Florentine economy.

origins that the commune did not grow out of the earlier public institutions for the regulation of town life but was grafted on to them at a later stage. Originally intended only to defend the common interests of their members, the communes were forced to take on political functions by the inability of existing institutions to represent the interests of the leading elements in the growing towns.[1]

The circumstances under which the effective government of the cities passed to the communes varied greatly from place to place; the scant records give an impression of a revolutionary movement accompanied by violence but this should not obscure the fact that there could be considerable continuity of personnel if not of institutions. Before the communes appeared, the cities had already a long tradition of regulating their own internal affairs. Where, as in most of Lombardy, the bishop was dominant, he had long been in the practice of sharing his temporal authority with the leading citizens. From the tenth century, the citizens enjoyed the right of electing the *visdominus*, the lay administrator of the bishop's temporalities; during a vacancy, the control of these assets passed to another layman, the *advocatus*. Although both these offices tended to become hereditary in the eleventh and twelfth centuries, in practice a bishop could do little without the support of his major vassals, and the episcopal *curia militum* was the nucleus from which the leading members of many of the early communes were drawn. So far as the lay authority was concerned, in many places the power of the count had declined to a point at which the public nature of the office had been lost sight of, so that the title and the remaining comital rights were allowed to pass by inheritance into the hands of more than one branch of the original comital stem, each of which tended to take its name from its principal castle. As a result, a commune might have among its members a number of titular counts; the Count Manfredino who ruled Padua in the year 1182 is described as a Paduan citizen, which almost certainly means that he was a member of the commune holding the office of sole consul.[2] But even where the comital powers

[1] For an introduction to the vexed question of the origins of the commune, see Sapori, *Le Marchand Italien*, pp. 77–80; in the main I have followed Chiappelli, *ASI* LXXXIV–LXXXVIII.

[2] *Liber Regiminum*, published as an appendix to Rolandino, *Cronica in factis et circa facta Marchie Trivixane*, ed. A. Bonardi, RIS VIII, i (1906), p. 294.

remained a reality in the hands of a single family, a violent clash was not inevitable and a wise nobleman might surrender on terms, as Duke Guelpho appears to have done to the young Florentine commune about the middle of the twelfth century.[1] In many cases, it would seem that the emergence of the commune represented a reallocation of power within an existing ruling class rather than a struggle between two mutually exclusive hostile groups.

Initially, the powers of the commune were no more than the private rights of its members, and only gradually did they develop an exclusive claim to the higher jurisdiction or *comitatus* within the city and its territory. But the process was inevitable if only because the Italian communes included among their members not only those whose interests were strictly urban and mercantile, but also many landowners and those whose interests were mixed; only those noblemen whose resources were so great that it was impossible to associate with them as equals were excluded. Because the members' rights and interests were so scattered from the start, it is quite misleading to represent the commune as an urban body which first consolidated its authority in the centre and then proceeded to conquer the contado; the rights which the communes acquired were so fragmented that the process of consolidation was bound to proceed in a piecemeal fashion in both town and country. The operations of the communal militia by which the more recalcitrant nobility were coerced into membership or subjection to the commune were only the most conspicuous part of the story; simultaneously, city and contado were being bound together by an increasingly complex web of private rights. Not only were wealthy citizens investing in land, but well-to-do members of the rural communities were being drawn into the towns without, however, relinquishing their interests in the land.[2] The intimate interdependence of town and country is one of the characteristics of the Italian scene. At the same time, the process by which the commune gradually suppressed rival jurisdictions was never complete. In country areas the administration of local affairs was often left to the rural communes and

[1] Davidsohn, *Geschichte von Florenz*, I, p. 659.
[2] The original statement of this view by J. Plesner, *L'Emigration de la Campagne à la Ville Libre de Florence au XIIIe Siècle* (1934), has been much criticised in detail, but is well supported by the Paduan evidence.

the jurisdiction of the nobility was tolerated *de facto* if not *de jure*. Even in the heart of the city, vital matters like the regulation of the port or the collection of tolls and taxes could be left in the hands of individuals or quasi-independent bodies.[1] The communes never quite lost the marks of their origins as private associations; throughout the period of their political dominance, they were remarkably tolerant towards the growth of organisations such as guilds, parties and *societates* which could come to wield considerable power, whose origins resembled those of the communes themselves.

From their emergence in the eleventh century, until the establishment of the *signoria* which was complete almost everywhere by the mid-fourteenth century, the internal evolution of the communes may be seen as revolving round two issues: the problem of representation and the problem of the executive. The first of these was a consequence of the urban growth which had brought the commune into being in the first place, which meant that at any time there were two elements among the substantial inhabitants of any Italian city: those who were regarded as old-established citizens, and the *gente nuova*, who were recent immigrants or newly enriched. The time-honoured summary of the development of the communes is to say that they were first aristocratic or patrician and then popular; a more accurate view would be that the social and political assimilation of new elements was proceeding all the time. The earliest records suggest that from the beginning the governing class of the commune included well-established landowning families from the contado side by side with newer urban elements; if the fragmentary evidence of the twelfth century gives little information about social conflict under the patrician commune, it should not therefore be assumed that it did not exist. On the other hand, there is nothing to suggest a clear-cut conflict of interests between these groups; investments in trade and land both urban and rural were not alternatives but complementary. If in the course of time urban interests came to be more strongly represented in the governing class, this was no more than the growth of an element which had been present from the start.

It is against this background that the emergence of the *popolo* must be viewed; it was a milestone on the road which the

---

[1] Herlihy, *Pisa in the Early Renaissance*, pp. 18–19.

communes were already travelling but it did not mark a major change of direction.[1] The various *societates populi* which took shape during the social conflicts within the cities from the turn of the thirteenth century onwards, were originally voluntary associations not unlike the communes themselves. They included mainly those who were excluded from full participation in the existing commune, the smaller property owners and masters of the greater guilds, who served in the city militia as *pedites* rather than *milites*, owners of rural land but not on such a scale as to carry with it the exercise of a feudal jurisdiction. Beginning as an association for mutual defence, the *popolo* gradually took on the nature of a political party which was often in armed conflict with a privileged *societas militum*. The outcome was the establishment of regimes dominated by the *popolo* which took place in the major cities of Lombardy in the first part of the thirteenth century and in the corresponding cities of Tuscany up to fifty years later. Wherever it took place, the advent of the *popolo* left a permanent mark on the institutions of the commune, for the *popolo* took over the commune in much the same way as the commune had taken over the pre-communal administration of the city, effectively but not completely. The officials and assemblies of the commune were supplemented with others representing the *popolo*. As a result, a much wider section of the population was admitted to political privileges and responsibilities. The lower classes, especially the unskilled labourers, continued to be excluded from power, and the *magnati*, great men who were distrusted because of their wealth or their political record, were placed under political disabilities. Attacks on the jurisdictions of the nobility and the clergy, and measures to secure a cheap and plentiful food supply for the urban population are characteristic of the *popolo*; taken at its face value, much of the legislation suggests a kind of dictatorship of the middle class. But the position of the *magnati* at least was not so intolerable as it appears; in war their support was indispensable to the commune and in peace they could no doubt make their influence felt through clients who were members of the *popolo*.

[1] For the rise of the *popolo* in general, see G. de Vergottini, 'Note sulla formazione degli statuti del popolo', *RSDI* XVI (1943), pp. 61–70, and *Arti e popolo della prima metà del secolo XIII* (1943); the development of the *popolo* in Cremona has been traced in detail by U. Gualazzini, *Il 'Populus' di Cremona e l'autonomia del comune* (1940).

The *societas populi* might be organised in a number of ways but the underlying basis was generally territorial; for the purpose of electing officials or in case of a civil disturbance, the *popolo* assembled by quarters or *sesieri*, by urban parishes or *centenarii*. In the course of the thirteenth century, the *popolo* in many cities was re-formed as a confederation of guilds.[1] In some places, the two alternative ways of ordering the *popolo* co-existed with separate or overlapping functions, but in some of the more highly developed industrial towns, of which Florence is the classic example, the *popolo* organised by guilds superseded the territorial *popolo* for all political purposes. When this occurred, there may have been an important shift in the centre of power within the commune, but there was no admission of new classes to political rights such as had followed from the victory of the *popolo*. Power passed to the guild masters and often a distinction between the rights of major and minor guilds ensured that control remained firmly in the hands of the former, so that, far from there being an extension of the franchise, a narrowing of the effective ruling class probably took place. The increase in the power of the greater merchants, financiers and industrialists in the commune may have been more apparent than real, for wherever guild membership became the passport to politics, the possibility of nominal membership, exemplified by the enrolment of the poet Dante in the guild of apothecaries, has always to be reckoned with.

Parallel to the changes in the membership and organisation of the commune was the development of various committees, councils and offices which represented attempts to solve the problem of the executive. The problem stemmed from the nature of the commune as an association of equals; for the exercise of any but the most rudimentary functions of government, it was necessary that the council of all the members of the commune should delegate authority to representatives empowered to act on behalf of the whole body and strictly responsible to it. The provision of a strong executive under increasingly exacting conditions was the most difficult problem which the communes had to face and it was one which all in the end failed to solve.

The main stages in the development of the executive cor-

[1] De Vergottini, *Arti e popolo*.

respond only approximately to the changes in the composition of the commune which have been outlined above. While the communes were growing up under the shadow of the pre-communal authorities, a very informal executive seems to have been sufficient; in general, the assumption of effective government seems to have antedated slightly the emergence of the consulate, the distinctive office of the early commune. At first, the title of consul was given to the chief officials of a number of departments of the city government, and the consuls who were in charge of overseas colonies, or the *consules de placitis* who continued to perform the function of assessors in criminal cases in the city courts until long after the end of the communal period, represent a survival of this early practice. But, as the twelfth century progressed, there was a tendency for the most important powers of the commune to be grouped in the hands of a decreasing number of consuls *par excellence*, who were elected annually and given wide judicial powers and oversight of the commune's property and taxation.[1] Between the consuls and the Consiglio Maggiore consisting of all the members of the commune, it was common to interpose a smaller council, while in exceptional circumstances, a *parlamentum* of all the inhabitants, the lineal successor of the pre-communal *conventus ante ecclesiam*, might be called.

In the last quarter of the twelfth century, the search for a strong but impartial executive led to the adoption of a new official as the head of the commune, the *podestà*.[2] The tendency to decrease the number of consuls, taken to its logical conclusion, could only lead to the appointment of a sole consul, but this expedient, though it was resorted to sporadically, failed to become a permanent feature of communal government. The factions within the communes were unwilling to see such wide powers vested in a single citizen as a regular practice but preferred to bring in a less interested outsider. The regulations governing the *podestà* were designed to make him as far as possible a completely detached and impartial executor of the law and the constitution. Legislation was framed to define his course of action in any foreseeable circumstance, and after his term of

[1] Davidsohn, 'Ueber die Entstehung des Konsulats in Toskana', *Historische Vierteljahrschrift*, III (1900), pp. 1–26.

[2] V. Franchini, *Saggio di ricerche sull'istituto del podestà nei comuni medioevale* (1912).

office had expired, his actions were subjected to a searching scrutiny. In practice, it was often necessary to allow the *podestà* a good deal of initiative, especially in time of war when he became *ex officio* commander of the communal army, but on paper he was always the servant of the general will of the commune, strictly responsible to its councils. The municipal codes of the period represent a sustained attempt to arrive at a system of general and constitutional law as far as possible impartial and impersonal in its application.

At first, the advent to power of the *popolo* brought little change to the formal organisation of the executive. The greater and lesser councils of the commune became in practice additional councils of the *popolo*, but the position of the *podestà* as the head of the whole administration of the commune remained unchanged. The most important innovation was the appearance of the *anziani*, a college of eight or twelve members of the *popolo* elected for a short term in various ways, whose function was to represent the wishes of the *popolo* to the *podestà*.[1] The *podestà* or his deputy presided in the councils, but proposals were initiated by the *anziani*. Sometimes, a *popolo* which felt threatened by some internal or external force would proceed to the election of an outsider as *capitano del popolo*. The overlapping powers of this office could serve as a check on a *podestà* whom the *popolani* did not entirely trust, and the office could become a more or less permanent feature of the constitution, as at Bologna, where *capitani* and *podestà* were elected to serve in double harness for a six-month term of office in the late thirteenth and early fourteenth centuries.

In retrospect, it can be seen that the appearance of the *podestà* only deflected for a time the persistent drift towards despotism. This tide was so strong and so general that its cause must be sought in conditions common to nearly all the communes. Monarchy was the most common form of government in the Middle Ages because it usually meant a strong executive and ensured that the interests of the ruler and the state would most nearly coincide; as the communes took on more and more the nature of city-states, the pressure to move in the direction of monarchy was correspondingly increased. While the intimacy

---

[1] I know of no comparative study of the institution of the *anziani*, which, like many other innovations of the time, seems to have originated at Bologna; see Davidsohn, *Geschichte von Florenz*, II, i, p. 371.

of city government made rule through councils and committees a possibility, this advantage was partly offset by the banes of small-scale politics, the intrusion of particular interests and the tendency to faction. Despite the elaborate efforts to control the magnates, the smaller communes in particular had the greatest difficulty in maintaining their independence from the great noble families of the region. In the larger cities, the growth of the urban population presented the communes with problems of public order unparalleled in mediaeval times. Wherever there was a large urban proletariat, there was a constant threat to the stability of the state and physical proximity made the government particularly vulnerable to sudden revolts. Above all, as each state consolidated its position, the competition between states became more intense; as wars became more serious and more professional, the disadvantages of corporate and amateur control increased. The inevitable difficulties of a civilian government in its relations with its military leaders appear in an acute form over and over again.

In passing from the commune to the *signoria*, each city went through a crisis in which the long search for responsible and representative government was finally abandoned as hopeless. Most *signori* rose as the leaders of a faction and maintained their position by playing off one faction against another. Despotism could be legalised in a number of ways. Sometimes the office of *podestà* or *capitano* was prolonged indefinitely and released from the shackles of the law, or a variety of other offices in the state could provide a springboard for a rising *signore*. Frequently, a new office with indefinite powers was created and formally ratified by the ancient *parlementum*, revived out of obscurity for the purpose, but sooner or later, most *signori* felt the need of some recognition from above, generally represented by a nominal vicariate from an emperor whose actual powers were small.[1]

---

[1] The best general study of the rise of the *signorie* is still E. Salzer, *Über die Anfänge der Signorie in Oberitalien*, Historisches Studien XIII (1910). For the imperial vicariate whose influence was underestimated by Salzer, see P. Torelli, 'Capitanato del popolo e vicariato imperiale come elementi costitutivi della signoria bonacolsiana', *Atti e memorie della R. Accademia Virgiliana di Mantova*, XIV–XVI (1923), pp. 73–166, reprinted in *Scritti di storia del diritto italiano* (1959), pp. 375–480. For a recent review of the problem, see E. Sestan, 'Le origini delle signorie cittadine, un problema storico esaurito?', *BISI* LXXIII (1962), pp. 41–69.

By the middle of the fourteenth century, a *signoria* of one kind or another had been established in all the major Italian cities north of the Appenines except Venice; in Tuscany some republics survived but even here there were many instances of concealed despotism. The republican commune was thus a passing phase in the development of the typical Italian state. Some communal institutions remained in being but were deprived of all real power; in a crisis, the commune might be resurrected if only to give legal form to the election of a new lord. But if the Renaissance was predominantly an age of princes, the tradition of the commune did not entirely die out. Dr Baron has seen in the Florentine republican tradition at the turn of the fifteenth century the key to an essential stage in the development of the Renaissance mentality;[1] Florence and Venice, the two greatest states of the fifteenth century both paid lip-service to republican ideals. Even in the period of the Italian wars, an undertow of local republican independence is perceptible. Burckhardt's despotic 'state as a work of art' is far from the whole story; beside the Macchiavelli of *The Prince* must be set the republican Macchiavelli of the *Discorsi*.

[1] H. Baron, *The Crisis of the Italian Renaissance* (1958).

PART ONE
THE GOVERNING CLASS

CHAPTER II

City and Contado

THE description of Paduan society must begin from its physical setting, from the topographical and economic structure of the city and its territory which exercised a persistent and sometimes a determinant influence over its whole development. Nothing is more characteristic of the modern historical outlook than its way of regarding the relationship between economy and society, and in the following pages some attempt will be made to answer the kind of questions which occur to the modern mind, even though this means that in many cases the sources have to be worked against the grain and made to yield up evidence on matters which they were not designed to record. For it goes without saying that the outlook of the thirteenth and fourteenth centuries was not ours, yet it would be a serious omission to ignore their ideas, for the contemporary understanding of the city and its environment is an integral part of the world we are seeking to recreate. And, in the case of Padua, the sources do permit a glimpse of the city as it appeared to contemporary eyes.

Padua is one of the few cities for which there exists a literary description from the mediaeval period. This is the *Visio Egidii Regis Patavie* of Giovanni da Nono, whose title refers to the opening passage, in which the author imagines Egidius, a mythical king of Patavium, a refugee at Rimini after the destruction of his city by Attila the Hun. The king falls asleep and is comforted by a vision in which an angel prophesies the rebuilding of the city and its future greatness. This device enables Da Nono to put into the mouth of the angel a description of Padua as he knew it in the early fourteenth century; internal evidence makes it possible to date the work with reasonable certainty between the years 1314 and 1318.[1] In

[1] For Da Nono, see G. Fabris, 'La cronaca di Giovanni da Nono', *BMCP* VIII (1932), pp. 1–33, and IX (1933), pp. 167–200; J. K. Hyde, 'Mediaeval Descriptions of Cities', *BJRL* XLVIII, ii, (1966). For the text of the *Visio*, the only part of Da Nono's works yet published, see *BMCP* X–XI (1934–9), pp. 1–30.

undertaking a formal description of his native town, Da Nono was placing himself in a long-standing but diffuse tradition of town-descriptions leading back to antiquity, most of which was unknown to him, for although he was a judge, it is evident that his literary culture was small. From this tradition, which probably reached him through the popular *Mirabilia Urbis Rome*, Da Nono drew the overall plan of the *Visio* which concentrates first on the gates and walls of the city and then on the chief 'palaces' or public buildings, but within this outline the writer was free to follow his own interests and inclinations, and to this extent the *Visio* is both a description of the city and a window into the author's mind.

The first part of the *Visio Egidii* is devoted to the major and minor gates of the city and the principal buildings and other features associated with them. Da Nono begins with the Porta Pontemolino, which took its name from the numerous mill wheels in the river below, which in his day numbered thirty-four. Standing at the head of the Via Maggiore which had been the principal north–south street of Roman Patavium, the gate gave access over a fine bridge to the suburbs of S. Giacomo and Codalunga. For Da Nono, each principal gate was associated with the territory beyond, which in the case of the Pontemolino meant the region beyond the Brenta, a fast-flowing river which, leaving the Alpine foothills at Bassano, ran south to within a few miles of Padua before turning east to the lagoon almost opposite Venice. The chief centre of the Paduan Oltrebrenta was the walled town of Cittadella, built by the commune in 1220 to guard the route to the north and the open north-eastern frontier with Treviso.[1] But the Pontemolino was also the gate for Padua's north-western neighbour Vicenza, which was reached by turning left at the head of the bridge and following the road which ran roughly parallel to the other major river of the Paduan territory, the slow-flowing Bacchiglione.[2] It was by this route, Da Nono remarks, that a Paduan expedition left to take control of the neighbouring city in 1266.

[1] *Liber Regiminum*, p. 340.
[2] The hydrography of the Paduan region is a complex matter as the courses of the rivers have been considerably altered in historical times. Padua stands on the low watershed between the Brenta and the Bacchiglione, so that sometimes the one, sometimes the other and sometimes both rivers have supplied the water which has flowed through the city.

The old western and southern gates of Padua were known as the Porta S. Giovanni and the Porta Torricelli, the latter taking its name from the many towers which stood in that quarter until the time of Ezzelino. These gates gave access to two of the most important parts of the Paduan contado: the region of the Colli Euganei, known in mediaeval times as the Pedevenda, and the plain beyond, between the hills and the Adige, to which the old name of the Scodosia was attached. The Colli form a striking contrast with the plain which makes up the rest of the Paduan contado, from which they stand out like islands. In Da Nono's mind, they were connected with the earliest history of Padua, for he believed that the first city, called Euganea, had been founded by the fugitive Antenor of Troy on the Monterosso; down to his own day, the Pedevenda was associated in a special way with the oldest Paduan nobility and it was there that they were reputed to have their castles and country houses. The importance of the Scodosia rested on the fact that in or near it were situated Monselice, Este and Montagnana, three of the four largest dependent towns in the Paduan contado which looked out towards the river Adige marking the natural frontier of Paduan territory.

The last of the four main gates was the Porta Altinate, through which the main roads passed for Venice and Treviso. Just outside the walls, the Via Altinate served the port of Ognissanti which was connected by canal to the lower part of the Brenta and Venice, while near by was the salt port from which it was possible to navigate to the salt pans near Chioggia by way of the lower Bacchiglione. Almost as important as the Porta Altinate was the Porta S. Stefano, a short distance to the south, from which the Via S. Margherita ran in a south-easterly direction to the Pontecorvo to form the backbone of that part of the town known as Rudena. Near the Pontecorvo were two of Padua's greatest religious houses, the Benedictine monastery of S. Giustina and the Franciscan church of S. Antonio which Da Nono describes in detail. The road continued from the Pontecorvo for some ten miles to Piove di Sacco, the chief town of the south-eastern part of the Paduan contado which was occasionally referred to as the Plebatus.

Despite its apparent comprehensiveness, the first part of the *Visio Egidii* presents a very incomplete picture of fourteenth-century Padua. The walls which it describes are the ancient ones, reconstructed about the end of the twelfth century, which enclosed the western island formed by the Bacchiglione, on which the cathedral and the centres of business and the administration were situated. But by the fourteenth century, this was less than half the built-up area of the city which extended for a considerable distance on all sides of the old walls, especially to the east on the island bounded by the Arena, S. Sofia and the Pontecorvo. In fact, there was probably never a time when the city was confined to the western island, for ancient Patavium had stood on both islands astride the Bacchiglione, which was spanned by Roman bridges, traces of which are visible to this day.[1] Legend derived the name Rudena from the ruins of Patavium which Attila had destroyed.[2] Thus Da Nono's description was realistic only in its details; as a whole it was highly stylised, the exact verbal equivalent of the city represented on the seal of the commune—walled, moated and four-square, while the surrounding inscription names the mountains, the sea and the rivers Adige and Musone as the ideal boundaries of the Paduan state. The city was thought of as a fortified square within the larger square of her territories.[3]

For indications of the probable course of Padua's urban development, it is necessary to turn to records of a very different kind. For the twelfth century, there is an inscription copied into the *Liber Regiminum* which records that in 1174 a fire destroyed 2,614 houses in the city, which are said to have been three-quarters of the whole. If these figures can be relied on, they would suggest a total population of the order of 15,000 at that date.[4] Eighty years later the next milestone is reached with the oath which Ezzelino da Romano ordered to be taken by all the citizens, promising to uphold his treaty with Oberto Pelavicino of Cremona. Altogether 665 members of the Consiglio Maggiore and 1,941 other inhabitants are named as having taken the oath.[5] While these figures cannot be used to

---

[1] C. Gasparotto, *Padova Romana* (1940), pp. 83–94.
[2] Rolandino Patavino, *Cronica in factis et circa facta Marchie Trivixane*, ed. A. Bonardi, RIS VIII, i (1906), p. 124. In a narrower sense, Rudena was and is the name of a street in the same part of the city.
[3] See Plate I.
[4] *Liber Regiminum*, pp. 291–2.
[5] AS Cremona, ASC 1772–90, 1793–4. For totals by *centenarii*, see below, p. 37.

From a seventeenth-century engraving

PLATE I

The Seal of the Paduan Commune

estimate the total population, they do give some indication of its distribution, as the names of the ordinary inhabitants, though not of the councillors, are listed under the various *centenarii* into which the city was divided. The administrative divisions are in themselves a sign of the development of the city; the four quarters of Pontemolino, Duomo, Torricelli and Ponte Altinate obviously derive from the gates of the old walls, but of the twenty *centenarii*, nine were mainly outside the confines of the western island. In 1254 the oath-takers in these extramural *centenarii* amounted to 1,135 as against 806 from within the gates, those showing the highest numbers being Rudena (234) and S. Sofia (207) on the eastern island, followed by the outlying suburb of S. Croce (137), separated from the city by the great open space of Prato della Valle. Even allowing for the fact that the great majority of the 665 councillors probably came from within the walls, while the lists reflect Ezzelino's reliance upon the lower classes of the city in the last years of his *signoria* when he had quarrelled with almost all the nobility and many of the substantial members of the *popolo*, it is probable that at least half the population lived outside the walls which had been reconstructed only fifty years before. 146 persons who took the oath, including 15 members of the council, were described as immigrants from the contado or from other cities.[1] Taken as a whole, it is likely that the first half of the thirteenth century was a period of considerable urban growth in Padua.

From 1254 to 1320 the evidence for the growth of Padua is almost entirely indirect; the political successes and the public works of the commune in this period suggest a prosperous and growing community. The eastern suburbs of the city were already fortified in 1256, when the Guelph army had to force an entrance near the Pontecorvo; the western arc of the new circuit known as the *murus spaldi*, was begun by the victorious army in the same year and completed in 1270.[2] Among the public buildings, the Palazzo del Podestà was erected in 1281, the hall of the Consiglio Maggiore in 1284; the Palazzo degli Anziani followed in 1285 and a communal archive was provided in 1297. The record with regard to bridges, markets, river-ports

---

[1] In Paduan documents, immigrants are sometimes distinguished by the description 'qui fuit de . . .' instead of the noncommital 'de'.

[2] Rolandino, pp. 118–19, 131; *Liber Regiminum*, p. 324; *Annales Patavini*, p. 203.

and the paving of streets in this period is equally impressive.[1] The early fourteenth century which saw the completion of the basilica of S. Antonio and the reconstruction of the Palazzo Comunale, which was decorated with frescoes ascribed to Giotto, was the golden age of mediaeval Paduan architecture.[2] Private documents provide some evidence for continuing immigration into the city. Most of the individuals found in these records were men of some property, who when they reached the city, particularly favoured certain occupations such as notary, taverner and university professor.[3] Behind them must be imagined an unknown mass of poor labourers who have left no mark on the records.

The most important evidence for the demography of mediaeval Padua belongs to the year 1320. It consists of a detailed survey undertaken by the communal authorities while the city was besieged by Cangrande which has survived through two independent transcripts made in the sixteenth and seventeenth centuries.[4] These give the number of men and/or families living in each street or *centenario*, together with the names of the leading inhabitants. Fortunately, unlike some other records of this kind, neither the names nor the figures seem to have been deliberately tampered with. Although there are some discrepancies and omissions in each manuscript, the survey appears to be substantially complete since the sum of the details tallies fairly well with the total, and the census leaves no obvious gaps when plotted on the map.

The real difficulties in the interpretation of the census of 1320 arise not so much from the nature of the record itself as from the circumstances in which it was compiled. At the time,

---

[1] Ibid. pp. 204–5, 263; *Visio Egidii*, pp. 19–20. For other public works, see especially *Annales Patavini*, pp. 261–5.

[2] *Visio Egidii*, pp. 8–9, 19–20.

[3] See examples below, pp. 135, 141, 148, 170, 176.

[4] MSS BP 253, II, and 1860, IX. The former was published by G. Grion, *Delle rime volgare, trattato di Antonio da Tempo*, Collezione di opere inedite o rare (1869), Appendix I, pp. 254–88. Grion also published two other lists from the same MS. The first, containing several hundred names and bearing the date 1276, is in fact an uncritical compilation of no independent value, based mainly on the matricula of the College of Judges *c*.1280–1349; the latter, dated 1321, appears to be more authentic, but is of little practical use, as it is a bare list of surnames only. These lists appear in several Paduan MSS, some of which are adulterated and unreliable.

Padua was closely besieged by the Veronese, and consequently the outlying parts of the city which were outside the defended area were omitted, while the population within the defences was undoubtedly swollen by an uncertain number of refugees from the contado. Thus an element of uncertainty is introduced into the use of the census to answer the question both of urban growth and of the total population in 1320. With regard to the former, the survey mentions three localities known as Borgo Nuovo in different parts of the city, and opposite these and several other streets in the outskirts is noted *omnes artifices*, probably indicating industrial suburbs of recent origin.[1] But the outer suburbs beyond the *murus spaldi* are omitted; in particular, the Borgo Ognissanti with its two ports, which had supported a considerable population in 1254, was not recorded.[2] The most important evidence bearing upon the population of the city is the figure of 11,131 men given by the census; if, as is most likely in the context, men of military age are understood, this would represent a total population of over 40,000. The problem is to decide how far this represents the normal population of the city and its suburbs. Some allowance must be made for the presence of refugees from the contado—162 families in this category are expressly recorded in the *centenario* of S. Nicolò—but against these must be offset a number of political exiles, as well as the inhabitants of the outer suburbs who should certainly be included in the normal population of the city. Bearing in mind that in a census compiled for military purposes under difficult conditions there are likely to have been some omissions, it seems reasonable to say that in 1320 Padua was a city of at least 35,000 inhabitants. This means that by population, Padua belonged to the middle rank among Italian cities, being about a third of the size of the great centres like Venice, Milan and Florence, and about half the size of contemporary Bologna. On the other hand, she was as large as almost any city north of the Alps, and about the equal of London in 1377.[3] The rates at

[1] Grion, op. cit. pp. 260, 263, 268, 285.

[2] There are listed under *centanario* S. Sofia in 1254 ten boatmen, a boat repairer (*calcator navium*) and four (glass?) vessel-makers (*verarii*) almost certainly from this suburb, as well as others described as *ab Omnibus Sanctis* (AS Cremona, ASC 1788).

[3] J. C. Russel, 'Late Ancient and Mediaeval Population', *Transactions of the American Philosophical Society* ns. XLVIII, iii (1958), pp. 109–11, and *Mediaeval British Population* (1948), p. 142.

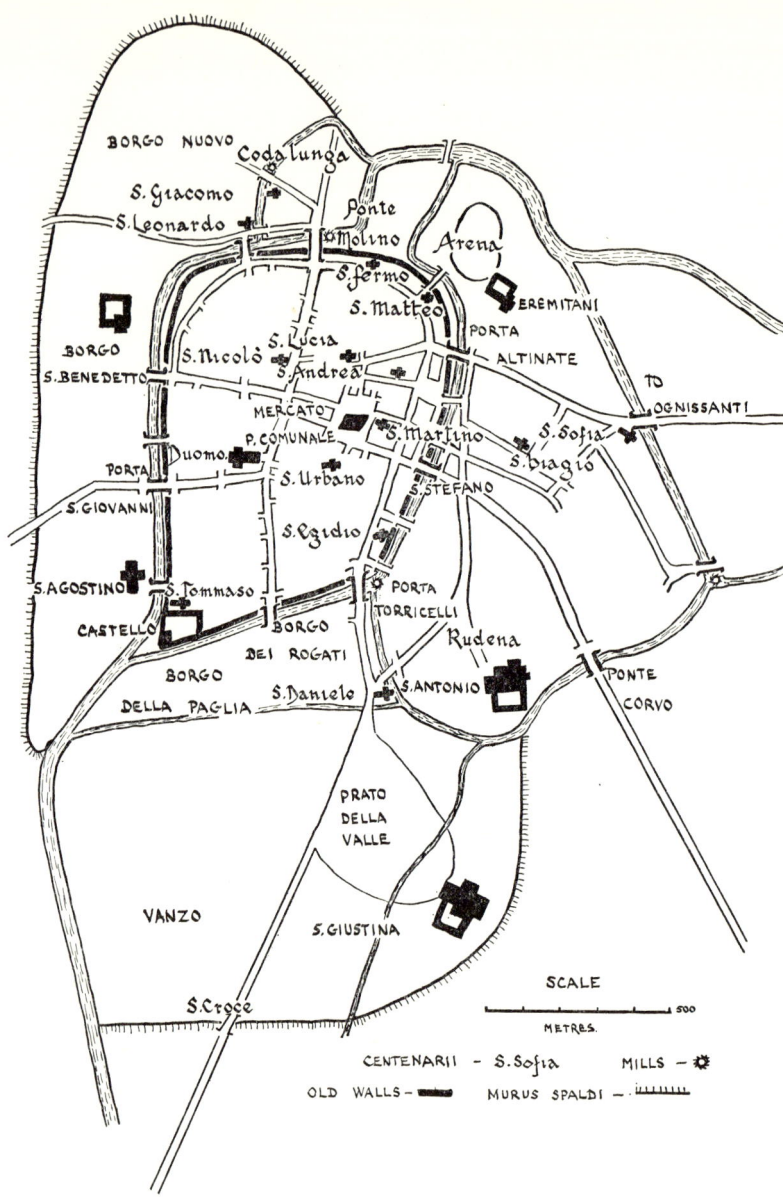

Map I. The City of Padua in 1320 (see table opposite)

CITY AND CONTADO 37

which monthly *collecta* were imposed by the Della Scala in 1332 suggest that Padua was thought to be as rich as Verona and twice as wealthy as Vicenza and Treviso.[1] The main problem relating to the Paduan economy is to discover how this wealth was created and this considerable urban population maintained.

It is commonly considered that from the economic point of view, mediaeval towns fall into two groups—those in which long-distance trade played a significant part in the economy, and those whose markets were predominantly local. All the indications are that despite its size, Padua belonged to the

[1] The rates for the chief cities of the Della Scala state were Verona and Padua £6,000 each; Vicenza and Treviso £3,000 each; Feltre and Belluno £1,200 together, and Bassano and Monselice £250 each (Verci, *Marca Trivigiana* doc. n. 1194).

The Territorial Distribution of Persons taking the Oath of 1254

Quarter	Mainly within Walls		Rudena		Suburbs	
DUOMO	Duomo	62				
	S. Lucia	88				
	S. Nicolò	107				
	S. Tommaso	87				
	S. Urbano	84				
TORRICELLI	S. Martino	61	Rudena	234	S. Croce	137
	S. Egidio	100	S. Daniele	93		
PONTE ALTINATE	S. Andrea	50	S. Biagio	103		
	S. Matteo	47	S. Sofia	207		
			Arena	100		
PONTEMOLINO	Pontemolino	36			S. Leonardo	85
	S. Fermo	84			S. Giacomo	96
					Codalunga	80
Total		806		737		398

The 665 persons who took the oath as members of the Consiglio Maggiori cannot be allocated to any part of the city, though it may be assumed that up to three-quarters probably came from within the old walls.

second group. In the first place, the city was not particularly well situated for long-distance trade. The main route from Venice to north-west Europe passed south of Paduan territory along the Po; the secondary route to the Brenner could be reached by way of the Adige and Verona, or by the shortest overland road through Treviso.[1] It is true that during the communal period, some attempts were made to improve communications with the north. In 1264 the commune of Vicenza undertook a survey of the mountain roads to Trento with a view to selecting one of them for improvement and, after the annexation of Bassano, the extensive works carried out by the Paduans on the Limena road suggest that the commune may have been interested in encouraging trade with the north by way of the Val Sugana.[2] Many Venetians did come to Padua, as may be inferred from the series of trade treaties between the two states and from the existence of a standing joint tribunal for the hearing of disputes between Paduans and Venetians.[3] But the Venetians who carried out transactions in Padua are more likely to have been those buying local products in the Paduan markets, rather than the long-distance merchants for whom Padua can have been little more than the last stage on the journey home. The Paduan share in the profits of long-distance trade must have been small unless they participated in it themselves. But no evidence has yet come to light of Paduans taking part in the trade to northern Europe. A Paduan guild of *mercatores* existed in 1287, but nothing more is known of it. Individual *mercatores* are rarely met in Paduan records; only five, none of whom was in the council, took the oath in 1254. *Negociatores* are a little more common, but some of these were also tailors or dealers in a wide variety of goods, apparently on a small scale.[4] The only leading Paduan citizen who can be connected with trade in any way is Enrico Scrovegni, mentioned in a Venetian document of 1312 as the owner of a barge-load of wool, cotton and cheese impounded by the customs at Mestre.[5]

[1] J. E. Tyler, *The Alpine Passes 962–1250* (1930), pp. 171–9.
[2] F. Lampertico, *Statuti del comune di Vicenza 1264*, Mon.RDVSP ser. II, i (1886), p. 151; Verci, *Marca Trivigiana*, doc. nn. 218–20.
[3] N. Rodolico, 'Di alcuni trattati di arbitraggio nelle questioni commerciali tra Venezia e Padova', *Raccolta di scritti storici in onore di G. Romano* (1907), pp. 117–40.
[4] For examples, see below, pp. 178–9.
[5] AS Venice, Consiglio Maggiore, Capricornii, f. 105.

Conclusive evidence for the restricted importance of Padua as a textile centre comes from a statute of 1301 which sought to revive the city's wool market by encouraging foreign merchants.[1] The preamble stating that the Paduan market had once been famous throughout Italy can probably be discounted as rhetoric; the admission of its decline means that the market was moribund at a time when the commune was at the height of its prosperity.

Industrial development in Padua in the communal period seems also to have been on a modest scale. The great industries of the thirteenth century were mostly textiles, and with the Paduan cloth market so weak, it is not surprising that the evidence for the large-scale manufacture of textiles is slight. Textile workers, weavers and the like, are rare among the witnesses to Paduan documents; even the oath of 1254 which mentions so many tradesmen, contains only fourteen persons described as *texatores*, with another thirteen *filaroli*. The Paduan textile guilds are obscure. The Arte della Lana has been the subject of a detailed study by Cessi, who showed that it was only founded, after much encouragement by the authorities, between 1276 and 1287, and that it did not grow into a major industry until the middle of the fourteenth century.[2] Da Nono, who devotes a lot of space to the goods sold in the Paduan markets, mentions Veronese but not Paduan cloth; the only native textiles which he notes are the linens of Piove di Sacco.[3] The oath of 1254 bears out the importance of the Paduan linen industry; forty *linaroli* are named, of whom twenty-nine are concentrated in Rudena and the adjacent *centenarii* of S. Sofia and S. Biagio, together with eight *spaolatores* who were probably also linen workers.

Another natural resource which was well exploited was the abundant water power provided by the various branches of the Bacchiglione which flowed through the city. There are many references to corn and fulling mills both private and public in the communal period, and thirty-three millers took the oath in 1254. That these mills could have more than a local importance

---

[1] *Statuta et Matricula Collegii Iudicum* (*Stat. Coll. Iud.*), Archivio Antico Universitario, MS n. 123, ff. 8v–9r; R. Cessi, *Le corporazioni dei mercanti di panni e della lana in Padova*, MRIV XXVIII, ii (1908), pp. 80–1.
[2] Cessi, op. cit. pp. 27–55.
[3] *Visio Egidii*, p. 18.

is shown by the licence granted in 1277 to a certain Leonardo of Venice to import grain and cloth to his mills in Paduan territory and re-export the product to Venice.[1] The Paduan fulling mills were considered sufficiently important for the Venetian authorities to exercise a strict control over the cloth being sent to Padua for fulling.[2] Another group of trades using the resources of the contado and the water supply of the city was the leather industries. The documents of 1254 list nine tanners but ninety-five shoemakers and cobblers. The same source shows sixty-one smiths, of whom ten were members of the council, not including two knife-smiths and a sword-maker. Clearly too much emphasis should not be laid on these figures, which may only show that certain industries were in the hands of many independent masters while others depended on a mass of poor labourers who have left no mark on the records. The obscurity of the Paduan industrial guilds may be partly fortuitous. On the other hand, if many Paduan families owed their wealth to investment in industry, it is remarkable that no record of the fact has survived.

Fourteenth-century Padua had an unsavoury reputation for usury. Not only did Da Nono and Mussato accuse their fellow-citizens of this vice, but Dante chose the Paduan Renaldo Scrovegni to speak on behalf of the usurers in Hell.[3] Despite the odds against documents not connected with real property being preserved, sufficient evidence has survived to show that this reputation was not undeserved. Paduans of all classes made loans at interest, and a few families and individuals stand out as professional moneylenders.[4] Two characteristics of the Paduans' moneylending activities emerge from the records. The first is the extreme rarity of commercial loans. In part this reflects the bias of the sources, where short-term contracts with private individuals were most likely to be destroyed. On the other hand, it must be of some significance that where a number of ephemeral contracts have survived, the two largest commercial loans

---

[1] *Statuti del comune di Padova dal secolo XII all'anno 1285* (*Stat. Com.*), ed. A. Gloria (1873), n. 833 I.

[2] Cessi, *Le corporazioni*, pp. 35–7.

[3] Da Nono, *Visio Egidii*, p. 3, *De Generatione, passim*; A. Mussato, *De Gestis Italicorum post Henricum VII*, RIS X (1727), col. 586; Dante Alighieri, *Inferno*, XVII, ll. 61–73.

[4] See below, pp. 181–90.

should be of no more than £500,¹ while other loans of thousands of pounds are not uncommon, and that there should be not a single reference to a *commenda* or a *cambio*, two of the most important types of contract in mediaeval commercial finance. Major loans by Paduans were either to communes or to ruling families, or were connected with the acquisition of land. The second point is the very restricted range of the financial activities of even the greatest Paduan moneylenders. So far as is known, they found their clients only in Padua and its dependent towns, or in Padua's immediate neighbours. The Paduans did not participate in the international banking operations of the Florentines and Siennese and they do not appear among the Papal bankers or the Italian bankers of Paris or London. Nor did the great banking houses have their Paduan branches or agents; in fact, the only evidence of contact is a single document linking a group of Paduans with the son of a Parisian banker, who may have been one of the Bardi of Florence.²

The organisation of the Paduan moneylenders appears to have been quite rudimentary. Loans were made by individuals or by *ad hoc* groups, but there is no indication that permanent partnerships were formed. Kinsmen generally worked together, and at one point the Scrovegni brothers can be seen accepting deposits from their well-married sisters.³ But, in general, Paduan documents do not distinguish between a deposit and a loan, and the only substitute for cash payment seems to have been the assignment of individual debts which was used from time to time but not systematically.⁴ At the more humble level of the moneychangers, the Paduans seem to have been equally back-

[1] For further details of these loans, see below, pp. 179–80, n. 7.
[2] Archivio Comunale, S. Vito di Leguzzano, Perg. antic., n. 5, published by G. Mantese, *S. Vito di Leguzzano dalle origini ai nostri giorni* (1959), pp. 231–7. This document of 1322 refers to an earlier loan of 3,625 florins received by Vitaliano Lemici and others from a certain 'd. Banchellum q.d. Bardi tabulatore seu campsore Parisiensi'. No-one of this description appears among the Bardi agents listed by A. Sapori, *Studi di storia economica medioevale*, 2nd ed. (1946), pp. 457–94.
[3] See below, p. 188.
[4] The practice was not restricted to commercial debts. For example, in 1314 the heirs of Aicardino da Villadelconte repaid his widow her dowry of £700 by this method (Bibl. Seminario, Padua, Documenti Famiglia Mussato III, n. 39), and in 1316 Zamboneto Cane assigned a debt of £1,000 to Gonberto da Vigodarzere for unspecified services to his father (Arch. Capit., Diversa II, n. 225).

ward. They had no guild, and the only partnership on record is a group of Florentines described as *socii campsores* in 1286.[1]

The currencies in use in Padua also indicate that the city was outside the main stream of the high finance of the period. The normal currency was Venetian, or occasionally Veronese deniers petty, or Venetian deniers gross.[2] Until the very end of the communal period, the Paduan mint had little more than a nominal existence, and Paduan coins are rarely mentioned. The new gold coins of the later thirteenth century, the florin and the ducat, hardly appear except in connection with Papal or Imperial taxation. While it would be wrong to assume that there could be no large-scale transactions without gold, this fact, in conjunction with the other evidence, points to the conclusion that Padua was not a major financial centre. The Paduans were moneylenders on a local scale only, and some of their notoriety may have derived from their being more associated with consumption loans than the financing of commerce. Usury played a large part in the advancement of certain Paduan families, but it is hard to believe that it made a very great contribution to the economy of the city as a whole.

For a clue to the basis of Padua's urban economy, it is necessary to return to the more impressionist picture presented by Da Nono's *Visio Egidii*. For the second part of his description, the author turns to the 'palaces' of the commune which, in order to compare with the *Mirabilia Urbis Rome*, he builds up to a total of fourteen by including not only the chief public buildings but also structures which appear to have been only covered markets, although there may have been apartments above.[3] The inclusion was not entirely unjustified as the distinction between *palazzi* and markets was not absolute, since goods were sold in the porticoes of all the public buildings. Thus there was ironmongery for sale under the Palazzo del Podestà and salt under the Palazzo degli Anziani. The Consiglio Maggiore of the commune met above the stalls devoted to the sale of Veronese and other cheap cloth. All these buildings adjoined the main square, which was divided into sections according to the wares on sale. On the north side were poultry, fruit, second-hand clothes and weapons; on the south, wines, tools, vegetables

[1] AD 3200.
[2] *Stat. Com.* 828.
[3] *Visio Egidii*, pp. 11–20.

and grain. On the edges of the square were a number of covered markets devoted to the sale of a further range of goods, particularly important being the corn market, the Fondaco delle Biade. There was also the communal prison, and a number of offices for the receipt of tolls and taxes. In the centre of the main square stood the Palazzo Comunale, its great roof, like an inverted ship, dominating the scene. Da Nono devotes a good deal of space to the description of this building, and with reason, for it was the heart of the Paduan state. On the first floor, next to the chapel of S. Martino, was the seat of the *podestà*, the head of the communal administration. Adjacent were the tribunals of the four judges of the *podestà*, who were mainly responsible for criminal cases; beyond were the fourteen benches of the ordinary judges. Each judge had a secretariat of five notaries. In the porticos on the floor below were stalls where good-quality cloth and clothing, hides and furs were sold. Other tradesmen had their places under the four staircases. Here, in the square, or in the adjacent streets of S. Urbano, S. Andrea, S. Martino and S. Lucia, the great majority of the public and private transactions of the city took place. Justice was administered in the market place and the conjunction points to a deep-seated interdependence. The administration could not have existed without the market, but without the administration, the market would not have been as large as it was.

Self-sufficiency was the ideal of the mediaeval city-state, and the goods listed by Da Nono drive home how much the city took from the contado. The wealth of the city was closely bound up with the wealth of its territory. In our period, the region directly subject to the commune coincided more or less with the modern province of Padua, except that it extended farther to the east to take in Mirano and Oriago, which are now part of the province of Venice. The whole made up a compact bloc with an area of about a thousand square miles, very little of which was irretrievably waste. From the economic point of view, it falls into two parts, the Pedevenda and the plain, which were largely complementary. The soil of the Pedevenda is rich and its valleys are sheltered, particularly suitable for the vine, as can be seen by the high prices paid for vineyards there; the *congola de Pedevenda* is the standard liquid measure in the Paduan documents. The hills were the only part of the Padovano where olives were grown, and they were the only considerable source of lime and building stone. While the Pedevenda was probably the first part of the Paduan contado to be intensively cultivated, the plain offered enormous opportunities for expansion once the initial problems of clearance and drainage had been overcome. Innumerable references to clearings and reclaimed land, and the comparative scarcity of references to woods and marshes suggest that much had been accomplished before 1256. Most of the plain seems to have been given over to arable and pasture though there were some vineyards. Large-scale sheep farming was not favoured, as there is only one reference to flocks of sheep and these were in an outlying part of the contado, on the meadows by the Adige at Lendenara.[1] For a time, productivity outstripped the growth of population, for in normal years the Padovano seems to have produced a surplus of grain during much of the communal period, and the commune was able to legislate encouraging peasants from other parts of Italy to settle on the land.[2]

A considerable part of the working population of the city was employed in the distribution of the products of the contado. In addition to the six main victualling guilds of butchers, bakers, cheesemongers, greengrocers, fishmongers and taverners, the oath of 1254 shows that there were other individuals like the corn chandlers or the oil merchants of S. Croce, who do not seem clearly to belong to any guild.[3] All these must have dealt mainly with the produce of the Paduan territory; only the spice and the salt merchants were, of necessity, importing guilds. It is significant that the guilds whose members individually were of some account were, after the notaries and physicians, precisely those which controlled the nexus between the city and the contado, particularly the butchers and the taverners, some of whom at least owned their own vineyards.[4] The statute forbidding the sale of fish by those who had not been responsible for catching them indicates that not all the city guilds carried on exclusively urban activities.[5] There was a guild of gardeners

[1] AD 5828.
[2] Newcomers were exempt from most taxation for five years, *Stat. Com.* 699.
[3] Thirteen corn-chandlers (*frumentarii, blavaroli*), including three in the council and four oil merchants (*olearii, qui facit oleum*), including one in the council, took the oath. For a full list of the Paduan guilds, see Appendix I
[4] For some examples, see below, pp. 179–80.
[5] *Stat. Com.* 856.

and a guild of *segatores* whose occupation was probably agricultural. The degree to which rural pursuits were carried on by citizens is underlined by the inclusion of three bird-catchers in the oath of 1254. Transport gave employment to the members of four Paduan guilds, the waggoners, the boatmen of Ognissanti, the boatmen of S. Giovanni and the wine porters. The routes connecting the city with the countryside were the lifelines of the urban population, and the commune provided for them accordingly. The Paduan canal system whose main lines were built by the commune between 1189 and 1212 was a remarkable achievement which must have considerably reduced the cost of urban living. The main canals ran from the port of S. Giovanni to Este, with branches tapping the Pedevenda at Arquà, Montegrotto and Galzignano, and from Ognissanti to Venice or Chioggia.[1] The preamble to a statute of 1308 ordering the removal of obstructions to navigation in the Bacchiglione above Padua shows that the river was chiefly valued as a means of bringing the victuals and timber of the north-western part of the contado into the city; few long-distance traders can have used this route, since the navigation to Vicenza was barred by the dam at Longare.[2] Apart from an obscure branch from Battaglia to Bovolenta, Padua was the hub of the whole system of waterways, and since all goods passing through the city had to be trans-shipped from the port of S. Giovanni to Ognissanti because of the change of level, they were almost physically forced into the city markets. The commune's road building was less spectacular than its waterways, but it served the same purpose. In the first quarter of the thirteenth century, new roads were built connecting the city with Piove di Sacco and Bovolenta, and in the 1270s the road to Limena was improved.[3] The statutes of the commune show the great care taken by the authorities to ensure that the roads and bridges of the contado were properly maintained, the main burden of this work falling upon the local communities.[4]

The Paduan commune not only facilitated the physical movement of goods into the city, it also legislated to prevent

[1] *Annales Patavini*, pp. 200, 261; *Stat. Com.* 886, 887, 896, 899.
[2] 'Ad hoc ut copia victualium habeant in, civitate Padue et etiam lignaminum', *Statuti Carraresi*, f. 230r.
[3] *Annales Patavini*, p. 261; Verci, *Marca Trivigiana*, doc. nn. 218–20.
[4] *Stat. Com.* 876–85, 1032–1118.

goods being carried elsewhere to the detriment of the Paduan market. Markets and fairs in the contado were closely controlled and were permitted only in a few privileged towns like Este and Cittadella.[1] The statutes forbade the export from Paduan territory of a wide range of goods, from precious metals to dung; in principle, all surplus goods, especially foodstuffs, had to be brought to the Paduan markets.[2] This was no more than the common practice of all Italian communes and Peyer's comparative study of grain policies has shown that in this regard the Paduan regulations were exceptionally mild.[3] The statues of 1276 allow grain to be freely exported until the price in Padua reached 8s. *per staio*, at which point the *podestà* was bound to consult the Consiglio Maggiore as to what should be done.[4] The critical figure is so low that free export must have been rare, but the aim of the controls in normal times was probably not to prohibit exports but ensure that they passed through the Paduan market and paid the tolls and taxes which were due. Until the end of the thirteenth century, it is likely that the Paduan state was on the whole an exporter of foodstuffs, but in the early fourteenth century there are signs that supplies were becoming less abundant. A series of laws was passed tightening up the administration of the regulations relating to foodstuffs, and their enforcement was made the chief responsibility of one of the judges of the *podestà*, assisted by one of his knights.[5] The building of the new cornmarket in 1309 probably indicates increased supervision by the state. To Da Nono's forensic mind, the Ponte Altinate suggested the smugglers who illegally carried victuals from Padua to Venice who, he remarks, if they were caught, forfeited half the goods to their accuser and half to the commune.[6]

Padua's main economic function with regard to the contado was as a centre of exchange and distribution; the exports and

[1] Ibid. 556 I, 565.
[2] Ibid. 800–11, 859.
[3] H. C. Peyer, *Zur Getreidepolitik Oberitalienischen Städte im XIII Jahrhundert* (1950), pp. 26–46.
[4] *Stat. Com*, 807, dated before 1236. But as early as 1204 11s. *per staio* had been considered a glut price (*Liber Regiminum*, p. 299).
[5] *Statuti Carraresi*, ff. 3–5, 13v–14r; M. Roberti, *Le corporazioni padovane d'arti e mestieri*, MRIV XXVI, viii (1902), pp. 97–9, 117–20.
[6] *Visio Egidii*, pp. 5–6.

imports of the whole territory were channelled through the city. Although it owed something to geographical and economic convenience, the monopoly of the Paduan market depended on force for its maintenance; it pre-supposed the political domination of the countryside by the city. The Paduan annals give some fragmentary information as to how this control had been consolidated in the late twelfth century and the first half of the thirteenth century; the statutes of 1276 show the process virtually complete. For administrative purposes, the contado began at a radius of two miles from the Palazzo Comunale, where stones were set up to mark the boundary of the *campanea Padue* which was administered with the city.[1] The rule of the Paduan commune over the contado was partly direct and partly indirect; not only were subject communes recognised in the larger towns like Monselice, Este and Montagnana, but some villages had their rural communes and there are sporadic references to meetings of local *vicinancie*;[2] the commune also accepted that certain areas were *de facto* under the predominant influence of local magnates. Jurisdiction in minor cases and the regulation of local affairs were left in the hands of these lesser bodies; in particular, rural communes were charged with the duty of protecting the property of citizens within their boundaries and with preventing the illicit export of foodstuffs.[3] What the Paduan commune reserved for itself was the higher jurisdiction or *comitatus*; for military service and criminal appeals, regions of the contado were attached to the administrative divisions of the city.[4] As a guarantee of its overall control, the commune sent out its *podestà* to the most important communities, twenty-seven of which are detailed in the statutes of 1276, and also maintained fortresses at strategic points, of which the most important were Monselice in the south and Cittadella in the north.

The measures by which the commune asserted its control and exacted services from the contado may be used to build up a political geography of Paduan territory. The salaries of the

[1] *Liber Regiminum*, p. 339.
[2] See list of extant statutes from the Padovano in the List of Sources below. They are discussed by A. Checchini, 'Comuni rurali padovani', *NAV* XVIII, i (1909), pp. 131–84. For *vicinancie* see AD 1829, 5757; Brunacci, *CDP* III, p. 1730.
[3] *Stat. Com.* 642, 687; *Statuti Carraresi*, ff. 136–41.
[4] *Stat. Com.* 471–2, 1010–30; *Statuti Carraresi*, f. lv.

podestà give some idea as to the relative importance of the main centres, and the economic strength of each locality is shown by the obligation to provide supply waggons for the communal militia imposed upon it; most important of all, a statute dated 1281 in the Carrara code of 1362 contains a hearth-assessment of the contado for the purpose of regulating contributions to public works on dykes and drainage canals.[1] These sources show without doubt that Monselice was the chief town in Paduan territory followed by Piove di Sacco and Este. The evidence relating to Montagnana is contradictory; probably the town was increasing in importance during the communal period. Cittadella enjoyed special privileges but its importance as a fortress was out of proportion to its modest development as a town; in general, the northern part of the contado seems to have been less rich than the south and west. In passing it should be noted that the fortified village was not a feature of the Paduan contado in our period; in Paduan documents, *castrum* means a fortified building or house, while a *villa* is a rural settlement. The relatively high salaries of the *podestà* of Conselve, Abano and Arquà suggest that they were responsible for a wider area than the villages concerned, but there is no evidence for a systematic division of the territory into *podestarie*. The compactness of the Paduan contado is underlined by the fact that no part of it, with the exception of the town of Montagnana, was considered to be more than a day's journey from the city for the purpose of making travelling allowances to officials.[2] It is tempting to take the further step and to try to calculate the population of the contado on the basis of the hearth assessment of 1281. Luzzatto gives the total number of *fuochi* as 12,660 which, multiplied by the usual coefficient gives a population of 57,000.[3] This figure would seem to be too low both in relation to the area of 1,000 square miles involved, and in relation to the urban population, which can hardly have been less than 30,000 at that date. Either, despite appearances to the contrary, the

---

[1] See below, key to Map III.
[2] *Stat. Com.* 394.
[3] G. Luzzatto, 'La popolazione del territorio padovano nel 1281' *NAV* III, ii (1902), pp. 373–84. Luzzatto estimated the rural population at 63,000 by using a coefficient of 5, but the evidence produced by R. Mols, *Introduction à la Demographie Historique des Villes de l'Europe* (1954–6), II, pp. 110–15 suggests that this should be reduced to at least 4·5.

assessment is incomplete, or the normal ratio of hearths to heads did not obtain.¹

The Paduan contado obviously contained some of the richest land in Italy, and very little waste; its products not only fed the city but normally provided a surplus for export. For the period, it constituted a considerable and tightly governed state whose administration offered substantial profits to those in a position to secure them. The ways in which these profits were distributed differed in the various periods of Paduan history. During the *signoria* of Ezzelino da Romano, the bulk seems to have accrued to the ruling family and a small body of henchmen and courtiers, of whom a few had some legal training, but after the restoration of the commune, administrative duties and their proceeds were spread much more widely among the citizens and the professional element increased enormously. Thus in 1254, under Ezzelino, only 14 judges and 86 notaries could be found to take the oath to uphold the alliance with Pelavicino, whereas forty years later there were at least 100 judges and probably 500 notaries in the city. The internal affairs of the commune were largely dominated by the lawyers and their lay relations. The College of Judges was one of the most important bodies in the city and the Guild of Notaries was without question the greatest of the guilds both in numbers and influence.² This swelling of the professional administrative class seems to have been particularly characteristic of the communal period, for after the establishment of the Carrara *signoria* in 1328, there are signs of a reaction against this class and the monopoly on which it depended. The number of judges declined and certain outlying areas and towns were released, at least in criminal cases, from the obligation of attending the Paduan courts.³

¹ There is one piece of evidence which suggests that this latter explanation may be the correct one. In 1295, the town of Bassano and its district was assessed at 586 hearths (P. M. Tua, 'Registro degli archivi bassanesi', *BMCB* VIII (1911), n. 646) indicating a population of about 2,640. But as early as 1175, about 800 men of Bassano between the ages of 14 and 70 took an oath of fidelity to the commune of Vicenza (Verci, *Storia degli Eccelini*, III (1779) doc. n. XL), which means that the population was already in the region of 2,400; it is hard to believe that the town had grown so little in more than a century.
² See Chapters V and VI below.
³ *Statuti Carraresi*, f. lv, dated 1320 but possibly later. For the number of Paduan judges at different times, see below, pp. 127-30.

Although administrative centralisation played its part, undoubtedly the greatest factor in the economic balance between the city and the countryside was the distribution of landed property. The overwhelming majority of the private documents of the period relate to land, and the impression which they convey, even when allowance has been made for their far from random survival, is that the greater part of the productive land of the Paduan contado was owned by individuals, families or corporations whose main home was in Padua. This situation had come about step by step with the growth of the city. The bishop, the cathedral chapter and the older religious houses which had once formed an important part of the nucleus of the urban population, still held considerable lands and tithes in the contado, the monastery of S. Giustina being particularly rich in lands. By the mid-thirteenth century, the landowning nobility were firmly rooted in the city. Many retained their castle or substantial country houses on their estates, but there was no great noble of the contado who did not have at least one *palazzo* in Padua in which he passed a part of the year. More humble immigrants to the city, of the kind who are found as notaries or members of the guilds, also maintained their links with the countryside. Men of this class are frequently found buying or leasing land, often in the localities from which they took their names; some of these holdings probably represent the property of the family before the move to the city took place. By an opposite process, men who made their fortunes in the town by moneylending, administration or trade, always invested in land, and the great Paduan usurers, when opportunity allowed, built up large estates by purchasing all the available land in certain villages, together with their castles and whatever jurisdiction still pertained to them. The ownership of small parcels of land extended to individuals quite low in the urban social scale, including obscure guildsmen with no obvious rural connections who can be found with holdings of a few *campi* which might be in the *campanea Padue* but might equally be situated a considerable distance from the city. It was felt necessary to try to restrict by law the time which a citizen might spend in the contado during the year.[1] Even an entirely urban association like the city Guild of Notaries sometimes invested its funds in rural land, though its natural preference was for

---

[1] *Stat. Com.* 692. The aim was to prevent tax evasion.

building plots and houses in the city.[1] The only major landowners who did not belong to the city were a few religious houses of the contado and a few which were outside Paduan territory altogether, mainly in Venice.

In town and country alike, the relations between landlord and tenant were almost always defined by a written contract known as a *livello*, in theory a lease for twenty-nine years which was in practice perpetual. The *livellarius* in the town paid a cash rent with certain customary gifts, but in the country his obligations were often expressed as a proportion of the produce of the land, generally between a third and a half. In addition, the tenant paid the tithe, originally due to the church but now almost always in the hands of a layman who was usually but not always identical with the landlord.

Since a man of almost any class might hold land by *livello*, class distinctions among the rural population must be defined in terms of wealth rather than tenure. At the top of rural society were those whose holdings were sufficient to release them from the exigencies of the agricultural routine. To this class must have belonged the notaries and petty moneylenders as well as some of the tradesmen of the towns or larger villages. Doubtless they played a leading role in the lesser communes and formed a rural bourgeoisie which was an important link between the city and the contado. Some, at least, were rich enough for the commune to demand mounted service from them in time of war.[2] Below these come the great mass of *livellarii* who were cultivators of the soil; villagers upon whose backs the whole economy ultimately rested, who are recorded only when they come to renew the *livello* by which they held the land from which they lived. Even less is known about the lowest classes of rural society; it is doubtful whether the unfree, who were disappearing at this time in the more developed parts of Italy, survived into our period in significant numbers. It is noticeable that the statutes which speak of *villani* who could be dismissed from the land at a

---

[1] *Statuti della Fraglia dei Notai 1260–1341*, (*Stat. Not.*) MS Archivio Notarile, Padua, ff. 51–8; the guild buys land with vineyards in Frassenedo in 1307 for £800.

[2] See references to *milites* in *Statuta et Ordinamenta Communis S. Georgii de Perticis*, nn. 16–17, 19, Checchini, *NAV* XVIII (1909), pp. 174–84. About a thousand of them served in the Paduan army in 1312 (Mussato, *Historia Augusta*, col. 429).

fixed time of the year, almost all date from the first half of the thirteenth century; on the other hand, a statute of 1283 forbade *servi* to hold office in the rural communes.[1] The problem is bound up with the question of the survival of the large estates as effective units of agricultural organisation, for the complete absence of labour services from existing contracts suggests either that demesne farming was carried on only with semi-free or hired labour, or that it had virtually disappeared. In favour of the latter alternative, one may cite the testimony of a Paduan witness in 1318 who defined a *domus dominicalis* as 'a house situated in a village in which the produce and rents of the lords are collected.'[2] The large estates of the period, such as those of the monastery of S. Giustina or the Carrara family, seem to have consisted of a multitude of small parcels of land scattered within the territory of one or more villages, linked only by their common ownership and the obligation of the tenants to render their dues to the lord's *gastaldione* at a convenient centre. The total effect of the property structure must have been to place great quantities of rural produce at the disposal of urban landowners every year, and it was primarily by this produce that the city lived.

It remains to consider the possible role played by taxation in the economic relations between town and country. Italian historians of the last generation, notably Salvemini and Checchini, asserted that the commune ruthlessly exploited the countryside by imposing a much greater burden of taxation on the contado than on the city, but this view has recently been challenged by Dr Fiumi.[3] The question has an important bearing on the nature of the urban economy, for a higher rate of taxation in the contado could have provided an incentive for immigration into the towns, and would have produced a kind of subsidy on urban living which would have contributed to the maintenance of the urban population. The Paduan evidence in this respect is not conclusive, but so far as it goes, it suggests that it is unlikely that differential taxation was an important factor in the growth of the city after 1256. If there was any serious exploitation of this kind, it would seem to have been introduced

---

[1] *Stat. Com.* 663–7; *Statuti Carraresi*, f. 143r.
[2] 'Domus posita in villa, in qua colliguntur fruges et redditus dominorum', Brunacci, *Appendice al CDP* (MS Seminario 583), II, n. 102.
[3] E. Fiumi, *ASI* CXIV (1956), pp. 18–68.

only in the 1290s and is mainly associated with the economic and political decline of the commune after 1311.

The regular income of the Paduan commune was obtained from the rents on its property. The inventory of the commune's possessions has not been preserved so no overall picture of the distribution of communal property is possible. The remaining references suggest that much of the commune's land had been acquired in connection with some particular public works of a special kind, so that although the commune had its *livellarii*, most of its capital was invested in unusual kinds of property. Thus the commune owned the hot springs of Montegrotto and Montenovo and retained land and mills lying adjacent to the Monselice canal.[1] Mills, which were farmed, formed an important part of the commune's property in the city.[2] Another important item was the rents obtained from the stalls in the city's markets which were generally leased *en bloc* to the appropriate guilds for distribution among their members. In 1273 the commune demanded from the butchers an annual payment of 12 per cent on the £4,224 13s. which it had spent on improvements to the meat market.[3] In the contado, the commune depended upon forced labour for the essential works on dykes, roads and bridges. In the three decades after 1256 a great deal of legislation was passed on this subject, closely defining the obligations of each village and hamlet.[4] It was most probably these services which the inhabitants of the village of Volta Brusegana wished to avoid when they petitioned for the privilege of being taxed with the city and the *campanea Padue* in 1322.[5] It is hard to believe that these two traditional ways of providing for the costs of government and public works, rents from communal property and forced labour in the contado, affected the balance of town and country to any significant degree, though the avoidance of the latter may have provided an incentive to migration into the city.

The normal word in the Paduan records for a tax of almost

---

[1] *Statuti Carraresi*, f. 213r; AD 3123.
[2] Da Nono, *Visio Egidii*, pp. 5–6, mentions eight mill-wheels belonging to the commune near the Porta Torricelli and another two near S. Leonardo; in 1254 the commune had a linen mill in the *centenario* of Rudena (AS Cremona, ASC 1785).
[3] *Stat. Com.* 1123–9.
[4] Ibid. 1032–1118, 908–1010, 1260–2; *Statuti Carraresi*, ff. 240–96r.
[5] Corona, 3269–70.

any kind is *dacia*, but the *dacia par excellence* was a personal tax similar to the Florentine *libra*, for which the citizens' individual assessments were kept in the *Liber Impositionum*.[1] It was these assessments which were used to define the qualifications for the holding of public office and the enjoyment of certain privileges. Although the assessments were supposed to be brought up to date every five years, the imposition of a *dacia* on the city and contado in 1290 was still sufficiently unusual to be recorded in the annals.[2] There is nothing to suggest that the rural areas paid the *dacia* at a higher rate; indeed, the contrary may have been the case, since in the 1270s it would seem that the assessment was based on movable property only, which must have struck the citizens more heavily than the peasants.[3] The most obvious injustice was the way in which persons whose assessment was high paid proportionately less than their poorer neighbours.[4] By 1317, however, the *dacia* was being levied on both real and movable property. This is shown by an assessment relating to Guidota Engleschi, a complete copy of which is still extant. Each piece of property is listed with its estimated value and its annual rent, whether in corn or cash; the total assessment is £2,803, the annual income is estimated at £149 0s. 4d., or just over 5 per cent.[5]

The commune also imposed taxes from time to time on a wide range of commodities, from horses, carts and cattle, to cloth, thread and salt, wine and cheese.[6] These taxes were farmed, and in a few cases there is a record of the sum raised. For example, the salt tax was sold for £7,110 in 1279 and for £8,505 in 1285; the corn tax (*dacia bladi*) brought in £2,808 at the same date.[7] In 1314, after a period of war, the *dacia*

[1] *Stat. Com.* 1187.   [2] *Liber Regiminum*, p. 340.
[3] This may be deduced from *Stat. Com.* 414, dated 1274, which lays down that *anziani della comunanza* should be 'in dacia communis Padue ad minus pro libris ducentis' but should have £500 'in bonis immobilibus'.
[4] In 1280, 2s. tax was due on an assessment of 20s., 50s. on £100 and a further 3d. in the pound over £100 (AD 566; another copy, with date, in *Statutum Magnifice Communitatis Cittadelle*, MS Biblioteca della Corte d'Appello, Venice).   [5] Corona, 340.
[6] E.g. 'dacia capiciorum, telle, filli et lini maioris' (AD 6333); 'dacia equorum' (AD 4854); 'dacia plaustrorum' (*Stat. Com.* 978); 'dacia bestiarum' (Corona, 3234).
[7] G. B. Verci, *Acta ad Patavinos Spectantia ex Membranis Tabularii Bassaniensis* (MS BP 818), pp. 149–50; AD 3182.

machinatarum, which was levied on most types of grain, was worth £17,265.[1] There are no clear indications of how these taxes were assessed and collected. The *dacia vini* which was one of the earliest, imposed to pay for the building of the *murus spaldi* soon after 1256, was rated at 20s. per waggon load.[2] This gives it the appearance of a toll, but this may be misleading for it was collected in both town and country and therefore cannot have been a market toll, and it may be doubted if any other kind of toll would have been practicable. The terminology of the statutes is very imprecise, but there seems to have been a general tendency to abolish tolls within the state, those remaining being vestiges of outdated feudal rights, like the *muda* of the city gates which was the property of the bishop.[3] It is possible therefore that the *dacia vini* may have been a sales tax, and that the taxes on commodities like salt and cloth, whose sale was closely regulated by a guild, may have all been raised in this way. On the other hand, some of the *dacie* must have taken the form of direct taxes imposed on special classes of movables. An obvious example was the annual road tax on carts (*dacia plaustrorum*); another was the *dacia machinatarum*, which in 1292 was collected by a commission who were to assess the stocks of grain held by individuals on a particular day.[4]

All these taxes on movables seem to have been imposed equally on the city and contado, but their incidence must have varied greatly according to the type of commodity taxed. The chief weight of the *dacia salis* and the *dacia machinatarum* must have fallen initially on the rural producers; this may have been balanced by the more obscure taxes on textiles but this seems unlikely. The final distribution of the tax burden would depend on whether the producer was free to pass on the increased cost to the consumers in the form of higher prices. Some communes in this period, such as Pisa, did control the price of grain in order to provide cheap bread for the citizens.[5] There is no positive evidence for this in Padua, but the building of the Fondaco delle Biade in 1309 is an indication that the commune

---

[1] Verci, op. cit. p. 373.
[2] *Stat. Com.* 973, 975–6; Verci, op. cit. p. 295.
[3] *Stat. Com.* 477, 1204–6.
[4] Verci, *Marca Trivigiana*, doc. n. 340.
[5] Herlihy, *Pisa in the Early Renaissance*, pp. 109–16.

was taking an interest in the grain market.[1] If price control was imposed at a time when the *dacia machinatarum* was increasing in importance, the last years of the commune may have seen an over-taxation of the contado which may have contributed to the collapse of the Paduan state after 1311.

The dichotomy which we have made between city and contado will have served its purpose if it has drawn attention to the problem posed by the existence of a city of 35,000 people which did not support itself to any great extent by long distance trade or urban industries. In fact, the distinction between the rural and the urban economy is to a large degree unrealistic. Padua and its contado formed a single economic unit in which production was spread throughout the territory, and distribution and consumption were concentrated in the city. A high proportion of the city's working population was employed in crafts organised on a small scale to meet local needs, most of the rest were in the victualling trades. But in the governing class, while a few were professional moneylenders, and a few may have had interests in trade, all were *rentiers* of various kinds living directly or indirectly on the resources of the contado. The nobility and many of the *popolani* looked to rents as their main source of income; others were to varying degrees administrators in the service of the commune, drawing a part of their livelihood from taxation or the costs of justice and administration. It was this common interest which provided the indispensable economic foundation for the Paduan commune.

[1] Price control would have been no innovation in Padua, since from 1277 the commune fixed the retail price of wine at certain times of the year (*Stat. Com.* 1207, I).

CHAPTER III

Nobles and Magnates

'IT is the walls which define the city, but it is the inhabitants and not the stones who make up the commonwealth.' Acting in the spirit of Isidore of Seville's definition, Da Nono completed his topographical description of the city with an account of the citizens of the Paduan commonwealth; indeed, of the two, it was the latter aspect which aroused the author's greater interest: the *Visio Egidii* is little more than an introduction to the *De Generatione aliquorum civium urbis Padue, tam nobilium quam ignobilium* which is Da Nono's *magnum opus*.[1] Often mistakenly described as a chronicle, the *De Generatione* in fact belongs to an entirely different genre in which the framework is made up not of events in chronological order but of families arranged according to their social position, well over a hundred, ranging from the noble Estensi and Carraresi down to quite humble guildsmen, being described in the four books. Within each family, Da Nono's treatment follows a fairly set pattern. Beginning with an account of the supposed origins of the family, there follows a description of the more important individuals of the author's own time, ending, where appropriate, with details of the family's houses in the city, its coat of arms and an estimate of its wealth. Among the sources are clearly a number of earlier 'chronicles,' popular legends enshrined in songs, folklore and gossip, but above all Da Nono drew on great personal knowledge of his contemporaries and their affairs which owed much to his professional experience as a judge. In writing in this way, Da Nono seems to have been following a local tradition of which only a few traces now remain, but the literary ancestry of the *De Generatione* is by no means as clear as that of the *Visio Egidii*. Whatever its antecedents, the *De Generatione* provides a

---

[1] Unedited; the basic MS to which all references will be made is Seminario Padua, n. 11, ff. 15–53. I am currently engaged in a complete edition of Da Nono's works which it is hoped will be published by the Deputazione Veneta di Storia Patria in the near future.

comprehensive picture of a mediaeval city seen as a corpus of families which seems to have been unique for its time.[1]

Since the *De Generatione* describes Paduan society in terms of its component families, it is essential to inquire first how the family was defined and what were the norms of family and inter-family relations. The family was a group of persons related in the male line, which was the only criterion of membership; there is no evidence of legal adoption, nor of brotherhoods including several different kin (*consorzi nobiliari*) found at an earlier period among the nobility of many parts of Italy.[2] In legal documents every individual was identified by his father's name in addition to his own, followed by the family name if there was one. The use of a surname was not universal, but was slowly spreading down the social scale from the nobles, all of whom had established family names by the end of the twelfth century, to the artisans of the town, only a few of whom had them by the end of the communal period. Families of all social classes often took their names from a place with which they were associated, occasionally from a trade, but commonly from the name or nickname of an individual. The Dalesmano who gave his name to the magnate Dalesmanini lived about the middle of the twelfth century; the judge Buzzaccarino, founder of the family which took his name, flourished a hundred years later. Approximately half the notaries mentioned in city documents had surnames by the early fourteenth century. Occasionally, a new family would appear through the fission of a greater one; thus the Papafava sprang from the Carrara and the Paradisi from the Capodivacca, both in the later thirteenth century. In an exceptional case, the descendants of Marco Zeno Badoer took the name Da Peraga from his wife Balzanella, through whom they had inherited the castle of that name.

The moral unity of the family under the monarchical rule of the *paterfamilias*, was recognised both by common law and local custom. The former laid down that all sons remained under their father's control until his death unless he formally emancipated them before a judge. The power of the head of the family is underlined by a Paduan statute which, while admitting that

[1] See J. K. Hyde, 'Italian Social Chronicles in the Middle Ages', *BJRL* XLIX, i (1966).
[2] F. Niccolai, 'I consorzi nobiliari ed il comune nell'Alta e Media Italia', *RSDI* XII (1940), pp. 116–47, 292–341, 397–477.

the father had a general obligation to provide for his sons, denied to the heirs any fixed proportion of the inheritance.[1] Among the nobility, it was customary for co-heirs to hold the estate in common (*pro indiviso*) at least until the partners had families of their own. Among the citizens, the right to sit in the Consiglio Maggiore passed, on the death of a member, to his nearest kinsman, and trades and professions were often hereditary.[2]

Families were supposed to maintain a united front against the outside world. The chronicler Rolandino reports with approval the opinion of those who, knowing the strength of brotherly love, refused to believe that the apparent break between Ezzelino and Alberico da Romano was real, 'for it was not credible that two full brothers should strive and struggle together so as to bear one another a mortal enmity'.[3] In fact, it is noticeable that the recurrent disputes within the Este family only became irreconcilable when they came to involve an illegitimate brother, and the Carraresi, despite disagreements as to the means to be employed, in the end worked together to secure the *signoria* of Padua. Both within the city, and at the wider provincial level, politics were seen in terms of family rivalries and alliances.

Marriage was seen as an alliance between families as well as a union between individuals. Rolandino notes how many believed that Ezzelino's marriage to Beatrice da Castelnovo indicated that he would make peace with the leading Paduan magnates.[4] At all levels of society, the power and prestige of a family was partly determined by its marriage connections. Ideally, marriage took place only between social equals, so that, in general, the marriages of the members of a family are a good guide to its social standing. Sometimes political or financial considerations would produce a marriage where the parties were not felt to be social equals; in Padua, as elsewhee, there were men who were believed to have made their fortunes by a lucky or a skilful marriage. The relative wealth and social standing of the families concerned was reflected in the dowry settled on the wife by her kin, which passed, with her, under the trusteeship of the husband for the duration of the marriage.

[1] *Stat. Com.* 589.
[2] See below, p. 210.
[3] Rolandino, p. 126.
[4] Ibid. p. 90.

Apart from a general tendency to increase during the period, which was much deplored by the moralists of the time,[1] the dowries within families, social and professional groups show a remarkable consistency; but, when there was a marked social disparity, as when the daughter of a newly enriched citizen married the son of a nobleman, a greatly inflated dowry would be paid.[2]

The social distinctions between families were thought of in terms of nobility, a concept which was so all-pervading that it was usually taken for granted and rarely explicitly discussed. In Italy, it is true, the exceptional social mobility noticed by Otto of Freising in the mid-twelfth century, does seem to have produced an undertow of social questioning which occasionally breaks the surface, as in the stories of the Emperor Frederick II's discussions of nobility, or in the preoccupation with *gentilezza* shown by the poets of the *Dolce stil nuovo*.[3] It cannot be said, however, that these scattered references reveal any coherent doctrine of nobility; the varied approaches of the poets, philosophers and lawyers only underline the elusiveness of the idea at the time. Social tensions were expressed in conflicting theories as to the nature of nobility.

Broadly speaking, there seem to have been two main approaches to the question of nobility: the literary and the legalistic. The writers in the literary tradition tended to stress the moral aspect of nobility: 'È Gentilezza dovunque è virtute' —often, as in Dante, in order to minimise the hereditary element. But this was not always so: Brunetto Latini, for example, while noting that *noblesce de lignie* is nothing without *vertueuses oevres*, can also say of the noble virtue of magnanimity, 'Et noblesce de naissance, signorie et richece, aident moult a home a estre magnanimes.'[4] The lawyers were naturally much more precise, but they were very slow to evolve a definition of nobility. The reason for this is not far to seek. Most ages discuss social questions through a terminology carrying overtones from the past; the mediaeval Italian jurists were using terms derived

---

[1] E.g. Dante, *Paradiso*, XV, ll. 103–5.
[2] For examples, see below, pp. 83 n. 3, 141, 169.
[3] Otto of Freising, *Gesta Friderici I Imperatoris*, ed. G. Waitz, MGH. SS. Rerum Germanicarum in usum scholarum, 3rd edn. (1912), pp. 116–17; G. Bertoni, *Il Duecento* (1910), pp. 165–8.
[4] *Li Livres dou Tresor*, ed. J. Carmody (1948), pp. 194, 295.

from Roman law whose original significance had been almost entirely lost. It is hardly surprising that the glossators, when they came to comment on the law *de dignitatibus*, failed to appreciate and bridge the gulf which divided their republican city-states from the autocratic monarchy of sixth-century Constantinople.

The classic discussion of the question of nobility by a mediaeval lawyer was produced by Bartolo da Sassoferrato in his commentary on the *Codex* about the middle of the fourteenth century.[1] It illustrates admirably the impossibility of producing a clear-cut and universally valid definition of nobility in mediaeval Italy; where Bartolo failed, lesser men may be excused who did not even try. He begins by ruling *nobilitas theologica* and *nobilitas naturalis* as outside the scope of his subject, which he takes to be *nobilitas politica et civilis*. This Bartolo defines as a quality conferred by a sovereign which raises a man above the level of the honest *plebs*. Occasionally an inferior grade of nobility may be conferred directly; normally what is conferred is an office to which the quality of nobility is attached. It remains to define what is a sovereign, and what offices carry nobility with them. For the first, Bartolo suggests that a king, a marquis, a duke or a great count, also a commonwealth is sufficient, provided it has the power to make laws for its subjects;[2] for the second, Bartolo is forced to conclude that this depends entirely on local custom.[3] Thus knighthood did not ennoble in Florence, though it did in Perugia. The unfortunate jurist is reduced to special pleading to prove that knighthood may carry with it nobility, even though it is not an office; the height of paradox is reached when Bartolo faces the objection that under the anti-magnatial laws, nobility, far from arising from a public office, actually meant legal disabilities and disqualification from office. He can only conclude that nobility depends on local custom and public opinion: 'In brief, nobility is what the prince or the commune have accepted it shall be.'

[1] *In Duodecim Libros Codicis Commentaria* (Basle, 1562), pp. 938–45.
[2] 'Rex, marchio, dux vel magnus comes qui habet potestatem condendi leges in suos. Et idem intellego de quolibet populo, qui habet potestatem condendi leges' (p. 943).
[3] 'Istud officium seu ille actus habet in se dignitatem sive nobilitatem annexam, quod in universitate illa ubi de hoc agitur, habere illam reputatur' (p. 944).

Bartolo's discussion of nobility is not entirely barren; great interest lies in the possible opinions which are tacitly or explicitly rejected. Thus the jurist, like the poet, refuses to recognise nobility as a hereditary caste based on a perpetual hereditary right; the most that he will admit is that it extends to great-grandchildren or until the descendants come to poverty and the practice of degrading occupations. Though it could be lost through poverty, it could not simply be acquired through wealth—a generation or two were needed to purge the line of *rusticitas*. By thus combining the idea of a nobility based on office with a limited hereditary element, Bartolo was able to move some way towards reconciling what he found in his texts with the view of nobility current in his day. But local customs varied, and even within the same city, different opinions might be found. 'If someone makes the point that someone was and is reputed to be noble, it is not sufficient, because the word "noble" is ambiguous.'

It is therefore pertinent to ask what nobility meant in thirteenth- and fourteenth-century Padua. As might have been expected, there is no simple answer to this question. In the documents of the period some titles, such as *magister* for a master of one of the guilds, or *sapiens et discretus vir* for a judge in office, are used with consistency and care, but this was not the case with titles denoting nobility. The notaries who recorded the oath of 1254 distinguish between those citizens and members of the council who are styled *dominus* and those who are not, but after 1256 this distinction progressively disappears, and *dominus* is applied to everyone above the status of a peasant or a labourer, up to the heads of the most powerful noble houses. The style *nobilis vir*, on the other hand, is comparatively rare and its use is quite unsystematic. A good deal depended on the circumstances, and the various writing offices in Padua and elsewhere followed slightly different practices. Sometimes the whim of the notary or his client seems to have been sufficient. All that can be deduced from an isolated use of the style *nobilis vir* is that the application of this title to the individual concerned was not so unreasonable as to be ridiculous.

The Paduan commune was not interested in defining nobility, which was a matter of reputation and prestige, but only with naming those who, through their preponderant power in the city or a part of its territory, constituted a danger to its public authority. It is important to keep this primarily legal and political category distinct from the social concept of *nobilitas*, even if the two are sometimes confused in the sources. In the statutes, the over-mighty subjects of the Paduan commune are described as *magnates, potentiores* or *male ablati*.[1] Generally, these were defined as powerful men who were not members of the political organisation of the *popolo*, but occasionally the statutes are more precise and list by name the persons falling within their scope. The statutes relating to the protection of life and property in the villages of the magnates include two examples: one, belonging to a statute dated 1225, contains names not inconsistent with that period, while the other, though appended to a statute of 1216, may be placed some time between the restoration of the commune in 1256 and the death of Uberto Dalesmanini in October 1266.[2] Both these lists are very short, including members of only nine and ten families respectively. A third statute, of 1278, is much longer and more informative as it gives the names of persons who, either individually or jointly, were to be held responsible for the arrest of outlaws in certain specified villages and districts.[3] These are drawn from some twenty families who were almost certainly regarded as *potentiores*, but there is no guarantee that the list is complete. The designation of a *potentior* was largely a political matter, liable to be influenced by matters of policy and reflecting the obscure shifts of power within the communal government.

Most of the Paduan writers of the communal period show themselves conscious of social distinctions but their remarks are, for the most part, too fragmentary to reveal the author's ideas of nobility. The historians were chiefly concerned with its political aspect: Rolandino shows a respectful deference towards the nobility and stresses the importance of class solidarity, and Mussato considers the Paduan constitution as one embodying a balance between the powers of the nobles and the *popolo*.[4] For a direct interest in social distinctions in their own right, it is necessary to turn to Da Nono's *De Generatione*. As the title

---

[1] *Stat. Com.*, nn. 10, 86, 461, 472 et seq. The primary meaning of 'male ablati' is ill-gotten gains, especially the profits of usury; its application to a class of persons seems to be restricted to Padua and some neighbouring cities.
[2] *Stat. Com.*, nn. 645, 635.   [3] See Appendix III, pp. 312–14.
[4] See below, p. 217; 'nobilibus plebeisque mixta', *De Gestis*, col. 587.

suggests, this is a description of families noble and ignoble, and, though nobility is nowhere explicitly defined, the author's views on the subject become clear as the analysis proceeds.

For Da Nono, a noble family was one which, at some time in the past, had been granted an Imperial *privilegium*. This would normally have conferred the right of higher jurisdiction, which he sometimes defines as jurisdiction of blood or *merum et mixtum imperium*.[1] In the case of the counts of Padua, Da Nono notes only that they had had the right to a loaf from each baker and a proportion of the wine sold by each taverner, and he believed that the jurisdiction of his own family had included a levy on all ships, mills and fish on the river Brenta, and the power to create notaries and judges.[2] But, in the last resort, even the grant of a purely ceremonial office was sufficient to ennoble, such as that of the Da Ronchi di Campanile, which was to carry a sword before the Emperor, 'although they had no jurisdiction in the Paduan district except their above-named privilege'.[3] It was essential, however, that the privilege, however small, should be exercised in Padua. Thus the De Doto, though descended from the nobility of Troy 'were reputed *populares*, since they do not seem to have had any jurisdiction in this city'.[4] Once conferred, Da Nono seems to have imagined that nobility continued indefinitely, though it could be lost either through poverty, as in the case of some of the Da Nono 'who became rustics through lack of wealth', or through the practice of a base occupation, as with the Scintilla who had had jurisdiction over fourteen villages; 'however, these powerful men were not considered nobles in Padua because they kept a moneylender's table in the Via Maggiore of the city'.[5]

The similarities between Da Nono's views on nobility and the theories of Bartolo are sufficiently apparent; despite the wide gap in learning and culture between the two men, they both belong to the same juristic tradition. But Da Nono's ideas were markedly more conservative and aristocratic, especially as he worked them out in practice in the course of the *De Generatione*. Circumstances and inclination made Da Nono seek for evidence of nobility only in the past. In the first place, when the

---

[1] E.g. *De Generatione*, ff. 34–5.　　[2] Ibid. ff. 29–30.
[3] Ibid. f. 36r.　　[4] Ibid. f. 39r.
[5] Ibid. ff. 31v, 33r.

De Generatione was written, few Imperial privileges had been granted in Padua for the past hundred and fifty years or so, and Da Nono seems to ignore even the few which had. Then, as the author remarks several times, the commune had taken away all higher jurisdictions in Paduan territory about a century before, and whatever vestigial rights may have remained in his day were not taken as sufficient to prove nobility. As Da Nono had access to very few records relating to the period before 1200, he was forced to rely largely on popular legends and folklore. As depicted in the *De Generatione*, the Paduan nobility were a diminishing class of ancient families, many of whom were extinct or declining into obscurity.

Da Nono was a romantic conservative; any doubts on this matter are removed by a consideration of his third work, the so-called *De Hedificatione Urbis Patavie*, most of which is concerned with the seemingly endless battles and jousts of the knights of the remote past in the war between Dardano, King of Padua, and the Tartars.[1] But there was another side to his nature which was passionately interested in his contemporaries and the realities of their wealth and power. In a remarkable chapter entitled 'Of the Paduan families who were the more noble and powerful at the time of Henry of Luxemburg', Da Nono discusses the rise and fall of the Paduan magnates of his own time almost entirely in terms of military and political power and wealth.[2] Throughout the *De Generatione*, Da Nono shows a keen interest in the wealth of his fellow-citizens, often giving a sum which he believes that they were 'worth'.[3] There is unfortunately no way of checking these figures: it would be interesting to know if they were derived from tax assessments.

Nobility, power and wealth are three strands which run through the *De Generatione* and give it unity. The plan of the work shows a half-resolved conflict between the author's passion for the past on the one hand, and his interest in the realities of power and wealth in his own day on the other. In the first book, Da Nono discusses three families only—the Estensi, the Camposanpiero and the Da Romano—families with diverse origins who together had dominated the social and political life

[1] Seminario MS 11, ff. 1–8.
[2] *De Generatione*, f. 38.
[3] E.g. 'Petrus de Scruffegnis habens valorem maiorem quam centum milia librarum . . .', ibid. f. 44r.

of Padua in the late twelfth century and first half of the thirteenth century. They are, in fact, three of the four families mentioned by Rolandino at the beginning of his chronicle, and the imitation is probably direct, since much of Da Nono's extended account of the rise and fall of the Da Romano is based on Rolandino and the more popular and sensational *Chronicon Marchiae Tarvisinae et Lombardie*. The *De Generatione* begins to break fresh ground in the second book, which is devoted to the old nobility of Padua, many of whom had declined to insignificance, though a few still maintained their position. In book three, Da Nono deals with those families which were powerful in his time, but whom he did not consider truly noble, though he calls some of them 'noble citizens'. The fourth book is devoted to the non-nobles, who fall into two groups: those good men of the *popolo* who might be prosperous but who knew their station, and those, epitomised by the infamous Scrovegni, who had recently enriched themselves by shameless usury and were seeking assimilation into the aristocracy.

The *De Generatione* is not a theoretical but a descriptive work; its value derives not so much from the theory of society implicit in it, as the way in which it is worked out in detail. Da Nono is a unique and invaluable guide to the nature of Paduan society, and that despite his manifest prejudices and eccentricity. Over the centuries, the attitudes of antiquarians and historians to the *De Generatione* have varied from complete and uncritical acceptance to outright rejection. It must be accepted that Da Nono's ideas of historical events before the thirteenth century were wildly inaccurate—they represent what was popularly believed to have happened—also Da Nono was constitutionally inclined to say little that was favourable to any family or individual. For most of the scandals he reports, there is now no proof either one way or the other. On the other hand, many of the complex family relationships which he describes can be checked against contemporary documents, and can be shown to be extremely accurate. Even when Da Nono seems to have been swayed by prejudice, he frequently gives a kind of summing up of both sides of the question before pronouncing his verdict.

Only a complete critical edition of the *De Generatione* can establish its reliability in detail; here, two examples alone must suffice. There were only two Paduan families whom Da Nono was predisposed to regard with favour—his wife's and his own.

Concerning the former, we have already noticed that although he makes the high claim that the De Doto had a gate named after them in Troy, he nevertheless has the honesty to admit that they were not considered noble in Padua. With regard to his own family, his claims are at first sight fantastic. The Da Nono, he says, are the same family as the Trevisan Castelli and Counts of Collalto, and used to be powerful throughout Lombardy, exercising rights in the whole March of Treviso which sound like a garbled recollection of those of a count palatine.[1] For all this, there seems to be no shred of supporting evidence, except for a curious entry in the *Liber Regiminum* under the year 1204:

And the commune of Treviso destroyed the lords of Nono because of their pride, and because of a great possession which they had in the district of Treviso. And the Trevisans sold the castle of Castelli which the lords Carmonesi bought for £30,000 and from that day onwards they were called the Castelli. And then the castle of Carturo, which is on the Musone, and Villanova were given to the lords of Nono as goods of the Trevisans which they had in the Paduan district, by the counsel of Lenzone and Guicemano, *procuratores* and *extimatores* of the Paduan commune. But this castle was afterwards destroyed by the Trevisans.[2]

Although the *Liber Regiminum* is a compilation of the mid-fourteenth century, this entry carries considerable weight, since it is not derived from the writings of Da Nono but almost certainly from a document of which the judge was entirely ignorant. If, as it suggests, the Da Nono really were a displaced and impoverished branch of the Castelli, then Giovanni's most unlikely claim, while much exaggerated, can be seen to have behind it a certain basis of truth.

While following Da Nono through the maze of Paduan family relationships, it is helpful whenever possible to check one's bearings with other evidence. A chance reference in a document or a literary source may have considerable significance when placed in the context of the *De Generatione*. The statutes of 1225, 1256–66 and 1278 are obviously important evidence of magnatial status. Moreover, the *De Generatione* does not quite stand alone. The only authority frequently cited by

---

[1] *De Generatione*, ff. 30–2.
[2] *Liber Regiminum*, p. 299.

Da Nono is that of the notary Zambono d'Andrea (fl. 1254–1315), some of whose verses relating to family relationships, castles and coats of arms are quoted in the *De Generatione*. Unfortunately, Zambono's poem has been lost, and a prose work on the model of the *De Generatione* which has sometimes been attributed to him is either a late-fourteenth-century fabrication, or has so garbled an earlier source as to render it quite worthless. Of much greater value are the fragments of the 'chronicle' of Antonio d'Alessio, which seem to represent an earlier work in the same genre which was unknown to Da Nono. No copy of this book has ever come to light, and it is known only through some brief notes made by Gianfrancesco Capodilista in 1434, which amount to little more than a list of some forty families and their castles, sometimes with a short remark such as *cum privilegio*. According to Capodilista, D'Alessio compiled his work in 1258 using earlier chronicles of the second half of the twelfth century, and the information which he gives seems to be entirely consistent with such a date. A castle *cum privilegio* in Antonio d'Alessio is therefore good *prima facie* evidence for nobility, and a castle without an Imperial diploma indicates a family which was at least well established.[1]

Since nobility was universally held to derive from public office, it will be best to begin our analysis of the Paduan aristocracy with those families which, holding the titles of count or marchese, claimed descent from the officials who had held public authority in the Regnum Italicum before the rise of the communes. In the Carolingian period, Padua had belonged, with her neighbours Verona, Vicenza and Treviso, to the March of Friuli; in the later twelfth century when the administrative unity of the region was no more than a dim memory, the name March of Treviso was used in a loose way to indicate the same area. The only *marchesi* in the region had strictly speaking nothing to do with the March but were descended from the Obertenghi, one of the great noble families of the ninth and tenth centuries. They took their name from the castle of Este in the southern part of the Paduan *comitatus*, but they had interests

---

[1] J. F. Capodilistae, *De Viris Illustribus Familiae Capodilistae*, MS BP 954. The D'Alessio list is printed with notes by V. Lazzarini, 'Un antico elenco di fonti storiche padovane', *Archivio Muratoriano*, I, vi, pp. 326–35. For an appraisal of the historical value of Capodilista, see J. K. Hyde, *BJRL* XLIX, i (1966).

which were scattered over a wide area of north-eastern Italy.¹ In 1208, Azzo VI d'Este was given the title of *Marchese* of the March of Ancona for himself and his descendants by Innocent III²; in 1264 the family established an early *signoria* over the city of Ferrara which thereafter became their chief home and the centre of their power.

The Estensi were the head of the social hierarchy not only in Padua but in the whole March of Treviso. Rolandino described Azzo VII as 'the greatest and most noble person of the Trevisan March, its very shield and guardian'.³ Da Nono, who was no partisan of the Estensi, whose grasping character he criticises more than once, takes their nobility for granted, saying that they were descended from the Trojan traitor Antenor, the founder of Padua.⁴ In fact, their eminence raised the Estensi in some respects out of the society of the March altogether into the social milieu of kings and the rulers of cities. Thus Beatrice d'Este married Andrew, King of Hungary, in 1234 and Azzo VIII married a daughter of the Angevin, Charles, King of Naples, in 1305. Other important marriage connections of the family in the thirteenth century included the Pepoli of Bologna, the Orsini of Rome, the Visconti of Milan and the Fieschi of Genoa.⁵

Within the March, the social pre-eminence of the Estensi was unchallenged, as can be seen by the leading role played by their court in the knightly festivals of the period. Their political position was never so secure, and political considerations were more important than social in their marriages with local families. Azzo VII (d.1264) and his grandson and successor Obizzo II (lord of Ferrara 1264–93) were closely linked to the leader of the Paduan Guelph aristocracy, through the marriage of the latter's natural sister Costanza to Guido da Lozzo. Obizzo's second marriage in 1289 to Costanza della Scala of Verona marked a reversal of the existing alliances and a *rapprochement* with Padua's traditional enemy. The della Scala

---

¹ For the origins of the Estensi and their relations with Padua up to the end of the twelfth century, see E. Zorzi, *Il territorio padovano nel periodo di trapasso da comitato a comune*, Misc. RDVSP ser. IV, iii (1929), pp. 162–94.
² Rolandino, *Cronica*, p. 23.
³ Ibid. p. 49.
⁴ *De Generatione*, ff. 15–17.
⁵ The basic history of the Estensi remains L. A. Muratori, *Delle Antichità Estensi ed Italiane* (1717–40).

were not *haute noblesse* in 1289, but they were rich and powerful, as was Enrico Scrovegni who married Giovanna, daughter of Obizzo's son Francesco, who had particularly close relations with the Paduan commune in the later years of his life. In the next generation, Renaldo d'Este married into the rising Paduan family of the Maccaruffi, forging a link which played an important part in the collapse of the Paduan commune in the years after 1311.

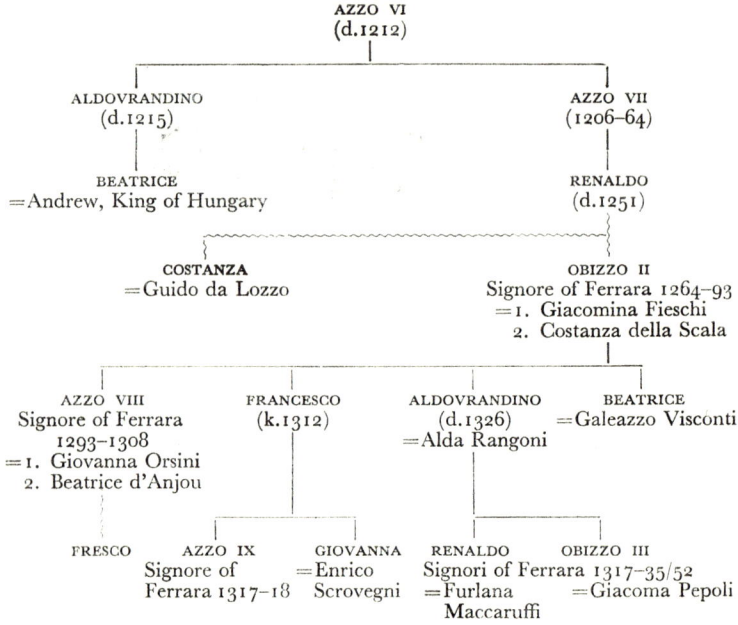

TABLE 1. Genealogy of the Estensi family.

With the Marchesi d'Este social standing and actual power still coincided to a remarkable degree, but in the Paduan comital family the case was very different. The family which had held both the counties of Vicenza and Padua in the eleventh century had gradually declined, mainly, it would appear, through the progressive splitting up of the rights and property of the family among many heirs, some of whom had established separate families. Thus, while some of the branches still flourished, there is no doubt that the original stem had withered, though the evidence for this decline is naturally somewhat elusive.[1] One indication is that while two of the Conti are named in the anti-magnatial statue of 1225, none appear in the statute of 1256-66: they are the only family thus dropped from the list of magnates. Antonio d'Alessio links them with the Schinelli in the possession of Mota in the Vicentino, *cum privilegio*, and of Rovolon on the northern slopes of the Pedevenda. In the statue of 1278 the Conti appear not in connection with Rovolon, but sharing responsibility with some of the Dalesmanini in Arquà. By 1297 when Agnese da Carrara, the widow of Giacomo Conti, left a quarter of the castle of Arquà *cum comitatu et iurisdictione* to the Paduan Inquisitors, half the jurisdiction was already in the hands of the Paduan commune which appointed a *podestà*.[2] This left the remaining quarter of Arquà in the possession of Engolfo Conti, a knight who served twice as *podestà* of Vicenza and was one of the last of the family to play a part in public affairs.[3] His son Demetrio was mentioned by the chronicler Cortusi as one of the leading Paduan property owners in the Vicentino at the time of the Vicentine revolt in 1311, but his surrender of the frontier castle of Montegalda to the forces of Cangrande della Scala in 1312 seems to have ended his political career, and with it the independent role of his family in Paduan affairs.[4]

It is indicative of the decline of the family that many members of the Conti merged with the citizen body, even to the point of taking minor office under the commune. The appointment of Count Manfredino as sole consul or *podestà* of Padua in 1182 is in itself ambiguous, though the description of him as 'citizen' probably indicates that he was a member of the commune and not a magnate brought in from outside.[5] In the period after 1256, some of his kinsmen were content to take much smaller posts; Giacomo Conti was *podestà* of Bassano in

---

[1] See E. Zorzi, *Il territorio padovano*, pp. 43-63. Miss Zorzi's evidence for the decline of the family at the end of the twelfth century (p. 63) is not convincing.
[2] AD 3872.
[3] Gennari, *CDP* IX (unnumbered page at end of book); *podestà* in 1282-3 and 1296, N. Smereglo, *Annales Civitatis Vincentiae*, ed. G. Soranzo, RIS VIII, v (1921), pp. 15, 17. One wonders what lay behind the chronicler's comment: 'iam erat quasi mentecaptus, sed tamen fecit bonum regimen'.
[4] Cortusi, *Chronica*, p. 13; Mussato, *Historia Augusta*, col. 421.
[5] *Liber Regiminum*, p. 294.

1294 and Manfredo held the office of *extimator* in 1271.[1] Social assimilation can also be traced through marriages with plebeian families, including not only the rich and rising Capodilista and Enselmini, but even the Lovesini who were 'poor men, having almost nothing' according to Da Nono.[2]

Da Nono clearly recognised the decline of the Conti, and devotes only a short chapter to them, which is mainly taken up with the story of how young Manfredino made a shameful marriage with a daughter of the poet Mussato, who was one of Da Nono's *bêtes noires*. In fact, he could hardly believe that they were the line of the true counts of Padua, and says they owed their jurisdiction to a gift of the Da Nono. He begins the noble families of book two not with the Conti, but with the legend of how a certain blacksmith, Alberto Allemanus, became the Count of Montebello in the Vicentino by deceiving Frederick Barbarossa as to the number of followers he had. From him are said to be descended the counts of Vicenza, the Da Carturo and the Maltraversi—in fact, almost all the branches of the Conti which were still of any importance.[3] In this way history and genealogy were adjusted to correspond with contemporary realities. Other great families descended from the Conti were extinct, like the Da Cero and Calaone, whose castles became important strongholds of the Estensi, the rich Da Baone whose estates were divided among eight daughters in 1183, or the line of Manfredo d'Abano, reputed the richest man of his time in the March, the marriage of whose heiress touched off the feud between the Da Romano and Camposanpiero at the end of the twelfth century.

In the case of the Da Carturo, there is documentary support for a link with the Montebello, since Count Pietro da Montebello, by his will made in 1259, made his kinsman Ugozono da Carturo his heir.[4] This did not prevent the decline of the family, who were rated as magnates in the statutes of 1225 and 1256–66, but were omitted from the statute of 1278. Perhaps they never recovered from the ravaging of their estates

---

[1] Tua, *Reg. Arch. Bassanesi*, nn. 638, 980; AD 2515.

[2] Antonia, daughter of Rolando Capodilista=Franzone Conti (AS Privati, Selvatico 772, Padova 2); Catterina Enselmini=Percivalle Conti (AD 5111); Antonia, daughter of Gherardo Lovesini=Tebaldo Conti (AD 3343); *De Generatione*, f. 49r.

[3] *De Generatione*, ff. 28–9.   [4] AS Vicenza, *S. Lorenzo*, 843.

by Frederick II and Ezzelino da Romano in 1236.[1] Uberto son of Ugozono da Carturo, who appears from time to time living in Via San Pietro in Padua, seems to have ended his life as a cleric attached to the church of S. Martino in the village of Saonara; his cousin Giacomo was a canon of Padua cathedral.[2] Da Nono speaks of Ansedisio da Carturo as the sole survivor of the family—presumably he meant to say in his generation, since by his will of 1316, Ansedisio divided his estate between four sons and a grandson, the share of each amounting to about four *mansi*, which was hardly the portion of a nobleman.[3] Perhaps it was with a view to supplementing his expected inheritance, that a fifth son, who predeceased his father, entered the Paduan College of Judges in 1305.[4]

It is noticeable that the various families tracing their descent from the counts of Padua all had their main estates either in the Pedevenda or in the north-west part of the Paduan contado towards Vicenza. The hills provided many sites suitable for the building of castles, and the position near the Vicentine frontier may have aided the preservation of independence from the control of either commune. At all events, the only branches of the comital family who remained in the magnate class until the fourteenth century, had their power centred on the north-western slopes of the Pedevenda, overlooking Vicentine territory.

The Schinelli of Rovolon were descended from Count Schinella, one of the *XVI podestà* elected by the Paduans to treat with Frederick II and Ezzelino in 1236. His sons tried to co-operate with Ezzelino but eventually suffered under his tyranny. Under the restored commune, the family was still strong in Rovolon and in the adjacent villages in Vicentine territory, where they held tithes in fief from the bishop of Vicenza.[5] One branch of the family, represented by the brothers Bartolomeo and Ansedisio, remained among the magnates,

[1] Rolandino, pp. 48–9.
[2] AD 3658, 4188, 5206, Corona 3273; Arch. Capit. Tomo Nigro, f. 77.
[3] *De Generatione*, f. 34; AD 5449. The *mansus* was the equivalent of about 20 *campi*.
[4] *Stat. Coll. Iud.*, f. 29r.
[5] Arch. Papafava 39, n. 6; Arch. Vesc. Vicenza, Feudorum, IV, f. 153v. The tithes were in Costa, near Róvolon, and Montecleda, neither of which appear on a modern map. Perhaps the latter was Montecello, midway between Rovolon and the Vicentine Colli Berici.

with strong interests in Vicenza as well as the Padovano.[1] Bonaccorso and his nephew Guglielmo, on the other hand, were closely asociated with the Paduan Franciscans, probably as tertiaries. They had a house near the basilica of S. Antonio and in 1300 they bought from the Franciscan inquisitors, land at Cervarese on the Vicentine border, which had belonged to Ziborga, countess of Vicenza.[2]

The Paduan family most closely associated in Da Nono's mind with the counts of Montebello was the Maltraversi, with whom they shared a common coat of arms. They were also the most powerful remaining branch of the Paduan comital family,

TABLE 2. Genealogy of the Da Castelnovo family.

and were themselves divided into two branches, the Castelnovo and Da Lozzo, which took their names from their chief castles. The statute of 1278 shows that the territory of the northern branch of the Maltraversi was contiguous with that of the Schinelli, extending southward from Rovolon to the villages of Boccon and Zovon, both dominated by the castle of Castelnovo. South of Boccon, at Cortelà, began the sphere of influence of the Da Lozzo which stretched from their castle at the foot of the isolated hill of Lozzo eastwards across the centre of the hills to Galzignano. Both branches also had their palaces in Padua, the Castelnovo near the Pontemolino, and the Da Lozzo in the Via S. Andrea, and both were among the most important and powerful families in the city. The Da Lozzo in

---

[1] See below, p. 236.
[2] AS Corp. Sopp. S. Antonio, 150, f. 92.

particular, played a leading part in Paduan politics until their rebellion and exile in 1312.

The status of these families is apparent from their marriage connections. The head of the Da Castelnovo in 1256 was Nicolò who, despite the liberal eating and drinking which earned him Da Nono's disapproval, survived until about 1311. He married Alessandra, sister of Tiso IV Camposanpiero, the leading Paduan magnate of his time.[1] One of Nicolò's aunts had been the wife of Ezzelino da Romano; another, Adelmota Maltraversi, married Giacomino da Carrara, the first to be surnamed Papafava, in about 1263.[2] She too was long-lived, surviving until 1321, and she is the only woman praised by Da Nono for her character and ability. She had a reputation for knowing cures, and her relations and friends often came to seek her advice; she was responsible for the division of her son Pierconte's estate in 1318.[3] Nicolò da Castelnovo's sons married into the most wealthy of the city families, the Scrovegni, the Lemici and the Negri.[4]

TABLE 3. Genealogy of the Da Lozzo family.

The marriages of the Da Lozzo were even more illustrious and politically opportune than those of their kinsmen of Castelnovo. Guido I da Lozzo, a contemporary of Nicolò da Castelnovo, was the reputed leader of the Paduan Guelphs, and was married to Costanza, the natural sister of Obizzo II

[1] *De Generatione*, f. 30.
[2] Arch. Papafava 38 (unnumbered document).
[3] *De Generatione*, f. 38r; *Documenti Carraresi* (MS BP 990), n. 25.
[4] *De Generatione*, f. 30.

d'Este.¹ Obizzo himself presided over a magnificent court held in the Palazzo Comunale in 1286 on the occasion of the marriage of Guido's son Nicolò to Agnese, daughter of Gerardo da Camino, *signore* of Treviso.² After his father's death about 1290, Nicolò's reputation and power rose rapidly, based to a considerable extent on his family connections, until, in the first decade of the fourteenth century, they were second only to those of Tiso Camposanpiero. One of his sons, Antonio, married a sister of Marsiglio da Carrara, the future *signore* of Padua, while the other, Guido II, after the dissolution of his first marriage with a daughter of Enrico Scrovegni, made a politic union with a daughter of Baiardino da Nogarolo, Cangrande della Scala's favoured lieutenant.³

The families tracing their descent from the counts of Padua were not the only families with comital connections in the Padovano. The claim of the Da Nono to a link with the nobility of Treviso has already been considered; another claim allowed by Da Nono was that of the Cumani who 'from olden times were counts of Monselice'.⁴ Behind this tradition, there may have lain a vague memory of the Carolingian period when Monselice rather than Padua was the seat of the county for a time; the tradition also bears witness to the military and symbolic significance of Monselice, the largest town and greatest fortress in Paduan territory. Whatever the truth concerning their origins, the records show that in the later thirteenth century the Cumani were a family of some importance in Monselice, with interests in Padua and a link with the Estensi. For example, Biagio Cumani was a vassal of the Estensi in respect of land in Este, and he also held the tithes pertaining to agricultural land and town building plots in and around Monselice from the bishop of Padua.⁵ His will, made in 1289, shows that he had a large crenellated house in Monselice, and another house in Via Maggiore in Padua.⁶ Both he and his son Guglielmo practised as judges in the city.⁷ In the troubles after 1311, it was the tie with the Estensi rather than that with the Paduan commune which proved the stronger, at least for some

---
¹ Ibid. loc. cit.   ² *Liber Regiminum*, p. 339.
³ *De Generatione*, ff. 30r, 40v.   ⁴ Ibid. f. 30v.
⁵ AS Modena, AMS VI, 9 (ii); Brunacci, *CDP* IV, pp. 2172, 2177.
⁶ Ibid. p. 2178.
⁷ *Stat. Coll. Iud.*, f. 4.

of the family. Guglielmo's son Giacomo was described as an inhabitant of Ferrara in his will of 1360, and a judge called Beloto Cumani held the office of viscount under the Estensi in Rovigo in 1335.[1]

Just as in Padua the original stem of the Conti had been eclipsed by other families of more recent origin, so in Monselice the Cumani were, by the later thirteenth century, inferior in power to the Paltinerii. Da Nono considered the Paltinerii to be noble, having been lords of Galzignano 'from olden times' and calling themselves counts of Tribano; a remark of Rolandino suggests that they may have originated as the hereditary castellans of Monselice.[2] Simone Paltinerii, Cardinal of S. Martino from 1261 to 1277, was the only Paduan churchman to reach that rank during the communal period.[3] The family was linked by marriage with the Malatesta of Rimini and in Padua with the Dalesmanini, Scrovegni and Capodivacca.[4] But, so far as the Paduan commune was concerned, they had a bad political record. Pesce Paltinerii surrendered the castle of Monselice to Ezzelino in 1249 and, when Padua rebelled against the Emperor Henry VII, Guglielmo Novello was the first citizen to be suspected of treason and removed by assassination. More than any other family, they were felt to personify Imperialist Monselice, *Imperii regalia et camera specialis*, the antithesis of traditionally Guelph Padua. Da Nono says that it was one of the Paltinerii who tried to betray Egidius, King of Patavium into the hands of Attila the Hun.[5]

A number of Paduan families of the thirteenth and fourteenth centuries were reputed noble through their supposed descent from lesser feudal families known as *capitanei* (*cattanei*) or *vavassores*. The most important of this group were the Cattanei of Lendenara, a noble family who, like the Estensi, were not exclusively attached to any one city. In the early thirteenth century they were active in Verona, closely allied to the

[1] Brunacci, *CDP* IV, p. 2181; *Liber Statutorum Com. Rodigii* (Bibl. Civ. Rovigo MS Silvestriani, n. 355), p. 91.
[2] Da Nono, *De Generatione*, f. 37r; Rolandino, p. 52.
[3] See A. Main, 'Il Cardinale di Monselice, Simone Paltanerii', *NAV.* XXXIX (1920), pp. 65–141.
[4] Main, art. cit. p. 68; Doniza, daughter of Fruzerino P=Marco Capodivacca, Arch. Capit. Diversa III, n. 254. For the other Paduan marriages of the Paltinerii and their significance, see below, pp. 257–8.
[5] Rolandino, pp. 50–2, 87–8; Da Nono, *De Generatione*, f. 37r.

Sanbonifacio, counts of that city.[1] After 1269, political circumstances drove them back to their ancestral castle of Lendenara on the Adige, with an outpost in Paduan territory at Cinto in the south-western Pedevenda, while they still had a house in Vicenza.[2] In the early fourteenth century, having sold their jurisdiction in Lendenara, some members of the family began to play an important part in Paduan life. Altegrado da Lendenara became a professor of law in Padua from 1289 and bishop of Vicenza, with Paduan support, in 1303.[3] Rizardo da Lendenara, nicknamed the Tartar, was one of the most violent of the supporters of the Carraresi, and his son married one of the Scrovegni with a dowry which, according to Mussato, was so high as to suggest that it was really a bribe for protection during the troubled period which attended the foundation of the *signoria*.[4]

Da Nono believed that the Cattanei of Limena had earned their title defending Padua against the raids of the Huns.[5] In the thirteenth century, the most famous member of the family was the saintly abbot Arnaldo of S. Giustina who died under Ezzelino's persecution in 1256.[6] His successor in office, though not apparently in sanctity, was his kinsman Giacomo who, in 1271, met a violent death as a result of an abortive plot to place his brother, who was the abbot of S. Felice in Vicenza, on the episcopal throne of that city.[7] His death revealed another member of the family, a layman called Aleardo, to be deeply in debt to the monastery, and he was ordered to repay a sum amounting to nearly £8,000.[8] This might well have ruined him unless the blow was softened through the influence of the new

[1] See below, p. 200.
[2] Ailice Menabobi, wife of Antonio Novello da Lendenara at his house in Vicenza, 4 Feb. 1284 (AS Modena, AMS IV, n. 19).
[3] See below, p. 226.
[4] Mussato, *De Traditione*, RIS X (1727), col. 758. The 'dowry' is said to have amounted to £8,000 *per annum*.   [5] *De Generatione*, f. 34r.
[6] Rolandino, pp. 64, 131.   [7] See below, pp. 146, 226.
[8] AD 2494 (formerly 2499), printed by L. A. Botteghi, 'La fine di Jacopo abbate di S. Giustina di Padova', *Atti dell'Accademia Scientifica Veneto-Tridentino-Istriana*, II (1905), pp. 8-23. My interpretation of this document differs radically from Botteghi's mainly because I hold that Aleardo was a kinsman of the abbot and not a member of the Zacchi family. The document itself is not clear, but I am convinced that Aleardo cannot have been involved in the murder because both he and his son appear subsequently in S. Giustina, e.g. Corona 1590, f. 52, 2206, f. 71r, AD 3287, 3295.

abbot, who was also a Da Limena, and a nephew of the famous Arnaldo.¹ At all events, Aleardo was in debt to the Scrovegni, Lemici and others some six years later, and his son Luppo had entered the College of Judges, a course not without parallel among nobles in straitened circumstances.²

None of the families known as *vavassores* were of any importance by the second half of the thirteenth century, though in the case of the Da Fontaniva the decline was comparatively recent, since in D'Alessio's list they had a *privilegium magnum cum castro*. A branch of the Da Fontaniva had settled in the Oltrebrenta to the east of Padua and had adopted the name of their castle at Peraga. In the later thirteenth century, their line ended in an heiress, Balzanella da Peraga, who is named among the magnates in the statutes of 1256-66 and 1278. She married Marco Zeno Badoer, a Venetian whose family had considerable interests in the *terra firma* and had provided several *podestà* of Padua, and their descendants, who took the name Da Peraga, remained a power to be reckoned with on the frontiers of Padua and Venice.³

In many Italian cities there were noble families who owed their position to the hereditary right to act as officials of the bishop, going back to the times when the bishop's court had been one of the most important nuclei of urban society. In Treviso, for example, the bishop's *advocati* became one of the leading families of the city. In Padua, the office passed through the hands of several families after the extinction of the original line in 1147.⁴ In the thirteenth century, a new line of *advocati* appear and are included among the magnates in the statutes of 1225 and 1256-66. The D'Alessio list mentions their fortress on the island of Calcinara on the lower Brenta towards Chioggia, but the statute of 1278 names only Margherita Schinelli, widow of Ugolino Avvocato, in connection with her own hereditary lands in Rovolon. Avezzuto Avvocato exercised the rights of his office during the episcopal vacancy in 1283, and appears in a document for the last time in 1303.⁵ Da Nono's comment

---

[1] Odorico, a doctor of canon law, see below, p. 146.
[2] Corona 1594, f. 100v; *Stat. Coll. Iud.* f. 2r.
[3] Da Nono, *De Generatione*, f. 34r; for the Badoer and Paduan politics, see below, pp. 202, 234, 252–3.
[4] E. Zorzi, *Il territorio padovano*, pp. 88–92.
[5] Brunacci, *CDP* II, pp. 1318, 1593; see also Dondi dall'Orologio, *Istoria Ecclesiastica*, VII, doc. n. 161 and VIII, doc. n. 6.

just over a decade later was that there were now no males known in this family, except perhaps one.¹

The remaining noble families described in the first two books of the *De Generatione* cannot be classified according to their origins, about which Da Nono really knew very little. Sometimes he was able to cite a story or legend to account for their nobility; in other cases he simply assumes it on the strength of a former *de facto* jurisdiction and long-standing respectability. In Da Nono's time, these families varied widely in power and wealth. Some were extinct or so impoverished as to have lost their nobility; others retained considerable wealth and shared in the activities of the citizen body. The examples of the Da Vigodarzere who were professional soldiers, and the Da Montagnone, who became judges, will be considered below.² But among the residual nobility there were some of the greatest families of the March who had dominated the political life of the region in the early thirteenth century: the Da Romano, the Camposanpiero and the Carraresi. These three families had similar origins, being reputedly sprung from eleventh-century German immigrants who had gradually built up a *de facto* authority based on a compact rural area. Their position was legalised by Imperial privileges during the twelfth century, and by the early thirteenth century they were ready to fight for the control of the major communes. The Da Romano were fated to enjoy a rapid rise followed by complete extinction; the Carraresi succeeded them after an interval of nearly a hundred years in the *signoria* of Padua, while the Camposanpiero always just failed to make good their prospects of becoming the *signori* of a major city.

There is a strong contrast between Da Nono's treatment of the Camposanpiero and the Carrara. He knew very little about the origin of either, but for him the nobility of the Camposanpiero was self-evident. In the time of Henry of Luxemburg, 'Tiso Camposanpiero was, on account of his own qualities and those of his predecessors, more noble and powerful than the other citizens of Padua', and despite the setback suffered by the family on his death in 1312, Da Nono still believed a prophecy that the family might found a new tyranny in Padua

---

¹ *De Generatione*, f. 39r.
² See below, pp. 97–9, 131.

a hundred years after the destruction of that of the Da Romano.[1] Their power was based on castles and estates lying to the northeast of Padua, straddling the frontier with the territory of Treviso. The statue of 1278 shows that they were powerful in seven villages of the Paduan contado, of which the chief was Camposanpiero itself. The D'Alessio list mentions two castles in the Trevigiano, probably Fonte and Treville. In 1261, on the

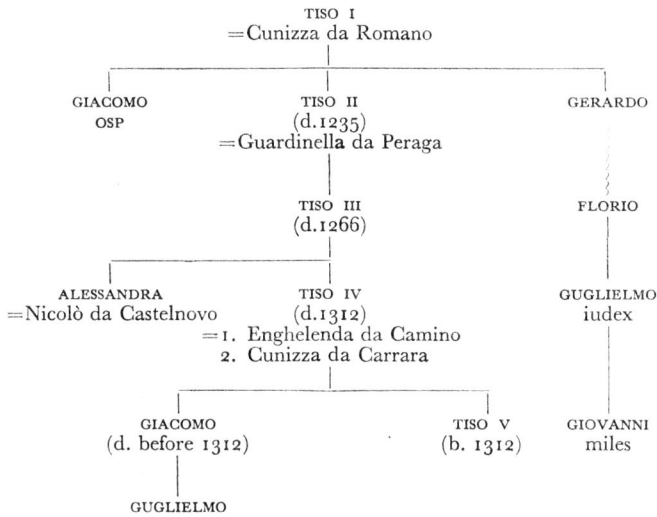

TABLE 4. Genealogy of the Camposanpiero family.

fall of the Da Romano, Tiso III Camposanpiero was enfeoffed by the bishop of Freising with the castle of Godego in the district of Treviso which had formerly been held by the Da Romano.[2] His son, Tiso IV, helped his brother-in-law Gerardo da Camino to establish a *signoria* in Treviso and bought further property in the Trevigiano.[3] A list of 1330 includes the Camposanpiero among the twelve noble families of Treviso, but the family was

[1] *De Generatione*, f. 17v, *Visio Egidii*, pp. 3-4.
[2] Verci, *Storia degli Eccelini*, III, doc. n. 257.
[3] 'In un gran fascio di pergamene della cancelleria del comune, ci sono molti istromenti di vendite di beni, che furono delli Da Romano, fatte dal comune a Tisone Camposanpiero.' *Raccolta Scotti* (MS Bibl. Civ. Treviso), IV, p. 308. A document of 1317 mentions a sum of £3,000 paid to the commune, and £6,000 to Rizardo da Camino (Verci, *Marca Trivigiana*, doc. n. 841).

equally at home in Padua, where their house was near the Pontemolino.[1]

According to the criteria established by Da Nono, the Carraresi had nearly as good a claim to nobility as the Camposanpiero. Because of their later importance, their early history has been more thoroughly studied than that of other families, and it has been established that in the mid-twelfth century the Carraresi exercised comital jurisdiction over an area south of Padua centred on Carrara and Pernumia.[2] In the period after 1256, though their power was rated inferior to that of the Camposanpiero and Da Lozzo, they still had vast estates near Carrara, with a secondary centre around the castle of Agna, near the Adige and the border with the county of Rovigo. The family owned a number of *palazzi* in Padua, as the census of 1320 shows, including the houses of Marsiglio da Carrara in Via S. Andrea and Giacomo Grande near the head of the Via S. Margherita, while the palace of the Papafava branch was opposite the church of S. Martino, right in the administrative and commercial centre of the city.[3] Finally, the marriage alliances of the Carraresi outside Padua, which included the Della Torre of Milan, the Fieschi of Genoa and the Gradenigo of Venice, show the unmistakable marks of nobility.[4]

Da Nono knew that the Carraresi were of German descent, and believed that they were an offshoot of the Da Montagnone, a family whose nobility he accepted. But he could not place the Carrara among the nobles with the same confidence as he had shown in the case of the Camposanpiero. The common people, he says, were of the opinion that the contemporary Carraresi were not of the ancient noble house of Carrara, but were Paduan citizens of the *popolo*; 'but I pass over what they say, because today they are noble and powerful Paduan citizens'. What was the reality which lay behind this popular opinion which runs counter to so many of the facts? Probably it was a reflection of the relative impoverishment and obscurity of some of the many members of this family, individuals of whom even

[1] R. Battistella, 'Il comune di Treviso e la cavalleria', *NAV* ns. VIII, ii (1904), pp. 286–7.
[2] R. Cessi, 'La signoria comitale dei Carraresi nel secolo XII', *BMCP* ns. I (1925), pp. 133–48.
[3] Grion, *Delle rime volgari*, pp. 256–8, 261, 264.
[4] *De Generatione*, ff. 37v, 38r.

the fourteenth-century family histories can find nothing very honourable to record.[1] In fact, there are signs that by the early fourteenth century, some branches of the Carraresi had already progressed some way towards the fragmentation of their estates which had brought so many great families to ruin in the past.

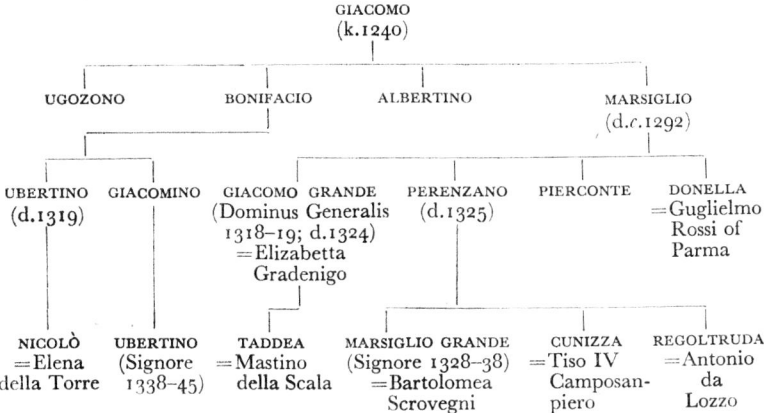

TABLE 5. Genealogy of the Carrara family.

A sign of the incipient break-up was the appearance of the Papafava as a separate family, originating with Giacomino Papafava da Carrara, who died about 1289 leaving his property to be divided among four sons.[2] Despite the extinction of one line in 1318, the descendants of one of these sons had run hopelessly into debt by 1332.[3] The same process was at work in the main stem of the Carraresi until a series of lucky chances reconcentrated some of the dispersed wealth in the hands of Giacomo Grande and Marsiglio da Carrara, under whose leadership the family attained power between 1314 and 1328.[4]

[1] E.g. Giovanni, Giacomino and Giacomo 'in urbe magnates' (*Gesta Magnifica Domus Carrariensis*, ed. R. Cessi, RIS XVII, i, vol. 2 (1942–8), p. 14) of whom, in fact, nothing more is known.
[2] *Documenti Carraresi* (MS BP 990, i), n. 12.
[3] The goods of Brisco and Ugucio Papafava, son and grandson of Bonifacio, were declared forfeit to their creditors on 21 May 1332. In 1304, Brisco had received the generous dowry of £3,000 on his marriage to the plebian Mabilia Linguadevacca (Arch. Papafava cod. 38).
[4] See below, pp. 276–7.

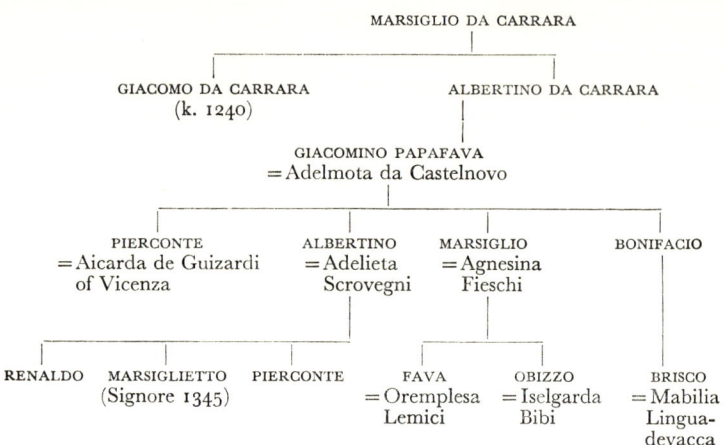

Table 6. Genealogy of the Papafava family.

The families placed by Da Nono in the third and fourth books of the *De Generatione* were those which he considered non-noble and in some cases ignoble. The majority were 'honest *popolani*', administrators or guildsmen, but a few were border-line cases: families whose power placed them in or near the magnate class, but whose rise was too recent for them to qualify for noble status. Da Nono generally describes the members of such families as *nobiles cives* or *nobiles populares*. It is important to understand what was meant by these phrases. Da Nono was not positing the existence of a noble-citizen class intermediate between the nobles and the *popolo*. Bartolo quotes Giacomo de Arena, who taught in the university of Padua between 1260 and 1300, to the effect that 'The *popolo* contains all except the nobles', and 'Everyone lacking *dignitas* is a *popolano*', so in theory there could be no status between noble and *popolano*.[1] Nor was Da Nono using the word noble in a loose sense, indicating that it had lost any precise meaning for him; rather he was using it in the sense of *nobilitas naturalis*, the excellence of any thing within its kind. A 'noble popolano' was a leading member of his class, just as Da Nono called high-quality cloth *nobiles panni*. The usage was not restricted to Padua; Villani described

[1] Bartolo, *In XII Lib. Cod. Commentaria*, p. 940.

Giano della Bella as 'un valente uomo, antico e nobile popolano, e ricco e possente'.[1]

Among the powerful families who, in Da Nono's view, just lacked the *dignitas* necessary for nobility, were the Forzatè and the Capodivacca. The former were a family of some antiquity, being apparented to the Transalgardini; a Transalgardino had been ruling consul of the city three times between 1176 and 1188.[2] Giovanni Forzatè, bishop of Padua from 1256 to 1283, was the only Paduan to occupy the episcopal throne in the communal period.[3] The family was represented in the magnatial lists of 1256–66 and 1278, which shows that they controlled a group of villages to the south-east of Piove di Sacco. Da Nono considered their claim to have been counts of Piove and Cona not proven; for him they were 'noble and powerful in the *popolo* from olden times and up to the present day'.[4] The Capodivacca had a much weaker claim to longstanding territorial power, as they were not mentioned in the anti-magnatial statutes, but according to the D'Alessio list they had a small fortress in Saletto, near Montagnana. They were a numerous family, so their original estates must have been much divided. Despite this, they rose steadily after 1256, some becoming knights, some judges and some at least making considerable loans, until by 1311 Da Nono rated them among the eight most powerful families in the city. For him, their name and coat of arms proved that they had been butchers, 'but what they were formerly I pass over, and say they are at present noble and powerful *populares* in Padua.'[5]

The name of the Dalesmanini was an important one in the history of Padua, since the revolt by which the city had achieved its freedom from the Imperial Vicar of Frederick I was said to have been organised by Dalesmanino, the son of the Dalesmano who had held the office of episcopal *advocatus*.[6] Subsequently, Dalesmanino was twice consul of the commune and in 1212 he

---

[1] G. Villani, *Cronica*, ed. I. Moutier (1823), III, p. 5. Cf. M. A. Zorzi, *L'ordinamento comunale padovano nella seconda metà del secolo XIII*, Misc.RDVSP ser. IV, v (1931), p. 55.

[2] *Liber Regiminum*, pp. 293–5.

[3] See below, p. 239.

[4] *De Generatione*, f. 40r.

[5] *De Generatione*, f. 43r; also f. 38v. For some members of this family, see below, pp. 108–9, 185, 225.

[6] 'The Legend of Speronella', see *Liber Regiminum*, pp. 291–2.

received a privilege from Otto IV bestowing on him the *comitatum et iurisdictionem* of a group of villages lying between Padua and the Venetian lagoon.[1] His son Giacomo was a magnate whose conduct was such as to cause the citizens to feel great relief when he died in 1228.[2] The D'Alessio list gives the family the castles of Camponogara and Noventa, and the statute of 1278 confirms that they were strong in that part of the contado. Da Nono adds the information that they had owned a considerable tract of urban property between the Ponte Altinate and Ognissanti; they are the only family for whom there is any evidence that they may have been enriched by urban ground-rents. Their power reached its apogee with Guecillo and declined rapidly on his death soon after 1295; in about 1317, Da Nono could write: 'But today the house of these powerful men is little heard of because their possessions have passed under the control of others, and because of the lack of good men.'[3]

Da Nono betrays no knowledge of the historic past of the Dalesmanini, whom he rated as only rich and powerful citizens. Probably the decisive factor which led him to deny their nobility was his belief that almost all of them had always been usurers. In fact, the certain evidence of moneylending by the Dalesmanini relates only to the period when the family was declining in the fourteenth century, but Da Nono makes the same charge against other important families which can be more fully corroborated.[4] Guglielmo Lemici, for example, can be shown to have been involved in some important loans in the later thirteenth century, and his son Vitaliano, who inherited a reputation for wealth and usury, was considered the fourth most powerful man in Padua in his day. Although a Giovanni Lemici had been a consul in 1181,[5] the family was not included in the anti-magnatial legislation, and there is no sign that there was any territorial basis to their power until Vitaliano began buying estates in the Vicentino in 1299. The other great Paduan

---

[1] Op. cit. pp. 294, 299; E. Winkelmann, *Acta Imperii Inedita* (1885), I, p. 62.
[2] 'De cuius audatia et maliciosa caliditate multum timebant Paduani pro statu civitatis.' *Liber Regiminum*, p. 308.
[3] *De Generatione*, ff. 38–9.
[4] For the financial activities of these families, see below, pp. 185–9.
[5] *Liber Regiminum*, p. 294.

moneylending family, the Scrovegni, first appear in the thirteenth century in the circle of the bishops of Padua.¹ In 1268, Bishop Giovanni enfeoffed the notorious Renaldo with the hill of Montecchia, 'where the castle used to be', and in 1283 he made a new grant of the tithes pertaining to some nearby villages 'in consideration of the many various and diverse services and gracious benefits which he had recently performed in the palace of the Paduan commune and in many other ways'². At some unknown date, Renaldo bought the *comitatus* of Selvazzano, which was held in fief from the bishops of Vicenza, from Manfredo Dalesmanini, and his son Manfredo bought the castle of Trambacche together with extensive rights in the same area in 1297, thus consolidating the family's power over a bloc of territory on both banks of the Bacchiglione between Padua and the Vicentine frontier. For Da Nono, the rise of the Scrovegni from a humble condition before the time of Ezzelino to a position of great wealth and power in his own time, due, as he believed, to usury, made him place them at the beginning of book four of the *De Generatione* as the very epitome of ignobility.⁴

Another family which rose at about the same time as the Scrovegni was the Maccaruffi. Da Nono asserts that they had formerly been known as the Visdomini, presumably because they had held that office in the bishop's *curia*, but he also records the opinion of Zambono d'Andrea that they had been butchers, which, he says, does not surprise him, since in his time many of the meanest condition had held important offices, though some of them were rich.⁵ Probably the Maccaruffi had attained a moderate standing among the citizens by the mid-thirteenth century. They were not among the magnates, but the D'Alessio

---

¹ Pietro and Guglielmo Scrovegni were canons of Padua cathedral in 1225–76 and 1260–8 respectively (F. S. Dondi dall'Orologio, *Serie cronologica-storica dei canonici di Padova* (1805), pp. 192–3). The home of the family was in Via Maggiore, near the cathedral.
² Brunacci *CDP* II, p. 1592; Arch. Vesc, Feudorum I, f. 20. Both grants were unusual in being *cum fidelitate*.
³ Arch. Vesc. Vicenza, Feudorum IV, f. 169; AS Padua, AD 3894a. Renaldo had also had possessions in Trambacche (e.g. Arch. Capit. Perg. XXX, Feuda Canonicorum, nn. 71–2) which according to the D'Alessio list included the castle, so perhaps the purchase of 1297 should not be taken at its face value.
⁴ *De Generatione*, ff. 43v–44r.
⁵ Ibid. f. 40v.

list records their castle at Brugine, near Piove di Sacco. The real founder of the family's greatness seems to have been Zilio Maccaruffi, who was active in the politics of the commune from 1256 to 1308. He was a knight and held the office of *podestà* in several cities, and he left his family so strong that for a short time between 1312 and 1317 they were able to compete for the control of Padua with the Carraresi.[1]

The Paduan magnates of the early fourteenth century, as they emerge from the *De Generatione* and the other records, can be seen to have sprung from families of diverse origins whose power had been established at different periods. Of the eight most powerful families of Da Nono's day, the Da Lozzo traced their status to their descent from the counts of Padua, and Camposanpiero and Carrara had been great names by the middle of the twelfth century. The Dalesmanini had come to the fore towards the end of the twelfth century. The Lemici and Scrovegni, the Maccaruffi and the Capodivacca, on the other hand, had all risen to the top by various means after 1256. But it would be wrong to see in these last a new ruling class which was about to replace the old. In the crisis of the early fourteenth century, it was some of the newer families like the Lemici, the Scrovegni and the Maccaruffi who were ruined, while the Carraresi and the Camposanpiero survived, with the Capodivacca and yet another rank of newcomers, like the Buzzaccarini and the De Doto. It was as if a new stratum of wealth and power was laid down with every generation and, with the passage of time, the weaker elements in each stratum were worn away, while the stronger or more fortunate families survived. This was the 'Game of Fortune' referred to in the title of one of the oldest manuscripts of the *De Generatione*,[2] where economic and political factors can be seen playing their part, while, in the background, the accidents of human generation exerted their persistent influence. Too many surviving children could be as disastrous for a family as to back the wrong political faction.

Analysis of the *De Generatione* makes it clear that there was a rapidly changing hierarchy of power and a more conservative,

---

[1] See below, pp. 268-70.
[2] 'Incipit Liber Ludi Fortune, sive De Generatione . . .', Bibl. Civ. S. Daniele di Friuli, cod. 264, p. 199.

less flexible, social hierarchy expressed in terms of nobility. Da Nono's nobles were, in fact, the magnates of the earliest period of which he had record, the mid-twelfth century. After his time, the criteria of nobility were widened to admit the new dominant families. Da Nono's conservatism is an aspect of the high social tension which accompanied the time of crisis in which he wrote.

It remains to consider whether there was any objective distinction between the magnate families which were accounted noble and those which were not, or whether nobility was simply ancient power and riches. So far as the evidence goes, there seems to have been no essential difference between magnatial families once their position was secure. The older noble families participated in the life of the city as fully as conditions allowed; the new families tended to drop the professions which had contributed to their rise and bought up country estates and castles whenever possible. Intermarriage between old and new families was the rule rather than the exception, especially in the generation which was young at the beginning of the fourteenth century. The difference was rather in the way in which the family fortunes were made. Before the thirteenth century, the great fortunes seem to have been made in the contado by families like the Da Romano who successfully amassed property and jurisdictions in rural areas.[1] With few exceptions, the older families took their names from the rural castles which were the centre and basis of their power.[2] With the establishment of the ascendency of the Paduan commune over the contado, the centre of opportunity passed to the city. The magnatial families which were new in Da Nono's day had all made their way in the

[1] See F. Cusin, 'Per la storia del castello medioevale', *RSI* V, iv (1939), pp. 491–542; and for the example of the Da Romano which was probably typical, see G. Fasoli, 'Signoria feudale ed autonomie locali', *Studi Ezzeliniani*, Istituto Storico Italiano per il Medio Evo, Studi Storici fasc. 45–7 (1963), pp. 7–33.

[2] The most important exceptions were two related families which took their names from the city churches of S. Andrea and S. Lucia. Though they were in decline by 1256 and virtually extinct by Da Nono's day (*De Generatione*, f. 36), in the early thirteenth century they had been rich enough for Dante to take the figure of Giacomo da S. Andrea as a typical spendthrift (*Inferno*, XIII, l. 133). Beyond the evidence of their names, there is nothing to indicate that these families belonged to the city in any special way, or that they had made their fortunes there.

city by means which were often all too well remembered. Given the slight development of industry and commerce in Padua in the thirteenth century, the choice was mainly between two roads to wealth: the honourable way through administration and the law, and the dishonourable way of usury.

CHAPTER IV

Knights and Podestà

THE contemporary writers who divided mediaeval Italian society into nobles and non-nobles were acting rather like a boundary commission drawing a frontier on a large-scale map; their rulings might be clear enough in theory, but could be related to the actual features of the ground only imperfectly, by reference to certain major social landmarks. Ancient jurisdictions were the most important of these, and their bearing on nobility has already been traced. Knighthood was another; though, unlike a jurisdiction it was not a necessary mark of nobility, and though its social significance seems to have varied considerably from time to time and place to place, it always had an important bearing on social status. If knighthood did not always indicate nobility, at least it generally showed that nobility was not far away.[1]

The normal mediaeval term for knight was *miles*, a word which, if used without qualification, could be even more ambiguous than *nobilis*. The root notion was, of course, military: a mounted soldier. Under early mediaeval conditions, there was a constant tendency for mounted soldiers to acquire the land necessary to maintain their costly equipment, so that *milites* often came to constitute a class of substantial landowners, holders of fiefs and jurisdictions. Thus most Italian bishops had a *curia militum* composed of their leading fiefholders, who were often the dominant element in the early communes. As a class with common political and economic interests, it was natural that the *milites* should form mutual associations, and in the later twelfth and early thirteenth centuries, many communes passed through a stage when internal conflicts revolved round

[1] Knighthood in mediaeval Italy is a neglected subject; the essential starting point is still Muratori's *Antiquitates Italicae Medii Aevi* (1738–42), IV, coll. 677–94. For knighthood in Florence, see G. Salvemini, *La dignità cavalleresca nel comune di Firenze* (1896), whose view was accepted and developed by Davidsohn, *Geschichte von Florenz*, IV, pp. 205–15. The most recent contribution to the subject is in Fiumi, 'Fioritura e decadenza', *ASI* CXV (1957), pp. 385–439.

the opposition of the *societas militum* and the organisation of *non-milites* usually known as the *popolo*. When this happened, the political distinction between *milites* and *pedites* ceased to correspond to the military division between horse and foot; it stands to reason that the *popolo* would have had little chance of success had they not been able to build up a mounted force of their own. In Piacenza in 1222, there were not only *milites* who adhered to the *popolo* but members of the *popolo* who adhered to the *milites*.[1]

The capture by the *popolo* of the dominant interest in the communes eventually put an end to the privileged status of the *milites*, but it did not alter the need for mounted troops to serve in the city militia. The *popolo* introduced the systematic conscription of all classes, who had to provide themselves with arms according to their means; the highest class was composed of *milites pro commune* who were obliged to keep a horse and armour, and who were to be found in the cities and contado alike. Following on this development, there emerges during the later thirteenth and early fourteenth centuries, a distinction between the conscript troopers of the communes and the dubbed knights, the *milites pro commune* as opposed to the *milites adobati* or *milites de corredo*.[2] The latter, for whom it will be convenient to reserve the term 'knight', were distinguished by having passed through an initiation ceremony which could take various forms, but which was always an important event. It has been commonly assumed by historians that thirteenth-century knighthood was essentially the same institution as twelfth-century *militia*, but the writers who do this do not produce any evidence to show that the *milites* of the earlier period had passed through the initiation ceremony. If the twelfth-century *milites* were all dubbed knights, then knighthood must have been a great deal more common than it later became.

In the thirteenth and fourteenth centuries, it is clear that dubbed knights formed only a small proportion of the *milites* of any Italian state. For example, Villani says that there were 300 *cavalieri de corredo* in Florence in 1283 and only 75 by 1338,[3] and

---

[1] Gualazzini, *Il 'Populus' di Cremona*, p. 297, who makes the case for a similar development at Cremona. For the social significance of the Florentine *milites*, largely ignored by Salvemini, see Davidsohn, II, p. 30.

[2] Muratori, *Antiquitates Italicae*, col. 677; Salvemini, pp. 28–9.

[3] *Cronica*, II, p. 281, VI, p. 184.

the Trevisan chronicler Liberale de Levada reports that in the army gathered for the relief of Padua in December 1319, there were '8,360 horse including good and bad, among whom there were three hundred and more knights'.[1] It is not possible to estimate the number of knights in Padua at any time during the communal period. The Paduan notaries were not very consistent in their use of the title *nobilis miles*, generally preferring *nobilis vir* where either was appropriate, and, except for Da Nono, the other sources mention knighthood only incidentally. In consequence, there are only about eighty knights known by name for the whole period from 1256 to 1328, though many must have escaped the records altogether. The *milites pro commune*, on the other hand, were numbered in hundreds. As early as 1242, Ezzelino da Romano was able to raise a force of 500 mounted troops in the city.[2] In a detailed and convincing account of the composition of the Paduan army in July 1312, Mussato gives the number of *milites pro commune* as 1,200, with the mounted troops from the contado making up about a thousand more.[3] It is probably no more than a coincidence that at each period the number of *milites* shows a constant relationship to the membership of the Consiglio Maggiore, which was 400 in 1242 and 1,000 in 1312; the significant fact is that throughout, the majority of the fully enfranchised citizens must have normally been *milites pro commune* during their active years. The knights, on the other hand were always a small minority.

The history of the Paduan *milites* in the crucial period of the late twelfth and early thirteenth centuries is extremely obscure, mainly because Rolandino, who must have known a great deal, seems to have deliberately expunged from his chronicle any reference to social conflicts between the citizens of Padua. Thus, he says nothing about the rise of the Paduan *popolo* and its organisation, the *comunanza*, which must have taken place in his time, and he is similarly silent concerning any association of the Paduan *milites* whose existence is extremely probable. In other cities, the *societas militum* had its own consuls, and

[1] 'De Proditione Tarvisii', R. degli Azzone Avvogari, *Memorie del Beato Enrico* (1760), II, p. 199.
[2] Rolandino, p. 76.
[3] 'Ex conscriptis civibus Paduanis equites mille ducentos', *Historia Augusta*, col. 429.

Rolandino mentions an official known as the *rex militum* at a mock battle held with the Venetians and Trevisans at Treviso in 1213, but this may have been only an *ad hoc* office for the regulation of the games.[1] The best evidence for a division between the *milites* and the *popolo* comes from a statute in the code of 1276, which lays down that there shall be two *podestà* appointed for the fortified town of Cittadella, one a *miles* and the other *de populo*.[2] A purely military interpretation of the provision would seem to be ruled out by the requirement that both *podestà* should have at least two horses; the use of the phrase *de populo* instead of *pedes* is unusual and significant. Although the statute bears the date 1267, it seems likely that the wording may go back to an earlier period, soon after the building of Cittadella by the commune in 1220, when it was the practice for certain offices to be divided between the *milites* and *popolani*. A few statutes which impose a higher fine on *milites* as opposed to *pedites* may go back to the same period.[3]

In the great majority of cases where *milites* are referred to in the statutes, *milites pro commune* are either specified or may be safely inferred from the context.[4] In many cases, as in the regulations concerning the communal militia and the appointment of captains and castellans, the significance is primarily military, but in others it is clear that the *milites* were also thought of in some degree as a social class, the wealthier element within the *comunanza*. The clearest example comes from the regulations for the election of the college of *anziani* which constituted the formal leadership of the *popolo*. Although the office was not a military one, it was laid down that the four *anziani* of the *comunanza* had to be *milites pro commune* and, in addition, they were to have a tax assessment of at least £200 and immovables to the value of £500; for the eight *anziani* of the guilds, on the other hand, who represented the lesser men of the *comunanza*, the sole requirements were a tax assessment of £100 and immovables worth £200.[5] The exact criteria which were used by the commune in imposing mounted service on its subjects do not emerge from the statutes of 1276, nor from a resolution of the Consiglio Maggiore of 1304, which ordered a new enrolment of

---

[1] *Cronica*, p. 25. [2] *Stat. Com.* 326.
[3] E.g. *Stat. Com.* 1.I, 31, 67.
[4] E.g. *Stat. Com.* 354–97, 867–74.
[5] *Stat. Com.* 414, 416, 416.I.

the citizens for military service in four classes, *milites*, heavy armed infantry, light infantry and archers.[1] No doubt the assessment depended on a number of personal factors which could not be reduced to a single formula in terms of income or property. But the general position of the *milites pro commune* is sufficiently clear. In some of the statutes, they are linked with the judges as representing the richer element in the *comunanza*. On the other hand, the numbers involved must have meant the inclusion of at least some of the guildsmen, and there is positive evidence that at least two notaries were *milites*.

It is sometimes stated or implied that in Padua or elsewhere, the *milites pro commune* represented a new kind of knighthood created by the commune as a rival to the existing *milites* and nobility.[2] In a situation in which a *popolo* was seeking to assert its position against the opposition of an entrenched body of *milites*, the enrolment of its own corps of mounted troops was obviously an important event in the political and military sphere; socially it seems to have been of little or no significance, at least so far as the Paduan evidence goes. In Padua, a *miles pro commune* was not a knight in the social sense at all, and no Paduan notary would have dreamed of giving a man the honoured style *nobilis miles* on this ground. To be a dubbed knight was to have a personal distinction shared by few: to be enrolled as a *miles pro commune* was to become liable for onerous and expensive duties. To an ambitious man of humble birth like Albertino Mussato, who mentions in an autobiographical poem that he entered the Consiglio Maggiore and was enrolled as *miles* in his thirty-fifth year,[3] the event was no doubt a source of a certain satisfaction, but the attitude of others who were less ambitious or less public-spirited was very different. Rolandino recounts how in 1242, when Ezzelino made a new enrolment of *milites*, he arrested and executed a judge called Renaldo de Bonello on the ground that he had complained of his 'election'

---

[1] A. Medin, 'Riforme del Maggior Consiglio del comune di Padova per l'estimo del 1304', *BMCP* ns. I (1925), pp. 37–42. In Arezzo in the early thirteenth century, a tax assessment of £500 was the necessary qualification for enrolment as a *miles* (Davidsohn, I, p. 686).

[2] M. A. Zorzi, *L'ordinamento comunale padovano*, pp. 51–2; Fiumi, 'Fioritura e decadenza' *ASI* CXV (1957), p. 405.

[3] 'His raptus iam factus eques loca celsia senatus/Sortius, me sic sorte ferente, fui', 'De celebratione sua diei nativitatis', ed. J. G. Graevius, *Thesaurus Antiquitatum et Historiarum Italiae* (1722), VI, ii, col. 62.

for mounted service.¹ Similarly, a Paduan annalist records that the *podestà* for 1279 showed 'such pride and intolerable officiousness' in his new assessment for mounted service, favouring the Guelphs and oppressing those whom he suspected of Imperialist sympathies, that the opposition secured the election of a *capitano del popolo* and the *podestà* was dismissed from his office before his term had expired.² The supposed desire of the *popolani* to become *milites* has been much exaggerated, to say the least.

When a commune was responsible for the creation of knights, the case was very different. In strict theory, there was nothing to prevent a commune or a *popolo* doing this. Bartolo makes it clear that in his view, any body which had the authority to make laws could also create knights, and he expressly states that the *popolo* of Perugia had this right.³ But in practice, knighthood was governed by customs which accorded very imperfectly with the ideas of the civil lawyers. The universal custom was that any knight could create further knights, and even *signori* like Azzo VIII d'Este and Gerardo da Camino seem to have conferred knighthoods by virtue of their own status as knights rather than in their capacity as rulers. If a commune wished to confer a knighthood, it must have been a simple matter to commission a knight to perform the ceremony on its behalf, and this is certainly what happened in some of the cases listed by Salvemini as knighthoods created directly by the Florentine commune.⁴ Only in the mid-fourteenth century does the custom seem to have changed in Florence, where some sort of an attempt was made to distinguish the knights created by the commune by making them bear the arms of the city, a development clearly related to the growth of the idea of distinct orders of knighthood which occurred about the same period. By this time, it is hard to believe that there was any distinct old knightly class which constituted any special menace to the government; the ideals of knighthood were in decay, and even the *milites*

---

[1] *Cronica*, p. 76.
[2] *Liber Regiminum*, p. 333.
[3] *In XII Lib.Codicis Commentaria* (1562), p. 943.
[4] E.g. nos 1 & 5 in the list given in *La dignità cavalleresca*, pp. 101–2. The author does not seem to have realised the significance of these instances; two other cases are mentioned from the mid-fourteenth century, pp. 109, 113.

pro commune were being superseded by mercenaries. In the earlier period, the aim of the communes in arranging for the creation of knights, seems to have been the honouring of individuals, and not the creation of a new social class.[1]

It is clear that in Padua knighthoods were conferred upon persons of widely differing social backgrounds. At one extreme there were representatives of the great noble families like the Estensi, the Da Lozzo, the Camposanpiero and the Carraresi; at the other there were individuals like Giacomo Torculi 'whose grandfather was a cobbler' and the humanist Lovato Lovati, whose father was a notary.[2] An example of a *nouveau riche* who became a knight was Pietro Murfi, who Da Nono believed had amassed a fortune amounting to £100,000 and who owned two great houses in the city, one with a great tower.[3] The probable source of his wealth is indicated by the provision in his will ordering the restitution of the usuries exacted by himself, his father and his two brothers.[4] But neither extreme was at all typical; it is chiefly in the lesser noble families and the greater families of the *popolo* that something like a tradition of knighthood is to be found.

Though little is known of their early history, it would seem that the Da Vigodarzere were a family which, like the Carrara and the Camposanpiero, had achieved wealth and power in a portion of the Paduan contado during the twelfth century. Da Nono relates that they were believed to have once been tenants of the church of S. Giulia of Brescia, which had property in Paduan territory, but he tacitly accepted their nobility.[5] Guerico da Vigodarzere, 'a bold and true knight', appears in the mid-thirteenth century as one of the Paduan exiles who played a part in the liberation of Padua and Treviso from the domination of the Da Romano. His appearance as a witness in the Consiglio Maggiore at Ferrara in 1251 suggests that he was an adherent of Azzo VII d'Este, who controlled that city;[6] in

---

[1] As in the case of Matteo dei Ternibili, first Executor of the Ordinamenti di Giustizia, 'fatto cavaliere per lo popolo', Villani, *Cronica*, III, p. 165.

[2] Da Nono, *De Generatione*, f. 50r; for Lovato, see pp. 134–6 below.

[3] *De Generatione*, f. 53r.

[4] Dated 8 Feb. 1325; copy of 1815, Corona 5111.

[5] *De Generatione*, f. 33v; see also f. 40v. In 1184, the church of S. Giulia owned tithes in Pernumia, in the Padovano (E. Zorzi, *Il territorio padovano*, p. 228).

[6] AS Modena, AMS II, nn. 62–3.

1259 Alberto bishop of Treviso enfeoffed him with the castle and jurisdiction of Rustega, near the north-eastern frontier of the Paduan contado, 'on account of the many services which he has performed and still performs daily for the said Lord Bishop and diocese of Treviso, and especially in the recovery of the city and bishopric of Treviso (from Alberico da Romano)'.[1] About a year later, Guerico was enfeoffed by the bishop of Vicenza with the tithes pertaining to a considerable area in the northern part of the Paduan territory, at Fontaniva, Cittadella, Rossano and Onara.[2] Both these properties had probably belonged to supporters of the Da Romano. Guerico lived to enjoy the rewards of his labours for nearly fifty years, appearing from time to time in the records, and serving a term as *podestà* of Vicenza once, and Belluno probably twice. Yet he did not found a leading family, and records are lacking concerning his nephews Uberto and Guerrino, who were his presumptive heirs in 1297.[3] There is a tradition that they took the name Da Rustega, but when Da Nono wrote, Guerico's great house in via S. Fermo had been sold to the Camposanpiero.

It is probable that Guerico represented a junior branch of his family, as in 1278 Vigodarzere itself, with its castle controlling an important crossing of the Brenta a few miles north of Padua, was in the hands of another knight, Onore, who served in that year with the Paduan army against the Veronese.[4] His son Simone was clearly a man of some importance. He was knighted by Azzo d'Este and served as *podestà* in Modena, Florence and Vicenza between 1296 and 1299.[5] In 1304, he was joint commander of the Paduan forces in service against the Venetians.[6] Da Nono says that he married twice, one of his wives being of the noble Cattanei of Lendenara. His brother Uberto was also a knight and a soldier; he was *podestà* of Bassano in 1315, and a leader in the defence of Padua against

---

[1] The document recording this grant, which was seen by Scardeone in the sixteenth century, has been lost, but there is a copy in the sixteenth century Da Nono MS, Marciana cl VI Ital., n. 45, p. 174.

[2] Arch. Vesc. Vicenza, Feudorum II, f. 181.

[3] Smereglo, *Annales Vincentinae*, p. 14; Piloni, *Historia di Belluno*, new ed. (1929), pp. 223, 227; MS.Marciana cl.VI Ital. n. 45, loc. cit.

[4] Verci, *Marca Trivigiana*, doc. n. 229.

[5] Da Nono, f. 33v; E. P. Vicini, 'I Podestà di Modena', *Giornale Araldico* (1913), p. 197; Davidsohn, IV, p. 541; Smereglo, *Annales Vincentinae*, p. 17.

[6] Ferreto Ferreti, *Opere*, ed. C. Cipolla, FSI (1908–20), I, p. 232.

Cangrande in 1320.[1] According to Da Nono, he enriched himself through his wives, one of whom was a daughter of Bellebono Guarnerini, a knight, and the other a daughter of Novello Sanguinaci, a rich citizen.

In contrast to the noble Da Vigodarzere, the De Doto are an example of a family with a tradition of knighthood who undoubtedly belonged to the *popolo*. Da Nono, as he was married to Dota de Doto, had a particular interest in them, and repeats legends connecting them with Troy and the foundation of Venice; consequently, his admission that they were not reputed noble is decisive.[2] In fact, the De Doto seem to represent perfectly the new class of men whose roots were essentially urban; they had no castle in the country, and no apparent attachment to any particular part of the contado. The fortunes of the family also suggest that they were careful not to commit themselves irrevocably to any particular political regime.

Zambono de Doto was already a judge in 1257 and appears in various city councils and holding a number of offices between that date and 1269.[3] Da Nono says that he was also a knight but this is not supported by any other evidence. His wife was Mecholda da Vigodarzere, who may or may not have belonged to the noble family of that name, and his son Paolo, who became Giovanni da Nono's father-in-law, married a daughter of Antonio Crosna, a judge. Paolo was a knight who played a leading part in the putting down of a Vicentine revolt in 1290, and who served a term as *podestà* of that city in 1302-3[4] His sons were Zambono II, a judge from 1302, and Schinella, successively a judge, a knight and a doctor of law.[5] The latter began his career as a judge in 1303 and soon after the outbreak of war in 1312 he achieved a position of considerable importance in the government of the commune. An indication of this are the numerous missions which he performed on behalf of the city between 1314 and 1327. During these years he was in Venice once and Treviso twice, and represented the commune before

[1] Verci, *Marca Trivigiana*, doc. n. 731; Mussato, *De Gestis*, ed. Padrin, Mon.RDVSP ser. III, vol. III, p. 79.
[2] *De Generatione*, f. 39.
[3] E.g. judge and *extimator* 1257-8 (Corona 2928); council of 60 and Consiglio Maggiore (Verci, *Marca Trivigiana*, docs. nn. 137, 149); *anziano* 1265 (*Stat. Com.* 1032).
[4] Da Nono, loc. cit. Smereglo, *Annales Vincentinae*, p. 17.
[5] *Stat. Coll. Iud.*, ff. 73v, 27v.

Frederick, duke of Austria, from whom he received his knighthood in 1321, and Henry, duke of Carinthia, in a last-minute attempt to save the communal regime in 1327.[1] At home, he was one of the twelve *sapientes* appointed to fix the salary of the *capitano del popolo* in January 1318, and six months later performed the same function after the election of Giacomo da Carrara to the *signoria*.[2] Two years later, after a further change of policy, he witnessed the oath of Ulric de Valse when he took office as Frederick of Austria's *vicegerens* in Padua.[3] Despite his close involvement in the affairs of the commune, he survived the coming of the *signoria* undisturbed, and continued to hold office as a judge until 1338. Another side to his activities was his connection with the university; he was a member of the university college of doctors of law and took part in the negotiation of a new agreement between the commune and the student body in 1321.[4]

Despite the existence of a few families with a tradition of knighthood, it is apparent that in Padua there was no longer a knightly class. Even among the higher nobility, it was far from universal. By the nature of the evidence, it is difficult to be certain that a given individual was not a knight, but when it is considered that Tiso IV Camposanpiero had been *podestà* of Treviso and Ferrara before he was knighted, and that Marsiglio da Carrara was elected *signore* of Padua before he was knighted by his protector Cangrande della Scala, it seems likely that many others of a similar social standing must have never become knights at all. For instance, there is no evidence that Giacomo Grande da Carrara, the first *signore* of Padua, was ever a knight. Knighthood was therefore largely an individual matter, and it is reasonable to ask what were the motives which led some men to seek for the honour and other men to grant it.

A dubbed knight was a noble knight, and the honorific

---

[1] R. Predelli, *I Libri Commemoriali della Repubblica di Venezia*, Mon.RDVSP ser. I, i (1876–8), n. 625; Verci, *Marca Trivigiana*, docs. nn. 982, 1058; Cortusi, *Chronica*, p. 39; *Annales Patavini*, p. 248.

[2] G. Bianchi, *Documenti per la storia del Friuli 1317–1325* (1844–5), I, n. 48; Arch. Papafava 39, n. 1.

[3] Mussato, *De Gestis*, ed. Padrin, p. 66.

[4] A. Gloria, *Monumenti della Università di Padova 1222–1318*, MRIV XXII (1884), pp. 287–8; H. Denifle, 'Statuten der Juristen-Universität Paduas 1331', *ALKM* VI (1892), p. 524.

element was always an important part of the attraction of knighthood. Its appeal, however, differed according to the various social classes. Those whose nobility was recognised and assured had no need of the extra prestige of knighthood, but for some of them the honour was a qualification for entry into the magnificent knightly festivals which were held from time to time, attended by the nobility of the March of Treviso and the neighbouring regions. For example, a great court was held in Ferrara at All Saints 1294, at which fifty-two knights were created, including nobles from Venice, Modena, Bologna, Florence, Mantua and Padua, as well as Ferrara itself. In, 1298, Alberto della Scala created twelve knights at the festivities in honour of the marriage of his son Cangrande, and in 1300 Azzo VIII d'Este presided at Modena when thirty-eight knights were made on the occasion of the marriage of Beatrice d'Este to Galeazzo Visconti.[1] Cangrande celebrated his occupation of Padua in 1328 with a *magna curia* at Verona, and prominent among the thirty-nine who received the accolade were a number of Paduans who had supported him, and whose help he no doubt wished to retain.[2]

To some of those just below noble rank, prestige may have been the chief motive in their seeking the honour of knighthood. Enrico Scrovegni is a case in point. Da Nono characterised him as a hypocrite and a trickster and the Paduan Augustinian friars (*Eremitani*) complained that he built the famous Arena chapel 'more for pomp, vainglory and gain than for the praise, honour and glory of God'.[3] Enrico's knighthood seems to have been inspired by the same motive as his ostentatious building activities and his noble marriage alliances, for he cannot be shown to have had any of the typical interests of a knight in arms or the law. He was not a judge and never served as *podestà*, and, so far from his being a soldier, during the crucial siege of Padua in 1320 he served with neither side but abandoned his property

[1] 'Cronaca de Romano', ed. C. Cipolla, *Antiche Cronache Veronesi*, Mon.RDVSP ser. III, ii, pp. 444, 453; *Chronicon Estense*, ed. E. P. Vicini and G. Bertoni, RIS XV, iii (1908–37), pp. 51, 56–7.

[2] Cortusi, *Chronica*, p. 56; *Annales Patavini*, p. 250.

[3] *De Generatione*, f. 43v particularly describes Enrico's histrionic performances in the Consiglio Maggiore. The complaint of the Eremitani recorded in AS Padua, Corp. Sopp., Eremitani 62, ff. 305–6, was directed against the building of the tower of the Arena chapel which tended to detract from their own church.

and took refuge in Venice, where he died in 1336.¹ It is consistent with the character ascribed to him that he should also have been associated with the so-called Knights of the Blessed and Glorious Virgin Mary, commonly known as the Cavalieri Gaudenti, a religious confraternity which had a bad name for ostentation and tax evasion.²

Enrico Scrovegni was, of course, the son of the notorious usurer Renaldo and the inheritor of one of the greatest fortunes and worst reputations in the March of Treviso; his apparent pursuit of knighthood for its own sake was exceptional. This may be related to the fact that in Padua knighthood in itself ennobled neither the individual nor his descendants. This is clear from Da Nono's description of Pietro Murfi as 'a man of the *popolo* although decorated with knighthood';³ and he would certainly have argued the nobility of the De Doto, if not that of the Capodilista and the Capodivacca, on account of the many knights in these families, had local custom given him any ground for so doing. But though knighthood in isolation did not create nobility, combined with long-standing wealth and a good reputation, it could contribute to raising the status of a family, and it is no coincidence that all three of the families named did succeed in establishing their claim to be considered noble during the fourteenth century. Yet in these cases, of which the De Doto are typical, knighthood does not seem to have been sought for itself, but was the ornament and symbol of a certain way of life and certain interests, particularly leadership in war and the holding of certain high offices in peace.

To be a professional soldier, it was not necessary or even customary to be a dubbed knight. The status of mounted mercenaries was not high; in fact, for men of some social standing, the occupation seems to have been the final refuge to those who were too poor to do nothing and too proud or too incompetent to do anything else. Da Nono tells the story of two impoverished noblemen, Bartolomeo and Tebaldo da Caldenacio who, having lost all their landed property, were reduced to keeping an inn in a Paduan suburb, which brought them no profit since they gave credit to everyone. But for the

---

¹ Cortusi, pp. 35, 74.
² See F. D. Federici, *Storia dei Cavalieri Gaudenti* (1787). For the Scrovegni as moneylenders, see below, p. 188.
³ *De Generatione*, f. 55r.

influence of Guglielmo Lemici they would have been outlawed for debt. Finally, they turned for help to their kinswoman Adelmota Maltraversi. She gave them horses and arms with which they left, without thanking their patron, and took service with a count in Sclavonia, so that they were eventually able to meet their debts.[1]

A case of a member of a respectable citizen family driven by misfortune to become a professional soldier, is that of Bartolomeo Enselmini, the son of Anselmino, who had been a prosperous knight and judge. In October 1324, Bartolomeo appeared before the Inquisitor in Padua as a suspected adherent of the excommunicates Renaldo and Obizzo d'Este who had seized Ferrara from the Holy See. Bartolomeo admitted that for two years he had been in the pay of the Estensi, standing guard and riding often with them, but he pleaded that he had done this under the compulsion of poverty, because he had been exiled from Padua.[2]

According to common opinion, a military man (*militaris vir*) could be recognised by certain outward signs which, according to the depositions of a number of witnesses in a case concerning Traverso Dalesmanini in 1318, included 'to associate with troopers and squires, and horses and arms and hawks' and to 'associate with *valorosi*, and delight in horses, dogs and hawks and go riding in the country'. Traverso was a member of the Consiglio Maggiore and had served as *anziano* for the *comunanza*; asked if he was literate, a witness replied that he knew a little, but was not learned in law.[3]

In the predominantly peaceful years of the later thirteenth century, the opportunities presented by a military career near home must have been limited. An honourable form of service was a term as one of the *milites* which every *podestà* of a major town was bound to bring with him. The records of the Paduans who served in this way outside the city are fragmentary, but what little evidence there is suggests that their status was not

[1] Ibid. f. 33r.
[2] Arch. Capitolare, Diversa III, n. 266.
[3] Brunacci, *Appendice al CDP*, II, n. 102. The relevant passages, which defy complete translation, are as follows: 'Quid est esse militaris vir, respondit: uti cum militibus et domicellis, et equis et armis et osellis, et facere corredos et bagordare et doare.' Another witness: 'Uti cum valorosis, et equitare, et se dellectare in equis, canibus et osellis, et ire equitando et ad cazandum et payssandum.'

high. For example, the three *milites* surnamed Da Vigonza who appear in Vicenza, cannot be shown to have been members of the minor noble family of that name.¹ Unlike some of the judges of the *podestà*, there is no evidence that any of them subsequently became *podestà* on their own account. That they were normally below knightly rank is shown by the style accorded to the *milites* of the *podestà* of Padua, which is always *dominus* and never *nobilis miles*; in most cases the notaries even omitted the family name.

Although it was not customary for an ordinary mounted soldier to be a dubbed knight, the connection between knighthood and proficiency in arms had not yet become entirely nominal. As the examples of Paolo de Doto and Simone and Onore da Vigodarzere already given show, the military leaders of the time were often knights. Another instance is provided by the life of Giovanni Camposanpiero, the son of Guglielmo, a judge belonging to an illegitimate branch of the noble family. Giovanni commanded a detachment in the defence of the approaches to Padua during Cangrande della Scala's attack in January 1318, and in 1321 he was knighted by Frederick of Austria, to whom he had been sent on an embassy by the Paduan commune.² Exiled about 1325 as an enemy of Marsiglio da Carrara, he attached himself to the Estensi in Ferrara, being described as a companion of the Marchesi Renaldo, Obizzo and Nicolò in 1330.³ Two years later, while commanding an army of the Estensi, he was defeated and taken prisoner outside Modena.⁴

Knighthood was commonly associated with military leadership, and in a few cases it is possible to go further and suggest a direct connection between a knighthood and the subsequent acceptance of a military command. The clearest example is that of Antonio da Curtarolo, the companion of Nicolò da Lozzo, who followed him into the Della Scala camp in 1312. Cangrande gave him the accolade before placing him in command of a force of German troops in the war against the Paduan

---

¹ Alberico, Garsilione and Giacomo da Vigonza, AS Vicenza, Arch. Torre 29, nn. 83, 87, 90; AS Padua, AD 4496.
² *Annales Patavini*, p. 264 (misdated 1320); p. 242. For Giovanni's place in the family, see Genealogical Table 4.
³ AS Modena, AMS XI, 19.
⁴ Cortusi, p. 62; *Chronicon Mutinense*, RIS XI (1721), col. 126.

commune.¹ In 1276, the annals record the knighting in Padua by an Angevin prince of Marsiglio Partinopei, the son of a judge. Two years later, Marsiglio was sent by the commune as *podestà* in Trento, where the bishop had called in the Paduans in an attempt to free the city and diocese from Veronese domination.² The supposition that Marsiglio's knighthood was an important consideration in his appointment to this front-line post is strengthened by the fact that it was in 1276 that the Paduan commune laid down that the *podestà* of the subject city of Vicenza was always to be a *miles adobatus*.³ Not only was this the most important appointment in the power of the Paduan commune to bestow on one of its own citizens, it was also an office where, in view of the smouldering discontent of the Vicentines, military action might be demanded at any moment. The provision that if the *podestà*-elect were not already a knight, he should have himself made one, is the only certain example of the commune taking a direct interest in the creation of knights.

Knights were prominent not only as military commanders, but also in a number of important governmental posts. One example was the frequency with which knights were chosen to represent the commune on embassies, especially those directed to the courts of important foreign princes. The statute dated pre-1236 which lays down that when more than one ambassador is to be sent, they must be chosen from the judges, *milites* and *popolani* clearly does not refer to knights but to *milites pro commune* or possibly members of the *societas militum*;⁴ nevertheless, in practice, dubbed knights were frequently employed. The Paduan embassy sent to the dying Azzo d'Este in 1307 consisted of Tiso Camposanpiero, Nicolò da Lozzo, Ubertino da Carrara and Enrico Scrovegni.⁵ All except Enrico Scrovegni were members of old noble families; except for Ubertino da Carrara, all were certainly knights. At the coronation of Henry VII at Milan in 1311, Padua was represented by four knights, a

---

¹ Cortusi, pp. 18, 23, and interpolation in Cortusi, RIS XII (1728), col. 800.
² *Annales Patavini*, p. 228; *Liber Regiminum*, pp. 332–3.
³ *Stat. Com.* 337.
⁴ Ibid. 302.
⁵ AS Modena, AMS VIII, 14, printed in G. Soranzo, *La Guerra fra Venezia e la S. Sede* (1905), pp. 239–44. The Ubertino da Carrara referred to was Ubertino di Bonifacio (d. 1319), not Ubertino di Giacomino, *Signore* of Padua 1338–45, see Genealogical Table p. 83 above.

judge, a doctor of law and Mussato the poet.¹ Each of the two missions sent by the commune to the Papal court in the following year was composed of a knight and a judge or doctor of law.²

The most important post in which knights were prominent, and for which knighthood appears to have been an important asset, was that of *podestà* of a major city. This office combined military, judicial and ceremonial functions; the *podestà* was the head and personification of the commune, he supervised the administration and the judiciary and in time of war he was generally appointed to lead the communal army. A similar office was that of *capitano del popolo*, whose task was to defend the special interests of the *popolo* within the commune, and who appears *de facto* to have been a check upon the *podestà*. Yet another was the *defensor artium et artificium* and the Executor of the *ordinamenti di giustizia* at Florence. The holders of all these offices had to be non-natives of the city in question, and they held an important and well-paid post for a limited period, normally a year or less. They are well documented, so that an analysis of the *podestà* and the careers and backgrounds of the Paduans who held this type of office is practicable, and will throw light not only on the knights, but on many other aspects of Italian politics and society.³

The towns and cities where Paduans served as *podestà* or in similar offices may be divided into three classes. Firstly, there were those places where the choice was restricted to Paduans, either because the communes in question were politically subject to the Paduan commune, in which case the appointment was made in the Consiglio Maggiore, or, in the case of Feltre and Belluno, the election was made by the local authorities but was limited to Paduans by the terms of a treaty of alliance.⁴ A second class of close neighbours and allies of the Paduan commune may be distinguished from the remaining cities which had no special tie with Padua. Although the line is not always easy

---

¹ Cortusi, p. 13.
² Mussato, *Historia Augusta*, col. 373.
³ A comprehensive general study of the *podestà* has still to be written. Two possible approaches are explored by G. Hanauer, 'Das Berufspodestat im 13 Jahrhundert', *Mittheilungen des Instituts für Oesterreichische Geschichtsforschung XXIII* (1902), pp. 378–426; and Franchini, *Saggio di ricerche sull'istituto del podestà*.
⁴ *Statuti Carraresi*, f. 299r; Verci, *Marca Trivigiana*, doc. n. 97.

to draw, the real distinction between the last two groups is that in the former local politics and family connections were of great importance, while in the latter election depended much more upon the personal abilities and reputation of the candidate. Each class of office appealed to somewhat different sections of the Paduan citizen body.

The offices in subject communes show a considerable gradation of importance and rewards, from the smaller villages where the *podestà* was paid between £25 and £50 for a six-month term, through the larger towns of the contado, where the salary ranged from £100 to £200, up to the major city of Vicenza where the *podestà* received £3,000 *per annum*, nearly as much as the *podestà* of Padua itself. As the rewards were graded, so were the qualifications for office. For the minor communes, a tax assessment of £50 was sufficient, but for the larger towns the qualifications were an assessment of £200 and £500 in immovables, the same as those for the *anziani della comunanza*. The *podestà* of Vicenza had to be a knight and place a deposit of 1,000 marks with the Paduan treasury. In addition, it must be remembered that the *podestà* of the larger cities had to provide from their salaries for a considerable staff of judges, *milites* and other retainers whom they were bound to bring with them.[1]

Very little can be discovered concerning the *podestà* of the smaller communes of the Paduan contado. By chance, it is known that in 1310, Marino Marini was *podestà* of Teolo, Villa di Teolo and other unspecified villages, and Pietro Gici was *podestà* of a group of villages south of Padua consisting of Pernumia, Tribano, Carturo and Riveria.[2] According to Da Nono, the Marini were rich *popolani*, *mercatores* and wine merchants; it may be no coincidence that Teolo was one of the chief communes of the wine-producing Pedevenda.[3] Pietro Marini, probably Marino's father, had held a minor post in the Paduan administration in 1265; Zilio and Ziraldo, probably his grandfather and uncle respectively, are described as *negociatores*.[4] The background of Pietro Gici is more obscure, but he appears

---

[1] *Stat. Com.* 326–53. For a list of *podestà* and their salaries, see below, key to Map III.
[2] J. Salomonio, *Agri Patavini Inscriptiones* (1696), pp. 183–4; Gennari, *CDP* VII, f. 254v.
[3] *De Generatione*, f. 46v.
[4] AD 2183, 2648, 3265, 3527, 3781–4.

to have been an employee of Marsiglio da Carrara, near whose lands the communes in question lay. In 1323, he was appointed Marsiglio's representative for some transaction, the records of which have not come to light, and he was one of those who administered the lands of the monastery of S. Giustina on Marsiglio's behalf between 1328 and 1334.[1] Another *podestà* of Pernumia was Giacomo Campanati, presumably the son of Giovanni, a notary, and brother of Aldovrandino and Engenolfo, who were judges.[2]

It seems likely that the majority of the *podestà* of the groups of minor communes were members of the Paduan administrative class, notaries, judges or their relatives. This is consistent with what is known of the *podestà* of the larger towns of the contado. Alberto da Brugine, *podestà* of Este in 1303, was a judge and the father of Buonaparte, who was also a judge.[3] Guglielmo Pipere, who held the same office in 1305, came from a family of judges and notaries long established in Prato della Valle.[4] Rolando da Piazzola, another judge, was *podestà* of Monselice.[5] It is in this important fortress town that members of rich, powerful citizen families near to the magnate class begin to make their appearance Such a person was Francesco Capodivacca, *podestà* in 1301; significantly, he had a local connection through his mother, Cunizza Paltinerii of Monselice.[6] Fairly good lists exist of the *podestà* of Bassano, a small town controlling a large and important piece of territory, whose *podestà* was paid £500 for a six-month term of office.[7] These were mostly *popolani*, often judges or the relatives of judges; a few were knights and a few were members of noble or magnate families. The list of *podestà* of Belluno which is complete but not

---

[1] AS Padua, Notarile 176, f. 28v; Arch. Vesc., Diversorum, f. 97v.

[2] Giacomo C. *podestà*, 9 April 1313; (AD 5171) son of Giovanni, in census of 1320 (Grion, *Delle Rime Volgari*, p. 285). For this family, see below, p. 136.

[3] *Liber Statutorum Communis et Hominum de Est* (MS Arch. Municip. Este), f. 60v. Alberto became a judge in 1300, and his son Buonaparte in 1329 (*Stat. Coll. Iud.*, ff. 24v, 40v).

[4] *Stat. Este*, f. 66v; for family, see 1320 census, Grion, *Delle Rime Volgari*, pp. 262–3.

[5] AD 5500. For further details of Rolando, see below, p. 300.

[6] *Stat. Coll. Iud.*, f. 70v; Arch. Capit., Diversa III, n. 254.

[7] Gennari, *CDP* VIII, pp. 693–8; *Annali di Bassano* II (MS Museo Civico, Bassano 33C, 15); G. Fabris, *Serie dei Podestà di Bassano* (MS Museo Civico 259D, 3).

entirely reliable, shows similar general characteristics.¹ The proportion of noble and magnate families is higher, but judges and judicial families are still well represented. Among the offices reserved for Paduans, that of *podestà* of Vicenza was in every way the prize; it offered the control of a major city about half the size of Padua, and a contado fully as large as the Paduan, with the corresponding prestige and innumerable opportunities to reap personal advantage. The office is very well documented, and the *podestà* can be seen to fall into the three familiar categories: the magnates, the substantial citizens and a few who had worked their way up from humbler origins. The latter were chiefly judges, the most important being Lovato Lovati, the humanist, and Aldobrandino Mezzabbati, another judge with a high reputation and literary interests, who had also been *Defensor Artium et Artificium* at Florence.² The well-established *popolani* predominate numerically; no doubt they were attracted by such a lucrative and honourable office which could be exercised so near home. Although the acts of the *podestà* were examined at the end of his term of office, the opportunities for pursuing private interests seem to have been greater than they would have been in a fully independent commune and, if the bitter comments of the Vicentine chronicler Nicolò Smereglo are to be believed, advantage was frequently taken of the opportunities for corrupt practices. Several of the *podestà* had interests in the Vicentino; some had married Vicentine wives. The sense of power carried by the office went to the head of at least one *popolano*. According to Smereglo, Giovanni Capodivacca had to be restrained from having the city alarum bell rung, just for the pleasure of seeing the citizens rush to arms in the square beneath his feet.³

Brunetto Latini described *signourie* as 'li plus nobles mestiers c'on puisse avoir au monde'; it was as absolute *signori* and not as constitutional *podestà* that the magnates wished to rule.⁴ The direct rewards of the office must have been relatively less important to them, and it is noticeable that most of the magnates

---

[1] F. Pellegrini, *Serie dei Podestà e Capitani . . . di Belluno, 1200-1400* (Belluno 1893), is partly based on G. Piloni, *Historia di Belluno* (1607) but not all the obvious errors have been eradicated.
[2] See below, pp. 134-5, 147, 150.
[3] *Annales Vincentinae*, p. 15.
[4] *Li Livres dou Tresor*, p. 301.

who became *podestà* of Vicenza seem to have had some special reason for doing so. The lands of Nicolò da Castelnovo, Nicolò da Lozzo and Manfredo Scrovegni were on the borders of the Vicentino, while Vitaliano Lemici had bought up considerable estates in Vicentine territory.[1] But the special sphere of the noble *podestà* was in the offices of the second class, those in the belt of independent cities near Padua whose nobility were close relations of the Paduans. The virtual exclusion of *popolani*, whether magnates or non-magnates, from these offices suggests that it was the family ties possessed by the nobles which were all-important.

A good example of a noble *podestà* is provided by Tiso IV, the head of the Camposanpiero in the later thirteenth century. As we have seen, Tiso was the holder of considerable property and rights in the territory of Treviso. Having helped Gerardo da Camino to found and maintain his *signoria* against his rivals the Castelli in 1283-4, Tiso was rewarded with the office of *podestà* in 1286.[2] Two years later, he served as *podestà* in Ferrara, then under the control of his kinsman Obizzo d'Este. He also served as *podestà* and *supracapitaneus* (presumably a military commander) in Vicenza in 1303-4.[3] The career of Nicolò da Lozzo as a *podestà* provides an almost exact parallel. He too was *podestà* of Treviso and Vicenza and held office under the Estensi twice, though in his case this was in Modena.[4] So far as is known, Tiso Camposanpiero never accepted office farther afield, and Nicolò da Lozzo only did so on one occasion, after he had left Padua as a rebel in 1312.[5] In this, both were typical of the Paduan nobility of their time.

The record of the Carraresi illustrates the disinclination of members of the great noble families to serve as *podestà* except in special circumstances. Only two of this very numerous family were *podestà* of Vicenza, and none appear among the *podestà* of Bassano. Three Carraresi are to be found in the list of office

---

[1] See above, pp. 74, 87, and below, p. 225.
[2] Verci, *Marca Trivigiana*, docs. nn. 273, 291.
[3] *Chronicon Estense*, p. 48; Smereglo, p. 16.
[4] G. B. Picotti, *I Caminesi e la loro signoria in Treviso dal 1283 al 1312* (1905), p. 335; Smereglo, p. 19; Vicini, 'Podestà di Modena', *Giornale Araldico* (1913), pp. 202, 207.
[5] He was *podestà* of Bergamo in 1314; G. Angelini, *Catalogo de'rettori di Bergamo* (1742), p. 24.

holders in Belluno, but one of these appears to be an error.[1] Marsiglio di Giacomo da Carrara, *podestà* of Vicenza in 1268–9, also took office in Ferrara, but only after an interval of twenty-two years.[2] Pierconte da Carrara was *podestà* of Ferrara in 1264 when Obizzo II was elected to the *signoria*, a fact not without significance for the relations between the two families.[3] Only one of the family is known to have taken office outside the region of Padua's immediate neighbours, and this was in the abnormal period of war and internal tension which preceded the establishment of the Carrara *signoria*. From January to June 1322, Nicolò da Carrara was *podestà* of Bologna; soon after he was rector of the Guelph party in Parma.[4] He owed the latter post to the Rossi family, who were his kinsmen by marriage; Marsiglio de Rossi had been present at the defence of Padua in 1320, and Pietro de Rossi was the first *podestà* of Padua under the Carrara *signoria* in 1328.

The great majority of the Paduans who took office near their native city were not in any sense professional *podestà* and did not take similar office elsewhere. Those who were prepared to serve far from home were almost all *popolani*. Among these, it would seem that some were occasional *podestà*, taking office only once or twice; others appear to have served as *podestà* incidentally to a career devoted to arms or the law in their native city. The Paduan chronicler Cortusi, looking back on the golden days of the commune, asserted that in the early fourteenth century, all Tuscany and Lombardy had sought Paduan governors; this was a gross exaggeration, for in fact, Paduans were much less prominent in this field than the citizens of some other communes like Parma, Piacenza and Cremona.[5] Only a very few Paduans were *podestà* so frequently as to justify their classification as professionals.

[1] No Giovanni Papafava was *podestà* of Belluno in 1261, as the first of the Papafava, Giacomino, cannot have been married much before 1263.

[2] Smereglo, p. 12; C. Cipolla, *Documenti per la storia delle relazioni diplomatiche fra Verona e Mantova nel secolo XIII*, Biblioteca Historica Italica (1901), pp. 229–30.

[3] Muratori, *Antichità Estensi* II, pp. 25–7.

[4] *Serie dei podestà di Bologna* (MS AS Bologna); *Chronicon Parmese*, ed. G. Bonazzi, RIS IX, ix (1902), pp. 170–1.

[5] 'Duces, immo reges, Paduanos preferebant. Tuscia, Lombardia, rectores de Padua supplicabant', *Chronica*, p. 12. Cf. Hanauer, 'Das Berufspodestat', p. 396 and Franchini, *Istituto del podestà*, p. 199 et seq. for towns which were the homes of many *podestà*.

The borderline between the noble and occasional *podestà* may be illustrated from the record of Simone da Vigodarzere and Guglielmo Camposanpiero. Simone's career as a knight has already been described; as a *podestà*, his appointments at Vicenza and Modena fit into the pattern normal among the nobility. On the other hand, he was not a great magnate and this may not be unrelated to his acceptance of the office of *podestà* of Florence.¹ Guglielmo Camposanpiero was also not a magnate, being the son of Florio of Mantua, an illegitimate son of Gerardo Camposanpiero, who had been comfortably provided for by his relatives in Padua.² Da Nono says that Florio married well, and this is confirmed by the fact that Guglielmo was invested by the bishop of Padua with widespread tithes which he inherited from his mother.³ Guglielmo had the resources to enable him to pursue a professional career, and he became a judge in 1276, appearing in various offices in Padua.⁴ His first office outside Padua seems to have been as judge and assessor to the *podestà* of Modena in 1289, and he returned there as *podestà* himself ten years later. He was *podestà* of the allied city of Belluno in 1302 and 1305. His only venture outside the Paduan sphere of influence which has come to light, was to Bergamo in 1310.⁵

Anselmino Enselmini is another example of a semi-professional *podestà*, this time from a rich, landed but non-noble background. His grandfather Anselmino I had been a favourite knight of Ezzelino da Romano, under whom he served as *podestà* of Verona in 1247; his father Bartolomeo was also a knight.⁶ Although, unlike his brother Giacomo who was *podestà* of Vicenza in 1275, Bartolomeo does not seem to have held any important office, the wealth and status of the family rose considerably in his time, for while his wife brought him a dowry of only £200, his son Anselmino II was able to marry a niece of Bishop Giovanni Forzatè with a dowry of £1,000; the expenses

¹ See above, p. 98.
² Da Nono, *De Generatione*, f. 17v. See Genealogical Table 4.
³ Arch. Vesc. Feudorum II, ff. 58–9; Brunacci, *CDP* III, p. 1972; Gennari, *CDP* VI, f. 202r.
⁴ *Stat. Coll. Iud.*, f. 2r.
⁵ Vicini, *Podestà di Modena*, p. 202; Piloni, *Historia di Belluno* (new ed. 1929), pp. 236–7; Angelini, *Catalogo de'rettori*, p. 24.
⁶ Rolandino, p. 107; 'Syllabus Potestatum', ed. Cipolla, *Antiche Cronache Veronesi*, Mon.RDVSP ser.III, ii, p. 398.

of the wedding, which amounted to £622 11s. 5d. were met by the bishop.[1] Anselmino's knighthood was in the family tradition but his study of the law was a new departure; he was admitted to the College of Judges some two years after his marriage in 1281.[2] His career outside Padua does not seem to have begun until 1301, when he became *capitano del popolo* at Pisa, but thereafter he was *podestà* of Trieste and Modena, as well as of Belluno twice, in the course of the next seven years.[3] His last service was an embassy to the Roman court on behalf of the Paduan commune in 1311, for which 100 florins were still owing when an inventory of his property was taken in January 1312. Da Nono says that the family were rich and powerful, having a large house near the cathedral in Padua, and this is confirmed by the inventory, which shows that Anselmino also owned several smaller houses in the city, a quarter share in a small tower, and considerable rural property.[4] The lands of the family were clearly concentrated in and near the village of Brentasecca, a few miles east of Padua, where Anselmino and some of his relations built and endowed a church in 1309.[5] There was a *domus dominicalis* there in 1271 but, significantly, no castle is mentioned. Although he left his daughter a dowry of £1,100, Anselmino also felt the large sum of £6,913 'for the restitution of his usuries'. The Enselmini were badly hit by the wars of the early fourteenth century, at least four of the family being in exile by the time of the siege of 1320.[6] Anselmino's son Bartolomeo was, as we have seen, compelled by poverty to become a mercenary of the Estensi.

An interesting man from a more humble background was the knight and judge Giovanni Caligine. The origins of the family are unknown, but Da Nono mentions an Alberto Caligine who was a tailor, and the fact that Giovanni's brother Giacomo practised as a notary before his admission to the College of Judges was exceptional, and suggests that the family was not

---

[1] Arch. Capit., Testamenti I, nn. 44 & 55; Brunacci, *CDP* II, p. 1595.
[2] *Stat. Coll. Iud.*, f. 15r.
[3] R. Roncione, *Delle Istorie Pisane*, ed. F. Bonaini, *ASI* ser. I, VI, i (1844), p. 655; Predelli, *Libri Commemoriali* I, n. 286; Vicini, *Podestà di Modena*, p. 239; Piloni, *Historia di Belluno*, pp. 236-7.
[4] Arch. Capit., Diversa II, 252; *De Generatione*, f. 41v.
[5] Salomomio, *Agri Patavini Inscriptiones*, p. 343.
[6] Cortusi, p. 34, AD 5735.

rich.¹ Giovanni entered the College, of which he was three times *gastaldione*, in 1273.² He must have been still a young man when he filled the important post of judge of the *anziani* in 1283.³ His experience in the duties of *podestà* was gained in Vicenza, where he was judge and assessor twice, before becoming *podestà* for six months in 1302–3.⁴ He was back in Padua just in time to be sent on a mission to Venice in connection with the dispute over the salt workings. After the short war which followed, he was one of the commune's representatives at the peace of Treviso.⁵ His Ghibelline sympathies must have become known by this time—it is probable that he had been involved in the Paduan-Veronese alliance of 1304—for in 1305 he became the *podestà* of Padua's traditional enemy, Verona.⁶ He followed this up with a term as *podestà* in Mantua, a commune controlled at that time by Passerino Bonacolsi, an ally of the Della Scala.⁷ By this time, Giovanni appears to have been an important man in the Paduan *popolo*. His brother had married one of the noble Schinelli family and, in 1308, Giovanni's son Prosdocimo married a daughter of Enrico Paradisi, a knight of the Capodivacca family, with the noble dowry of £1,245.⁸

The arrival of Henry of Luxemburg found Giovanni Caligine in Modena as *capitaneus libertatis communis populi Modene*, and though he was displaced by one of Henry's Imperial vicars, he was compensated almost at once with the vicariate of Arezzo.⁹ With an Emperor once more in Italy, his Ghibelline allegiance must have quickly led to a break with the government of his native city, as, while he was still at Arezzo, he was granted Venetian citizenship, for which he was allowed to take the necessary oath by proxy.¹⁰ He was *podestà* of Modena in 1314, in

---

¹ *De Generatione*, f. 37r; AD 1990; *Stat. Coll. Iud.*, f. 13r.
² Ibid. ff. 2v, 14r, 18r, 65v.
³ AD 3021.
⁴ *Iudex potestatis*, Sept. 1290 and Feb. 1298: AS Vicenza, Torre 29, n. 127 & 32, n. 48; *podestà* Nov. 1302–May 1303, Smereglo, p. 18.
⁵ Predelli, *Libri Commemoriali* I, n. 123; AS Venice, Pacta IV, f. 32r, printed in Picotti, *I Caminesi*, pp. 282–3.
⁶ *Syllabus Potestatum*, p. 406.
⁷ C. D'Arco, *Studi intorno al municipio di Mantova* (1871–4), VI, pp. 51–2.
⁸ AD 3712–3; Brunacci, *CDP* IV, p. 2144.
⁹ Vicini, *Podestà di Modena*, p. 236; *Annales Aretinorum*, ed. A. Bini and G. Grazzini, RIS XXIV, i (1909), p. 14.
¹⁰ Predelli, *Libri Commemoriali* I, nn. 530–1.

which year it is recorded that his daughter, well married into the Capodilista family, gave birth to a son at her father's house in Venice.[1] Giovanni was clearly a professional and largely self-made man who had become attached irrevocably to a political party, and he suffered in consequence. In 1320 his house in Padua was given to the convent of S. Anna, his sons being listed among the rebels. In 1338, his son Prosdocimo was described as living in Vicenza.[2]

The most professional *podestà* among the Paduans of his time, the career of Simone Enghelfredi was in many ways unique. He was educated at Bologna, and was already a doctor of law when he entered the Paduan College of Judges in 1286. Four years later, he began his wandering life, and during the space of the next twenty-one years, he is known to have been a *podestà* or the equivalent ten times.[3] Although with a normal term of office of only six months, this represents only five years actually in office, it must be remembered that the records are unlikely to be complete, and that throughout, Simone was taking his turn in office as an ordinary judge in Padua. It was no doubt his legal training which fitted him to hold so many responsible offices, but his knighthood, which must have preceded his installation as *podestà* of Vicenza in 1293, may have been an additional recommendation to the bodies who nominated or elected him.

Like Giovanni Caligine, Simone was one of the few Paduan

[1] Vicini, *Podestà di Modena*, p. 236; Arch. Papafava 39, n. 39.
[2] AS Padua, AD 5735; Monasteri Veneti, S. Lorenzo III, H. ii, n. 1.
[3] The public life of Simone Enghelfredi 1286-1311: April 1286, *Doctor Legum*, enters Paduan College of Judges (*Stat. Coll. Iud.*, f. 18r); 1290, *Podestà* of Bergamo (Angelini, Catalogo de'rettori, p. 21); Jul.-Oct. 1293, *Iudex ordinarius* in Padua (*Stat. Coll. Iud.*, f. 103r); Nov.-Nov. 1293-4, *Podestà* of Vicenza (Smereglo, p. 16); 1295, *Capitano del Popolo* at Todi (G. Ceci, *Todi nel Medio Evo* (1897), p. 316); 1296, *Podestà* of Orvieto (G. Pardi, 'Serie dei magistrati e reggitori di Orvieto', *BRDSPU* I (1895), p. 378); Nov.-Feb. 1296-7 and Mar.-June 1300, *Iudex ordinarius* in Padua (*Stat. Coll. Iud.*, f. 105v and f. 108r); 1302, *Podestà* of Trieste (A. Hortis, *Gli antichi podestà di Trieste* (1895), p. 13; July-Sept. 1303, *Iudex ordinarius* in Padua (*Stat. Coll. Iud.*, f. 110v); 1304-5, *Podestà* of Bologna (MS *Serie dei podestà*, p. 32); Jan.-June 1306, *Podestà* of Vicenza (Smereglo, p. 18); 1307, *Podestà* of Verona (Cipolla, *Relazioni Verona-Mantova Sec. XIV.* Misc.RDVSP ser.II XII, i (1907), p.139); Sept.-Feb.? 1307-8, *Capitano del Popolo* at Modena (Vicini, 'I Capitani del Popolo di Modena', *RDSPER(M)* IV, p. 237); 1311, Dies in office as Imperial Vicar at Arezzo (*Annales Arretinorum*, RIS XXIV, i (1909), p. 13).

notables with Ghibelline sympathies, which were already sufficiently pronounced in 1293 to be remarked upon by the Vicentine chronicler Smereglo. In view of this, it is natural to find him holding office in a Ghibelline city like Verona, and he was Imperial Vicar in Arezzo at the time of his death. On the other hand, he was not so much a partisan as to preclude his holding office in traditionally Guelph cities like Bologna and Orvieto. His timely death in 1311, before the break between Henry VII and the Paduan commune, spared him the necessity to choose between his city and the Emperor.

Simone's family background is of considerable interest. Da Nono places the Enghelfredi among the families of the *popolo*, late in book four of the *De Generatione*:

Enghelfredo, a tailor and second-hand clothes dealer, was the third treasurer of the noble and powerful Ezzelino da Romano, when he was lord of Padua and the March. He, when he lost Padua, said 'I am leaving in Padua the richest notary, that is Alberto Bibi, the richest barber and the richest tailor in the whole of the March of Treviso'. These men divided Ezzelino's treasure into three parts, and each of them became a moneylender.

Enghelfredo begot Simone, Giovanni Cane and another. Simone, a knight, received a doctorate of law at Bologna, and was twice *podestà* there. In his time, he held the office of *podestà* many times. This good and law-abiding governor died, leaving no son, inhabiting the great palace with an arch, which is without a tower, in Contrà S. Lucia.

Giovanni Cane Enghelfredi, decorated with knighthood by the king of Hungary, begot . . . and the sons of these murdered each other. . . .[1]

In its general lines, this account is supported by independent evidence. In his testament, Simone is described as the son of Enghelfredo, the son of Paduano.[2] Although this Enghelfredo is never himself called a tailor, he is twice designated as the son of Paduano *negociator*, and once as the son of Paduano *sartor*.[3] The allegation of usury would seem to be supported by Simone's direction that the ill-gotten gains of his father, his grandfather and of Pierconte his brother, are to be repaid on his behalf by

---

[1] *De Generatione*, f. 51r.
[2] Corona, 608
[3] Arch. Capit; Perg. XXII, nn. 114–15; Arch. Vescovile, Feudorum, I, f. 33.

his surviving brother Antonio. Da Nono must have overlooked at least one of Simone's brothers, but neither Antonio nor Pierconte were public figures, and both may have been dead when Da Nono wrote. The Giovanni Cane named by Da Nono appears in several documents under that name, and may have been the Giovanni who entered the College of Judges with his brother Anselmino in 1281.[1] Since Simone does not mention him in his will, we cannot be certain whether Anselmino was a brother, a half-brother or possibly a cousin of Simone, but he resembled him in being also a knight and *podestà*, holding office in Bassano in 1292, and in Vicenza, where he died, in 1304.[2] It is surely no coincidence that he too lived in the Via S. Lucia and

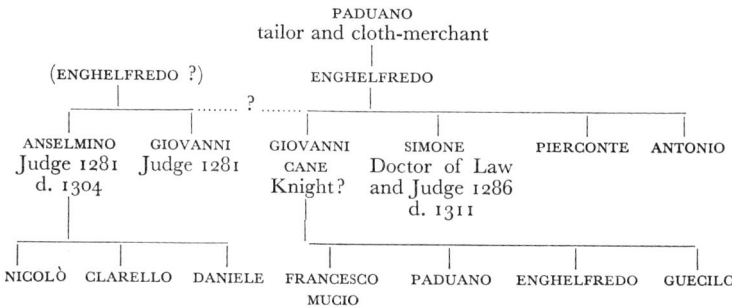

TABLE 7. Genealogy of the Enghelfredi family.

that he owned some second-hand clothes stalls which were bought by the commune in the year of his death.[3]

Though there are many obscurities, the general lines of the family's progress are fairly clear, In the first generation, an artisan succeeds in establishing himself as a merchant and moneylender. His son may have made a fortune as the tyrant Ezzelino's treasurer. The active members of the third generation were judges, knights and *podestà*, Simone standing out by reason of the extraordinary number of external appointments he held. Unfortunately, it is impossible to judge what his career meant in terms of social advancement, as he left no children to inherit it, but his nephews could be described as *nobilis vir* in

[1] *Stat. Coll. Iud.*, f. 15r.
[2] Tua, *Reg. Arch. Bassanesi*, n. 592; Smereglo, p. 18.
[3] *Statuti Carraresi*, f. 214r.

documents without absurdity: Nicolò, son of Anselmino as early as 1309, and Francesco Mucio, son of Giovanni Cane, in 1333.[1]

The outstanding example of a knight and occasional *podestà* who did succeed in advancing his own position and establishing that of his family is Zilio Maccaruffi. This knight begins to appear in the records soon after 1256, and like many Paduans of his day, his first experience of the office of *podestà* was obtained at Vicenza, where he served in 1273.[2] In 1279 he was in Modena, and in 1285, Florence; he held office in Brescia in 1288, Mantua in 1293 and again in Florence in 1296.[3] In the same period, he seems to have been active in Paduan political life, and was twice an ambassador on behalf of the commune. He died in 1308 or soon after.

When Zilio began his public career, the Maccaruffi were a powerful citizen family, possibly on the fringe of magnatial status; at his death he left his sons among the few most influential men in Padua, and between 1312 and 1318, the power of the family was comparable to that of the Carraresi themselves.[4] As the only active member of the family in the crucial years of the last quarter of the thirteenth century, it is obvious that Zilio must have been at least partly responsible for the spectacular rise of the Maccaruffi, but unfortunately, lack of records make it difficult to see in detail what his contribution was. For instance, it is not known whether he was able to invest some of the profits of office in land, possibly consolidating his ancestral holdings in the south-east of the Paduan contado, where the main strength of the family lay. The accidents of inheritance may have been equally important; in particular, the execution for murder of Bartolomeo Maccaruffi, who may have been Zilio's brother, in 1265, could have had the effect of concentrating the leadership and resources of the family on Zilio at a vital period.[5] On the other hand, Da Nono notes that the Maccaruffi could look for strong support to the horse and foot of the city militia, and it is reasonable to suppose that Zilio's

---

[1] AD 4885; AS Verona, Famiglia Bevilacqua 139, n. 59.
[2] Smereglo, p. 13.
[3] Vicini, *Podestà di Modena*, pp. 150–1; D'Arco, *Municipio di Mantova*, p. 47; Davidsohn, IV, pp. 540–1.
[4] See below, pp. 268–9.
[5] *Liber Regiminum*, p. 327.

long association with the affairs of the commune may have contributed something to the building up of this allegiance.

In one respect at least, it is possible to show that Zilio, if he was not the originator, was certainly the fomenter of the link with the Estensi which had an important influence on the policy of the family in the early fourteenth century, and thus indirectly contributed to the fall of the Paduan commune. In 1255, Rolandino mentions that the sons of Maccaruffo and their mother had already gone into exile from Padua with the partisans of the Church and the Marchesi, but this need not imply a close connection with the Estensi themselves.[1] The next point of contact which can be established was in 1284, when Zilio was among the witnesses to a trade agreement between the Paduan commune and the Estensi in Ferrara.[2] Zilio's term as *podestà* in Modena took place before the city passed into the hands of the Este family, but his appointment as *podestà* in Mantua less than two months after peace had been made between Pinamonte Bonacolsi and Obizzo d'Este, suggests that it was probably due to the influence of the latter.[3] Zilio's last mission, in November 1307, was to the dying Obizzo d'Este in Ferrara, to protest about disorders on the frontier of the Paduan contado and the county of Rovigo.[4]

It is an indication of the rising social status of the Maccaruffi, that before 1318, Zilio's grand-daughter Furlana had married the Marchese Renaldo who, with his brother Obizzo III, had recovered Ferrara with the help of some of the Maccaruffi in 1317.[5] When the Maccaruffi were driven out of Padua, it was naturally to Ferrara that they went, and Zilio's grandsons became professional soldiers and administrators under the patronage of the Estensi. In 1321, Nicolò di Maccaruffo Maccaruffi was leading a force of twenty-five knights in the service of the Marchesi, and he commanded the army of the Estensi at the siege of Argenta in 1333-4, where he returned as

[1] *Cronica*, p. 109.
[2] AS Modena, AMS IV, n. 23.
[3] The peace was made on 10 May 1292 (*Annales Mantuani*, ed. G. H. Pertz, MGH.SS XIX, 1866, p. 30), and Zilio took office about the middle of the same year.
[4] AS Modena, AMS VIII, n. 14, printed in Soranzo, *Venezia e la S. Sede*, pp. 239-44.
[5] Mussato, *De Gestis*, ed. Padrin, p. 52; Cortusi, p. 26.

visconte in 1341.[1] In addition, he was twice *podestà* of Modena, and also of Parma and Brescia.[2] His brother Bernabò was *podestà* of Modena in 1351–2, and was knighted by Obizzo III in the latter year.[3]

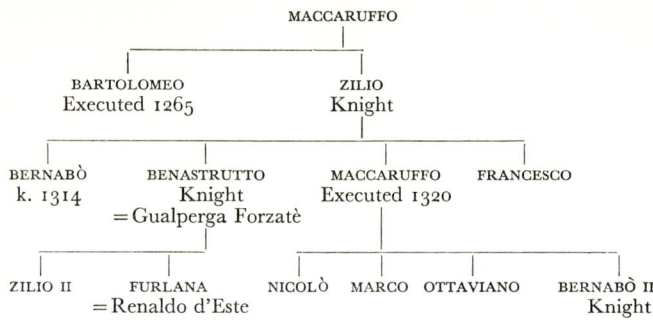

TABLE 8. Genealogy of the Maccaruffi family.

In conclusion, it may be affirmed that in Padua, knighthood was not the prerogative of any particular social class, and it was only rarely pursued simply for the indefinable social prestige which it bestowed. On the other hand, it was not in itself a profession, but was a personal distinction, generally obtained incidentally in the pursuit of certain activities. The occupations most closely associated with knighthood were military leadership and the highest offices in the administrations of the major communes, and for these, knightly status seems to have been a definite advantage. Until the onset of almost continuous war in 1311 upset the prevailing pattern, knighthood and its associated occupations were chiefly a sign of social mobility and the marks of men seeking to improve their wealth and status. For men of noble or near noble status, arms and the administration of cities was one of the honourable roads to self-improvement which could be followed without loss of caste; the other was the law.

[1] Cipolla, *Relazioni Verona-Mantova Sec. XIV*, pp. 236–7.
[2] Vicini, *Podestà di Modena*, pp. 150–1; P. I. Affò, *Storia della Città di Parma* (1793), IV, p. 333; A. Valentini, *Il 'Liber Poteris' della città e del comune di Brescia* (1878), p. 195.
[3] Cipolla, *Relazioni Verona-Mantova Sec. XIV*, p. 237.

CHAPTER V

Judges and Doctors of Law

IT is a commonplace that mediaeval society was to a large extent dominated by legal ideas and by lawyers. At no time was this more true than in the thirteenth century, when the revived study of Roman law was exerting its strongest influence on the traditional structures of church and state. Largely under its influence, law came to be regarded less as a conglomeration of immemorial customs, and more as an articulated and rational system, and its administration ceased to some extent to be regarded as a rightful attribute of property and lordship, and became the concern of trained men. As academic jurisprudence, and its application through legal institutions developed, so the lawyer's profession was bound to become increasingly distinct and technical, containing within itself several further specialisations. The law and the legal profession grew together; and yet historians have not yet extended to the men the attention which they have lavished upon the system.

Italy occupied a cardinal position in the development of mediaeval law. Her schools, which had been the fountainhead of the revived civil and canon law in the eleventh and twelfth centuries, remained the main training ground for the lawyers of much of Europe. The academic study of law had a more direct influence on the life of the Italian communes than was possible in the rest of Europe. Roman law became for them the *lex communis* which prevailed unless overridden by local statutes or customs.[1] Canon law, too, did not exist in isolation as the concern of the clergy alone. At the universities, civil and canon law were studied together, and laymen not only learnt the law of the church, but taught and administered it as well.

One of the first and most lasting impressions which emerges from the Paduan records of the communal period is of the

---

[1] The basis of Roman law is assumed in communal statutes, especially in the sphere of private and criminal law (see *Stat. Com.* 35, 589). In 1314 the commune claimed the legal privileges of the *respublica Romana* (*Statuti Carraresi*, f. 50v).

ubiquity of lawyers. In part, this may be attributed to the bias of the sources, for judges and notaries are naturally prominent in the legal records which comprise the bulk of the documentary material; it is more significant that they were also responsible for virtually all the literary evidence produced in the period as well. At all levels, from the popular chronicling of Da Nono and Cortusi to the classicising erudition of Mussato, the intellectual life of the commune was dominated by notaries and judges. Paduan literary culture was a spare-time activity of lawyers. It is not entirely due to chance that the two Paduan corporations which have left the fullest records are the College of Judges and the Guild of Notaries, for each was in its sphere outstanding, being directly concerned with the chief activity of the city, which was administration. Lawyers and their relations were the leaders of the Paduan *popolo*, appearing over and over again as ambassadors, leaders of political factions and military commanders.

There seem to have been two distinct ways in which the legal profession was organised in the Italian communes, which may conveniently be described as the Florentine and Bolognese systems. In the former, the judges and notaries together formed a single guild which, at Florence, was one of the seven Arti Maggiori; in the matricula of this guild, dated 1290, the majority of the members are described as judge and notary and only a few as notary only.[1] At Bologna, on the other hand, judges and notaries belonged to separate associations, and the two professions were clearly divided.[2] The Bolognese system was followed in Padua; in theory, and to a large extent in practice, membership of the College of Judges and the Guild of Notaries was mutually exclusive and it was an anomaly for notarial and judicial functions to be performed concurrently by the same individual. The professional distinction was deepened by the fact that the judges and the notaries represented two separate though contiguous social groupings within the Paduan *popolo*, for while the notaries, both individually and corporately, were the obvious leaders of the Paduan guildsmen, the judges formed the only professional group within the upper ranks of the *popolo* and, as such, were the natural spokesmen of the more

[1] A. S. Florence, Arti, Giudici e Notai, n. 5.
[2] A. Gaudenzi, 'Le società delle arti in Bologna nel secolo XIII', *BISI* XXI (1899), pp. 26, 29.

substantial members of the *comunanza*. Consequently, though the whole legal and administrative profession in Padua has many common characteristics, it is reasonable to treat it here in two parts, dealing first with the judges, professors and doctors of law and placing the notaries with the other guildsmen in a later chapter.

The legal institutions of thirteenth-century Italy represented a mixed heritage, comprising a long-standing tradition with vulgar Roman and feudal elements which was gradually being transformed or supplanted by the revived Roman law of the schools and universities. According to the older tradition, a judge was a man who, by right of property or appointment, had the duty and authority to give counsel and pronounce judgement in a court which might be communal, feudal or ecclesiastical. In mid-thirteenth-century Padua it was still possible to describe a member of a feudal court, who might have no legal training at all, as a judge. For example, on 7 May 1258, Ugolino Avvocato held a court of his vassals at his house in Padua, at which Guerico Matosavio, Ottaviano the goldsmith and Ottolino di Mandello are recorded as the judges (*iudices curie vasallorum*).[1] Again, in 1269, Renaldo Scrovegni confirmed the grant of a fief in Trambacche in the presence of Aldrico Vescia and Pietro Manfro, peers and judges of his feudal court (*paribus et iudicibus curie vasallorum domini Rainaldi*.)[2] In both cases, the judges presumably exercised their office as fiefholders of the lord in question, and there is no evidence that any of them had any special legal training.

By the mid-thirteenth century, feudal jurisdictions had long been formally abolished in the Padovano, and secular feudal courts were fading away. The two examples above are among the last recorded cases of feudal courts held by laymen, but in the ecclesiastical sphere, these institutions retained their vigour until much later, partly because custom dictated that tithes should be held in fief and not by any other form of tenure. The central organisation of the diocese of Padua thus included at least two feudal courts, those of the cathedral chapter and of the bishop himself, and each presumably had its 'peers and judges'. A record has survived of the appointment of three judges to the bishop's feudal court in 1256, two being nominated

[1] Brunacci, *Appendice al CDP II*, n. 155.
[2] Arch. Capit., Rotuli Capit., vol. XXII, *sub anno*.

by Ugolino Avvocato and one by Bishop Giovanni Forzatè. Two of those named are described as *iudex*, meaning that they were judges of the commune and therefore men with some legal training, but the third, Rolando Engleschi, was not.¹

The complex administration of the Paduan diocese, of which the feudal courts were only a small part, absorbed the services of a considerable number of laymen, some of whom are recurrently described as *iudex* or *iurisperitus*. Some of these were certainly trained men, doctors of law or members of the College of Judges, but the status of others cannot be determined. A large proportion of the *iudices* and *iurisperiti* associated with the ecclesiastical administration were not native Paduans and were therefore generally debarred from membership of the College of Judges and the holding of office under the commune, but there are a few examples of Paduans who either lacked the qualifications or preferred to restrict themselves to ecclesiastical business.

An important reservoir of trained judges which could be drawn upon by the ecclesiastical authorities was the university. Every year, the commune appointed three doctors of canon law and two civilians to be salaried professors.² An amendment to the law, dated 1276, laid down that no Paduan citizen was to be eligible for any salaried university appointment, and though some exceptions were made from time to time, the great majority of the law professors were not Paduans, and as such were excluded from office under the commune. They could plead in the city courts only on behalf of their own students but their only other official function in the municipal administration was to give counsel for the commune *gratis* when required to do so.³ The effect of these regulations was to create a considerable degree of separation between the lawyers of the university and the judges of the commune. The only institution which brought them together was the College of Doctors of Law, whose membership included Paduans and non-Paduans, canonists and civilians, clerks and laymen—in fact, probably all the university graduates in law resident in the city. It is unfortunate that, apart from a list of members, very little is known of this interesting body during the communal period.⁴

¹ Ibid. vol. XIX, n. 5.
² *Stat. Com.* 1249.
³ Ibid. 1253; *Statuti Carraresi*, f. 228v.
⁴ See Appendix III, pp. 315–17.

To a remarkable extent, the professors of law formed a cosmopolitan group who passed from one school or university appointment to another without striking roots, even when they stayed in the same city for many years. This may be illustrated by the example of the Malombra family, who originated in Cremona. Nicolò Malombra first appears in Padua in 1267, when he was enrolled in the College of Judges, but at some later date the note 'struck off because a foreigner' was entered opposite his name, and he seems never to have held office under the commune.[1] In 1268–9 he was in Bologna in the service of the bishop of Cremona, and in 1271 he was assessor to the *podestà* of Arezzo, but in 1275–81 he was back in Padua, being described as professor of both laws in 1279. He was buried in the Dominican church of S. Agostino.[2] His son Giovanni appears as a witness many times in the circle of the bishops of Padua between 1283 and 1308 and was designated *iurisperitus*.[3] His brother Riccardo, who begins to appear in the same circle at about the same time, served as vicar to Percivalle Conti and Bishop Pagano della Torre. He became one of the leading law professors of his time, teaching in the university of Padua in 1295 and 1300; he may also have taught at Bologna. Despite their long residence in Padua, neither brother seems to have achieved citizenship and did not join the College of Judges. About 1311, probably because of the disturbed conditions in Padua, Riccardo moved to Venice where he became *consultore*, or official legal adviser to the republic; he died there in 1334.[4]

Though for a comprehensive picture of the Paduan judicial class it is essential to remember the lawyers of the university and the judges in the service of the bishop and the cathedral chapter, these groups were numerically insignificant compared to the judges of the city who were employed by the commune. The great majority of these were Paduan citizens and members of the College of Judges, the sole exceptions being the judges of the *podestà*. By the code of 1276, each *podestà* had to employ a staff of four judges, and in 1300 this number was increased to five.[5]

[1] *Stat. Coll. Iud.*, f. 13v.   [2] Gloria, *Università*, pp. 231–3.
[3] E.g. Arch. Capit, Canonici XVI, n. 164; Corona 3314 bis.
[4] E. Besta, *Riccardo Malombra, professore dello studio di Padova, consultore di stato in Venezia* (1894); Gloria, *Università*, pp. 243–7.
[5] *Stat. Com.* 11, 12; Verci, *Marca Trivigiana*, doc. n. 418; Da Nono, *Visio Egidii*, p. 16.

It was the duty of these judges to deputise for the *podestà*, to administer the criminal law and to supervise certain vital departments of the administration where a native judge might be unable or unwilling to act impartially. To ensure that, so far as possible, the judges of the *podestà* should be disinterested, it was laid down that they should be non-Paduans and each was to be chosen from a different city. No doubt these men exerted an important hidden influence by spreading ideas and standardising the customs of the various cities, but since detachment was their most important quality, it is not surprising that no evidence can be found of their personal impact on Paduan government and society in the communal period.

The main burden of the judicial work of the commune was carried on not by the foreign judges of the *podestà* but by native Paduans who were members of the city College of Judges. The most important posts filled by them were the twelve offices classified as 'ordinary'; that is the eight benches dealing with civil cases presided over by the eight 'judges of the *palazzo*', and the four permanent administrative commissions, each headed by a judge and a layman, known as the *cataveri*, *procuratores*, *ingroxatores* and *extimatores*.[1] There were in addition a number of 'extraordinary' offices reserved for judges, including the head of the communal archives and the supervisor of the fairs in Prato della Valle.[2] Admission to these offices could be obtained only through the College of Judges, whose members were the Paduan judges *par excellence*, whom the notaries styled *iudex* in every document, regardless of the capacity in which they appeared. They are central to any description of the Paduan judicial class, firstly because they were professionally trained; secondly because they were almost invariably fully enfranchised citizens, able to participate in the political life of the commune, and finally because they were so numerous as to form, with their relations, almost a distinct social class within the citizen body.

The regulation of the judiciary was a matter of the highest importance to the communal government, and the requirements for admission to the College were laid down by statute. These were not unduly exacting. It was necessary to be a Paduan citizen living in the city, of at least twenty years of age with the

[1] *Stat. Com.* 230.
[2] Ibid. 265–79, 563.

modest tax assessment of only £100. No university degree was required, but six years' continuous legal study and the possession of the customary books, that is to say, at least the Codex, the Institutes and the Old Digest, was expected. Candidates were to be examined by a judge of the *podestà* in the chapter of the College of Judges, in the presence of the four *gastaldiones* and at least two-thirds of the members.[1] In practice, this procedure seems to have been modified in detail, and admission took place in two stages. First, the candidate was proposed by an existing member, and proved that he possessed the necessary qualifications; then this was ratified by the judge of the *podestà*, so that some kind of external check on the College was retained.[2] Steeped as they were in Roman law, it is remarkable that the judges did not make even the most formal recognition that they were in theory Imperial officials. There is no evidence of an investiture ceremony of any kind.

It is typical of the ways of the communal government that the detailed regulation of the judicial body was left to the judges themselves, acting through the College of Judges, its chapter and officials. This association, though it was regarded as superior to the artisan guilds, carried out essentially the same functions on behalf of its members, looking after their spiritual and temporal welfare, and regulating their employment and conditions of work. Its most important function was to see that communal offices were filled by qualified men in due rotation as the statutes demanded. Fortunately, more of the records of the College are extant than those relating to any of the Paduan guilds, and they make possible a more detailed analysis of the Paduan judiciary than can be attempted for any other group in the communal period.[3]

Despite the comparative wealth of evidence, it is no easy matter to ascertain the number of the members of the College of Judges during the communal period. Prominent among the

[1] *Stat. Com.* 253, 254, 256.
[2] See record of numerous judges *recepti* and *approbati*, *Stat. Coll. Iud*, ff. 19r et seq. and 63r et seq.
[3] The statutes of the College, from about 1274, together with several lists of members, a partial record of admissions from 1275, lists of office-holders from 1289 and miscellaneous resolutions of the chapter of the College from the early fourteenth century, are all contained in the unpublished MS. Archivio Antico Universitario, Padua, n. 123, cited as *Stat. Coll. Iud.* throughout.

College records is an extended matricula of 387 names, listed under the four administrative quarters of the city.[1] It is undated, but comparison with the record of admissions shows that those who entered the College before 1280 are listed in no particular order, while those received after that date are placed in order of seniority, up to the year 1349, which would appear to be the date of compilation. Clearly, this was in no sense a working list, but when checked against other sources, it appears to be generally reliable though not quite complete, probably because judges who were expelled, but of whose expulsion no record has survived, were generally omitted. Consequently, though the matricula cannot be regarded as a complete list of the judges of the communal period, it has a certain value as a fairly representative sample of the College membership of the time.

The gross number of judges is of little significance unless it is possible to determine, at least approximately, the effective membership of the College at various times during the communal period. In 1254, under the Da Romano tyranny, 14 judges swore to uphold the treaty with Cremona, a surprisingly small number even if allowance is made for a few absentees.[2] Twenty-six years later, the long matricula suggests that membership of the College had risen to 85, since this is the number of judges not named in order of seniority. These included 25 who had entered the College in the single year 1276, a record intake no doubt related to a statute of that year reducing the term of office for most officials of the commune from four to three months.[3] Although this statute was repealed the following year, admissions to the College were reduced for only a short period; in the early 1280s they again reached a high level, a total of 76 candidates being accepted in the five years from 1281 to 1285. Even allowing for some exceptional wastage, possibly through a purge of judges with non-Paduan origins, it is hard to see how the judiciary in 1285 can have been much less than 120.

The effect of these inflated numbers can be seen from the

[1] *Stat. Coll. Iud.*, ff. 4r–7v.
[2] Thirteen of these were listed as members of the Consiglio Maggiore, and one was not (AS Cremona, ASC 1781, 1794).
[3] *Stat. Coll. Iud.*, f. 2; *Stat. Com.* 264.I.
[4] *Stat. Coll. Iud.*, ff. 15r–17v.

lists of judges in office which begin in 1289.[1] These comprise the names of fourteen judges for each four-month period, opposite the name of the bench to which each was allotted. Although there are some difficulties in relating all these offices to those mentioned in the statutes of the commune, and though the names of the office-holders do not always agree with those found in other documents, there is no reason to doubt that these lists are an authentic record of *de jure* office-holders, the discrepancies being due to the substitution of one judge for another, although this was expressly forbidden by statute and by resolutions of the chapter.[2] The examination of the lists shows that, in accordance with the statutes, judges were placed in office more or less in strict rotation, with a maximum of two novices taking office in each four-month period, so that groups of judges tend to recur in office together. Thus, of the fourteen named for the period from November to February 1289–90, ten reappear in the terms beginning November 1292 or March 1293, and eleven of the original group are found in office again in March or June 1296. In the intervals, the benches were filled by a further eight groups of fourteen judges, indicating an effective total of some 126 judges at this period. By the first years of the fourteenth century, the average interval had increased by four months, giving an active membership of the College of 140. The intake of new judges to the College, which in the ten years 1296 to 1305 averaged nine per year, was clearly still in excess of the wastage through death or resignation.

The declining fortunes of the commune after 1311 are reflected clearly in the College records. Recorded admissions fall at once to not more than four per year, and the rotation of offices becomes more rapid and irregular; in the years 1324–6, during the internal crisis which preceded the establishment of the *signoria*, there are lists of judges who had refused office, but who were to be counted as if they had served. Attendances at the chapter, which for the seventeen occasions on which they are known between 1287 and 1305, average about 50, drop to 23–5 at three recorded meetings in 1315.[3] Sixty-eight judges are named in the census of 1320, probably a high proportion of

[1] Ibid. ff. 100–71r.
[2] Ibid. ff. 90r, 177, 181r; *Statuti Carraresi*, f. 41v. Four repetitions between 1307 and 1329 suggest that the measure was not easy to enforce.
[3] *Stat. Coll. Iud.*, ff. 12r, 66v–86v, 93r, 172r, 174r, 176r, 182r.

those remaining in the city during that year of siege. The coming of the *signoria* did not bring any permanent recovery. A matricula dated February 1347 shows that just before the Black Death, the College had 41 members, indicating that the Paduan judiciary had declined to under one-third of what it had been in the peak years of the early fourteenth century.[1]

The great majority of the members of the College of Judges were, as the statutes demanded, natives of the city or its territory. Of the twelve apparent exceptions in the period up to 1328, the majority were probably immigrants to the Paduan state in the process of naturalisation. Some, like the two members of the Lambertazzi family of Bologna, received in 1282-3, and Bonmassario da Colle of Vicenza, who entered the College in 1312, were almost certainly political refugees.[2] Others may have had Paduan blood, like Enselmo da Barbarano of Vicenza who, having been accepted by the College in 1260 and subsequently expelled, successfully appealed for readmission in 1295 on the ground that he was a member of the Consiglio Maggiore and a Paduan citizen by right of inheritance on his mother's side.[3] In this, as in other respects, the year 1328 marked a turning point. Of the thirty-three entrants to the College between 1329 and 1347 named in the matricula, eight or nine appear from their surnames to have originated outside Padua and its contado.

Among the Paduans, the legal profession appealed to the established magnates not at all, and to the nobles only in special, that is generally straitened, circumstances. There were, for example, no judges among the Carraresi, Castelnovo, Da Lozzo, Dalesmanini or Lemici; among the Camposanpiero, the only member of the College of Judges was Guglielmo, who belonged to an illegitimate branch of the family.[4] One of the Cattanei of Lendenara did enter the College, but in exceptional circumstances. This was Nicolò, who was received at the

[1] Ibid. f. 8r. This contains a total of 48 names, but the last 7 are later additions. The earlier list found on ff. 1v-2r is very rough and incomplete.
[2] *Stat. Coll. Iud.*, ff. 15v, 16v, 37r.
[3] Ibid. ff. 12v, 68v. He appears in the matricula, f. 5r, with those who entered the college in 1300.
[4] See above, p. 112. The Tisolino da Camposanpiero who was received into the College in 1269 (*Stat. Coll. Iud.*, f. 13r) cannot have been a legitimate member of the noble family; his son Guglielmo is described as a tailor in 1310 (AD 4982).

express request of Giacomo da Carrara in October 1318, during the latter's brief period as *signore* of Padua.¹ The explanation of this unusual procedure is almost certainly related to the fact that Nicolò's father Rizardo was one of the most ardent supporters of the Carraresi. There is no evidence for Nicolò's ever taking office.

It was not uncommon for some members of lesser or declining noble families to take up a judicial career, presumably as a means of supplementing their limited resources. In the case of Traversino di Ansedisio da Carturo and Luppo di Aleardo Cattanei da Limena, which have already been described, there is evidence that the families in question were in a decline which, for one reason or another, was not arrested. The Cumani of Monselice, on the other hand, are an example of a family with a claim to nobility who seem to have stabilised their position in the judicial class.² However, the best instance of a once-noble family being assimilated into the professional class is provided by the Da Montagnone. This family enjoyed a secure reputation for nobility, which is reflected in Da Nono's story that the Empress Bertha, the wife of the Emperor Henry II, had granted their ancestor as much land as could be enclosed by the thread in the ball which she was spinning.³ In the twelfth century, Fulcone da Montagnone held the office of Prior of the consuls of the commune,⁴ and in 1278 the family still ranked among the magnates, Michele da Montagnone and his nephews being made responsible for the arrest of outlaws in a group of villages centred on the family seat at Monte Ortone.⁵ Yet three sons and two grandsons of this nobleman became judges and pursued careers apparently similar to those of their professional colleagues.⁶ The only one to achieve any special distinction was Geremia da Montagnone, and this had nothing to do with his noble origins but was on account of his intellectual interests as a member of the Paduan pre-humanist circle.

If, on the one hand, the judiciary was an acceptable career

---

[1] 'Secundum petitionem factam per d. Jacobum de Carrara, caput civitatis Padue', *Stat. Coll. Iud.*, f. 38v.
[2] See above, pp. 73, 76, 78.
[3] *De Generatione*, f. 36r.
[4] Roberti, *NAV* ns. III (1902), p. 78.
[5] See Appendix II, p. 313 below.
[6] *Stat. Coll. Iud.*, ff. 15, 33r. For Geremia, see below, pp. 300–1.

for the lesser nobility, it was also one to which the sons of guildsmen might successfully aspire. Taking the 354 names in the matricula of the College of those who became judges before 1328, some 47 were the sons of guildsmen. Of these, 34 were the sons of notaries, and the remaining 13 were drawn from seven other guilds, of which the largest group consisted of four sons of taverners. These figures make clear the outstanding position of the notaries which in part reflects the dominance of their guild over the other artisan corporations, and in part demonstrates the affinity of the two branches of the legal profession. No-one, for example, seems to have tried to combine the profession of judge with the membership of an artisan guild, unless it was the strangely styled *Dominus et Magister Johannes*, the son of Magister Marco the tailor, who entered the College in September 1305 but who does not appear to have taken office.[1] But the separation of the judicial and notarial professions, which was an important characteristic of the organisation of the Paduan administration, was maintained only at the cost of considerable vigilance on the part of the authorities. Although there was no statute to this effect in the 1276 code, the principle of separation was probably already in force, since it can be established that the expulsion of Giacomo de Veglo from the College 'because he tacitly renounced his judgeship by taking office as a Notary of the Seal' took place probably in 1278 and certainly before 1284.[2] However, in October 1306, a resolution of the chapter of the College called for the appointment of a committee to find out which members had taken office as notaries since the passing of a statute on this matter, and the action of this committee seems to have resulted in the resignation of some half-dozen members who elected to remain notaries.[3] Although the law forbidding judges to be members of a guild in the code of 1362, which bears the date 1316, has a clause exempting the guild of notaries from its provisions, this must be a later amendment since the College records show a

---

[1] *Stat. Coll. Iud.*, f. 31r.
[2] Ibid. f. 2r. The *gastaldiones* named in the record of the expulsion are known to have held office in September 1278, and one of the witnesses, Dino di Egidio, died in January 1284 (Salomonio, *Urbis Patavini Inscriptiones*, p. 76).
[3] *Stat. Coll. Iud.*, f. 87v. These expulsions are recorded in marginal notes which cannot always be dated.

judge resigning in order to become a notary as late as October 1321; in all probability the separation of the two professions remained in force until the end of the communal period.[1] Though these measures speak only of the taking of office as notaries or membership of the guild, the evidence of the documents is that judges did not even practise as notaries privately, for in the few cases where a judge is found acting as a notary, he does not subsequently appear in office as a judge, so that his resignation or expulsion from the College may be assumed.

A natural way for double membership of the College of Judges and the Guild of Notaries to arise would be through notaries graduating to the judicial bench, but although there are a number of instances where this can be seen to have happened they are too few to suggest that the practice was at all general. With Enrico da Terrarsa and Enrico de Cacio, both sons of notaries, who made copies from their fathers' registers before they entered the College, training in their father's profession would be a natural stepping stone to the higher office of judge, but the examples of Istriano a Solario, the son of a judge, and Pietro di Parisio, the son of a fishmonger, show that this approach to the judiciary was not restricted to the sons of notaries.[2] The fact that their appearances as notaries only precedes their reception into the College by two or three, or at the most, nine years, suggests that all these were young men who were working as notaries while completing the longer legal training necessary for the bench. The case of Andrea da Terradura, who was in practice as a notary at least seventeen years before he became a judge, is exceptional, and may account for his being referred to as a notary on two occasions after that time.[3]

Although many of the judges from notarial backgrounds do not appear to have been in any way outstanding, and some were among those who resigned or were expelled from the College, there are a few individuals falling into this category

[1] 'Salvo quod non preiudicet iudicibus qui sunt vel erint notarii vel de fratalia notariorum', *Statuti Carraresi*, f. 75v. Cf. resignation of Ongarello Ongarelli 'qui elegit tenere et habere pro notario', *Stat. Coll. Iud.*, f. 35v.

[2] AD 2417, 2964, 2252, 2478. See also the case of Giacomo Caligine, above, pp. 113-14.

[3] AD 2162; Arch. Vesc. Feudorum II, f. 235v; Verci, *Marca Trivigiana* n. 324. Andrea entered the College in 1282 (*Stat. Coll. Iud.*, f. 16r) and appears in various offices until 1302.

whom even the bare records of their careers suggest were men of remarkable ability who used the judicial profession to advance their fortunes and influence. Remarkable among these successful judges was Lovato Lovati, otherwise famous as the founder and leader of the Paduan humanist group. He was the son of Rolando di Lovato, a notary, and his brother Alberto was also a notary; the fact that the family name established itself only in Lovato's generation suggests that the family background was a modest one.[1] Lovato himself first appears in 1257 as a notary, making copies from his father's register; ten years elapsed before he was received into the College of Judges, suggesting that his education may have been prolonged by his activities as a notary.[2] Even after he became a judge, it was several years before his abilities began to receive recognition. In 1273 he was *gastaldione* of the College and in 1282 *podestà* of Bassano, an appointment which led to his nomination as an arbitrator between the communes of Bassano, Solagna and Piove in the following year.[3] His success was sealed in 1291 when he became a knight and *podestà* of Vicenza.[4] Soon after, he stood surety with, among others, Giacomo da Carrara, for a series of major loans to the bishop and commune of Feltre, and in the first years of the fourteenth century, until his long career ended in 1309, he was clearly a judge of considerable distinction, serving in cases involving reprisals with the communes of Milan and Treviso and appearing as a witness to the Paduan alliance with Verona in 1304.[5] Unfortunately, it is not possible to say what this career meant in terms of personal wealth and family

[1] Rolando di Lovato is named in a few documents between June 1247 (Arch. Capit. Pergamene XXII, Padua I, n. 97) and January 1259 (AS Padua, Monasteri Veneti, S. Michele di Murano 11, n. 296). Alberto Lovati appears as a notary in many documents between 1265 (AD 2183) and 1307 (AS Padua, Archivi Privati 99 (Dalla Porta), f. 18r).

[2] For Lovato as a notary, see Corona 7192, 9723, 9725. This part of Lovato's early life was first brought to light by Dr Guido Billanovich, 'Veterum vestigia vatum', *Italia Medioevale e Umanistica*, I (1958), p. 156, n. 2. He entered the College of Judges on 6 May 1267 (*Stat. Coll. Iud.*, f. 13v).

[3] *Stat. Coll. Iud.*, f. 17r; Tua, *Reg. Arch. Bassanesi*, nn. 498, 500.

[4] Smereglo, *Annales Vincentinae*, p. 16.

[5] AS Padua, Archivi Privati 99 [Dalla Porta], f. 18r; *Statuti Carraresi*, f. 146v; Picotti, *I Caminesi*, doc. n. XXI, pp. 270–1; P. Sambin, 'Le relazioni tra Venezia, Padova e Verona all'inizio del secolo XIV', *AIV* CXI (1952–3), pp. 212–14.

advancement. In 1316, Lovato's heirs held land in Albignasego, a village a few miles south of Padua, but his son Rolando seems to have died young.[1] One would like to know why it was that Lovato's widow, Giacomina da Solesino, left her possessions, including land in Monselice and Solesino, to Elizabetta Gradenigo, widow of Giacomo Grande da Carrara, in 1331.[2]

Another leading judge from a notarial family was Paolo da Teolo. His father Bartolomeo was a notary who had migrated from the village of Teolo in the Pedevenda before 1254, and settled in the south-western suburbs of the city near the Dominican church of S. Agostino, where he was buried in 1295.[3] Of his two sons, Paolo became a judge in 1283 but Antonio, although he appears in the matricula of the College, does not seem to have taken office as a judge, but is always described as a notary.[4] Both brothers, but Antonio particularly, figure as witnesses and agents for the Venetian house of S. Giovanni Evangelista and also for the Dominicans of S. Agostino who, after 1302, administered the Inquisition in Padua.[5] They were also connected with the bishop's circle both as vassals, holding tithes in fief in their native village, and through their uncle Stefano who was *custos* of the cathedral until about 1307.[6] Although Paolo did not achieve a knighthood, he was an exceptionally active judge, serving twice as judge of the *podestà* in Vicenza and acting for the Paduan commune in negotiations in Venice in 1312 and 1314.[7] He also appears arbitrating and giving counsel in the communal courts, and assisted in the drawing up of legislation.[8] He was one of the advisers appointed to

---

[1] AS Padua, Archivi Privati, Sala, June 1316. Rolando di Lovato appears as a witness to a transaction in which his uncle Alberto was notary, 31 March 1297 (AD 3894).

[2] AD 7737. Cf. Pietro d'Abano who left his estate to Giacomo da Carrara and Corrado da Vigonza because he was threatened by the Inquisition, see his testament, AD 4627.

[3] Bartolomeo 'qui fuit de Titulo' took the oath of 1254 in the *centenario* of S. Egidio (AS Cremona, ASC 1773); his death is noted in *Obituario S. Agostino di Padova*, ed. G. Mazzatinti, Misc.RDVSP ser. II, ii (1894), p. 39.

[4] *Stat. Coll. Iud.*, ff. 16v, 6r.

[5] AS Padua, Monasteri Veneti, S. Giovanni Evangelista 1, A 4, 6, 7 C I–II, *passim*. AD 4078, 4167, 5541, etc.

[6] AD 4121; 4742.

[7] AS Vicenza, Arch. Torre 31, n. 46; 33, n. 78; Verci, *Marca Trivigiana*, doc. nn. 545, 699.

[8] AD 4188, 5500, 4102, 3818.

the commission set up to dispose of the property of rebels in 1314 and was a member of the body nominated to decide the salary of Giacomo da Carrara when he was elected to the *signoria* in 1318.[1] In 1320 he witnessed the oath of Frederick of Austria's lieutenant when he took office as *capitano* in Padua.[2] By his death in 1325, he avoided the worst of the troubles of the last days of the commune; in his epitaph in S. Agostino, he was described as 'Iuris apex, urbis consiliumque suae'.[3] Though no writings of his have come to light, he was connected with the pre-humanist circle through his sister, who was the wife of the judge Egidio da Solesino, Lovato's brother-in-law, and Mussato addressed one of his verse letters to him.[4]

The rise of the Da Teolo can be traced through the move from the contado to the city and through the rise from the profession of notary to that of judge; with the Campanati, a similar process can be observed over three generations. Paduano Campanati of the Pontemolino quarter appears in 1285 as a minor official, the captain of the *cavalcatores de Ultrabrenta*, a mounted police force whose task was to prevent smuggling in the Paduan contado.[5] Da Nono says that he was a notary but he is never described as such; in 1304 he is mentioned as a tax collector for the *centenario* of S. Fermo.[6] However, he had two sons who were notaries and one of these, Giovanni, was the father of Aldovrandino and Enghenolfo who became judges in 1310 and 1314 respectively;[7] Giacomo Campanati, whom we have already met as *podestà* of Pernumia, was probably their brother. Enghenolfo subsequently resigned from the College and reverted to notarial status, but Aldovrandino continued to be active as a judge until at least 1348, and his son Bonfrancesco joined the College in 1334.[8]

Such being their background, it is not surprising that Da Nono, with his aristocratic prejudices, had little good to say of

---

[1] AD 5291, 5295; Arch. Papafava 39, n. 1.
[2] Mussato, *De Gestis*, ed. Padrin, p. 66.
[3] Salomonio, *Urbis Patavini Inscriptiones*, p. 90.
[4] AD 6054.
[5] Verci, *Marca Trivigiana*, doc. n. 283.
[6] *De Generatione*, ff. 47v–48r; AS Padua, Corp. Sopp., S. Agostino 168, n. 39.
[7] Da Nono, loc. cit. confirmed by AD 5421 and Archivi Privati, Frigemelica 10, n. 5; *Stat. Coll. Iud.*, ff. 36r, 37v.
[8] AD 6065; *Stat. Coll. Iud.*, f. 41v.

the Campanati. In his opinion they were *popolani* of little standing, and he relates that Aldovrandino, though not very learned in the law, tried to cash in on the reputation of the excellent doctor Aldovrandino Mezzabbati by calling himself Aldovrandino the second. Learned or not, Aldovrandino Campanati's success was rapid and lasting. In 1312, he was *podestà* Albertino da Castelnovo's vicar in Treviso; two years later he was judge of the *anziani*, a member of the committee on the property of rebels and an ambassador for the commune in Venice.[1] In 1318, he represented the Paduan government in

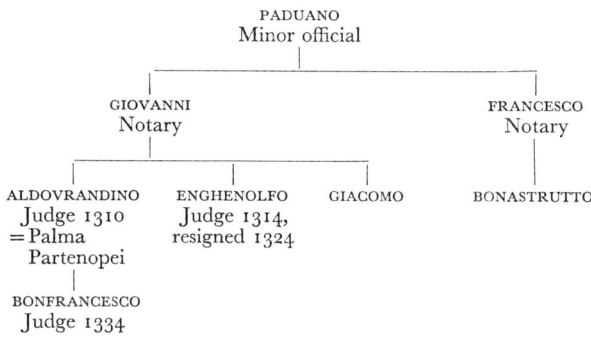

TABLE 9. Genealogy of the Campanati family.

Treviso.[2] The disorders which accompanied the establishment of the *signoria* do not seem to have disturbed Aldovrandino's career: he continued in various offices and in 1330 was a witness to the treaty between the Della Scala and the Venetians.[3] About this time, he married, presumably as his second wife, Palma Partinopei, a granddaughter of Marsiglio the knight.[4] The crisis of 1337, when Marsiglio da Carrara revolted against the domination of the Della Scala, found Aldovrandino in the centre of events as judge of the *anziani*, and it was he who delivered the formal speech of thanks on behalf of the Paduan *popolo* to the representatives of their Florentine and Venetian

---

[1] Picotti, *I Caminesi*, p. 340; AD 5254, 5265; Predelli, *Libri Commemoriali*, I, n. 625.
[2] Verci, *Marca Trivigiana*, doc. n. 880.
[3] Verci, *Acta ad Patavinos spectantia*, p. 436.
[4] AD 6393.

allies. He was later a witness to the treaty by which the independent Carrara *signoria* of Padua was recognised by the two great republics.[1]

While it is clear that some men from notarial families led a highly successful career as judges, it is perhaps surprising that there were others who, having invested in an expensive legal training and gained admission to the College of Judges, later chose to resign in order to continue as notaries. As the status of the judge was higher, his obligations appear to have been greater, possibly too great for some individuals to meet. A marginal note in the College records shows that Giacomo Matosavio was expelled because he ceased to be assessed for mounted service with the militia of the commune: later he is found in practice as a notary.[2] Another possible explanation is that the judiciary did not offer greater rewards to everyone, but only to those with the necessary talents.

Where the sons of notaries so often failed, it is not surprising that few of the sons of other guildsmen succeeded in entering the College of Judges and even fewer were able to establish their position there. Both the social and the professional gap was greater; it is, for example, rare to find brothers who were judges and members of the artisan guilds respectively. Not unnaturally, the thirteen sons of guildsmen named in the matricula of the College fall into two groups—those who barely maintained their position as judges, some of whom even lacked family names, and those whose successful careers are a measure of the degree of social mobility which was possible in the best years of the Paduan commune.

It might have been expected that the physicians, as members of a learned profession, might have provided some sons as candidates for the judiciary but in fact the matricula names only two, who were brothers, the sons of Magister Giovanni da Terradura.[3] Da Nono says that the family had been *contadini* of Terradura, but that by his time they owned a great and beautiful *palazzo* in Via S. Clemente; they continued to hold tithes in Terradura and other villages of the contado.[4] In fact, three

---

[1] Cortusi, p. 85; V. Lazzarini, 'La storia di un trattato tra Venezia, Firenze e i Carraresi', *NAV* XVIII (1899), p. 273.
[2] *Stat. Coll. Iud.*, f. 14v; AD 3049.   [3] *Stat. Coll. Iud.*, f. 4r.
[4] *De Generatione*, f. 48v; Arch. Vescovile, Feudorum II, f. 235v; Corona 2371.

of Giovanni's sons were enrolled in the College between 1267 and 1282, though the last of them, Andrea, must have obtained his promotion late, as he had been practising as a notary some seventeen years before.[1] The most interesting of the brothers is Ailino, an active judge in several spheres. In 1283, he appears among the witnesses to the purchase of a share in the jurisdiction of Lendenara by the commune, and he was also the agent employed by Gerardo da Camino to raise a substantial loan in Padua soon after his seizure of power in Treviso in the same year. These two events were not unconnected, and suggest that Ailino was closely involved in the political life of the commune at the time.[2] He crowned his career by becoming *podestà* of Vicenza, possibly with a knighthood, in 1301.[3] Ailino had a number of sons, among whom Galvano followed his father's profession, entering the College in 1306 and serving as *podestà* of Bassano in 1316.[4] Two years later, his career in Padua was cut short when he and his brothers went into exile as members of the Maccaruffi faction.[5]

The remaining guilds which provided the background for one or two of the judges in the matricula are a miscellaneous collection, comprising tailors, shoemakers or cobblers, fishmongers, glassworkers and *negociatores*. Paduano Rossi, the sole son of a *negociator* to be found in the list, established his position sufficiently to enable his son Alberto to follow in his steps, but another son, Azzo, remained a notary.[6] One or two were the sons of outstanding master craftsmen, like Principe Schalchi, who belonged to a family of 'old and good Paduan citizens', his father Bernardo being described by Da Nono as 'a poor man, but one of the best tailors in Padua, who became a very rich moneylender'.[7] Similarly, Da Nono speaks of the Verarii as

[1] *Stat. Coll. Iud.*, ff. 13v, 14r, 16r.
[2] A. Medin, 'I documenti originali dei primi acquisti di Padova nel Polesine', MRIV XXVII (1907), p. 22; AS Venice, *Codex Tarvisinus*, f. 331r. For the political background, see below, pp. 230–1, 239–40.
[3] Smereglo, p. 17.
[4] *Stat. Coll. Iud.*, f. 32r, 86v; Verci, *Marca Trivigiana*, doc. n. 804. The Bartolomeo di Trento da Terradura who also entered the College in 1306 and who served as judge of the *podestà* in Bassano under Galvano, was no relation, so far as can be ascertained.
[5] See below, p. 268.
[6] Paduano, received into the College 1284, in various offices until 1318; Alberto, received 1307 (*Stat. Coll. Iud.*, ff. 17r, 33r); Azzo notary, AD 6151.
[7] *Stat. Coll. Iud.*, f. 30v; *De Generatione*, f. 49r.

'excellent craftsmen, making ladles, phialls and other vessels' in the suburb of Ognissanti.[1] Flessio Verarii had a son and two brothers who became judges, and one of the latter, having served as *podestà* of Bassano and judge of the *podestà* of Vicenza, became *podestà* of Vicenza in 1301.[2] But the most remarkable success was that of Pietro di Parisio who, as the son of a fishmonger, must have made his way against considerable disadvantages in the traditional Paduan society of the later thirteenth century. Beginning as a notary, Pietro entered the College in 1272 and established himself as a respected member of the judiciary, serving three times as judge of the *podestà* in Vicenza as well as on several judicial or administrative commissions.[3] He was able to build himself a fine *palazzo* opposite the church of S. Giovanni delle Navi and married into the neighbouring Da Rossano or Tadi family, who had been leading citizens since the twelfth century, several of whom were knights, judges and professors of law.[4] From them, Pietro came to possess extensive tithes in Rovolon and Rossano, held in fief from the bishop of Vicenza.[5] His son became a judge in 1310.[6]

The notorious judge Pietro Altichini, who was torn to pieces by the Paduan mob in 1314 on account of his alleged extortions and usuries, was the son of a rich taverner.[7] He entered the College in 1277 and his brother Antonio also appears in the matricula, although there is no record of his holding office.[8] With a family fortune which Da Nono believed amounted to £100,000, and considerable ability, Pietro pursued a successful career which gave him an important position in Paduan politics in the early years of the fourteenth century. He seems to have been made the scapegoat of an unsuccessful and unpopular administration and no record of his infamous usuries has been

[1] Ibid. f. 52v.
[2] *Stat. Coll. Iud.*, ff. 2r, 13v, 25r; Verci, *Acta ad Patavinos Spectantia*, p. 152; AS Vicenza, Torre 29, n. 100; Smereglo, p. 17.
[3] *Stat. Coll. Iud.*, f. 13(a)v; AS Vicenza, Torre 29, n. 90; 43, n. 1; AS Verona, Bevilacqua 174, n. 5; *Statuti Carraresi*, ff. 146v, 240v; Verci, *Acta ad Patavinos Spectantia*, pp. 151–5; AD 5265.
[4] *De Generatione*, f. 48r. Typically, Da Nono thought him 'non multis legibus imbutus'. For the Tadi, see below, pp. 147–9.
[5] Arch Vescovile, Vicenza, Feudorum III, f. 209, IV, f. 85.
[6] *Stat. Coll. Iud.*, f. 36r.
[7] *De Generatione*, f. 51v. For the events of 1314, see below, p. 266.
[8] *Stat. Coll. Iud.*, ff. 2v, 7r.

preserved. There is no doubt as to his wealth for he was able to settle the exceptional sum of £1,500 on his second wife, a daughter of the jurist Giacomo de Arena, and he gave his daughter, who married Nicolò Capodivacca, the noble dowry of £3,500.[1] Like all upstarts, the Altichini were obvious magnets for jealousy and suspicion, but they were not the only sons of taverners to enter the judiciary. Also in the matricula of the College is Vendramo Berni the son of Berno, 'a very rich taverner' according to Da Nono, and Domenico di Brazaro de Iza.[2] Domenico's grandfather, before he moved into the city, had been a taverner in the village of Galzignano where his descendants continued to hold land.[3] They may have been tenants of the Da Lozzo, who it is known were landowners in that region, since in 1313 Brazaro and Domenico were declared rebels against the commune, as followers of Nicolò da Lozzo.[4]

While an exceptional interest attaches to those judges who notably advanced their status and that of their family through a judicial career, it must not be imagined that they were in any way typical of the judicial class. The majority of the Paduan judiciary was recruited from families whose power was less than that of the magnates and whose status was less than noble, but which were generally superior to those from which the notaries and guildsmen were drawn. Like other occupations, a judicial career was traditional in some families over several generations, and although a few of these families, like the Buzzaccarini and De Doto, were on their way to establishing their position as nobles and magnates, while others, like the Verarii, were climbing up from the artisan class, the majority were established members of the Paduan *popolo* whose fortunes neither rose nor fell sufficiently to make any impression on the records. To a considerable extent, the judges and their families formed a compact social class; of the 354 named in the matricula, at least half can be shown to have been closely related to at least one other judge. While their numbers are insignificant when compared to the total population of the city, most of them must have been members of the Consiglio Maggiore and their weight in

[1] Corona 1265, f. 85r; Brunacci *CDP* III, p. 1874.
[2] *De Generatione*, f. 40v. Both entered the College in 1302 (*Stat. Coll. Iud.*, f. 26v).
[3] AD 1966, 1982, 2686, 5165, 5183.
[4] See below, p. 264.

this body, which had a maximum of a thousand members, could have been considerable.

The descendants of Onore da Prato were an apparently typical judicial family, exceptional only in the number of judges which they produced. Three, and possibly four, of Onore's sons entered the College, and in the next generation there were three more.[1] The only one who, from the documents, appears to have been in any way outstanding, was Paduano,

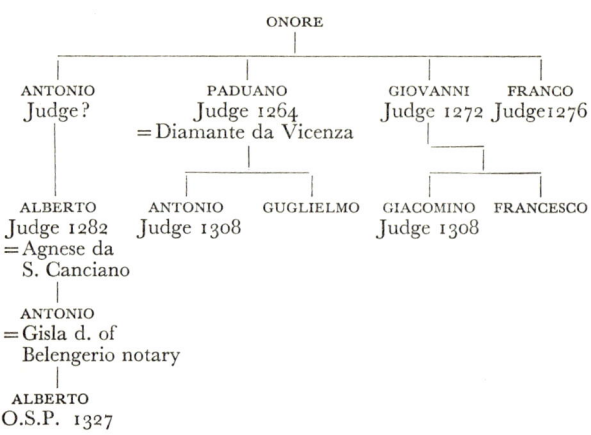

Table 10. Genealogy of the Da Prato family.

who was twice among the judges of the *podestà* in Vicenza, and in 1293 and 1299 was *podestà* of Belluno.[2] In 1291 he received the high dowry of £1,000 from a widow of Vicenza who was probably his second wife.[3] By contrast, his nephew Alberto married Agnese da S. Canciano, the daughter of a notary and the widow of another, with a dowry of only £400. In 1327, Agnese had an inventory drawn up of the property of her deceased grandson, her son being already dead, which shows

[1] *Stat. Coll. Iud.*, ff. 2r, 12v, 13(a)v, 33v, 34r. The doubt concerning Antonio di Onore arises because although he is several times posthumously described as a judge (e.g. AS Venice, Monasteri Padovani, S. Maria de Porcilia, I, n. 372; AS Padua, Archivi Privati, Frigemelica 80, nn. 2–3) he is never so designated during his lifetime.
[2] AS Vicenza, Torre 29, n. 110; 32, n. 44; Piloni, *Historia di Belluno*, pp. 236–7.
[3] Arch. Capit. Diversa II, n. 191.

that this branch of the family enjoyed only moderate means. Beside their house in Prato della Valle, they held half the tithes of the village of Conselve, 34 *campi* and two houses there, and a further 60 *campi* in Candiana.[1]

The most complete inventory of the property of a Paduan judge comes from the division in 1331 of the estate of Aicardino Mascara, a member of the College from 1285. After various legacies had been found, including all his cattle which he had in partnership (*soceda*), plus £50, which he left to his daughter for her marriage, there remained a total of $87\frac{1}{2}$ *campi* and two house-plots, all situated near the city. Since Aicardino is known to have bought 32 of these *campi* with a plot of land in Bagnolo for £1,000 in 1298, and a further 22 *campi* in 1307 for £51 each, £3,000 would be a reasonable guess for the value of this estate, and his total fortune had, no doubt, been greater than this. A codicil of 1311 mentions other land near Padua and in Este, as well as a bible, formerly the property of canon Tommaso Guarnerini, which was at that time in pawn. Aicardino had been well connected—his mother was Andriota Tadi—and, if the £700 which he left his widow in the event of her marrying again are any indication, he was moderately wealthy for a judge, since the dowries paid and received in the judicial class were generally between £500 and £1,000.[2]

The majority of the Paduan judiciary were the sons of men with no obvious professional interests, well-to-do *rentiers* who could afford the six years' study necessary to qualify for admission to the College. Moreover, most of the judges probably remained *rentiers* at heart: their professional activities occupied only a small part of their time and brought in proportionately small returns. Membership of the College gave a judge the right to hold ordinary office in due rotation and to share in the extraordinary offices which came up from time to time.[3] The work of giving counsel in the communal courts was distributed among the judges by lot.[4] Normally, ordinary office was limited to a four-month period every three or four years and it must have been rare for extraordinary offices to supplement this to any

---

[1] AS Padua, Archivi Privati, Frigemelica 86, n. 2; 10, n. 8.
[2] Corona 1249, nn. 108–9; 1338, 1380.
[3] *Stat. Com.* 257, 302, 563.
[4] The names of expelled members were extracted 'de saculis . . . pro consiliis dandis et habendis' (*Stat. Coll. Iud.*, f. 87v).

great degree. The official fees for the offices distributed through the College were limited by statute to £12 for a term in ordinary office and between 1d. and 9d. gr. for giving counsel.[1] Even allowing for a good deal of extra income from bribes and the like, it is hard to see how the profits from these offices can have amounted to very much. In addition, a judge could seek employment as an advocate and no doubt a man with ability could earn fame and rewards in this field, though the lack of records make it impossible to say how frequently this was done. Yet competition must have served to reduce the rewards of all but the most able, and a great deal of the less important legal business was generally entrusted to notaries. The inflated numbers characteristic of the communal period must have meant that most of the Paduan bench was composed of part-time judges who could have considerable time to spare for other activities. The trades controlled by the guilds were closed to them though like every other class in Padua, they could and did lend money at interest. But public affairs were the obvious outlet for their further energies. The ways of the commune are inexplicable unless it is remembered that the *popolo* could at any time call on the services of a large number of men with judicial training and experience.

While membership of the College of Judges was hardly in itself a profession, it was desired by some of the most active elements in the Paduan *popolo* because it could open the way to positions of power, profit and prestige. For some, like Lovato Lovati and Aldovrandino Campanati, it was the door to the politics of their own city; to others like Anselmino Enselmini and Simone Enghelfredi, it was the preliminary to a career outside Padua as professional *podestà*. Success in either of these spheres could lead to knighthood, and of the fifteen certain cases of judges who were also knights, the majority were also *podestà* at some time in their career, and belonged to the more professional part of the judiciary. As always in Padua, professionalism was a sign of insecurity or of outstanding ambition; the only exceptions in this case seem to have been members of two powerful citizen families, the De Doto and the Buzzaccarini, which maintained a strong judicial tradition for a generation or two after their circumstances had made a professional career superfluous.

[1] *Stat. Com.* 230, 521.

Another path open to a judge led through graduation at a university. A university degree was not demanded for admission to the College of Judges: this required an additional two years of study in civil law and another three years in canon law, if a doctorate in both laws was desired, ending with a public and private examination before the bishop and the doctors of the university. This was an expensive business compared with the procedure for admission to the College, with dues of one florin each payable to the rectors and doctors present, up to a total of fifteen.[1] A doctorate therefore represented a considerable outlay in time and money. Only two candidates were doctors of law at the time of their reception into the College, and only a small number, no more than 24 out of the 354 named in the matricula before 1328, went on to obtain a doctorate after their admission. A university degree would therefore seem to be *prima facie* evidence for an exceptional degree of professional interest; the advantages which it conferred, however, are not easily ascertained. In local affairs, no doubt personal reputation was more important than academic qualifications, but the example of Simone Enghelfredi suggests that in a wider sphere, a doctorate may have been a useful qualification for a potential judge or *podestà*. But the only advantage which seems to have followed graduation automatically was membership of the College of Doctors of Law, which in turn might lead to employment as a salaried professor in a university.

The most important record relating to the College of Doctors in the communal period is a list of members said to have been drawn up in 1349 which has been preserved in a sixteenth-century manuscript based on a copy dated 1382.[2] The doctors are listed in roughly chronological order, from some who are supposed to have taught in Padua in the twelfth century, up to the middle of the fourteenth. Such a document must naturally be treated with great caution, and the earlier part, in particular, is highly suspect. Fortunately, for the communal period it is possible to check its accuracy against the doctorates mentioned in other records and, for the doctors who were also members of the College of Judges, the list appears to be both complete and accurate, except for the interpolation of three members of the

[1] Denifle, *ALKM* VI (1892), pp. 429–41.
[2] See Appendix III. The indispensable guide to the jurists of the university of Padua is Gloria, *Università*, pp. 146–53.

Capodilista family who should have no place there. However, it should be remembered that with some of the canonists named, it is not always possible to confirm from other sources that they were in fact doctors.

While the lack of fuller documents relating to the College of Doctors is to be regretted, the bare list of members is itself quite illuminating when placed in the context of the rest of the Paduan judiciary and of Paduan society as a whole. The doctors may be divided into Paduans and non-Paduans; the latter, all of whom probably taught in the university, and some of whom also appear in the bishop's circle, do not concern us here. The Paduans may be further divided into doctors of canon and civil law and those who were purely canonists. The majority of the canonists were clerics and, in contrast to the other doctors, form a predominantly aristocratic group in the communal period, comprising five men from noble or magnatial families, one from a judicial background and only two whose families may have been at all humble or obscure. The aristocratic canonists were in fact the class from which bishops and the abbots of the greater houses were drawn. The first name is that of Giovanni Forzatè, bishop of Padua from the restoration of the commune until 1283. Percivalle Conti, who belonged to an obscure branch of the Paduan comital stem, was elected to succeed him by half the canons, and maintained himself as bishop-elect for some four years, until displaced by a Papal nominee, and he died as bishop of Cagliari in 1295.[1] Another member of the College, Altegrado Cattanei da Lendenara, after teaching in the universities of Padua and Bologna, became bishop of Vicenza in 1303. The remaining noblemen were Giacomo and Oderico Cattanei da Limena, both abbots of S. Giustina; the non-nobles were Meliadusio Buzzaccarini, abbot of the Benedictine house of Praglia, and two canons of Padua cathedral, Simone Boatino and Onorato de Brandello.[2] In sharp contrast, the three laymen listed as doctors of canon law were obscure men, two of whom had close notarial connections.[3]

[1] AD 3044–5; Brunacci, *CDP* II, pp. 1320–2; *Registres de Honorius IV*, ed. J. M. Prou (1888), n. 743. All that is known of Percivalle's father Bonifacio is that he came from the Torricelli quarter, with which the Conti were traditionally associated (AD 2799).

[2] Gloria, *Università*, pp. 329–32.

[3] Viz. Stefano Sasso, Albrighetto da Montagana and Nicolò da Piove; Gloria, op. cit. pp. 245–6, 275–8.

The Paduan doctors of both laws, who between 1256 and 1328 numbered twenty-four, represent a fair cross section of the Paduan judiciary, from the noble Luppo Cattanei da Limena at one extreme, to Compagnino a Sale, of a family with notarial and tradesman connections at the other. Only the poorest class of judge, the sons of guildsmen, seem to have been excluded by reason of the expense of a university degree. Clearly, the doctorate did not have the same significance in the lives of all these. For some, like the six members of the Buzzaccarini family or the brothers Pace and Giovanni Tadi, family tradition seems to have been very important. The doctorate of Simone Enghelfredi must be related to his career as *podestà*, yet his example is practically unique. Among the five other doctors who were also knights, three were members of the Buzzaccarini family and the other two, Schinella de Doto and Giovanni Tadi, were not professional *podestà*.

Despite the fortuitous nature of the evidence, for a university professorship was regarded as a temporary appointment which was often unrecorded outside the university context, it is clear that only a minority of the Paduan doctors of law used their degrees to take a teaching post. Notwithstanding the substantial salary of £300 *per annum* paid by the commune to professors of law, most were apparently content to remain *doctores non legentes*.[1] It is true that from 1276, a statute forbade the appointment of Paduan citizens to salaried positions in the university, but this could be, and was, waived when necessary. No Paduan doctor of civil law seems to have taught at Bologna.

The six Paduans who can be proved to have taught civil law at the university were Buzzaccarino, Aldovrandino Mezzabbati, Tebaldo Tebaldi, Giovanni Tadi, Pace Tadi and Belcaro Brognacci. These men were of quite diverse origins. Giovanni and Pace Tadi were the sons of Tado, a judge, and came from a long-established city family which had provided active members of the bishop's curia in the twelfth century; the gate of the city which stood near their house took its name from the family.[2] Aldovrandino Mezzabbati represented the third generation of his family to serve on the Paduan bench. His father Ugo, was an exceptionally active judge who appears in all kinds of legal

---

[1] *Stat. Com.* 1251.
[2] Bonardi, *ARAP* XV (1898–9), pp. 1–38; Da Nono, *Visio Egidii*, p. 6.

business from his reception into the College of Judges in 1259 until his death in office in 1305.¹ He was also a doctor of law and may well have taught in the university. By contrast, Tebaldo Tebaldi was the son of a judge of indeterminable standing while Belcaro Brognacci was the son of Bartolomeo, a notary, formerly of the village of Boccon in the Pedevenda.² Finally, there is the enigmatic Buzzaccarino whose father is never named and whose background cannot be divined from any contemporary record, though early in the fourteenth century both Da Nono and Mussato repeat the story that he had begun life as a baker.³ In addition, Da Nono believed he was the father of the notorious astrologer Salione, adviser to Ezzelino da Romano; it seems much more likely that he was in fact the brother of this mysterious character.

Appointment to a university professorship argues both aptitude and a certain degree of professionalism, for the nominating committee had a wide field to choose from and the duties involved were comparatively exacting.⁴ Consequently, a special interest attaches to the careers of the six Paduans who taught civil law at the university in the communal period. Tebaldo Tebaldi had a rather short career as a judge from 1276 to 1293, and all that can be said is that he maintained his position; his son Giovanni, representing the third generation of his family to serve on the bench, entered the College of Judges in 1305.⁵ Similarly, Pace and Giovanni Tadi, despite active careers as judges, do not seem to have advanced their family to any significant degree. Both served as *podestà* of Vicenza, and Giovanni at least was a knight.⁶ A third brother, Zilio, and a nephew, Pantaleone, became judges in 1282 and 1297 respectively.⁷ Although they clearly belonged to the class from which the leaders of the *comunanza* were drawn, none of the Tadi seems to have played any significant part in the political life of the commune. Paradoxically, at a time when a number of essentially urban families were making their way into the

¹ *Stat. Coll. Iud.*, ff. 12v, 111v.
² AD 5125.
³ *De Generatione*, f. 49v; *De Traditione Patavii*, col. 756, n. i.
⁴ *Stat. Com.* 1250; *Statuti Carraresi*, f. 228v.
⁵ *Stat. Coll. Iud.*, ff. 2r, 13v, 81r; *Obituario S. Agostino*, p. 43.
⁶ Smereglo, pp. 17, 19.
⁷ *Stat. Coll. Iud.*, ff. 15v, 20v. For further information on the Tadi, see Gloria, *Università*, pp. 220–2, 235–6.

magnatial class, this old city family was adopting the name Da Rossano, from a village where they had property.

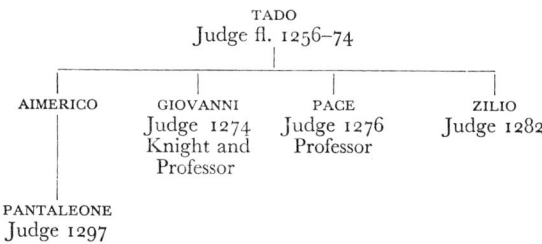

TABLE 11. Genealogy of the Tadi or Da Rossano family.

The recorded facts relating to Belcaro Brognacci are suggestive of a highly successful career, especially when his humble notarial background is borne in mind. A judge in 1293, and a judge of the *podestà* in Vicenza in 1302, his professorship dates from 1308, when he also appears giving counsel in the bishop's *curia*.[1] Another sphere of his activities is indicated by Bishop Pagano della Torre's prohibition of his leaving Padua in 1310, on the grounds that he was 'useful and necessary' to the Inquisition which was at that time administered by the Dominicans.[2] In 1311, Belcaro was one of the Paduan ambassadors to the court of Henry VII and in 1314 he was judge of the *anziani* and a member of the important commission for disposing of the goods of rebels.[3] The height of his political career was his negotiation of the unpopular peace with Cangrande della Scala in 1318, as a result of which his house was pillaged by the mob.[4] His last public act was to assist in the arrangement of a new agreement with the student body in 1321 and his will was drawn up two years later.[5] This shows that he had considerable

[1] *Stat. Coll. Iud.*, f. 19r; AS Vicenza, Torre 33, n. 33; G. Morelli, *Notizie per servire alla storia dello studio di Padova*, Bibl. Univ. MS n. 1675, I, p. 134; Brunacci, *Appendice al CDP*, II, n. 208.
[2] Bianchi, *Documenti per la storia del Friuli*, I, n. 10.
[3] Mussato, *Historia Augusta*, col. 373; Bianchi, I, n. 12; AD 5291, 5295.
[4] Cortusi, p. 26.
[5] Denifle, *ALKM* VI (1892), p. 524; Arch. Capit., Testamenti I, n. 63; AD 5923. For further details of Belcaro's career see Gloria, *Università*, pp. 250–3.

property over and above the fief in Boccon held from the bishop of Padua, which he had inherited. He left his wife several houses in the city, a great house with a cloister, an orchard and land in Boccon, rights in a mill and ten *campi* which he had bought in Fossato. His residuary legatee was his son Bongiovanni, who had been a judge since 1310, but he appears only in routine offices and seems to have died rather young.[1]

The career of Aldovrandino Mezzabbati also shows some marks of success, although his attainments were more intellectual than political. Enrolled in the College of Judges in 1277, Aldovrandino is referred to as a professor of both canon and civil law in 1289. In 1290 and 1292 he was *defensor artium et artificium* in Florence and in 1295 he served as *podestà* in Vicenza.[3] He should therefore have been a knight, though there is no documentary proof of this. Aldovrandino is unique among the Paduans of the period in being described as a professor of both laws, and Da Nono, who did not bestow praise lightly, called him a most excellent doctor.[4] Another of his accomplishments was the writing of vernacular verse. Only a few fragments of his poems have survived, but they earned the commendation of no less a critic than Dante himself.[5] The son and grandson of a judge, Aldovrandino had two brothers who were canons of Padua cathedral, but there is no evidence that he was married or had children.[6]

The only professor to found a great family was Buzzaccarino. The early part of his career is lost in the obscurity of the Da Romano period, but it is known that he was a judge by 1241, and in 1253 he was already a man of some importance, as he is named as joint vicar for Ezzelino in Verona.[7] His association with the previous regime did not prevent the commune from accepting his services in both the administration and the university little more than two years after the capture of the city.[8] He appears intermittently as a professor and in

---

[1] *Stat. Coll. Iud.*, f. 35v; he was dead by 1332.
[2] *Stat. Coll. Iud.*, f. 2v; Brunacci, *CDP* IV, p. 2177.
[3] Davidsohn, IV, p. 553; Smereglo, p. 17.
[4] *De Generatione*, f. 47v.
[5] See below, p. 289.
[6] AD 5199; F. S. Dondi dall'Orologio, *Serie cronologica-storica dei canonici di Padova* (1805), p. 71.
[7] *Syllabus Potestatum*, p. 394.
[8] AS Padua, Monasteri Veneti, S. Giorgio Maggiore XVI, pp. 32–3.

various offices until 1275, which was probably the year of his death.

Bartolo held that a doctor who taught law for twenty years automatically became *comes et illustris*;[1] Buzzaccarino may not have fulfilled this condition to the letter, but he left his sons well established among the leading citizen families. Both Fulcone and Salione were leading members of the Paduan judiciary and, according to Da Nono, also notorious usurers. They were knights, and Fulcone, who is styled *nobilis vir* in a document of 1288, was *defensor artium et artificium* in Florence in 1289-90 and *capitano del popolo* in Bologna in the following year.[2] Although both were doctors, there is no evidence that either of them taught in the university; Meliadusio Buzzaccarini, abbot of Praglia, who is listed among the doctors of canon law, was presumably their brother.[3]

The Buzzaccarini of the third generation followed the family tradition and became lawyers, churchmen, administrators and soldiers. Salione's son Buzzaccarino shares with Simone Enghelfredi the distinction of being a doctor of law at the time of his reception into the College; Albrighetto di Fulcone was also a doctor and his brothers Simone and Oderico were judges.[4] Buzzaccarino di Fulcone was a Dominican friar and his brother Salione became bishop of Adria from 1315 to 1327.[5] Yet another of Fulcone's sons, Pantaleone, was a knight who would seem to fall within the category of professional *podestà*, since he held office in five cities—Cremona, Lucca, Modena, Florence and Bologna—in the eleven years from 1299 to 1311.[6] He married the noble Anna Cattanei da Lendenara.[7] Dusio di Salione was also knighted in 1328.[8]

The Buzzaccarini were one of the most successful Paduan

[1] *In XII Lib. Cod.*, p. 939.
[2] Arch. Vescovile, Vicenza, Feudorum II, f. 182r; Davidsohn, IV, p. 553; AS Bologna, MS *Serie dei podestà*, p. 18.
[3] He may probably be identified with Aledusio, prior of Praglia in February 1275 (AD 2654).
[4] *Stat. Coll. Iud.*, ff. 24v, 13r, 24r.
[5] AD 4244, Gloria, op. cit.
[6] Vicini, *Podestà di Modena*, p. 212; Davidsohn IV, p. 544; AS Bologna, *Serie dei podestà*, p. 40; A. Cavalcabò, 'I rettori di Cremona', *BSC* XX (1955-7), p. 120.
[7] Da Nono, *De Generatione*, f. 49v.
[8] *Annales Patavini*, p. 250. For the political role of the Buzzaccarini in the last years of the commune, see below, pp. 278-9.

families of the communal era. Beginning in the early thirteenth century with a single individual who may have begun life as a baker, by 1311 they had become one of the leading families in the Paduan *popolo* and by 1328 they were well on the way to attaining the place in the Paduan nobility which they were to retain for many centuries to come. While this phenomenal rise may have been due to factors which have left no mark in the records, like their alleged moneylending, their concentration upon the legal profession can hardly have been accidental. In three generations the family produced one professor of law, five

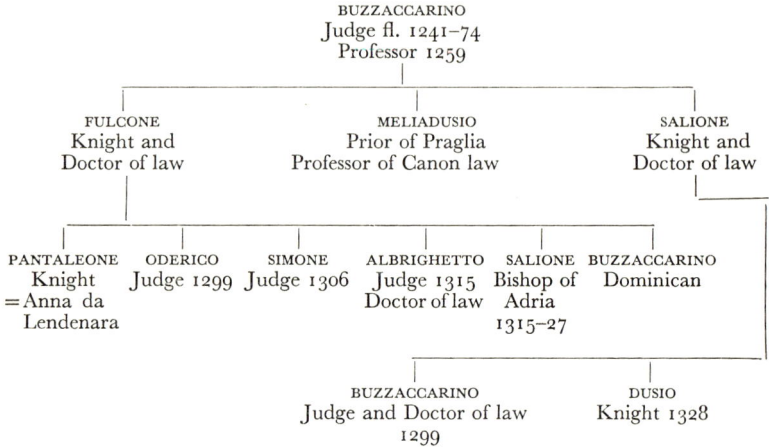

TABLE 12. Genealogy of the Buzzaccarini family.

doctors of law and two judges, and their varied careers illustrate most of the specialisations and opportunities within the contemporary legal profession. They were, moreover, an essentially urban family. Although they owned land, there is no evidence that they had a castle or a country seat; the family headquarters remained the 'large and beautiful *palazzo*' built by Fulcone and Salione in the Via S. Urbano near the heart of the city. Like all families which rose rapidly, the Buzzaccarini were not popular. Da Nono says that by nature they were not good lawyers but singers and *quasi ioculatores*; Mussato, more plausibly, describes a leading member of the family in his generation as 'crafty, envious, lying and scurrilous, but flattering, smooth-speaking and astute; popular with the crowd and appointed to many offices, but odious'.[1] Nevertheless, they were the greatest family to arise within the Paduan administrative class during the communal period, and they epitomise the greatness of the Paduan judiciary in the days when the judges were the leaders of the commune.

[1] 'Dolosus, invidus, mendax, maledicus, sed assentator, blandiloquus, astutus; omnis vulgo acceptus et ad officia quaeque admissus sed odiosus.' This refers to the knight, Pantaleone; his kinsman, Dusio, is given a slightly better character: 'Alter Duxius nomine visus honestior, tectus, insidiosus; sed in se se succelando prudens, potentioribus predetenim adhaerens, statu deficientibus deficiens, fortunae hominum imitator', *De Traditione Patavii*, col. 756.

CHAPTER VI

The Guildsmen

The Notaries

ONE of the most significant changes which accompanied the revival of Italian law and commerce in the twelfth century was the transformation of the office of the notary. The classical *tabellio* had been little more than a scribe, whose acts derived their force from the testimony of the witnesses. About 1150, after a gradual development which had lasted for centuries, the notary emerged as a fully public official whose instruments, authenticated by his sign and subscription alone, were recognised as binding in law and valid in any court at any time. The appearance of a universally valid notariat contributed inestimably to the commercial revival, serving as a kind of international currency which did much to counterbalance the political fragmentation of the time. In the maritime cities and larger commercial centres of Italy, the principle of giving legal validity to a notary's acts came to be extended to cover his rough drafts as well, though there is no trace of this in a conservative inland city like Padua. But over a wide area of the western Mediterranean and its hinterland, the notarial act came to eclipse every other form of legal document, and notaries monopolised the secretariat of the church and the Italian states. Consequently, it is no exaggeration to say that, with the exception of the literary sources—and a surprising proportion even of these were the work of notaries—the historian approaches Italian history in the thirteenth and early fourteenth centuries almost exclusively through the writings of notaries.[1]

The power to create notaries pertained in law to the Emperor, and in the early years of the restored commune there were one or two notaries practising in Padua who subscribed themselves 'notary of the Emperor Frederick' or 'notary of King Conrad'.[2] What the Emperor could do, the Papacy claimed it

---

[1] H. Bresslau, *Handbuch der Urkundenlehre* (1889), I, pp. 631, 656 et seq.

[2] E.g. 'Marchesinus f.q. Egidii qui fuit de Cantone, domini Friderici imperatoris notarius' (AD 1921); 'Ugolinus f.q. Viviani, domini Conradi regis notarius' (Verci, *Marca Trivigiana*, doc. n. 209).

could do also, and in the same period there was at least one 'notary of the Holy Roman Church' working in Padua.[1] Like other Imperial prerogatives, the power to create notaries had been delegated from time to time to certain palatine counts and had been usurped by others. At least six instances of the investiture of a notary by a privileged count in Padua during the communal period are on record: three by the Milanese counts of Lainate, one by Enrico, count of Lomello, and one each by Lodovico and Simone Vicinguerra, counts of Verona.[2] But although the older form of investiture did not entirely die out, by the mid-thirteenth century it was the commune which normally created notaries, and the great majority of the Paduan notaries who subscribed themselves 'notary of the sacred palace' had most probably become public officials by its authority. There is no evidence of a formal investiture ceremony in these cases; notarial status seems to have followed automatically on the passing of an examination before one of the judges of the *podestà* and reception into the notaries' guild.[3] While the validity of this procedure seems to have been unquestioned on the local plane, a passage in the Bolognese statutes of 1288 shows that in that city, which was the centre of notarial studies for the whole of Italy, there was some doubt as to whether the commune could authorise notaries to practise outside its own *comitatus*. It was proposed that the officers of the Bolognese guild should try to procure as many privileges to create notaries as they could, and have them entered in the communal registers, so that any notary might have a copy of them to carry with him wherever he might wish to go.[4]

---

[1] Viz. 'Ildebrandus f.q. magistri Gualterii medici, Sanctae Romanae Ecclesiae notarius' (AD 2158–9).
[2] AD 2835, 3232–3, 5489; Arch. Vescovile, Diversorum, ff. 6r, 31v.
[3] *Stat. Com.* 165–8.
[4] 'Sed ad hoc ut notarii qui creati sunt et creabuntur predicto modo, auctoritate communis Bononie, possint non solum in civitate Bononie vel comitatu conficere acta, instrumenta, et alias scripturas publicas, sed etiam extra comitatum per universum orbem, dicimus quod preconsul et consules societatis notariorum teneantur et debeant procurare omnino quod privilegia regum, comitum de Panico et comitum Mantue et omnium et singulorum aliorum qui privilegia habent creandi tabelliones, qui haberi potuerint, habeantur et scribantur in registro communis Bononie, insinuata auctoritate domini potestatis, ita quod quolibet qui meruit vel merebitur fieri seu creari tabellio ab aliquo de predictis habentibus predicta privilegia, possit habere copiam ipsorum privilegiorum et ubicumque voluerit hos-

The Paduan commune regulated the notarial profession in much the same way as it controlled its judges, in part directly and in part indirectly through the officials of the guild. The statutes suggest that in the early thirteenth century the keeping of the list of authorised notaries was the direct responsibility of the commune, but that later this duty was delegated to the guild; examination by an external judge, however, was always enforced.[1] The custody of the notaries' registers, which contained a record of all the documents which they had drawn up, and which therefore was the ultimate safeguard against loss or forgery, was a matter of the greatest public concern. Often they were passed from father to son, and in normal cases it would appear that the commune entrusted their transfer to the officials of the guild;[2] sometimes, however, it is recorded that the registers of a deceased notary were handed over publicly to a colleague during a session of the Consiglio Maggiore.[3] Another example of the commune's close supervision of the notaries' professional activities was the insistence that copies of an instrument originally drawn up by another notary had to be authenticated at the bench of one of the civil judges of the commune.

The claim of the communes to create notaries obviously embraced the lesser right to authorise or forbid particular notaries to practise within their territories or hold office in their administrations. Like the majority of governments, the Paduan commune laid down a residential and a taxation qualification for those whom it employed.[4] Some of the larger communes, like Florence and Bologna, went further and tried to prevent 'foreign' notaries from working within their borders,[5] but this does not seem to have been the case in Padua, where a number of outsiders are found following the profession over a long period. Alien notaries were particularly favoured by ecclesiastical bodies and notaries of Veronese origin were especially prominent in the bishops' circle in Padua. In fact, in

---

tendere vel portare exemplum ipsorum.' Gaudenzi, *Statuti delle società del popolo di Bologna*, FSI (1896), II, pp, 480–1.
[1] *Stat. Com.* 165–8; *Statuti Carraresi*, f. 27r.
[2] *Stat. Com.* 177.
[3] E.g. AD 1917, 2254, 2268.
[4] *Stat. Com.* 238, 260.
[5] Gaudenzi, op. cit. p. 481; R. Caggese, *Statuti della Repubblica Fiorentina* (1910–21), I, xx, 105.

1299, the Consiglio Maggiore passed a resolution trying to force the bishop to employ only Paduan notaries in future.[1] However, this measure must be interpreted in the context of the involved three-cornered struggle between the commune, the bishop and the inquisitors which was in progress at the time. Quite probably this tactical move was never put into effect and if it was, it was certainly not enforced for long. All this was a far cry from an attack on the status of an alien notary as such; to refuse to recognise the office of a foreign notary and the validity of his acts would have made inter-city relations and long-distance trade extremely difficult, and would ultimately have undermined the whole notarial system.

In recent years there has been an increasing realisation of the importance of notarial records for the historian of mediaeval Italy. Notarial archives, hitherto untapped, have already provided the material for a number of studies of the economic history of particular regions. But while notarial instruments have come to be appreciated for the light which they shed on many facets of the life of the times, the figure of the notary himself and the role which he played in the spread of literacy and culture among the laity has been given much less attention.[2] Yet the existence of a numerous and skilled notariat is obviously a factor of the greatest importance in accounting for the rise of lay culture in Italy. Although the *ars notaria* did not become a higher faculty in the universities, the profession demanded a thorough grounding in both grammar and law and where there was no university, as at Florence, the notarial school tended to take its place. In these, as in all legal studies, the school of Bologna took the lead and the *Summa Artis Notarie* of the Bolognese, Rolando Passaggeri, became the standard textbook on the subject. Formularies showing the uninstructed notary how to draw up various kinds of letters and contracts were produced everywhere.[3]

[1] Arch. Capit. Pergamene XXII, Padua I, n. 142, printed in M. A. Zorzi, *L'ordinamento comunale padovano*, pp. 213–14.
[2] For the use of notarial archive material, see above, p. 8. On the notary himself, there is a slight but stimulating essay by F. Novati, *Freschi e minii del dugento* (1908), pp. 299–328 and some brief notes by R. L. Reynolds, 'In search of a business class in thirteenth century Genoa', *JEH* Suppl. V (1945), pp. 1–19.
[3] Two Paduan examples are the formulary of the notary Corradino of 1223, and one of the early fourteenth century originating in the episcopal

Despite the notaries' undoubted position as 'public persons' and their need for at least a modest level of literacy and education, there are indications that the social position of notaries in general was not high. The conservative friar Giacomo de Cessolis, writing in the early fourteenth century, classifies them rather unexpectedly with the other trades whose raw materials were to be found in the body of a sheep. 'These are all called by the name of wool-workers (*lanifici*), whether they be notaries, or skinners, or tanners who work with the skin itself; or cutters, dressers, dyers or weavers who work with the fleece and hair; or slaughterers and butchers who deal with the meat.'[1] This was probably a rather severe view of the notaries' position but it is unlikely that it was wholly unrealistic. The notaries' guilds were generally grouped with those of the artisans and, where they achieved a predominant position, this was probably due to their administrative experience rather than any social superiority. Socially close to the artisans and small tradesmen, the notaries were well placed to become the spokesmen of the lesser members of the *popolo*: they were the natural tribunes of the *plebs*.

What is known of the origins and personal relations of individual Paduan notaries is consistent with this view of their social position. The nobility—even the lesser nobility—did not become notaries; nor did members of the leading families of the *popolo*. One would not expect to find a notary in a leading judicial family; the Rolando Buzzaccarini who was *gastaldione* of the Guild of Notaries in 1316 was not, according to Da Nono, a Buzzaccarini at all but the son of a priest.[2] The lesser judges, on the other hand, were frequently closely related to notaries, and a few had once practised as notaries before their admission to the bench, while others resigned in order to return to the notarial profession. Evidently an outstanding notary like Zambono d'Andrea, Matteo Filarolo or Aleardo Basilii could

---

curia, MS BP 2228, xli. See M. Roberti, *Un Formulario padovano di un notaio padovano*, MRIV XXVII (1906), and idem 'Intorno ai frammenti di un formulario notarile etc.', *ARAP* XXII (1906).

[1] Jacobo de Cessolis, *Liber de Moribus Hominum et Officiis Nobilium*, ed. E. Köpke, Mittheilungen aus den Handschriften der Ritter-Akademie zu Brandenburg, II (1879), p. 19.

[2] *Statuti della Fraglia dei Notai*, MS Archivio Notarile, Padua (hereafter cited as *Stat. Not.*), f. 75r; *De Generatione*, f. 31v.

establish his son as a judge; the great notarial families of the city, the Scarabelli, the Basilii and the a Rio all produced at least one judge, though in some cases they do not seem to have held office.

While one wing of the notaries mingled with the judges, the other was closely related to guildsmen and even to one professional group who did not have a guild of their own, the *precones* or court messengers. The general lack of family names in this class, and the poor documentation relating to the guildsmen make these relationships hard to trace, but a few selected examples may be given. In a document of 1269 there appear three brothers, the sons of Guariento, living in the suburb of S. Croce: Tebaldo, a notary; Ailino; and Zambono, a shoemaker. Four years later Tebaldo, who had moved to the Via S. Lucia in the heart of the city, is described as the son of Guariento di Bernardo, a court messenger.[1] Antonio and Prosdocimo de Pauleto, the sons of Giordano, were described as notary and butcher respectively.[2] The notary Antonio Plegaforte, the son of Antonio *preco*, was married to Cunizza, daughter of Primadezio, a butcher, and Meiorino, notary and parchment-maker (*cartolarius*), the son of *magister* Paduano the mason, was the son-in-law of a master shoemaker. Even more significant than these instances of kinship and intermarriage are those cases where individuals are described as both notaries and tradesmen. The combination notary-apothecary occurs several times, a notable example being master Antonio *specialis* who was *gastaldione* of the Guild of Notaries in 1320.[4] Paduano Lazara, described as notary and *negociator*, supplied robes to the Guild of Notaries for the celebrations of the death of Henry VII in 1313.[5] Other mechanical arts of a more obviously plebeian character were not excluded, such as notary and weaver, skinner or linen-worker.[6] Some of the more unusual descriptions include master Paolo Plumbioli, notary and smith, Galeazzo,

---

[1] AD 2379, 2564.
[2] AD 2538, 2542, 3270, 3377.
[3] AD 2881, 6131.
[4] See the census of 1320. Grion, p. 266.
[5] *Stat. Not.*, ff. 71v–72r.
[6] 'Americus notarius et filarolus f.q.d. Johannis de Casale' (AD 5810); 'Bonacursius notarius et pelliparius' (AS Padua, Archivi Privati, Selvatico 559, n. 8); 'Petrus notarius et linarolus de Plebe saci' (Arch. Capit. Diversa II, n. 262).

notary and miller, and Guglielmo, notary and taverner, the son of master Tiso the blacksmith.[1]

How the artisan-notary divided his interests is not clear. No act drawn up by one of them has been preserved, but this may be due to chance; it is unlikely that the apothecary Antonio would have been accepted as *gastaldione* of the notaries if he had not been actively engaged in the profession. On the other hand, there was nothing to prevent a notary actively pursuing another occupation, even when this implied membership of a second guild. The holding of office in more than one guild was forbidden by statute in 1291, and in 1305-6 there is evidence that action was taken to prevent notaries from participating in the election of *gastaldiones* in more than one guild, but double membership as such was clearly tolerated.[2] Although it cannot be proved, it seems likely that some men whose primary interest was in trade or manufacturing found it worth while to qualify as notaries, presumably on account of its general value as a business education.

The artisan-notaries indicate a group within the profession closely related to the trade guildsmen of the city; another section who are not well documented but very important may be described as the rural notaries. A statute of the early thirteenth century assumes that there will normally be at least one qualified notary in most villages, and the surviving contracts of the communal period bear this out.[3] The typical village notary is found at work only within his local area which was rarely far from the village from which he took his name. To judge by their handwriting, some of them were much inferior in training and experience to the notaries of the city, and they can hardly have hoped to support themselves by their professional activities alone. Even so, their literacy and official status must

---

[1] 'Magister Paulus notarius et faber de Plumbiolis' (AD 5306-7); 'Dominus Galeazzus notarius et pistor de Padua' (Brunacci *CDP* IV, p. 2191); 'Guillielmo notario et tabernario f.q. magistri Tysonis ferratoris' (Corona 2356).

[2] *Stat. Not.*, ff. 22r, 50v.

[3] 'Per publicum instrumentum factum manu boni et legalis notarii de civitate si factum fuerit in civitate, et si in villa, per manum boni et legalis notarii de villa' *Stat. Com.* 158 (before 1236). Examples of village notaries include 'Ugolinus notarius . . . de Revolone' (AD 1884, 2210); 'Jacobus notarius . . . de Spaxano' (AD 2163); 'Rolandus notarius . . . de Galzignano' (AD 2706) and 'Vandus notarius . . . de Arquade' (AD 2530).

have made them influential members of the rural middle class and one of the main channels of communication between the villages and the outside world. The towns of the contado also had their notaries who could find additional employment in the administration of the limited local jurisdiction permitted by the Paduan commune. The sixteenth-century records of the Guild of Notaries of Cittadella open with a copy of a privilege of the Paduan commune dated June 1256, granting the *podestà* of Cittadella limited jurisdiction over certain villages 'so that notaries living in Cittadella ought to be put in office at Cittadella to administer justice there'.[1] The statutes of the commune of Montagnana, drawn up in 1366, show quite clearly that by that date the town had a guild of notaries whose *gastaldione* was responsible for the selection of notaries to serve in the local administration.[2]

The Paduan notariat, territorially spread throughout the city and its district, evidently embraced a number of socially and economically diverse groups. On the one hand there were the well-established notaries of the city who stood close to the judges, owners of rural and urban property who were wealthy enough to be assessed for mounted military service by the commune.[3] At the other extreme were the poorer notaries of the city who had little but their literacy and modest legal training to distinguish them from the other guildsmen. The rural notaries are difficult to place but by urban standards their position was not high. The range of social and economic standing within the profession is illustrated by the dowries known to have been received by notaries or given by them on behalf of their daughters or sisters. These could be as high as £800, paid in cash or land, or as low as £350–250 in the case of artisan-notaries; the dowries of between £200 and £150 received by Zambono and Francesco da Carturo, or settled on Boneta the daughter of Pietro, a notary of the village of Pernumia, would seem to indicate that the rural notaries were a good deal inferior to the average notary of the city.[4]

It is a difficult matter to estimate the numbers of such a

[1] AS Padua, Collegio dei Notai di Cittadella I.
[2] *Statuta Communis Montagnanae 1366*, Archivio Municipale, Montagnana.
[3] Antonio a Solis, notary, assessed for service *ad equum ab armis* 1279–80 (AD 3054); see also Albertino Mussato, above, p. 95.
[4] AD 3550, 4624, 5364, 5795, 6131.

large and scattered profession as the notaries of Padua and its district. A start may be made with the inner core who belonged to the city guild and were qualified to hold office under the commune. The statutes of the commune show the number of offices to be filled by notaries; the 'ordinary offices' which comprised the backbone of the administration were 91 in the code of 1276, while by an undated amendment contained in the code of 1362, they were raised to a total of 106 [1] As in the case of the judges, the normal term of office was four months, but there is nothing to indicate how rapidly these offices circulated, except for the provision that the twelve notaries who served the consuls at the benches where criminal justice was dispensed, could not be reappointed to that particular office for ten years.[2] This implies that the legislators envisaged that there would be 360 notaries available for this office in the period. Unfortunately, the records of the guild do not contain any matricula or any list of notaries in office before 1345. The statutes of the guild required a quorum in the chapter of 100, 150 or 200 for different types of business and, in fact, attendances, which are known for eighteen occasions between 1289 and 1327, range from 112 to 278, following no discernable pattern.[3] If the average attendance, which was about 200, represents the same proportion of the members as was the case with the judges, then the total membership should have been in the region of 600, which is a not unlikely figure in view of Bologna's estimated 2,000 notaries in 1294, Milan's 1,500 in 1288, or Treviso's 487 in the guild matricula of 1327.[4]

The full members of the guild, who took office with the commune, were by no means the whole notariat of Padua and its district. Those of non-Paduan origin, like many of the notaries of the bishop's circle, and those who had not been resident in the city for several years, which would include all the notaries of the contado, were excluded from serving in the administration and cannot therefore have been full members of

---

[1] *Stat. Com.* 231; *Statuti Carraresi*, f. 38v.
[2] *Stat. Com.* 264.
[3] *Stat. Not.*, ff. 6, 10, 19; for attendances at chapter, see ibid. ff. 22–87, *passim.*
[4] Gaudenzi, *BISI* XXI (1899), p. 30; Bonvesin della Riva, 'De magnalibus urbis Mediolani', ed. F. Novati, *BISI* XX (1898), p. 86; *Statuta Scole Notariorum Civitatis Tervisii 1327*, Archivio Notarile, Treviso, MS n. VI, f. 16v et seq.

the guild, though there may have been associate members, as was the case in Treviso.[1] The analogy with the judges suggests that there may have been others, perhaps the artisan-notaries among them, who could have qualified for full membership but preferred not to do so. How many there were in these categories who should be added to make up the whole notariat of the state there is no evidence even for guessing. If every village had its notary, and each of the four towns of the contado had enough to form a guild, then the notaries of the contado were a far from negligible proportion of the whole profession.

It would be fruitless to attempt a picture of a typical member of so large and heterogeneous a group as the Paduan notaries. Although as a body the notaries played an important role in many aspects of Paduan life, the average notary was a lesser member of the *popolo*, individually of little account. But no description of the profession would be complete without the recognition that notarial circles produced some of the most brilliant minds, and provided the setting for some of the most remarkable careers of the period. The pre-eminence of the notaries is most clearly marked in the field of letters. The two great Paduan historians, Rolandino and Mussato, were both notaries, and among the lesser writers there was Andrea da Tribano, a vernacular poet, and Zambono d'Andrea, a member of the pre-humanist circle who may have been the author of a lost verse chronicle.[2] Zambono belonged to a notarial family, having two brothers and four sons in the profession. The two great Paduan philosophers of the communal period also came from notarial stock. Pietro d'Abano, the scientist and astrologer, was the son of an obscure notary, probably an immigrant from the contado; his son and nephew were notaries also.[3] The political philosopher Marsiglio Mainardini was also the son of

---

[1] The Trevisan matricula of 1327 includes *non habitatores, iudices, fratres, banniti* and *nobiles*.

[2] For Andrea da Tribano, see below, p. 289. Zambono d'Andrea appears in numerous documents between October 1254, when he was already a member of the Paduan Consiglio Maggiore (AS Cremona, ASC 1794) and October 1315, when he made his will in Venice (AD 5370). The most important documents relating to him and his family are cited by L. Padrin, *Lupati de Lupatis, Bovetini de Bovetinis, Albertini Mussati necnon et Jamboni Andreae de Favafuschis Carmina Quaedam* (1887), pp. 51–5.

[3] Gloria, *Università*, pp. 353–9; the chief document on Pietro and his family is his testament, AD 4627.

a notary, Bonmatteo, and had an uncle, Corrado, and a brother, Giovanni, who were a notary and a judge respectively.¹

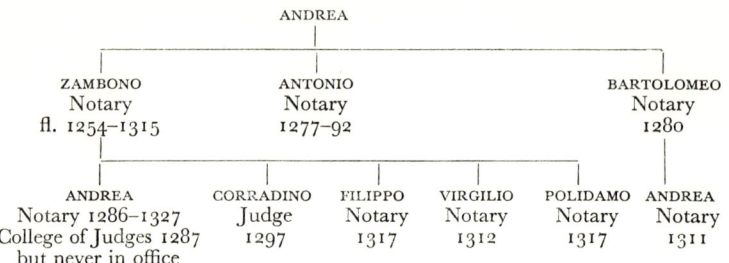

TABLE 13. Genealogy of the D'Andrea family.

In the political sphere, the role of individual notaries is not easily perceived, since their influence normally depended on the patronage of a magnate or a group of magnates whom they seem to have served as agents within the commune. Some relationship of this kind probably linked the magnate Guido da Lozzo and the notary Martino de Guidoto who are named in the annals as the leaders of the Paduan Guelphs in 1279.² Matteo Filarolo, a notary from an artisan background, who represented Guido in the bishop's curia in 1288, was in 1311 a respected member of the Guelph faction, which had passed under the leadership of Tiso Camposanpiero.³ His son Antonio, a member of the College of Judges from 1295, was castigated by Mussato as 'devoid of all strength of human courage' on account of his failure to resist the Veronese in the key post of *podestà* of Montagnana in 1317; his disgrace ended what appears to have been a promising career.⁴ The post of Defensor Populi, created

¹ Bonmatteo di Giovanni Mainardini figures in some half-dozen documents between Feb. 1264 (AD 2110) and Feb. 1307 (Arch. Vesc. Vicenza, Feudorum IV, f. 58v); for Corrado di Giovanni, see *Stat. Not.*, ff. 21v, 38v; Corona 99, n. 79; and AS Venice, Liber Commemorialis I, f. 58v (Predelli, n. 205). For Marsiglio's brother, see *Stat. Coll. Iud.*, ff. 7r, 19(a)v.
² *Liber Regiminum*, p. 333.
³ Arch. Vescovile, Feudorum II, f. 43; Matteo was also employed professionally in Guido's house in Padua in 1284 (AD 3087-8). For his position in 1311, see below, p. 253.
⁴ *Stat. Coll. Iud.*, f. 19(a)v; Mussato, *De Gestis*, ed. Padrin, p. 27. Antonio had also served with Mussato on a mission to Treviso in 1315 (Verci, *Marca Trivigiana*, doc. n. 767).

THE GUILDSMEN 165

in 1315 and suppressed in 1318, was one in which outstanding members of the lesser *popolo* might make their influence felt, and nearly every known holder of this office was a notary.¹ With the establishment of the *signoria*, the need for magnatial patronage asserted itself even more strongly. Sachetto da Campagnola, for example, was the notary who attached himself most closely to the fortunes of the Carrara. During the short-lived *signoria* of Giacomo Grande, he served as secretary and treasurer and in the following years gave his professional services to Ubertino

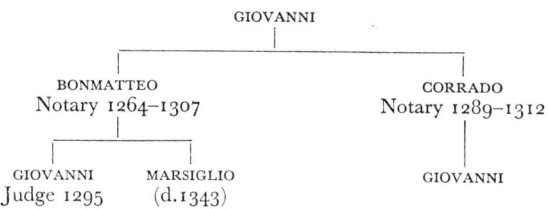

TABLE 14. Genealogy of the Mainardini family.

and Marsiglio da Carrara.² He was one of the principal ministers during Marsiglio's rule in Padua, and represented the city at the treaty of alliance with the Venetians in 1337.³ In Marsiglio's will, he was left a life annuity of £100.⁴

The strength and weakness of the notary's position, the possibility of advancement and the dependence on patronage, stand out most clearly in the career of the poet and historian Albertino Mussato.⁵ Mussato was of poor and humble origins; his acknowledged father was Giovanni Cavalieri, a court messenger

¹ Of the known holders of this four-monthly office which existed from June 1315 until January 1318, the following were notaries: June 1315, Pietro Berni (Brunacci, *Appendice al CDP* II, n. 239); Oct. 1315, Albertino Mussato (Verci, *Marca Trivigiana*, doc. n. 767); Aug. 1316, Martino de Caseta (*Stat. Not.*, f. 75r); Jan. 1318, Enrighetto d'Ambrosino (Bianchi, *Documenti per la storia del Friuli* I, n. 48); and, date uncertain, Pietro di Giustiniano (Da Nono, *De Generatione*, f. 47v). The non-notaries were Ubertino di Zante *linarolo* (AS Modena, AMS X, n. 30), and Marino Maroni (Mussato, *De Gestis*, ed. Padrin, p. 76).
² Brunacci, *Appendice al CDP* II, n. 102; AD 5622, 5666, 6077.
³ AS Venice, Pacta IV, ff. 54–5.   ⁴ *Documenti Carraresi*, I, n. 35.
⁵ The details of Mussato's life and family background have been the subject of a considerable literature during the last century, but the most satisfactory biography is still A. Zardo, *Albertino Mussato* (1884). While I

who lived in the northern suburbs of the city.[1] He passed his early years under the protection of a rich neighbour, Viviano Muso, whose family were reputed to have been boatmen and millers.[2] It is probable that Viviano stood godfather to Albertino, since his name was that of Viviano's own father; in later life Albertino took the name Muso, which he subsequently lengthened to Mussato, probably as a compliment to his patron.[3] In these circumstances, it is hardly surprising that stories circulated, which were later reported by Da Nono, to the effect that Albertino was really the son of an adulterous union between Viviano and Giovanni Cavalieri's wife.[4] A curious

---

accept the conclusions of M. Q. Dazzi, 'Intorno alla nascità di Albertino Mussato', Parts I and II, *Archivio Muratoriano*, II (1915), pp. 263–72, concerning the date and place of Mussato's birth, I cannot agree with the view expressed in Part III, Misc.RDVSP, ser. IV, vol. 4 (1930), pp. 1–105, that Mussato's father was a member of the Muso family, possibly a brother of Viviano Muso, since it is inconceivable that a person with such a background should have become a court messenger. Of course, a distant or possibly an illegitimate link between the two families cannot be ruled out. The primary sources for Mussato's life are his own writings, especially the *Elegia, de Celebratione suae Diei Nativitatis vel non*, Graevius, *Thesaurus Antiquitatum et Historiarum Italiae*, VI, ii, coll. 61-4, and the *De Lite inter Naturam et Fortunam* and *Contra Casus Fortuitos*, of which an edition is projected; see Guido Billanovich and G. Travaglia, 'Per l'edizione del "De Lite inter Naturam et Fortunam" e del "Contra Casus Fortuitos" di Albertino Mussato', *BMCP* XIV–XXVI (1942-54), pp. 279–96. Two strictly contemporary accounts of Mussato, Da Nono, *De Generatione*, f. 45v, printed by P. Rajna, 'Le origini delle famiglie padovane e gli eroi dei romanzi cavallereschi', *Romania*, IV (1875), pp. 182-3 and Guizzardo da Bologna and Castellano da Bassano, 'Commentum super Ecerinide', printed in the edition of the *Ecerinide* by L. Padrin (1900), are to be preferred to later traditions, especially those stemming from the so-called Favafuschis chronicle, which are misleading and worthless.

[1] In all his notarial work, Mussato signed himself 'filius Johannis cavalerii'; 'natus in suburbio Paduane civitatis cui Gadium dicitur', *Commentum super Ecerinide*, ed. Padrin, p. 70.

[2] Da Nono, *De Generatione*, f. 44v.

[3] Mussato signed himself 'Albertinus Muxus' in a notarial act dated 10 Oct. 1282, but 'Albertinus dictus Muxatus' on 30 April 1284. For the family of Viviano Muso, see Documenti della Famiglia Mussato, Seminario Padua MS n. 746, vols. I & III, *passim*. It will be noticed that the name Gualpertino was also common to both families. To add to the confusion, from about 1311, Gualpertino di Viviano Muso adopted the name Mussato, presumably to identify himself with Albertino, who was by that time a person of some importance.

[4] *De Generatione*, f. 45v.

remark in an autobiographical poem by Albertino tends to support this view. The poet says that he was only adolescent when the loss of his father left him alone to care for his two brothers and a sister.[1] Giovanni Cavalieri was alive in April 1284, when Albertino was twenty-three years old, but Viviano Muso can be shown to have died in 1276–7 when the future poet was in his fifteenth year.[2]

For Albertino, the death of Viviano Muso marked the beginning of a period of poverty from which he escaped only after years of hard work. He himself describes how he was compelled by need to take on the drudgery of copying texts for students. He first appears as a notary at the age of twenty-one, in October 1282, drawing up a document for Armerina, the widow of Viviano Muso, and by 1293 he was of sufficient repute to be given the important task of listing the property of the Este family in Paduan territory for the commune.[3] Mussato considered his thirty-fifth year (1296), when he became a member of the Consiglio Maggiore and a *miles pro commune*, as the year in which he finally achieved a reasonable place in Paduan society. At about the same time, we find the first evidence that Albertino had acquired new patrons in the Lemici family, the notorious moneylenders. Da Nono relates the beginning of this association in the following words:

But when he [Mussato] being well-learned in grammar, was working constantly in the Palazzo Comunale so as to enrich himself from notarial offices, he attracted the attention of Guglielmo Dente [Lemici]. When, one day, Albertino Mussato was going past Guglielmo Dente's house, he called out to him and asked if he

---

[1] Bina mihi fratres series adjuncta sorori
Et tamen illorum de grege maior eram.
His pater ut maior, patris post fata relinquor,
Quam fierem pubes, sic pater ante fui
Ipseque cum minimis alui, fovique minores
Augebant vires Numina sancta meas.
(*Elegia, col.* 63.) Cf. *De Lite*, f. 26r.

[2] Mussato signed himself 'filius Johannis' in 1284 (AD 3099), and 'filius quondam Johannis' from 1293 (Modena, Biblioteca Estense MS 1271 Lat. f. 1). The approximate date of Viviano Muso's death may be deduced from a notarial act dated 14 June 1277, in which Armerina is described as the widow of Viviano but pregnant (Doc. Fam. Mussato, III, n. 9).

[3] Doc. Fam. Mussato I, n. 28; Modena, Biblioteca Estense, *MS cit.* ff. 1–42 were written by Mussato.

wanted to get married. When he replied that he did, Guglielmo said 'I will give you a natural daughter of mine and four hundred pounds'.[1]

In the course of time, Albertino moved into the short Via S. Polo, where the Lemici *palazzo* stood, and when Guglielmo's son Vitaliano died in 1310, Mussato became the legal guardian of his son Guglielmo II.[2]

Mussato's emergence as a leading figure in the commune about 1310 was no doubt largely due to his ability as an orator and diplomat; he also served with the communal army in the field, though there is not enough independent evidence to judge his position as a military commander. But though Mussato never mentions the fact, there is reason to suppose that he was still dependent on the support of the Lemici. Changes in the ruling party, in the constitution and in the nominal overlordship of the commune, even the violent rising against him in 1314, did not permanently shake his position; it was only in 1325, when the power of the Lemici was broken by the Carraresi, that Mussato retired into exile and was unable to negotiate his return. Information concerning Mussato's personal resources is fragmentary. It is known that he held land adjoining the Carrara estates in Concadalbero and other villages in the south-eastern contado, and he owned one of the mills at Pontemolino.[3] By his will, he left a charitable bequest of £666 which was realised in 1340 from four *mansi* in Cona and eight *campi* in Vaccarino.[4]

Outstanding careers like those of Matteo Filarolo, Sachetto da Campagnola and Albertino Mussato, while they were numerically insignificant, contributed greatly to the contemporary image of the notarial profession. Da Nono nowhere discusses the notaries as a group; nevertheless, he rarely mentions the profession unless it is to say how a great notary managed to enrich himself by some means or other. His view, which is all the more telling because it was not consciously worked out by

---

[1] *De Generatione*, f. 45v. Mussato first appears associated with the Lemici, as a witness in their house, 3 Dec. 1297 (AS Vicenza, Torre 32, n. 42).

[2] AS Padua, Archivi Privati 61, n. 13; Arch. Vescovile, Vicenza, Feudorum IV, f. 168v.

[3] *Documenti Carraresi*, I, n. 25; AS Padua, Archivio Correzzola 50, n. 47; Corona 4010, f. 271; 4338.

[4] AD. 7139.

him, was that the notaries shared the propensity to rapid advancement which he usually attributed to usurers. He speaks, for example, of Vivarotto Guicemanni, the son of one of Ezzelino's knights, as 'a well-known notary in the city of Padua who acquired great wealth and kin in a short time, to the value of £10,000'. Bonadomane Bazalerii, whose father, a miller from Treviso according to Da Nono but elsewhere described as a notary, was another great *tabellio* 'who acquired handsome riches for himself'. The Bobi family, 'who were always shoemakers and heralds (*tubatores*)' produced Beldomando, a herald, notary and a great orator in the Consiglio Maggiore who 'became a rich man through his three wives, to whose property he succeeded'. Guglielmo da Censano, the son of a fishmonger, 'made great riches because he freely extorted money from everyone'.[1]

For Da Nono, the epitome of the enriched notary was Alberto Bibi whom he believed had been Ezzelino da Romano's treasurer and to have made a fortune of £40,000 by usury after his master's fall.[2] A book of miscellaneous contracts which is still extant shows that in the last ten years (1297–1308) of what must have been a long life, Alberto Bibi was a man of considerable wealth which he was in the process of investing in landed property.[3] He had a small castle at Torreglia in the Pedevenda, he held tithes from the bishop of Feltre and Belluno, and he was building up a considerable estate at Montegalda, just inside the Vicentino, whose final extent can be appreciated from the inventory made by the Vicentine authorities when they confiscated the property in 1311.[4] His son Antonio, who added to the Montegalda estates by his marriage to a daughter of Salamone da Montegalda, was a judge and later a knight, serving a term as *podestà* of Belluno in 1298.[5] His daughter married Obizzo da Carrara with a dowry of over £3,000, one of the highest recorded in Padua in the communal period.[6] His son Marsiglio is entitled *nobilis vir* in a document of

---

[1] *De Generatione*, ff. 47r, 50v, 52v.
[2] Ibid. f. 51v.
[3] AS Padua, Archivi Privati 99 (Fam. Dalla Porta).
[4] AS Vicenza, Torre 35, nn. 8–9.
[5] *De Generatione*, f. 51v; *Stat. Coll. Iud.*, f. 7v; Piloni, *Historia di Belluno*, pp. 235–6. Piloni confused the names of Alberto and Antonio; Antonio is clearly meant.
[6] Archivio Papafava 39, n. 27.

1334.¹ The prosperity of the family is obvious; the only doubt is whether Alberto was ever a notary as Da Nono believed, but from the point of view of the image of the notary, the truth of the story is comparatively immaterial. Paduan legend made everything connected with Ezzelino larger than life, so Ezzelino's notary had to be the greatest notary of all, but to be credible he had to conform to type.

The nature of the evidence makes it difficult to find conclusive support for Da Nono's stories of wealthy notaries. The large number of notaries whose sons became judges must be significant in this respect, especially in those cases like Bartolomeo da Teolo and Belcaro Brognacci of Boccon where a move from the contado to the city can be shown to have taken place. Another example of a notary from the contado, who was described by Da Nono as *rusticanus* but who was certainly a rich man, was Bellengerio da Conselve.² By chance, a series of surviving documents show that Bellengerio the notary 'who was from Conselve' married three of his daughters into substantial judicial families, each with the ample dowry of £800, in addition to providing for at least one son, who was also a notary.³ Unfortunately, these examples cannot be used to illustrate the opportunities of the rural notary as there is no proof that the individuals in question entered the profession before they left the contado, but they do at least suggest that a notarial career was one of those associated with some of the more active and successful elements in the community.

The large numbers and occasional brilliance of the Paduan notariat can only be explained by the assumption that the profession attracted the most lively members of a wide section of the *popolo* in both town and country, but it is not easy to show exactly why this was so. A notarial education must have been shorter, cheaper and more easily obtained than that required of a judge, thus opening the profession to a much wider section of the population. The large numbers who entered the notariat show that it was attractive to many; since the prestige acquired was negligible, the flock of candidates must have been impelled by the hope of more concrete advantages. For a few at least, the

---

¹ Arch. Vescovile, Feudorum V, f. 113v.

² *De Generatione*, f. 39r.

³ AS Padua, Archivi Privati, Frigemelica 66, n. 3; 80, n. 3; 86, n. 5; 92, n. 1.

profession did serve as a ladder by which they climbed in wealth and influence. The problem is to show exactly how this was achieved.

The notary's staple work was the recording of private contracts. The fees for this work were regulated by statute, the basic rate being 2s. for every £50 involved in the contract, up to a maximum of 20s.[1] The only way in which a notary could amass a great income from this source would be by writing a very large number of contracts. Although it was the custom to commit every conceivable kind of agreement to writing, the main source of notarial business must have been provided by commercial contracts. Padua's development as a commercial centre would seem to have been quite inadequate to sustain the throng of notaries in the city centre, not to mention those of the suburbs and the contado. This conclusion is supported by the evidence of the only general register of a Paduan notary which is extant for the communal period. This belonged to Sachetto da Campagnola and relates to the year 1323; it consists of seventy-six pages of miscellaneous contracts made at a rate of little more than one a week. If this represents Sachetto's entire output, it is very small compared with the rate of four to five contracts per day achieved by some notaries in other Italian cities.[2]

It is equally unlikely that fortunes were to be made by notaries through the exercise of regular office in the communal administration. Ordinary offices were regulated by the guild and probably did not recur very frequently. Remuneration was limited to £40 per term to buy materials with additional payment at a fixed rate for work done.[3] Although the volume of business provided by the precociously bureaucratic administration must have been considerable, the various departments were grossly overstaffed, no fewer than five notaries being allotted to each judge, each of whom had a right to an equal share in the fees obtained. Some 'extraordinary' offices may have been more profitable, and some occasional commissions

[1] *Stat. Com.* 187–90.
[2] AS Padua, Notarile, n. 176. Cf. Appuliese da Siena, who wrote 547 instruments in a little over ten months, 1221–2, *Liber Imbreviaturarum Appuliesis*, ed. D. Bizzarri, DSSCDCI IV, p. xii, and Guglielmo Cassinese, a notary of Genoa, who wrote 1,500 acts in the year 1191; V. A. Vitale, 'Vita e commercio nei notai genovesi dei secoli XII–XIII', *Atti della Società Ligure di Storia Patria*, LXXII (1949), p. 19.
[3] *Stat. Com.* 191–3, 197, 206, 211.

such as embassies to neighbouring cities. It may also have been possible or customary to take bribes, though it seems more likely that these would have gone to the judge rather than the notaries.

The cathedral administration provided an alternative field of employment for notaries. Two examples have survived of the formal appointment of notaries to the bishop's curia and the names of other notaries recur so often in the episcopal records as to suggest that they were permanently employed there.[1] A register of Galvano Beldomandi, 'notary and official of the episcopal curia of Padua', has been preserved containing miscellaneous documents relating to the years 1323 to 1344;[2] the same notary was responsible for a part of the volume of enfeoffments known as *Feudorum IV*, belonging to the years 1321–8. The register of Enrico da Marostica shows that he was particularly associated with the canon Corrado da Concoreggio, who served as vicar to the bishop of Padua on several occasions.[3] Like many of the notaries employed in the bishop's circle, Enrico was not a Paduan citizen by origin.

The university of Padua must have favoured the development of the Paduan notariat in a number of ways. The demand for books had to be met, and as there was no guild of parchment-makers, it seems likely that the work of book-production was shared between members of the guilds of skinners and notaries. Copying was no doubt left to poor aspirants to the profession, like the young Mussato; the retailers were presumably the *notarii-cartolarii* who appear in the general records from time to time, the *stacionarii* of the university statutes.[4] Yet none of these stationer-notaries appear from the records to have achieved even moderate distinction. Another potential link with the university was through the masters of grammar, who were a part of the paid staff of the university. Only a handful of the Paduan notaries, however, possessed the necessary qualifications and

---

[1] Arch. Vescovile, Diversorum, f. 11; AS Padua, Notarile, 407, f. 17v.
[2] Arch. Vescovile, the volume known as Diversorum.
[3] AS Padua, Notarile 407.
[4] *Notarii-cartolarii* figure in the following documents, among others, AD 3502, 4698, 5795, 6131. For regulations concerning university *stacionarii*, *ligatores* and *scriptores*, see University Statutes, ed. Denifle, *ALKM* VI (1892), pp. 452 et seq. The presence among the witnesses of the will of *magister* Deomedisio *notarius et correçarolus* of Enrico *correçario, qui stat in stacione testatoris*, (AD 2783) suggests a combination of the notariat with tanning and book-production.

normally the commune brought in outsiders, as in the case of the doctors of law. The only notaries who clearly combined a university appointment with an active career in the city were the historian Rolandino, who became a professor of grammar and rhetoric late in life, and *magister* Pantaleone di Marchabruni of S. Sofia, who was active from 1299 to 1328 and is referred to as 'gramatice professor' in 1310.¹

The office of the notary was a comparatively humble one, but as the preamble to the statutes of the guild pointed out, it was an absolutely essential one for any kind of administration in church and state.² Every religious house in the city and contado employed secular notaries from time to time, not only to make records but also to represent their interests in the courts and to act on their behalf in all kinds of business. Some of the larger houses were able to employ the same notaries on a more or less regular basis, and in some cases a close family connection was built up. Thus Giovanni and his son Nicolò a Rio appear frequently in the service of the convent of S. Pietro where, in 1319, Giovanni's sister Catterina was elected abbess.³ An enormous amount of secular business passed through the hands of the Franciscans of S. Antonio who were frequently nominated as the executors of wills, and who claimed all bequests made to 'the poor of Christ'. Much of this was carried on by the Scarabelli, another notarial family related by marriage to the a Rio. Gerardo Scarabelli, for example, was described as the *gestor negociorum* of the Friars Minor in 1290; his son Antonio became a member of the order.⁴ The Franciscans also administered the Inquisition in Padua, which offered further employment for notaries. In 1302, when the Holy Office was transferred to the Dominicans, the brothers Aleardo and Vitaliano Basilii obtained a declaration from the Franciscans to the effect that they were fully satisfied with their services.⁵ The transfer

¹ For the masters of grammar etc., see Gloria, *Università*, pp. 368–83.
² 'Scimus enim quod nulli provinciarum principes vel rectores, nulli quoque pontifices vel prelati, possunt absque notarie officio procedere recto calle, nec utique perficere, tam canonice quam civiliter, viam suam. Sunt enim notarii quasi navium instrumentum taliter remi, sine quibus nauta, quamvis providus et discretus, complere non poterit iter suum.' *Stat. Not.*, f. 2.
³ AD 3822–5, 3874, 4137, 5563–4, 5583, 5589.
⁴ AS Padua, Corp. Sopp., S. Antonio 150, f. 6; see also ff. 102–5; AD 3586.
⁵ AS Padua, Corp. Sopp., S. Antonio 151, f. 533v.

of the Inquisition to the Dominicans of S. Agostino must have favoured those families, like the Da Teolo, who were associated with that order, but detailed evidence is lacking.

Every one of the innumerable secular associations in Padua and its territory required the services of a notary from time to time. Among the more obscure were the rural communes and the purely religious confraternities. Each of the thirty-six trade guilds must have had a notary to keep the records and possibly to act as treasurer as well. The best documented example is Francesco de Crespo who was notary and beadle to the College of Judges from 1287 until his retirement about 1310; for a good deal of this time he was treasurer of the College also. Francesco was the son of a notary, and was followed in the profession by two sons and a grandson.[1] It would appear that all the leading notarial families had at least one corporation, religious or secular, within their orbit.

The loss of nearly all the family archives of the communal period has made obscure one of the most important fields of notarial activity, employment by a leading family for the keeping of the records relating to its property and business agreements, and also its representation in business and in the courts. Where the family concerned fell into the magnatial class, the notary's responsibilities probably included representation of the client's interests in the Consiglio Maggiore and possibly in the other councils of the commune from which the magnates were excluded. It must have been potentially very profitable to become indispensable to an important family. The selection of the low-born Mussato to be the guardian of his heir by the great Vitaliano Lemici, is an example of what could be achieved; Sachetto da Campagnola was no doubt amply rewarded for his services by Marsiglio da Carrara during his lifetime, as well as after his death.

All in all, the greatest asset of the notarial profession was the diversity of the opportunities which it offered. Every association and every individual of any account needed the services of a notary from time to time; the greater families and organisations could employ a notary regularly. But the most important employer of notaries was the great administrative machine of the commune, and the most able and ambitious notaries were

---

[1] *Stat. Coll. Iud. passim*, esp. ff. 12r, 65v. For Enselmo and Nicolò, sons of Francesco, see AD 3301, 3360; and Francesco II, see *Stat. Not.*, ff. 90–1.

drawn inevitably to the centre of the political and economic life of the city, the great Palazzo Comunale and the adjacent squares and streets. The main prizes were probably to be found outside strictly notarial tasks. Notaries became tax-farmers, moneylenders and the treasurers of the commune's revenues.[1] In whatever they did, the notaries had the advantage of working near the heart of the commune, where they might, for example, hear of an advantageous loan or buy for a favourable price the property of a bankrupt, a heretic or one who had left it to be sold for the poor of Christ. The notary, with the judge and the moneylender, were the typical Paduan figures of the communal era.

Doctors and Physicians

The only remaining group to stand out from the mass of Paduan guildsmen and tradesmen was the small but interesting medical profession. Like the lawyers, the doctors were superior to the 'mechanical guilds' in that they were a learned profession divided into two distinct though probably not entirely exclusive groups. On the one hand there were the professors of medicine and natural science who, having no college of their own at this period, were members of the university College of Artists, and on the other there were the doctors and surgeons of the city, usually with the title of *magister*, who must have belonged to the guild of *medici*.

Medicine no less than law was the special province of the Italian schools and universities in the Middle Ages. It is therefore curious that in Padua, the statutes relating to the appointment of professors make no reference to medicine, although by the agreement with the dissident Bolognese students in 1321, the commune promised to appoint 'two ordinary masters in medicine and one extraordinary, one in surgery and one in physics[2]'. There were certainly professors of medicine in the university before this date, and eleven of them are known by name.[3] Of

---

[1] E.g. Onore da Vaccarino, farmer of the *dacia machinatarum* in 1295 (Tua, *Reg. Arch. Bassanesi*, n. 645) and Tommaso di Azzone, farmer of the *dacia equorum*, 1304–5 (AD 4854). For moneylending, see below, pp. 184–5; *massarii* and *caniparii*, AS Padua, Corp. Sopp. Eremitani 23, f. 205 et seq.
[2] Denifle, 'Statuten der Juristen-Universität', *ALKM* VI (1892), p. 534.
[3] Gloria, *Università*, pp. 347–65.

these, four were certainly not Paduans and two are doubtful; the remaining five all took their names and presumably their origin from villages in the Paduan contado. We know little more concerning the antecedents of Matteo da Roncajette and Pietro da Bagnolo than what their names tell us; Avezzuto *physice doctor* was the son of the notary Antonio from Roncaglia in the south-eastern contado. The celebrated Pietro d'Abano, professor of medicine, philosophy and astrology, clearly belonged to the same background with his rural and notarial connections. With these it is uncertain whether the father or the son was responsible for the move from the contado to the city, but there can be no doubt of the immigrant status of Albertino Anselmi since he is always described as 'of' or 'who was from Piazzola' even in his will, where it is added 'who now lives in Contrà Braide'.[1]

From the evidence, it would appear that the teaching of medicine did not attract members of established city families at all, but only newly arrived immigrants from the contado. Nor, in spite of a salary from the commune, which in the case of Pietro d'Abano amounted to £500 a year, is there anything to suggest that professors were able to make a fortune and found a rich citizen family. Albertino Anselmi had no sons, and left his four daughters the moderate dowry of £500 each; Giovanni Mondino of Friuli, who had come to Padua as a student and remained as a professor, also left his daughter a dowry of only £500.[2]

Turning from the university professors to the ordinary physicians and surgeons, there is not sufficient evidence to give more than a tentative impression of their status. The guild of *medici* was one of the body of the artisan guilds, although its members enjoyed some privileges. Doctors and surgeons were exempt from the property tax, but the *gastaldiones* of the guild had to provide doctors to give professional evidence in the courts when required free of charge, travelling expenses only being paid by the commune.[3] Unfortunately, no records of the guild have survived from the communal period, and little more is known of it from other sources. This obscurity was probably due

---

[1] AD 5545. There is no evidence that he was any relation of the judge Rolando da Piazzola, the nephew of Lovato and friend of Mussato.
[2] Arch. Vescovile, Diversorum, f. 61.
[3] *Stat. Com.* 61, 1210.

in part to the small number of the members. The census of 1320, which names 264 notaries, mentions only 17 *medici*.

Doctors in Padua were not drawn from leading citizen families and did not apparently succeed in founding them. Master Giovanni Sanguinacci, 'the best doctor to be found in the whole world' according to Da Nono, who was said to have died in prison under the suspicion of heresy, may have been an exception as the Sanguinacci certainly became very wealthy, married into leading citizen families and began to pass as nobles towards the middle of the fourteenth century. Unfortunately, *magister* Giovanni cannot be identified in any existing document, and to judge by the extraordinarily large sums which some of the Sanguinacci left in their wills for the restitution of ill-gotten gains, it would seem that the family owed its fortune to usury, as Da Nono said, rather than to any professional activities of Giovanni.[1]

The scattered evidence available is not sufficient to show whether the doctors were socially nearer to the judges, the notaries or the other guildsmen. Master Giovanni the physician of Terradura, the father of three judges, was obviously exceptional; though Alessandro the son of Giovanni *doctor fysici* entered the College of Judges in 1274, he does not appear again.[2] Domenico, the brother of the judge Giacomo Berti, was a doctor who held extensive tithes in Arquà and confessed to extorting £300 by usury in 1318.[3] Two physicians are known to have been closely related to notaries; Rainerio de Cacio had three brothers who were notaries, and another doctor is described as Antonio the son of Bartolomeo the notary, of Via S. Lorenzo.[4] Guarino Museragli, who was both a physician and a notary, chose in 1305 to adhere to the Guild of Notaries for the election of *gastaldiones* but his right to belong to both guilds was not questioned.[5]

A final glimpse at some of the relationships of one particular physician is provided by the will of Giovanni Clericelli of Via S. Canciano, drawn up in October 1281. The £1,000 dowry which he left the child which his wife was expecting if it proved to be a

---

[1] *De Generatione*, ff. 51–2; AD 4246, ff. 41r, 44r.
[2] *Stat. Coll. Iud.*, f. 14v.
[3] Arch. Vescovile, Feudorum II, ff. 137–9, IV, f. 200.
[4] Brunacci, *CDP* IV, p. 2155; *Stat. Not.*, ff. 24r, 36r, AD 5113, 5804–5.
[5] *Stat. Not.*, f. 50v.

daughter, indicated that for a guildsman he was a wealthy man. There are references to land in the villages of Costa, Carbonara and Rovolon, as well as ten *campi* in Roveda valued at £200. He made bequests to two nieces, the daughters of Lorenzo the doublet-maker and also to a niece of his wife, the daughter of Antonio the apothecary. His medical books were left to Bosio, the son of Pace the notary, who was one of the executors.[1]

Other Guildsmen

From the point of view of social analysis, the members of the remaining thirty-four Paduan guilds are of little interest. It is not simply that the records of these guilds and of their individual members are comparatively sparse; there is enough evidence to make it abundantly clear that the leading Paduan citizens did not belong to the guilds, and that the guildsmen, with negligible exceptions, did not succeed through either wealth or influence, in making their way into the ruling cliques of the commune. The guild masters, who are styled *magistri* in the documents, to distinguish them from the apprentices and labourers, made up the mass of the members of the lesser part of the *popolo*. The majority perhaps were members of the *comunanza* and the Consiglio Maggiore but some would be enfranchised only in so far as they participated in the election of the officials and representatives of their guild. Many did not have family names.

There was in Padua no great merchant guild which the members of leading families might have joined; instead there are traces of a group of mixed traders and retailers, described as *negociatores* in the documents, who were the social equals of some of the notaries and judges. Alberto Rossi, *negociator*, was the father of Paduano, the judge; Ordano and Gomberto Enveradi are an example of two brothers, one a merchant and the other a judge.[2] Sachetto da Campagnola had a cousin Marco, *negociator*, who was among the witnesses to the will of Marsiglio da Carrara in 1338; his father Francesco had been *podestà* of the town of Este in 1318.[3] The a Rio family, described by Da Nono as rustics 'who afterwards became merchants of cloth and other

---

[1] Corona 1352, f. 46, another copy AD 5232, f. 53r.
[2] For the Rossi, see above, p. 139; for the Enveradi, Doc. Fam. Mussato III, nn. 27, 39, 40; Corona 1590, *Stat. Com.* 1155.
[3] Documenti Carraresi I, n. 35; *Decreta et Privilegia Magnificae Communitatis Este*, MS Arch. Municipale, Este, f. 7r.

things' were, as we have seen, also notaries.[1] Some *negociatores* were quite considerable landowners, raising doubt as to how far they were dependent on commerce alone for their livelihood. Graziadeo *negociator*, for example, left his sons, one of whom was a notary, 38 *campi* in Gazo and 30 near Padua on the Limena road, 24 in Tribano, 10 in Carturo and 64 in Pernumia, as well as a town house and several house-plots in the city.[2] Not all were as rich as this; Bartolomeo da Campolongo, notary and *negociator*, received a dowry of only £300 with his wife.[3]

The obscurity of the Paduan textile guilds is unrelieved by a single individual of even moderate importance. The notary Matteo Filarolo was no doubt descended from a weaver to whom he owed his name, but how many generations had elapsed is not known. The few noteworthy individuals were on the retailing, not the manufacturing, side. The remarkable descendants of Paduano Enghelfredi, tailor and used clothes seller, have already been described; his only rival in this respect was Aiperto Magnaspissi, a dealer in cloaks, whose sons became a judge and a knight respectively.[4] Bonaccorso de Spina *negociator*, whose business interests are revealed by the loan of £500 which he received to trade in new cloth, was a man with considerable property which he seems to have pledged to various creditors, as their rights had to be bought out when his sons sold lands and tithes to the value of £3,500 after his death.[5]

A third of the Paduan guilds were concerned with the production and distribution of victuals, but on the whole little is known of their members. There were two or three well-known families of butchers, including the De Manzio, who were also *negociatores* and moneylenders; the celebrated Antonio Pellegrino locally revered as a saint and miracle worker, belonged to this family.[6] Da Nono mentions 'the rich Giustiniano who did not exercise the butcher's trade himself, but had it carried on for

---

[1] *De Generatione*, f. 52v; see above, p. 173.
[2] AS Padua, Corp.Sopp., Eremitani 23, ff. 7v, 9v.
[3] AD 5761.
[4] *De Generatione*, f. 48v.
[5] 'in societate ad artem draperie nove'; Arch. Capit., Diversa II, n. 224; Villarum III, Campolongo 10.
[6] *De Generatione*, f. 46. *Negociatores* were Giacomo, *anziano* in 1261 (*Statuti del Comune di Vicenza*, ed. Lampertico, p. 245–6) and two of his sons, Bartolomeo and Pietro (AD 3066, Picotti, *I Caminesi*, docs. vii–ix). A kinsman, Enrico, had been a tax collector under Ezzelino (Rolandino, p. 102).

him' but the bills at least were made out in his name, since Federico Capodilista died owing him £30 for meat.[1] His sons Giovanni and Pietro were notaries, and Pietro served a term as Defensor Populi.[2] The taverners also included a few remarkable individuals. Altichino, Brazaro de Iza and Berno Berni have already been mentioned as the fathers of judges. Little is known of Altichino, beyond that he was a *tabernarius* and *hospitator* of Via S. Matteo, but Brazaro and Berno were connected with the Pedevenda, the chief wine-producing area of the Padovano.[3] Brazaro came from Galzignano and Berno was described by Da Nono as a rustic from Rovolon; he nevertheless served the commune on an embassy to Venice in 1303.[4] Like the butchers, these men were in a position to control an important nexus between the city and the rural areas; the leading taverners probably owned their own vineyards. Another branch of their activity seems to have been moneylending. Da Nono groups the Berni and De Iza with the Ferro and De Mariota as families which he considered to be wealthy innkeepers and usurers.[5] No information concerning moneylending by these particular families is available, but a similar pattern of life can be glimpsed from the will of Perenzano Torculi, which provided that 'all contracts of usuries and sureties belonging to the men of Pedevenda are returned and are null and void, and also all taverner's contracts relating both to the Pedevenda and to other parts, by occasion of wine sold to them, are also null and void'.[6] The mixture of interests, with production rooted in the contado, is typical of the Paduan economy.

Some potentially interesting groups are shrouded in obscurity. The water mills of the city and contado must have been an important economic asset, but the millers appear to have been only humble craftsmen. Some mill owners, like Fruzerino Lanzaroti, who traded in salt, oil and cheese and owned a mill with a fulling plant at Terranigra, were also merchants;[7] other

---

[1] *De Generatione*, f. 47v; '£30 pro carnibus', Arch. Papafava, 39, n. 37.
[2] Verci, *Marca Trivigiana*, doc. n. 379; *Stat. Not.*, ff. 66v, 75r, 78v.
[3] See above, p. 141.
[4] AS Venice, *Liber Commemorialis*, I, f. 43 (Predelli, n. 137).
[5] *De Generatione*, ff. 49v–50r.   [6] Corona 2964.
[7] In 1295 Fruzerino received a loan of £12. 10s. gr. from Aleardo Basilii, acting on behalf of the Paduan Inquisitors, 'fruendi et negociandi in mercatione salis, olei, et casei' (AS Padua, Corp. Sopp. S. Antonio 150, f. 256). For his mill, see Corona 671.

mills simply augmented the income of citizens whose main interests lay elsewhere. Similarly, one has only to consider the great public works of the communal period, the Palazzo Comunale and the basilica of S. Antonio, to realise that building and brick-making must have been considerable industries in Padua. As many as eighty-six masters attended the chapter of the Guild of Masons and Brick-makers in the early fourteenth century, but none of them left any significant mark on the records.[1] Some of the brick works were owned by the commune, and the bulk of the profits presumably went to the proprietors.[2]

A number of *precones* or court messengers are known by name, chiefly, it would appear, because they were often standing about when witnesses were required. The communal administration employed twenty *precones* at a time for the usual four-month term of office, and for their duties, which included the taking of sureties and the arrest of outlaws, they were paid 10os. and had a right to customary gifts.[3] The court messengers had their own *gastaldiones* but their guild was not among those recognised by the commune. Although they must have secured an income sufficient to buy and maintain the horse and armour which was essential to their work, their position was undistinguished. But at least they worked close to the centres of wealth and power; though they occupied the bottom rung of the administrative ladder, one or two, at least, saw their sons advance one step into the notariat.

Moneylenders and Usurers

Moneylending and landowning were the two most persistent characteristics of the Paduan citizen body in the communal period. Examples are to be found of loans at interest being made by Paduan laymen of every social class of which there is record, from the noble magnates Marsiglio da Carrara and Nicolò da Lozzo to a certain Giustina di Paduano in the village of Villa.[4] Clearly, only a tiny fraction of those who made occasional loans

[1] Gennari, *CDP* IX, pp. 1370–88.
[2] 'terra ubi sunt fornaces communis Padue' near S. Antonio, AD 2617.
[3] *Stat. Com.* 212–26.
[4] Loan of £50,000 by Marsiglio da Carrara (AS Padua, Archivi Privati, Obizzi 295, ff. 33–41). Loan of £32 gr. by Nicolò da Lozzo to Gerardo da Camino (AD 3998). Giustina di Paduano lends £40 for six months at 20% (AD 2969).

were in the remotest sense professional moneylenders. Many apparent contracts of loan were not primarily such at all, for nominal loans formed a part of many complex transactions whose full implications were often left intentionally obscure. But even when the numerous individuals who cannot be shown to have made more than occasional loans for special purposes have been discounted, the habitual moneylenders and those who can be assumed for other reasons to have been in some degree professionals, are still drawn from so many social groups as to prove that in Padua there was no moneylending class. Nevertheless, moneylending was of the greatest social significance. Usury was both the most commonly alleged cause of the enrichment of a family, and the most common reason for denying a family the honour otherwise due to it.

The identification of professional moneylenders is dependent upon several kinds of evidence, some of which present considerable difficulties of interpretation. The documents directly relating to loans are of several kinds, chiefly instruments of debt, repayments of loans, assignments of debts or, more rarely, prosecutions for debt, and loans or debts listed in inventories of property. The fact that the ecclesiastical laws against usury generally prevented a true statement of the rate of interest or the real term of the loan is among the least of the pitfalls presented by this kind of evidence. Sometimes it is uncertain whether a genuine loan is being made at all, and even then it is no easy matter to identify the real creditors and debtors. A distinction was not always made between a deposit and a loan; for reasons best known to contemporaries, the debtor often chose to conceal his identity by acting through an agent, and since the law demanded that there should be only one creditor, the partners in a joint loan often appear as sureties, *fideiussores*. Assignments of debt incidental to the purchase of real property often do not mention the sum involved. One is on surer ground with explicit confessions of usury, but these are rare and generally relate to small sums and rather obscure individuals. More useful are the implicit confessions of usury found in the provisions for the restitution of ill-gotten gains (*male ablata*) found in many of the wills of the period, though these can be disappointingly vague. Finally, the allegations of the chroniclers, especially Da Nono, are an additional guide to the notorious usurers. Though only about half Da Nono's accusations of usury are supported by other evidence, there is no reason to doubt that on the whole he reflects the common opinion of the families and persons concerned.

With this warning delivered as to the difficulties of the evidence, an attempt may be made to distinguish the various categories of professional moneylenders in Padua and its contado in the communal period.

The lowest class of professional moneylenders, who appear to have been of about the same status as the guildsmen, though they did not have a guild of their own, were to be found scattered throughout the city, towns and villages of the Paduan state. Often described as moneychangers (*campsores*), many of them were Toscani, usually of Florentine origin. Most of these, like the three *socii campsores* referred to in a document of 1286, make only a fleeting appearance in the Paduan records.[1] The Florentine Bentacordi, who were presumably related to Uguccione Bonaccorsi Bentacorde, who became a partner in the Peruzzi bank in the early fourteenth century, were exceptional in taking root in Padua.[2] Forzeto di Gallina, described as a Florentine now living in Padua, first appears in 1278-9 when, with a group of his compatriots living in Bassano, he helped to advance money to pay the Bassanese troops mobilised for service against Verona.[3] His son, known as Lapo da Firenze or Bentacordi, was styled a Paduan citizen in 1287, and is found in a number of financial transactions associated with Bonifacio Papafava.[4] Another member of the family, Ruggiero 'who was from Florence', was a judge in the bishop's court in Padua in 1286 and 1288, and by 1302 was sufficiently naturalised to be admitted to the College of Judges.[5] His son Tauro lent money to the commune of Vicenza in 1294 and 1298.[6]

The native Paduan moneylenders often combined this activity with a wide variety of other trades and professions. A few are described as *negociatores*, like Guglielmo Mandugavillano

[1] AD 3200. For Tuscan moneylenders in the Veneto, see A. Medin, 'La coltura toscana nel Veneto durante il medioevo', *ARIV* LXXXII (1922-3), pp. 83-154.
[2] Sapori, *Studi di storia economica*, p. 283.
[3] Verci, *Marca Trivigiana*, docs. nn. 228, 232.
[4] AD 3257; Arch. Papafava 38, *passim*.
[5] Arch. Capit. Villarum III, Campolongo, n. 7; Corona 1310; *Stat. Coll. Iud.*, f. 27r.
[6] AS Vicenza, Torre 32, n. 85; 42, n. 22.

who, according to Da Nono, 'made £20,000 by usury', or Pietro de Manzio who appears as agent or *fideiussor* for a number of loans raised in Padua for the commune of Treviso.¹ But other occupations are equally represented. Among the self-confessed usurers was Domenico Berti, a physician, whose brother was a judge, and Liberale Museragli whose brother Guarino was a physician and notary.² The evidence for the combination of innkeeping and usury, which may have involved the advancing of credit to wine producers and retailers, has already been given. Da Nono's allegation that the tailor Bernardo Schalchi was a usurer is confirmed by his will, which makes provision for the restitution of *male ablata* to those making claims within two years of his death.³ The conclusion to be drawn from these examples is that capital derived from whatever source could provide the basis for profitable moneylending. This is certainly what Da Nono believed, as he relates that the Bellarini set themselves up as moneylenders with the fine paid in compensation for the murder of one of the family, while the a Ferro, he says, obtained their capital by collecting and selling the old iron which fell off carts in the city.⁴

The legal profession created no bar to engagement in moneylending. The notary Matteo de Pipere, alias de Vitaclo, the son of Gerardo, a judge, clearly made loans on more than a casual basis, since in his will 'he ordered and commanded that the usuries received by him and all his *male ablata* be restored and paid in full from his goods to all persons making just requests, according to the pure truth as it is written in his three books of memoranda'. To his wife he left her dowry of £800 which 'really and in pure truth he had from her, notwithstanding that in her marriage contract . . . it is declared that he had from her in dower £1750'. This is a subterfuge found elsewhere among mediaeval *entrepreneurs* for securing a reserve in case of bankruptcy, when the preservation of the dowry would have a prior

---

¹ *De Generatione*, f. 51r; Picotti, *I Caminesi*, docs. nn. vii–ix, AS Venice, *Codex Tarvisinus*, ff. 333–4.
² See above, p. 177. For Liberale's confession, see AS Notarile, 407, f. 35v.
³ *De Generatione*, f. 41r; AD 5475.
⁴ *De Generatione*, ff. 49v, 50v. The chapter on the Bellarini is missing from the Seminario MS but is found in Bibl. Civ. S. Daniele di Friuli Cod. 264, p. 264 which is also of the fourteenth century. The style and sentiments are exactly those of Da Nono.

claim over all the creditors.¹ Vivarotto da Candiana, a notary, who was a kinsman and executor of Bernardo Schalchi, the tailor and usurer mentioned above, had one of his loans cancelled as usurous by the episcopal authorities in 1319 .With his brother Pietro, a judge, he advanced large sums to the Estensi.² Tristano d'Este, who was no relation to the *marchesi* d'Este, confessed in 1328 to having extorted 100 florins by usury. He had two brothers in the College of Judges, one of whom, Mezzoconte, stood surety for their restitution but was not blameless in the matter of usury himself.³ In 1335, the commune of Este had to impose a special tax to raise £8,000 due to him, and two years later he was imprisoned by the Della Scala *signori* of Padua who extorted £10,000 from him before he regained his freedom.⁴

The practice of moneylending extended equally to the knights and the leading citizen families of Padua. Palamede Vitaliani, a knight and judge, in his will ordered the restoration of his usuries, as written by his own hand in his three books of memoranda.⁵ His brother Vitaliano, a doctor of law who has been mistakenly identified with the Vitaliano of Dante's *Inferno*, was also a usurer, as his heirs were ordered to pay the monastery of S. Maria da Polverara £3,120 in restitution of his usuries.⁶ Da Nono considered the Capodivacca family, who were climbing steadily towards noble and magnatial status throughout the communal period, to be notorious usurers. Owing to the loss of records, it is possible to substantiate his charge only in the case of Tavanello, who made a loan to the commune of Vicenza, and Zamboneto Paradisi who, in addition to loans to Vicenza, was also involved in the provision of financial assistance to Gerardo da Camino, *signore* of Treviso.⁷

The three Paduan moneylending families which stand out

---

[1] AD 3037. The Bonsignori of Siena defended a part of their property in this way, G. Arias, *Studi e documenti di storia del diritto* (1920), pp. 5, 34.
[2] AD 5656; AS Modena, AMS VIII, n. 47; X, n. 15.
[3] Arch. Vescovile, Diversorum, f. 75; *Stat. Coll. Iud.*, ff. 22v, 26r.
[4] Arch. Municipale, Este, *Decreta et Privilegia*, f. 70v; Cortusi, p. 79.
[5] 'secundum quod scriptum est manu mea in libris memorialibus rationum mearum, qui sunt tres libricolli autentici', AD. 5801, excerpt only, fuller copy Gennari, *CDP* VIII, p. 718.
[6] AS Notarile, 407, f. 23r.
[7] Picotti, *I Caminesi*, pp. 157–8, n. 4; AS Vicenza, Torre 32, n. 12; 33, nn. 90, 98; 42, nn. 85, 95.

above all the others both by reason of their power, which placed them in the magnatial class, and by the scale of their financial operations, were the Dalesmanini, the Lemici and the Scrovegni. The evidence relating to the moneylending activities of these families, though it is naturally very incomplete, suggests a contrast between the Dalesmanini on the one hand, and the Lemici and Scrovegni on the other. Despite Da Nono's remark

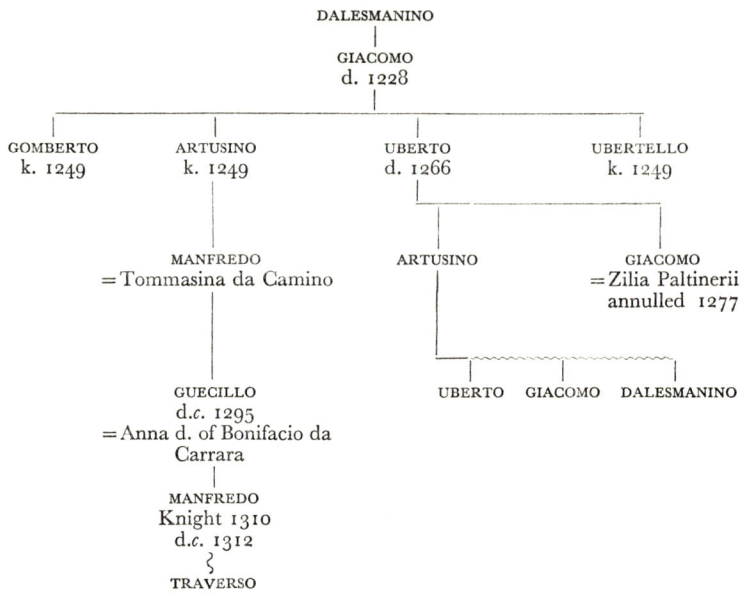

TABLE 15. Genealogy of the Dalesmanini family.

that they had nearly all always been amassers of usuries, there is no evidence to show that the Dalesmanini, who had been an important Paduan family from the later twelfth century, engaged significantly in moneylending before the fourteenth century. It is only after the death of Guecillo, the most powerful member of the family, without legitimate heirs between 1295 and 1300, that the records begin to show a remarkable series of loans by Artusino Dalesmanini and his sons Uberto, Giacomo and Dalesmanino. The debtors include the communes of Feltre, Bassano and Treviso, but above all Vicenza, where the

Dalesmanini appear to replace the Scrovegni as the chief creditors of the commune from 1302 to 1309.¹ The sums involved were very high by local standards: £16,000 in 1302, £30,000 in July 1308 and a further £15,000 in December of the same year. Some idea of the interest obtained can be gained from the fact that Artusino and Dalesmanino received £2,458. 10s. in respect of one year's interest in May 1304, and £3,112. 19s. 10d. to complete other interests still outstanding in the following October. Yet even an income on this scale does not seem to have halted the rapid decline of the family.

By contrast, the Lemici and the Scrovegni, the families chosen by Dante to represent the Paduan usurers in Hell, made their fortunes by usury in the course of the thirteenth century, abandoning this ill-famed activity when their position was secure. Of the two, the Lemici had the longer history, having been, like the Dalesmanini, a leading city family in the late twelfth century, but the evidence for their moneylending begins with Guglielmo I, who raised two important loans for Gerardo da Camino, the *signore* of Treviso, in 1283–4.² His son, the notorious Vitaliano, is on record as lending £2,000 to the commune of Vicenza in 1296, but thereafter appears as a *fideiussor* only.³ Too much weight should not be placed on this, since the evidence is obviously fragmentary, and Vitaliano may well have worked through agents. However, from 1299, it is clear that Vitaliano was investing heavily in real property in the Vicentine contado, and in 1301 he sold land near Padua for at least £20,000.⁴ The motive behind these transactions is no longer clear, but Vitaliano's last years do not appear to have been very successful financially, that is, if the application by the guardians of his heir, Guglielmo II, to sell lands to the value of £15,000 to meet outstanding debts is taken at its face value.⁵ At all events, the revolt of Vicenza in 1311 must have created difficulties for the young Guglielmo. Though his estates do not appear to have been among those confiscated at once by the Vicentines, by

---

[1] AS Padua, Arch. Privati, 99, f. 18r; Tua, *Reg. Arch. Bassanesi*, nn. 754, 763, 808–9; AS Vicenza, Torre 33, nn. 30, 49, 59, 119, 121, 123; 33, n. 77; 34, n. 26; 35, n. 2; 42, n. 93.
[2] Picotti, *I Caminesi*, doc. nn. vii, ix, see below, pp. 230–1
[3] AS Vicenza, Torre 34, n. 25. For Vitaliano as *fideiussor* see AD 3898; AS Padua, Monasteri del Territorio, Praglia 165, f. 243v.
[4] See below, p. 225; AS Padua, Archivi Privati, Frigemelica 10, n. 5.
[5] AS Padua, Archivi Privati, fam. Sala.

1322 a Vicentine court had declared part of his holdings in S. Vito di Leguzzano forfeit to the widow of a certain Crescimbene, *negociator* da Montagnana, in satisfaction of a loan of 3,625 florins for which Vitaliano had stood surety. In 1325, a year of acute party strife in Padua, Guglielmo sold another part of his S. Vito estates to the men of S. Vito for £1,800.[1] These facts throw some light on the circumstances in which the Lemici were decisively defeated by the Carraresi in the struggle for the control of Padua.

The Scrovegni, as we have seen, can be traced back no further than the early thirteenth century, and make their first appearance in the circle of the bishops of Padua. Renaldo Scrovegni, who spoke to Dante in Hell, is recorded as making a number of substantial loans to Gerardo da Camino and the commune of Vicenza between 1282 and 1297, the largest being £670. 11s. gross (about £21,457 petty), to Gerardo da Camino in June 1284, for which interest was charged at the rate of 20 per cent.[2] Renaldo employed his kinsmen Gonfredo and Ugolino Lispea Scrovegni as his agents, and his sons Manfredo and Enrico, and his grandson Pietro, all made considerable loans.[3] A series of documents show Manfredo, Pietro and Enrico in about 1290 borrowing jointly sums of between £2,000 and £3,000 from each of their four sisters.[4] This looks like a systematic exploitation of family connections for the purpose of raising capital, and is the nearest thing to a family bank to be found in Padua in the communal period. The ladies in question were married into the Papafava, Forzatè, Capodivacca and Linguadevacca families, the first three being of magnatial or near-magnatial status, and the last two having a reputation for usury. However, between 1297 and 1300, the evidence for large-scale lending by the Scrovegni comes to an end, their place as financiers of the commune of Vicenza being taken by the Dalesmanini. Where the records are so incomplete, it is extremely hazardous to argue from negative evidence, but it is

---

[1] Arch. Comunale, S. Vito di Leguzzano, Perg. Antic., nn. 5, 6, 8.

[2] Picotti, *I Caminesi*, doc. viii; AS Venice, *Cod. Tarvisinus*, f. 331r; AS Vicenza, Torre 29, nn. 85–7, 90, 96–7, 111, 113, 115–16.

[3] Manfredo: Arch. Capit. Diversa II, n. 175; AS Vicenza, Torre 29, n. 83. Enrico: AD 3438; Arch. Capit. Diversa II, n. 200. Pietro: AS Vicenza, Torre 29, n. 119.

[4] Arch. Capit. Diversa II, nn. 180–6.

probably significant that Da Nono, who wrote a good deal about Enrico Scrovegni, whom he hated, does not accuse him personally of being a usurer.

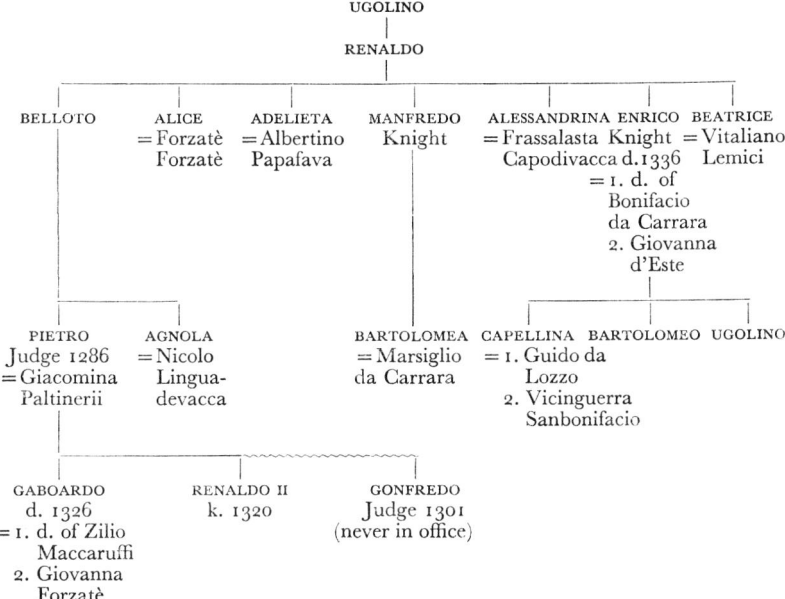

TABLE 16. Genealogy of the Scrovegni family.

The social significance of moneylending was related to the fact that the church defined virtually all gain derived from loans as usury and therefore intrinsically sinful.[1] In theory, manifest usurers should have been prosecuted by the ecclesiastical authorities, but in practice, the only confessions of usury recorded were made by comparatively unimportant men in respect of fairly small sums. Only the small fry were caught in the ecclesiastical net; there is nothing to suggest that the great

[1] For the theory of usury see T. P. McLaughlin, 'The Teaching of the Canonists on Usury', *Mediaeval Studies* I (1939), pp. 81-147; II (1940), pp. 1-22; and J. T. Noonan, *The Scholastic Analysis of Usury* (1957). For some indications of the policy of the church in practice, see B. N. Nelson, 'The Usurer and the Merchant Prince; Italian Businessmen and the Ecclesiastical Law of Restitution', *JEH* VII Suppl. (1947), pp. 104-22.

moneylending families suffered any censure by the church. Enrico Scrovegni's building of the famous Arena chapel and his endowment of the convent of S. Orsola may have been intended in part to expiate the sins of his father, but there is nothing to suggest this, even in the attacks on Enrico's character made by Da Nono and the friars of the Eremitani, both of which concentrate on his hypocrisy and vainglory.[1] The Scrovegni, at least. seem to have had powerful friends in ecclesiastical circles, Renaldo was the trusted agent of Bishop Giovanni Forzatè, and Enrico was described as *familiarius noster* by the Trevisan Pope, Benedict XI.[2]

The secular view of moneylending was somewhat different. Da Nono lables many individuals and families as moneylenders (*feneratores*), but when these were *popolani* and not too rich, there is nothing to suggest disapproval.[3] With a magnatial family like the Dalesmanini, usury seems to disqualify from nobility, but with the Scintilla it seems to have been the moneylenders' table, constituting the public practice of a kind of base art, which dishonoured the family. Da Nono's hate was reserved for those who, like the Scrovegni, had built up an enormous fortune by usury in a comparatively short space of time. Mussato's attack on his former political allies, the Altichini and the Ronchi, shows the same point of view.[4] These sentiments seem to have been directed not against usury as such, but against it in so far as it was a means by which a dangerous concentration of wealth could be amassed too quickly. In the long run, wealth could create nobility, and was certainly necessary to maintain it, but too rapid change violated the instinctive belief in social stability upon which Paduan social values were based. The idea of the degrading nature of usury, which nullified any claim to nobility, represented the defensive reaction of a conservative society to a period when rapid social mobility had become possible.

[1] The documents relating to Enrico's pious foundations are A. S. Padua, Scuole religiose soppresse, SS. Annunciata, n. 1, and Brunacci *CDP*, II p. 1350. For contemporary reactions to them, see above, p. 101.

[2] See above, p. 87, and C. Grandjean, *Le Registre de Benoit XI* (1905), n. 126.

[3] 'Populares et feneratores de progenie rusticana ville Campilongi, sunt satisque dilecti in populo'; *De Generatione*, f. 52r; see also f. 52v.

[4] *De Gestis*, col. 607; for a general denunciation of Paduan usury see *De Traditione*, coll. 715–16.

Fresco, Arena Chapel, Padua

PLATE II

Giotto: Enrico Scrovegni presenting the Arena Chapel to the Virgin

PART TWO

THE GOVERNING CLASS IN ACTION

CHAPTER VII

The Commune and the Pars Marchionis

DESPITE the many gaps in the evidence, the preceding examination has established the general pattern of Paduan economy and society by showing a certain consistency between the different facets of Paduan life. The salient features of this pattern can best be described by contrasting them with the accepted picture of Florence, the largest and the best known of the inland Italian communes. In population, Padua was between a half and a third the size of Florence, but the contrast rests not so much on size as upon the degree to which the Tuscan commune had evolved a truly urban economy and society. In Padua, commerce, manufacturing and even finance were relatively undeveloped, so that the purely merchant classes were comparatively unimportant; the international bankers and the great merchants of the Lana and the Calimala guilds had no equivalent in Padua. The agricultural products of the countryside, on the other hand, played a much larger role in the Paduan economy than they did in Florence; the entire ruling class supported itself primarily by the exploitation of the contado, either directly through the ownership of rights over the land or its products, or indirectly through the administration of the state. The most powerful elements in Paduan society were the landowning magnates and the inflated administrative class, dominated by the professionally trained notaries and judges. As on the economic, so on the social plane, the division between town and country was much less marked than at Florence. There, a largely urban society developed its own hierarchy and values; trade, for example, was not considered dishonourable even for the leading families. But this society was very exclusive; the common reproach against *parvenus* was that they were aliens from Fiesole or the contado. There is no trace of this feeling in Padua, where socially the city and the contado were one. Rural origins were not, in themselves, anything to be ashamed of; indeed, the possession of a rural jurisdiction and its visible symbol, the castle, represented the strongest possible claim to nobility. Direct participation in trade, on the other hand, dishonoured a noble family in Padua, and upstarts were attacked as usurers.

It is the purpose of this and the two succeeding chapters to follow out the pattern of Paduan society as it manifested itself in the political life of the city from 1256 to 1328. To do this, it will be necessary to look once more at the institutions of the Paduan state which obviously have many points of contact with the social structure, but our examination cannot be restricted to the formal constitution which, if taken in isolation, would be both incomplete and misleading. In the first place, such a treatment, being necessarily based on the statutes of 1276, is bound to be largely static, while it is clear that continual change, at least in details, is one of the most striking features of the political life of the period. But even if the records existed from which the bewildering flux of legislation could be followed in detail, it is doubtful if they would bring us much nearer the heart of the matter, for not only is there abundant evidence that many of the laws were never observed to the letter, but it is clear that the constitution was in many respects no more than a façade concealing the real forces which controlled Paduan political life. Like all small-scale politics, Paduan affairs were dominated by pressure-groups which, being informal and ephemeral, tend by their very nature to leave few direct traces of their existence; in Padua, the ideals of the commune, which favoured impersonal government in the common interest, provided a strong incentive for the factions to conceal their activities. Their hidden influence can be uncovered, if at all, only by the examination of those events which show the Paduan governing class in action. This and the following chapters will therefore contain an element of narrative, but they are not intended as a history of the Paduan state; their purpose is the further elucidation of the nature of Paduan society as demonstrated in political organisation and action.

Although the Paduan commune was in practice a fully autonomous state, recognising no temporal superior except a distant Imperial claimant for the greater part of our period, Padua was too small a political unit to be comprehensible by itself; much of the city's political life was shaped by reactions to movements originating outside its own territories. Sometimes, as in the crises of 1237, 1256 or 1311, the commune would be caught up in events of national or even European significance, but these inruptions were rare and generally of short duration, though their consequences might be felt for a long time. Under normal conditions, Paduan political life was little affected by the vicissitudes of the Empire and the Papacy, and the great cities like Milan and Florence had not yet come to dominate Italian affairs; even Venice, for all its proximity and economic importance, was politically aloof from 1260 to the first years of the fourteenth century. Certain political ideas seem to have come from Florence and especially from Bologna, presumably through the agency of the jurists and *podestà*, but on the whole the commune's political relations were only spasmodic beyond the circle of neighbours' neighbours. The turbulent regions of Friuli and the Romagna touched Paduan life mainly through intermediaries, which in the one case were the patriarchs of Aquileia and the Da Camino, and in the other the house of Este; Feltre and Belluno, the twin cities of the Alpine foot-hills, were closely linked to Padua by treaty, while Trento and Mantua generally fell within the Veronese orbit. But the influence of these was far outweighed by that of Padua's four immediate neighbours, Verona, Vicenza, Treviso and Ferrara, whose territories constituted the region which was the intimate environment of the Paduan political organism. Not only were commercial and diplomatic relations within this inner circle more frequent and intense, but they were reinforced by social and political contacts of a less formal kind for, as we have shown, Paduan society at its upper limits merged with the society of the March.

When, during the first half of the thirteenth century, historical writing in north-eastern Italy emerged from the level of bare annals, the form which it took was not that of city-histories but histories of the region; citizens themselves, the historians of the period were in fact and often in name historians of the March.[1] At least three writers of differing interests and intellectual attainments attest to the vitality of the region as a political unit; it was this political reality rather than its dim historical origins which gave the phrase 'March of Treviso' a renewed currency in the twelfth and thirteenth centuries. The

[1] See G. Arnaldi, *Studi sui cronisti della Marca Trevigiana nell'età di Ezzelino da Romano*, Istituto Storico Italiano per il Medio Evo, Studi Storici, fasc. 48–50 (1963), especially pp. 22–5, 56–63.

special unity of the region had no constitutional form, nor did it derive from the relations between the communes, close as these were; what linked the territories of the March together were the operations of the factions headed by a handful of leading families who belonged exclusively to no one city but to the whole March. The political attitudes of the chroniclers give evidence of a dual loyalty to city and to party in which the city did not always come first. For example, Gerardo Maurisio was a Vicentine judge, but his *Chronicon dominorum Ecelini et Alberici* was dedicated to Beatrice da Romano and was written to the greater glory of her house, so that Gerardo can rejoice over a defeat of his fellow-citizens at the hands of the Da Romano party. The authorship of the *Chronicon Marchiae Tarvisinae et Lombardie* is disputed, but an element which links those parts originating in the Paduan monastery of S. Giustina with those which seem to betray a Veronese background is a passionate attachment to the cause of the Estensi.[1] Rolandino was not only the most intelligent historian of the March in the period, he was also the most convincing civic patriot among them. There can be no doubt that the Paduan notary's first loyalty was to the commune and the good Paduan *popolo* to which he belonged, and his attachment to the Estensi was strictly subordinate to this; yet even he opened his carefully planned history not with the communes but with the four great families, the Estensi, the Da Camino, the Da Romano and the Camposanpiero, 'who in my time were sufficiently distinguished in fame and deeds'.

It is well known that the Florentine traditions of the time of Dante traced back the unhappy divisions in the city to the outbreak of the feud between the Buondelmonte and the Amidei in 1216. In Rolandino's history, the role of the Buondelmonte murder is played by the conflict over Cecilia, the daughter of Manfredo the Rich, which broke out in the later twelfth century. Cecilia, heiress of the Abano branch of the Paduan comital family, was the intended bride of Gerardo Camposanpiero, but while the terms of the match were still under discussion, she was seized by the Da Romano and hastily

---

[1] The most recent editions of these chronicles are by G. Soranzo, RIS VIII, iv (1914), and L. A. Botteghi, RIS VIII, iii (1916). For a bibliography of the discussion concerning the authorship of the latter, see Arnaldi, op. cit. p. 205.

married to Ezzelino II. The Camposanpiero were deeply offended, and the young Gerardo took his revenge by seducing Cecilia when she was on a visit to her Paduan possessions.

Therefore, from this spark of offence there grew a flame and an ardent fire, whence today (1262) the whole March lies subject to war, destruction and ruin. Between brothers and kinsmen, fellow-citizens and neighbours, were sown strife and hatred, fraud and deception, quarrels rapine and mortal enmity, as will be shown below.[1]

From this opening, Rolandino proceeds, with few of the digressions common in the work of most mediaeval historians, to unfold the history of the March for the next sixty years in terms of the Da Romano-Camposanpiero feud and its widening ramifications.

In going back to this particular event, Rolandino was doubtless following a popular tradition which, as so often, did not quite correspond to the facts. As the dispute proceeded, the main conflict came to lie not between the Da Romano and the Camposanpiero, but between the Da Romano and the Estensi and it was this division which established itself as the axis of political alignments within the March in the first half of the thirteenth century. But this in no way invalidates the point which Rolandino was making when he made the tradition into the ground-plan of his history. For him, it was not the cities but the great families who shaped the history of the region.

In the *Cronica*, it is the noble families which are the protagonists throughout. The role of the communes is strictly subordinate; at best, they are important allies for a noble faction, at the worst, mere prizes in the contest, as passive as Cecilia d'Abano. As the historian remarks at one point, 'In quarrels and wars, it is more than half the battle for the magnates to have control of the communes of the citizens'.[2] Even the Empire and the Papacy are subordinated to the local theme; Frederick II is represented as the dupe of Ezzelino III, who uses the Emperor as a cloak in order to accomplish his aim of gaining control over Padua, and the Papal crusade which eventually liberated Padua is shown as initiated at the request

[1] *Cronica*, pp. 15–17.
[2] 'Est enim plus quam facti dimidium ad magnates in discordiis et werris habere communia civitatum'. On the expulsion of the Estensi from Verona, ibid. p. 33.

of the local leaders Azzo d'Este and Tiso III Camposanpiero.[1]

In weighing the value of Rolandino's views, it must be remembered first of all, that except for the first pages, he was not embroidering a verbal tradition, but relating events which had occurred in his own lifetime. From 1223 to 1262 he was apparently resident in Padua and in practice as a notary, an eyewitness of much that took place there. His history was written in 1260–2, not from memory but from notes kept by himself supplementing others confided to him by his father and on completion it was publicly read before the university, within two years of the last events recorded in it.[2] Then, the so-called chronicle was not a simple piece of popular history showing the tendency to personalisation common to the popular history of all times, but a serious example of learned history. Rolandino was a graduate of Bologna, where he had been a student of the celebrated rhetorician Boncompagno, and was a doctor of grammar at the university of Padua, writing consciously in a learned rhetorical tradition. Indeed, the chief reservations about accepting all that Rolandino says at its face value arise not from his simplicity but from the subtlety which he conceals beneath his frank exterior. Rolandino was a propagandist who knew that history could be made to serve political ends. His admitted aim was to teach by example the evils of tyranny and government *per partem,* so that the citizens would value and uphold the government *ad communem* which had just been restored to them.[3] Hence he exaggerated the atrocities perpetrated by Ezzelino and, in the interests of solidarity between citizens of all classes, he minimised or suppressed the evidence for conflicts between them. For example, one would never realise from his account that the Paduan commune had taken over the jurisdictions of the nobility in the period of which he wrote. Yet these interests and prejudices strengthen rather than weaken the force of Rolandino's testimony on the main point, his analysis of regional politics not in terms of cities or social classes, the Empire and the Papacy, but primarily in terms of the rivalry of a few leading families and their supporting *partes.* If Rolandino is to be trusted, the nobly led *pars*—to translate this

---

[1] Ibid. pp. 87, 111, 172.
[2] Ibid. preface, pp. vii–ix.
[3] Ibid. pp. 5, 19, 109, 172–3.

ambiguous term 'party' or 'faction' would be to beg a very open question—was the most important and formative element in the political life of the March in the first half of the thirteenth century.

The *partes* described by Rolandino were loose-knit associations of families and clients whose composition varied from time to time and place to place. The most constant factor in the ever-changing political scene was the hostility of the Da Romano and the Estensi. The Da Romano came from the Alpine foot-hills near Bassano, and the Estensi from the southern part of the Paduan contado, but their influence was felt throughout the March as well as at Ferrara, Mantua and the surrounding regions. The main bone of contention was the control of the commune of Verona. Here, though the issue hung in the balance for nine years, the Estensi and their friends never succeeded in reversing their defeat of 1227, and the final triumph of Da Romano influence in 1236 was soon followed by the fall of Vicenza and Padua which brought the Estensi between 1238 and 1240 to their lowest ebb, reduced to a few fortresses in the southern Padovano. The capture of Ferrara in 1240 gave the Estensi a base and a refuge in which they could weather the long period of Da Romano dominance until its sudden collapse, begun by the crusade which recovered Padua in 1256 and ending with the extermination of the last of the Da Romano in August 1260.

Immediately surrounding the Da Romano and the Estensi was a small circle of noble allies whose sphere of influence, though rarely extending over the whole region, was yet considerably wider than the territory of a single city. The outstanding example on the Da Romano side was Ezzelino II's brother-in-law Salinguerra. He first appears as an ally of the Da Romano in Verona in 1207, but in 1220 he drove the Estensi from Ferrara and held the city until 1240, giving valuable help to the Da Romano during a critical period in their history; he was, for example, a leader against the Estensi during his tenure of office as *podestà* of Verona in 1230. In the opposing camp, a similar role was played by the Sanbonifacio, counts of Verona, who, when driven from their native city in 1227, managed to establish themselves in Mantua. Here, in spite of the formation of a popular *comunanza* against them in 1260, and a split with the local supporters of the Estensi in

1269, they managed to hold out until 1272 when they were finally displaced by the Bonacolsi. Other leading members of the Estense faction were the Cattanei da Lendenara who, though their family home was on the lower Adige, were also active in Verona, and the Camposanpiero and Da Camino whose main strength was in the area north-east of Padua, including the Trevigiano and parts of Friuli.[1]

While the noble leaders gave each of the *partes* a common element throughout the whole region, each had its more local adherents and allies who gave a different complexion to the party divisions of each of the major cities. The sources are not very informative about the lesser members of the great factions, but a few generalisations may be made. In Verona, the partisans of the Da Romano were known as the Montecchi, the historical prototypes of Shakespeare's Montagues, and they seem to have had the support of the leading elements among the citizens; the opposing party, known as the *pars Marchionis et Comitis*, had a more aristocratic complexion. In Mantua, and probably Ferrara too, the Este party was opposed by the *popolo;* in Vicenza, on the other hand, the comital family was generally allied to the Da Romano, and the Estensi enjoyed the support of the commune. The lack of a local chronicle makes the situation in Treviso obscure, but up to 1239 it would appear that the Estensi and the Paduan commune were normally in league with the Da Camino against the Trevisan commune. In 1239, Alberico da Romano gained control of the city with the help of some of the Da Camino and he held it independently, in opposition to Ezzelino III, until 1256, when he finally came to his brother's aid, only to share in his ruin. The make-up of the parties in Padua is obscure for another reason: Rolandino's reticence in naming the Paduan friends of the Da Romano. Most of the nobility, except perhaps some branches of the comital family, seem to have followed the lead of the Camposanpiero and the Marchesi, but the commune,

[1] The main sources for this and the following paragraphs are, in addition to the chronicles cited above, the *Annales* of Parisio de Cereta, MGH.SS XIX (1866), pp. 2–18 and *Annales Mantuani*, ibid. pp. 19–31. In the absence of an early chronicle from Treviso, see Picotti, *I Caminesi*, pp. 31–73. For a recent survey of Ezzelino's political career and its significance see R. Manselli, 'Ezzelino da Romano nella politica italiana del sec. XIII', *Studi Ezzeliniani*, Istituto Storico Italiano per il Medio Evo, Studi Storici, fasc. 45–7 (1963), pp. 35–79.

though usually loyal to the Estensi did on occasion reverse its allegiance and side with the Da Romano against its traditional allies. It is significant that the words Guelph and Ghibelline are rarely found in the local sources of the March. Rolandino, for example, prefers *pars Ecclesiae et Marchionis* and *pars Imperii* or *Eccelini*, and the Paduan statutes use almost identical words.[1] The local parties originated quite independently of the interests of the Empire and Papacy, and the alignment of the *pars Marchionis* and the *pars Eccelini* with the Guelphs and the Ghibellines took place at a late stage and almost accidentally, as a matter of expediency. Although the Estensi had been the allies of the church in the early thirteenth century, when Azzo VI was enfeoffed with the March of Ancona by Innocent III, this did not prevent his successor Azzo VII from trying to compete with Ezzelino for favours from Frederick II in 1238. Both were present with the Imperial forces at the battle of Cortenovo and it was only in the following year, when Azzo's suspicions of the Emperor grew too strong for him, that the Estensi left the Imperial camp.[2] Their unswerving opposition to Ezzelino thereafter brought them a reputation as the champions of the church, and as such, they were highly commended by Innocent IV in 1247.[4] In 1256, Rolandino described Azzo d'Este as 'the principal member of the Church in these parts' yet one suspects that the Guelphism of the Estensi was to a great extent only the accidental by-product of Ezzelino's superior skill in handling Frederick II.[4]

On the other side, it has long been noted that once his position was assured, Ezzelino's attitude to Frederick II was much more like that of an independent ally than a faithful subject. Rolandino clearly held this view, but the care with which he exculpates the Emperor from Ezzelino's misdoings has another aspect to it, illustrating that Rolandino's hostility to the Da Romano did not lead him to reject the Empire. Not only is Frederick's personal character spared as far as possible from criticism, but the Empire as an institution is

[1] *Cronica*, pp. 52, 109; cf. 'parti Ecclesiae et domini Marchionis Estensis', *Stat. Com.* 1191.
[2] Rolandino, pp. 23, 58, 68.
[3] Muratori, *Antichità Estensi* II, pp. 8–9.
[4] 'Dompnus Marchio erat in hiis partibus membrum Ecclesiae principale', *Cronica*, p. 127.

never questioned or attacked. The Paduan historian even went so far as to 'reconstruct' an Imperial letter in which Frederick is made to praise the Estensi for their services to the Empire and himself in the early thirteenth century.[1] The enmity of Azzo and Ezzelino was, as far as we can tell, absolute, but their Guelphism and Ghibellinism was only contingent.

While many of the party struggles which took place in the March of Treviso in the first half of the thirteenth century were strictly local affairs, from time to time there would be a major campaign in which forces from outside the region would be called in until the conflict took on the complexion of a Guelph-Ghibelline contest of almost national significance. On these occasions, the wider ramifications of the Guelph party can be seen coming into play. For example, at the capture of Ferrara from Salinguerra in 1240, the *pars Marchionis* was led by Azzo d'Este, Biaquino da Camino and Riccardo da San Bonifacio leading a Mantuan contingent. But the initiative for the campaign appears to have come from the bishop of Ferrara, and the attacking forces included an apostolic legate, Gregorio da Montelongo, and the Venetian Doge, Giacomo Tiepolo, as well as Alberico da Romano who was at that time opposed to his brother's party. The Venetian Stefano Badoer, who had led the Paduans against the Da Romano in 1228, was appointed the first *podestà* of the captured city.[2]

The recapture of Padua from Ezzelino's lieutenant in 1256 and the subsequent four-year war to the death against the Da Romano, show an even wider combination of forces. The initiative was Papal, and the crusaders assembled in Venice under the leadership of the legate, Filippo, archbishop of Ravenna. The Venetian supporters of the expedition included Marco Quirini, who was elected *podestà* by the Paduan exiles before they left Venice, and Marco Badoer, the marshal of the army, whose son became a magnate in the Paduan contado through his marriage with the heiress Balzanella da Peraga. Giovanni Badoer, the son of Stefano, became *podestà* of the liberated city in 1257–8 and 1261–2, and the Tiepolo too were evidently friends of the restored commune, since Lorenzo Tiepolo was chosen as *podestà* in 1264–5.[3] At the beginning of

---

[1] *Cronica*, pp. 62–3; see also pp. 87, 172.
[2] Ibid. pp. 71–2.
[3] Rolandino, p. 111; *Liber Regiminum*, pp. 323–6.

the campaign, the Marchese Azzo was defending Mantua against an attack by Ezzelino in person, but within a week of the fall of Padua he had received the submission of his fortresses in the Paduan contado, and within a month he was commanding a mixed force, which included Venetian and Bolognese contingents, which was defending the city against a threatened counter-attack.[1] The part played by the Sanbonifacio in these events does not seem to have been recorded, but in 1258 Count Lodovico was with the legate, the exiled bishop of Verona, and the Mantuans in an ill-fated expedition to relieve Brescia.[2] The defeat of this force by Ezzelino precipitated a crisis, as the tyrant was now in a position to threaten not simply the whole March but much of Lombardy and even Milan itself. The response was a council of the *pars Ecclesiastica* of the threatened region which succeeded in enlisting the help of Ezzelino's former allies, Oberto Pelavicino and Buoso da Dovara, the rulers of Cremona. In return for this support, this nominally Guelph alliance agreed to recognise the Emperor Frederick's successor Manfred, though the parties promised to try to bring about his reconciliation with the church. It was to this combination that Ezzelino finally succumbed in 1259, leaving his brother Alberico to be dispatched by the Paduans, Vicentines and Trevisans in August 1260.[3]

The campaigns of 1256–60, in so far as they affected the March of Treviso, represented a decisive victory—a rarity in that kind of warfare. The Da Romano family, which formed the nucleus of the party opposed to the Estensi, was exterminated and the party had to grow up again on a new basis. But the local situation differed in each city and district; the triumph of the *pars Marchionis* was not equally complete throughout the March.

In Verona, on the death of Ezzelino, power passed not to the Veronese *pars Marchionis et Comitis* but to Mastino della Scala, the head of the *Societas Mercatorum*, representing the trading element among the *popolo*. At first, Lodovico da San Bonifacio and his supporters were allowed to return, and a

---

[1] *Chronicon Marchiae Tarvisinae*, p. 27; Rolandino, pp. 127, 130.
[2] *Chronicon Marchiae Tarvisinae*, p. 32.
[3] Rolandino, pp. 150–71; for the text of the alliance against Ezzelino see Cipolla, *Relazioni Verona-Mantova Sec. XIII*, pp. 65–83.

treaty was signed between Verona and the Mantuan commune, which they controlled. But in the September of the following year, 1260, Count Lodovico and his friends were expelled again and, though there is some obscurity in the chronicles on this point, it seems most likely that they never returned to the city, although, supported from their main base in Mantua, they campaigned intermittently in the Veronese contado until 1269.[1] The rejection of the *pars Marchionis* on the morrow of its victory, by one of the great cities of the March under the leadership of a man who had held office under the Da Romano, was certainly a major setback which boded ill for the peace in the future. At first, however, Mastino della Scala showed no wish to quarrel with the neighbouring cities where the *pars Marchionis* was dominant, nor had he any immediate desire to follow Ezzelino's example and reveal his control of the commune openly, for in April 1262 he allowed Verona to join the communes of Padua, Treviso and Vicenza in a defensive alliance in which the governments pledged themselves to try to prevent the domination of any one person in any of the cities concerned.[2]

In Vicenza and Treviso, the two smaller cities of the March, the elimination of the Da Romano left the magnates still divided into two roughly equal factions. In Vicenza, Ezzelino's lieutenants fled on the news of his death, the exiles returned and, in the words of the chronicler Smereglo, 'there was a great peace between almost everyone'. But rivalries soon developed between the noble families in the relatively large Vicentine contado which the small commune proved itself

[1] Apart from the bare chroniclers' accounts in Parisio de Cereta, pp. 16–17, and the *Annales Mantuani*, p. 23, events in Verona in these critical years are not well recorded. The cryptic remarks of the *Chronicon Marchiae Tarvisinae*, pp. 57–8, that on the death of Ezzelino, 'Accidit namque Veronensibus quod dicit Job; quia dum nimis timuerunt pruinam, irruit super eos nix immo grando et glacies infernalis, et dum quesierunt equi fortitudinem declinare, in dentes leonis sevissimi incurrerunt', seem to represent the disgust of a supporter of the *pars Marchionis* at the transfer of power to the Della Scala. For further discussion, see C. Cipolla, 'Il Conte Loisio di San Bonifacio, podestà di Piacenza nel 1277', *ARIV* LXIV, ii (1904), pp. 285–303; L. Simeoni, 'La formazione della signoria scaligera', *AAV* V, iii (1926), pp. 117–67; and idem, 'Lodovico da San Bonifacio e gli inizii della signoria scaligera', *ARIV* XCII, ii (1932–3), pp. 1389–414.

[2] 'Omnes civitates predictas in statu pacifico et tranquillo manutenebunt sine dominio alicuius persone', Lampertico, *Statuti del comune di Vicenza*, p. 245.

unable to control. For a time, peace was preserved by Bishop Bartolomeo da Breganze, who was granted special powers by the commune, but in 1262 a flare-up in the intermittent war in the contado between the commune and the magnates of the *pars Marchesana sive Guelfa* on the one side, and the *pars Imperialis* on the other, led to Veronese and Paduan intervention and the loss of Vicenza's independence.[1]

In Treviso, the ending of the tyranny of Alberico da Romano, which had been nominally Guelph for the greater part of its existence, and the return of the Da Camino and Camposampiero, also Guelph, must have created a situation even more difficult to reconcile with the idea of two 'national' parties than usual. It is not without significance that the Trevisan parties had their own local names, the Reds, with allegedly Imperialist and Da Romano connections, being led by the Castelli family, while the Whites, headed by the Da Camino, were aligned with the *pars Marchionis*. Like Vicenza, Treviso was a comparatively small city with a large contado and in the long run the commune proved too weak to control the factions. Some kind of balance was maintained until 1283 when Gerardo da Camino, with Paduan help, expelled the Castelli and set up a *signoria*.[2]

In comparison with the other cities of the March, the strength of the *pars Marchionis* among the Paduan nobility in 1256 was overwhelming. From the early years of the thirteenth century at least, the majority of the Paduan aristocracy seem to have accepted the social and political leadership of the Estensi and Camposanpiero, and many were prepared to follow Azzo VII's lead and break with Ezzelino as soon as the Emperor had left the region. The heads of the Carraresi, Avvocati and Da Lozzo were all considered friends of the Marchese in the late 1230s; Giacomo da Carrara and his cousin Avezuto Avvocato, who deserted Ezzelino's camp together in 1238 were both captured and executed by him in 1240.[3] During the nineteen years of Ezzelino's rule in Padua, most of the noble families tried at some time to work with the

---

[1] Smereglo, pp. 8–12. There is confirmation that Bishop Bartolomeo held special powers in the treaty of 1264, Lampertico, loc. cit. For the Paduan acquisition of Vicenza see below, pp. 221-7

[2] Picotti, *I Caminesi*, pp. 74–105.

[3] Rolandino, pp. 58–9, 61, 68–9, 73.

tyrant, but the experiment was always disastrous. Guglielmo Camposanpiero did not break with Ezzelino until 1240, when he retired to his castle of Treville, in Trevisan territory, where he remained under the protection of Alberico da Romano until 1246, when a reconciliation with Ezzelino took place. The Dalesmanini, a family not particularly associated with the Estensi, survived until 1249 when three leading members of the family came under suspicion and were killed. Their fall involved Guglielmo Camposanpiero, who was their kinsman by marriage, and he was eventually executed in 1251, by which time his successor as head of the family, Tiso III, was already with the Marchese in Ferrara.[1] Rolandino records that Bontraverso Maltraversi, of the Castelnovo branch of the Paduan comital family, deserted the Estensi to whom his line had previously been most faithful in 1241 and joined Ezzelino, his daughter becoming the tyrant's wife in 1249. In 1253, Giacomino Schinelli, who belonged to a neighbouring branch of the family, saved Ezzelino from an attempt to assassinate him in Verona, but soon after he was rewarded with exile, and other members of the family were exiled or killed. The documents relating to the successive alliances with Oberto Pelavicino show the paltry support which Ezzelino was able to obtain from the Paduan nobility.[2] In the negotiations of 1252, members of the Schinelli, Castelnovo and Da Lozzo families are named, but in October 1254, the native nobility were represented in the Consiglio Maggiore by only two individuals, Bontraverso da Castelnovo and Guido da Lozzo. Even Bontraverso and his sons suffered imprisonment during the last months of the Da Romano regime in Padua.[3] In these circumstances, when the *Liber Regiminum* reports the return to Padua in 1260 of certain noble adherents of Ezzelino, it is hard to believe that they can have been very many or of much account.[4] Even allowing for the universal bias against the Da Romano, it seems incontrovertible that by 1256 Ezzelino had largely destroyed his own party among the Paduan nobility.

[1] Rolandino, pp. 72, 81, 94–5; *Liber Regiminum*, pp. 314–15.
[2] AS Cremona, ASC 1794–5.
[3] Rolandino, pp. 75, 90, 103–5; *Chronicon Marchiae Tarvisinae*, p. 26.
[4] P. 325. Neither Rolandino, nor any of the other chronicles throw any further light on these noble followers of Ezzelino. The young Guido da Lozzo may have been one of them.

Resistance to the Da Romano seems to have been particularly strong among the more substantial members of the Paduan *popolo*. In this connection, the oath of 1254 provides the most valuable evidence as to the state of the commune in the last years of Ezzelino's government. As has already been remarked, the relatively small number of judges and notaries which appear there is susceptible of more than one explanation; more conclusive is the rarity with which the great names of the communal period are met with among the 2,606 individuals who took the oath.[1] A few individuals like Buzzaccarino or Tommaso da S. Lucia did not appear because they were in Ezzelino's service elsewhere in the March, but the absence of great families like the Forzatè-Capodilista, Lemici and Capodivacca, not to mention the large number of lesser families whose names are common in the communal period, must denote a rift between the government and a substantial part of the population. Some of the rich *popolani* were in prison or in exile; many must have found ways of avoiding an oath which tied them to an unpopular regime, for only 2,606 names were collected in Padua compared with about 8,000 in Verona. Thus the Cremonese documents tend to confirm Rolandino's account of the general detestation which the Da Romano tyranny aroused in Padua. Although the historian exaggerated the numbers put to death, his stories of individuals and families imprisoned, exiled or killed must have been broadly accurate, since the audience at the first public reading of the history in 1262 was in a position to know whether he spoke the truth. Even some of those who tried to serve the tyrant eventually fell prey to his suspicions. Anselmino Enselmini, *podestà* of Verona in 1247, 'who, for a long time, Ezzelino held dearer to him than all his other knights' was imprisoned in 1254; Tommaso da S. Lucia, *podestà* of Vicenza from 1252 to 1254, was finally suspected of treason, arrested and killed.[2]

If Ezzelino did succeed in retaining any significant body of supporters in Padua, it would be among the lesser members of the *popolo*, the guildsmen and artisans, that they are most likely to have been found. During a part, at least, of Ezzelino's period of rule, the city was growing and prosperous and it

[1] See above, pp. 33, 128.
[2] *Syllabus Potestatum*, p. 393; Rolandino, p. 107; Smereglo, p. 7.

would be natural for the newly enriched classes to attach themselves to the regime. Ezzelino's Paduan ministers Enghelfredo the tailor and Buzzaccarino the judge both seem to have belonged to this category. Though it would be naïve to assume that they were all whole-hearted supporters of the government, the number of tradesmen among the oath-takers of 1254 is impressive. Ezzelino seems to have deliberately followed a policy of widening the franchise in the cities he controlled, for the Veronese Consiglio Maggiore was raised from 525 to 1,285 members between 1252 and 1254.[1] Of the 665 Paduan councillors named in 1254, nearly 150 were recognisably of the guildsman and artisan class, and since after 1256 the council was reduced to 600 members, and room had to be found for the Guelphs, many of these must have been disenfranchised until the council was increased to 1,000 members in 1277. The possibility that there was an element in the Paduan *popolo* opposed to the *pars Marchionis* in the years after 1256 cannot be ruled out; all that can be said is that there is no evidence that they ever constituted a serious danger to the restored commune.

There is nothing to suggest any serious resistance to the restoration of the Paduan commune after the fall of the city to the *pars Marchionis* in June 1256. Strictly speaking, the term restoration is inappropriate as, in theory, the commune had not ceased to exist during the Ezzelino period though, in fact, its independence had no doubt been severely curtailed. But a commune was not simply a legal structure, it was primarily an association of people, and the capture of the city must have been followed by a considerable change in personnel. The new commune formed by the Paduan exiles before they left Venice had to be grafted on to the stump of the old commune which remained in Padua. Almost nothing is known of how this was accomplished, but the indications are that there were no serious difficulties. Rolandino stresses that by the time the city fell, the exiles and those left within the walls felt as one; consequently, though there was some pillaging, there was hardly any bloodshed.[2] The victorious party does not seem to have

---

[1] These are the actual numbers who took the oath in those years; see L. Simeoni, 'Nuovi documenti sull'ultimo periodo della signoria di Ezzelino' *Rendiconto della sessione della R. Accad. di Scienze dell'Istituto Bolognese*, ser. III, iv (1929–30).

[2] Rolandino, p. 124.

been unduly vindictive towards the lesser members of the *par. Eccelini*. Some citizens who had been members of the Consiglio Maggiore in 1254 continued to hold public office after 1256; the judge Buzzaccarino, who had been Ezzelino's vicar in Verona, was employed by the new commune as early as 1258. Even Enghelfredo and Alberto Bibi, who are said to have been Ezzelino's treasurers, suffered no permanent disabilities.[1] The vast Da Romano estates provided ample booty to be divided among the victors, and the only other confiscation which has been recorded was the property of Antonio Ardenghi, *podestà* of Vicenza, who was killed fighting against the *pars Marchionis;* this was granted by the Papal legate to Giacomo Conti of Arquà in 1257.[2] This moderation may do much to explain why the Paduan commune was not threatened by bands of irreconcilable exiles during the crucial early years of its existence.

The indispensable source for the Paduan constitution is the code of statutes compiled in 1276, twenty years after the restoration of the commune. As a guide to the details of its organisation at an earlier date, the code is not entirely reliable, for although the statutes are dated, they were often amended without any record being made of the fact. However, the general similarities to the Vicentine code of 1264 suggest that the changes introduced after that time were not very radical. The Paduan statutes are arranged in four books, after the pattern normal in the Italian communes of the period. Although most of the statutes of a constitutional significance are to be found in the first book, they present at first sight a formidable mass of detailed regulations. As in the case of the topographical layout of the city, a contemporary guide is called for. Unfortunately, Rolandino will not serve us here, for although he had a firm grasp of political realities, he never once discusses the Paduan constitution. In part, he may have felt that the discussion of such a technical matter would have been out of place in a literary history, but mainly one suspects that the omission was due to the recognition that the details of the communal organisation were not important, compared to the question of who was in control of them, while the fundamental lines of the constitution changed so rarely that he probably

---

[1] See above, pp. 116–17, 150, 169.
[2] Verci, *Storia degli Eccelini*, III, doc. n. 232.

took them for granted. The only Paduan writer to produce a radical discussion of the communal institutions was Marsiglio Mainardini; it is doubtful if his analysis can be improved upon.[1]

As Marsiglio recognised, the essence of the Paduan state was the citizen body, the *universitas civium*, or rather its *pars valentior* or weightier part. This was the Legislator, and in Padua its embodiment was the Consiglio Maggiore. The exact criteria by which members of the council were selected are never stated; although a minimum tax assessment of £50 was required, the additional qualifications were probably personal and indefinable; it must not be forgotten that Paduan politics operated on a very small scale. Apparently the membership of the council was revised at irregular intervals, but in the meantime, vacant seats were generally passed to the next of kin, or could be bequeathed by will.[2] Marsiglio's point that the legislative body must be sufficiently numerous really to represent the *universitas civium* was admirably met by the Paduan Consiglio Maggiore which, after it had finally been increased to a thousand members in 1277, must have included at least one in ten of the adult male population, twice the proportion of enfranchised citizens in the united Italy of 1861.[3] Another way in which the Paduan council was clearly the prototype of Marsiglio's Legislator was that it really was the sole legislative power in the state, and when Marsiglio wrote had been so for the previous sixty years. While it is true that some of its power, notably the fixing of the method of selection of the *podestà*, were delegated to a smaller council chosen from the members, the sovereignty of the greater council was never impaired, and one wonders whether the complicated regulations defining the relative powers of the two councils were ever observed in practice.[4] For obvious reasons of convenience, the

---

[1] The close connection between Marsiglio's analysis of the state and the Paduan constitution of his time has rarely been recognised except in the most general terms; by far the most thorough attempt to trace the parallels to date is A. Gewirth, *Marsilius of Padua* (1951–6), I, pp. 23–31.

[2] *Stat. Com.* 16, 16.I, 17, 19. Examples of places left by will, AD 4476, 4959, Corona, 1133.

[3] 'Quia enim lege debent omnes cives mensurari secundum prop‾rcionem debitam, et nemo sibi scienter nocet aut vult iniustum, ideoque volunt omnes aut plurimi legem convenientem communi civium conferenti', *Defensor Pacis*, ed. R. Scholz, MGH Leges VII (1933), pp. 68–9.

[4] *Stat. Com.* 15, 18, 29, 31.

detailed drafting of legislation was delegated to *statutarii*, but it was given legal force only by a vote in the Consiglio Maggiore. The other part of the Marsilian state, the *pars principans*, was composed in Padua of two elements: the foreign *podestà* and his staff, and the native Paduans who served as *podestà* or garrison commanders in the contado, or as judges, notaries or laymen in the central administration. The laymen, that is the *podestà, capitanei* and others were appointed either directly or indirectly in the councils, or by lot; the professional men were selected in rotation by their professional organisations.[1] The function of the *pars principans* was to administer the law, which was framed as far as possible to meet every foreseeable situation, and not to make it; a committee of four *cataveri* was charged with seeing that officials from the *podestà* downwards did not exceed their powers or accept bribes.[2] The only occasion when the *podestà* and the officials in office might take independent action was in time of war or in other emergencies, and even then the citizens generally set up an executive committee with closely defined powers as soon as was practicable. The statutes are permeated with the mistrust of uncontrolled power.

It remains to describe the part played in the Paduan constitution by the association of the *popolo* which in Padua, as in some neighbouring cities, was known as the *comunanza*. Although its early history is obscure, it would seem that the *comunanza* was formed among the substantial citizens who did not possess feudal jurisdictions in the early thirteenth century, for the protection of their mutual interests against the nobles and *milites* who controlled the commune, and in the course of time became the instrument through which the *popolo* came to exercise, in law at least, a dominant role in the affairs of the city. The statutes in the code of 1276 relating to the *comunanza* contain many traces of the early militant period, when the *popolo* was still fighting to acquire its rights. Members were still required to take a long oath annually, and their names were enrolled by quarters; each *centenario* had its banner and the whole *popolo* its standard, to which members were sworn to rally in case of any civil disturbance.[3] At the same time, it

[1] *Stat. Com.* 228–31.
[2] *Stat. Com.* 94–109, 613–27.
[3] *Stat. Com.* 442–64.

is clear that by 1276, the commune and the *comunanza* were largely identified. The oath of the *comunanza* bound members equally to uphold the city and commune, and the *podestà* promised to act 'for the good and peaceful state of the *comunanza* and the whole city of Padua'.[1] From being an association of the less privileged, the *comunanza* had become a privileged body within the state. Members enjoyed special protection in the courts against non-members.[2] Apparently, although the statutes are not quite explicit on this point, enrolment in the *comunanza* was a necessary condition for a seat in the Consiglio Maggiore and for any full participation in the public life of the city.[2] The relationship with Marsiglio's idea of the *pars valentior* of the *universitas civium* is sufficiently clear. Unfortunately, no record of the numbers or the conditions of membership is extant. Clearly, the *comunanza* was a wider group than the thousand members of the Consiglio Maggiore; on the other hand, not all of the guildsmen were members. In addition to the indefinable criteria of loyalty and political reliability, there was probably a minimum property qualification and possibly maximum also, in order to exclude the magnates.

The dominance of the *comunanza* within the restored commune was ultimately guaranteed by the armed force of its members, and the statutes provide for the formation of special corps of horse and foot ready to go into action against any threat to the security of the *popolo* or the state.[4] But in normal circumstances, the *comunanza* exerted its influence over the organs of the commune through the *anziani* who were its own elected representatives. The twelve members who, until about 1300, made up this very important body within the Paduan state, were selected every two months by a process of indirect election, in the presence of all the members of the *comunanza* congregated about the Palazzo Comunale. On the

---

[1] *Stat. Com.* 60. There is a long discussion of the *comunanza* in M. A. Zorzi, *L'ordinamento comunale*, pp. 5–47.

[2] *Stat. Com.* 461–2.

[3] This is the logical conclusion to be drawn from *Stat. Com.* 636 which begins 'Statuimus quod nullus de male ablatis et nullus qui non est de comunancia debeat coram potestate Padue vel eius assessoribus et consulibus et eorum notariis aliisque officialibus ire vel stare . . .'; but when the qualifications for office or the council are directly stated, as in *Stat. Com.* 16, 16.I, 232–51, enrolment in the *comunanza* is not mentioned.

[4] *Stat. Com.* 447–8, 456.

first day, electors who were selected by lot chose the four *anziani della comunanza*, one for each quarter of the city, who represented the *popolo* organised on a territorial basis. On the second day, electors from among the councillors co-opted by the existing *anziani* named the eight guilds held to be 'meliores et utiliores', and from each of these a man was chosen to represent the members of the *comunanza* who were also guildsmen.[1] The *anziani* thus elected had considerable powers. They could impose a ban on members of the *comunanza* and could report crimes for investigation directly to the *podestà*. With their co-opted councillors, the *anziani* were required to meet at least twice a week to consider matters of common interest; in 1283 a *palazzo* was built for them. The *podestà* was bound to show them all letters of public interest within two days of their receipt.[2] Most important of all, by a statute dated 1257, the *podestà* was required to swear that he would allow the *anziani* to assemble 'their *comunanza*' whenever they wished, and likewise call the Consiglio Maggiore or Minore for them when requested.[3]. Most of the recorded resolutions and legislation passed by the Consiglio Maggiore were initiated by the *anziani*, who also supervised the secret ballot. In case of emergency, the *anziani* could consult with the *podestà* over the appointment of an outside *capitano del popolo* to protect their interests. The main checks on the abuse of their powers was their short term of office, the necessity for corporate action, and a subsequent scrutiny of their acts by four *cataveri ancianorum* specially elected in the Consiglio Maggiore.[4] Even subject to these limitations, it is clear that the *anziani* were in a very strong position to exercise a directing influence over the many councils and

[1] *Stat. Com.* 408–20.
[2] *Stat. Com.* 421, 425, 437, 33.
[3] 'Et ut societas et comunancia populi Paduani maneteneatur, conservetur et augmentetur in suo statu et honore, bona fide operam dabo secundum quod ancianis melius et utilius videbitur expedire; et quandocumque predicti anciani suam comunanciam voluerint congregare, ut congregare possint ubicumque eis videbitur congreganda, permittam et operam dabo. Et si predicti anciani a me pecierint conscilium sexcentorum vel sexaginta eis dabo, et faciam proponi et proponam in dictis consciliis ea que a me requisierint, et permittam super hiis consuli per eos qui consulunt. Et faciam in conscilio seu in consciliis reformari et refformata inviolabiliter observari, et hoc faciam sine dilacione ad voluntatem dictorum ancianorum, non obstante aliquo statuto'. *Stat. Com.* 111.
[4] *Stat. Com.* 27, 422, 430, 465, 432.

officials among whom the authority in the Paduan state was diffused. More than any other body, they were the connecting link between the *universitas civium* and the *pars principans*.

The communal organisation detailed in the code of 1276 is typical of the kind of constitution found in the Italian cities from the first half of the thirteenth century onwards; apart from the large numbers employed in the administration, it has no unusual features. Perpetuated rather than adopted in 1256, it was essentially conservative, it was the kind of constitution which in almost every comparable city was being superseded, in fact if not always in law, by new political forms based on the *signoria* of a single man or family, or, in an exceptional case, by a commune organised through the guilds. In Padua, though there were pressures in both directions, the commune survived with comparatively minor changes, not simply *de jure* but as a working constitution, until 1318 and in some respects until 1328. The reasons for this unusual stability lie not in the constitution but in the nature of Paduan society, assisted by the city's favourable position and a degree of good fortune. The next chapter will trace some of the episodes in that survival; here we shall consider only some of the factors which enabled the commune to find its feet in the years immediately following 1256, while Padua's neighbours all lost their freedom, in one way or another, within twenty-five years.

The stability of the Paduan commune may be seen as a reflection of the strength and unity of the elements within it and the relative weakness of the forces pressing upon it from outside. The essence of the Paduan commune was the *popolo*, bound together in the *comunanza* and represented in the Consiglio Maggiore. We do not know exactly how wide the membership of the *comunanza* was, but it clearly embraced two economic and social classes. Signs of this are the distinction for the purpose of military service between the *milites pro commune* and the *pedites*, which probably corresponded very roughly to the division between the non-guildsmen and the guildsmen. The two classes are also reflected in the difference between the *anziani della comunanza* (*de comunancia*), who had to be *milites* with a tax assessment of over £200 and immovables worth £500, and the *anziani* representing the guilds (*pro frataleis*), for whom the property qualification was immovables worth £200 and a tax assessment of £100.¹ The names of the *anziani* which are known bear out that this distinction was a real one; members of old feudal families like Ugolino Avvocato and Enghelerio da Montagnone, knights like Zilio Maccaruffi and powerful citizens like Caroto Capodilista and Traversino Dalesmanini must have belonged to a very different class from the majority of the tailors, skinners and shoemakers, many of whom lacked family names, who served as *anziani* for the guilds.²

There is very little evidence bearing upon the delicate question of the relative power of the two groups within the *comunanza*. The constitution of 1276 weighted the vital college of the *anziani* two to one in favour of the guildsmen, but in practice this must often have been offset by the superior status and experience of the *anziani della comunanza*. One of the latter was always a judge, known as the *iudex ancianorum,* and he was the *ex officio* president and spokesman of the group, which must have counted for a lot.³ Although in the course of time, the constitutional balance was tilted still more in favour of the guildsmen, there is no evidence that this was ever the occasion for violent disagreement. This must be attributed to the overlap of interests and personnel in the two groups. On the economic plane, the predominance of agriculture and administration in the Paduan state meant that there was no clear-cut division between the urban consumers and the rural producers; most guildsmen had some agricultural interests, and the prevailing food surplus in the Paduan contado, which seems to have lasted until the beginning of the fourteenth century, must have removed one possible bone of contention. Similarly, there was no social gulf between the guildsmen and the other citizens,

---

¹ *Stat. Com.* 411, 416.I.
² AS Padua, Fruttaroli I, f. 5r; Verci, *Acta ad Patavinos Spectantia,* p. 49–53; AS Venice, *Codex Tarvisinus,* f. 11v; Verci, *Marca Trivigiana,* doc. n. 170; AS Modena, AMS IV, nn. 8–11; Brunacci, *Appendice al CDP* II, n. 102. The fullest lists of *anziani* still extant (only one complete) are to be found in Lampertico, *Statuti del Comune di Vicenza,* pp. 245–6, and AS Modena, AMS IV, nn. 8–11.
³ *Stat. Com.* 412; *Statuti Carraresi,* f. 49v. The leadership of the *iudex ancianorum* may be inferred from the report in the *Liber Regiminum,* p. 342, that it was he who carried the standard of the *comunanza* in the celebrations of 1300, and also from the fact that he was made responsible for the conduct of the other *anziani della comunanza* by a statute of 1321 (*Statuta Specialorum,* MS BP 940, f. 14v, Roberti, *Le Corporazioni,* p. 85). For changes in the number of *anziani* see below, p. 245.

and there was some social mobility between one group and the other. But most important of all, the *popolo* was held together by the administrative class. The professional administrators were divided, as we have seen, into judges and notaries. While the College of Judges was not considered to be one of the guilds, the *fratalea notariorum* was the dominant guild both in numbers and influence, the one guild from which an *anziano* was always chosen. However, under normal conditions, the common interests of the two professions as parts of the administrative class made the differences between them of comparatively little account. The commune had created this class, and its members in their turn had an overriding interest in preserving the commune. They were in a strong position to do so, for their daily business kept them near the centre of power. One suspects that a high proportion of the 150–250 members of the Consiglio Maggiore who most frequently voted were notaries, judges or laymen employed in the administration. The statutes also mention a body called the *curia officialium* which consisted of the notaries, and presumably the judges, currently in office. This was responsible for the appointment of ambassadors, and may have had an important say in the formation of policy behind the scenes.[1]

The elements excluded from power in the Paduan state fall into two unequal groups. On the one hand there were those whose estate was too low for admission to the *comunanza* and to political rights. Essentially, they were those who did not have the necessary minimum tax assessment of £50 for membership of the council or £25 for minor administrative offices.[2] This class amounted to perhaps nine-tenths of the population of the city, and practically all the inhabitants of the contado, and unless they happened to be guildsmen, in which case they might exert some influence through their guild and its officials, they were entirely without a voice in public

---

[1] *Stat. Com.* 36, 37, 201, 613.
[2] *Stat. Com.* 16.I, 248, 403. M. A. Zorzi, *L'ordinamento comunale*, pp. 18–32 discusses this aspect at length, laying great emphasis on *Stat. Com.* 412.II which laid down that certain types of manual labourer, and others who were not economically independent, should not be present at the election of the *anziani*. Since such persons would not have been members of the *comunanza* in the first place, the effect of the statute cannot have been to disenfranchise them as Zorzi suggests; the most likely aim would be to prevent their being used to overawe the electors.

affairs. Generally they were purely passive members of the commonwealth, powerless unless led in arms by the leaders of a faction. So far as is known the *parlamentum*, the ancient assembly of the whole population, met only once in the communal period, and that was to confirm the election of Giacomo da Carrara to the *signoria*, which had already been carried out in the Consiglio Maggiore. The Paduan commune saw no rising of the Ciompi, probably because Padua had no large industrial proletariat. The workers were employed in small workshops or trading establishments which were easily controlled by the guild masters.

The other class which was excluded from the *comunanza*, as it were by definition, were the *magnates, potentiores, magni homines* or *male ablati*.[1] They were those nobles and non-nobles who were believed to be too powerful or insufficiently reliable to be allowed to participate in the government of the commune. The lists which have been preserved suggest that in the period 1256–66 the *male ablati* were drawn from only nine families, the Carrara, Camposanpiero, Carturo, Da Lozzo, Castelnovo, Schinelli, Avvocato, Da Peraga and Dalesmanini, but that by 1278 the number of families had increased to about twenty. It is doubtful, however, if the number of persons involved ever exceeded a hundred. They might nevertheless have been a considerable menace to the new political order, as the unhappy fates of the communes of Vicenza and Treviso show.

In fact, the restored commune never seems to have been in serious danger from the local magnates for at least the first twenty years of its existence. In part, this must be attributed to the attitude of the citizens. If Rolandino is to be trusted at all, they emerged from the yoke of the Da Romano determined never again to suffer the tyranny of any individual. As the historian went out of his way to stress, Ezzelino's victims had included 'some who were knights, and some more than knights, some burghers and some who were honourable *popolani*'; all classes were united by a common history of suffering.[2] So,

---

[1] The main statutes relating to *male ablati* are *Stat. Com.* 628–45. For the subsequent development of Paduan anti-magnatial legislation, see below, p. 238. *Magnati* and *nobiles* should not be confused, see above, p. 63.

[2] 'Horum autem aliqui milites et aliqui plus quam milites, aliqui burgenses et aliqui fuerunt honorabiles populares. Studiosus namque totis viribus Eccelinus Paduam deformare, non ponebat curam ad minimos; quamvis eciam et de illis aliqui perierunt', Rolandino, p. 108.

although the commune revived the anti-magnatial measures which had been in force in the early thirteenth century almost at once, the statutes were moderate and were probably applied with discretion. There was a considerable circumstantial element in the definition of a magnate, as is shown by a document of 1300 which records that, in response to a petition by an injured *popolano*, the council ruled that Antonio Cane 'be understood to be a great and powerful noble, and be enrolled among the *male ablati* and be liable to their penalties'.[1] The lot of a magnate was much more tolerable than it would appear from the statutes, taken at their face value. In the early fourteenth century, when class conflict was in some ways more acute, there is evidence of the commune defending strenuously the interests of men who undoubtedly belonged to the magnate class.[2]

Mainly, however, the Paduan commune escaped the fate of its neighbours because of the conditions prevailing among the magnates themselves. They were overwhelmingly of one party and remarkably free from major feuds. Of the generation alive in 1256, many could look back on long years of exile together. It is known, for example, that Tiso III Camposanpiero and Guerico da Vigodarzere were in Ferrara in 1250-1, and the tradition of the good Marchese Azzo and his generous hospitality to exiles survived into the fourteenth century, when it was recorded by Da Nono.[3] Many shared the additional bond created by service under the same banner. Tiso Camposanpiero fought with Azzo d'Este and the Papal legate at Argenta in the March of Ancona in 1254; in the crusading army of 1256, he was standard-bearer. Rolandino mentions three of the Carraresi as members of the victorious host.[4] These exiles had suffered severely not only from the destruction of their property but also, less tangibly, from the interruption of their customary control over their estates. Their first concern seems to have been to build up again their old spheres of influence in the contado, and their power in the city seems to have suffered an eclipse in the first years of the commune from

---

[1] 'Dominus Antonius intellegatur esse magnus nobilis et potens, et scribatur in numero maleablatorum et subiaceat poenis eorum', AD 4220.
[2] See below, p. 260.
[3] AS Modena, AMS II, nn. 62-4, 67, 71; *De Generatione*, f. 16v.
[4] Rolandino, pp. 112, 118.

which it only gradually recovered. Above all, power and wealth were fairly evenly shared among a number of leading families so that none of them was strong enough alone to threaten the commune. The Estensi were the undoubted leaders, but they were chiefly interested in consolidating their grip on Ferrara. Similarly, the Camposanpiero were distracted by their interests in the Trevigiano. Guido da Lozzo's leadership of the Paduan Guelphs cannot be discerned before 1278; Guecillo Dalesmanini did not achieve a dangerous pre-eminence until the early 1290s.

Such were the circumstances in which the revived Paduan commune, formed within the matrix of the *pars Marchionis* and protected by the favourable environment which its victory created, took root and flourished through over half a century of almost unbroken political success.

CHAPTER VIII

The Expansion of the Paduan Commune

THE political history of the Paduan commune, from its restoration in 1256 until the coming of Henry of Luxemburg in 1310, may be summarised as a story of dramatic external expansion accompanied by a much less radical internal reorganisation. The former was accomplished in two main stages. In 1266, the Paduans gained effective control of Vicenza and its large territory, including the subject town of Bassano; then, after years of effort, the commune finally succeeded in 1308 in extending its power southwards over the Adige by annexing the county of Rovigo. Internally, the initial reduction of the franchise when the Consiglio Maggiore was brought down to 600 members, was finally reversed in 1277, when membership was fixed at 1,000. After this, there was no further extension of political rights but, beginning in 1293, an attempt was made to give the guildsmen a greater influence within the *comunanza*. The Union of the Guilds and its councils and officials became an accepted part of the Paduan state, supplementing but not superseding the existing constitution.

It has been suggested that any approach which concerns itself only with the communes and their policies is inadequate to explain the political life of the March and its adjacent regions during the first half of the thirteenth century. Alongside the communes, and in some cases overshadowing them, were the great families and the *partes* made up of their followers. The period of intense party strife which culminated in the destruction of the Da Romano *signorie* in Verona, Padua, Vicenza and Treviso between 1256 and 1260, might have been expected to shift the balance of power decisively in favour of the cities, which were steadily growing in wealth and population all the time. In fact, the change brought about was far from radical. The two smaller communes of Vicenza and Treviso continued to be dominated by magnatial factions, and even the policies of Verona and Padua, both great cities, are incomprehensible without reference to the nobly led *partes*. As the decades passed, the lines of the old divisions became blurred, but it was not until 1311 that the natural antagonism of Verona and Padua and their struggle for the domination of the region, emerged as the axis of political alignment within the March.

The expansion of the Paduan commune to the north and north-east through its control of Vicenza and Bassano, illustrates the commune and its citizens acting in co-operation with its traditional allies of the *pars Marchionis*. The fall of the Da Romano, as we have seen, left the Vicentine magnates still divided into hostile factions, the *pars Marchesana* being led by Count Guido and the *pars Imperialis* by the Trissino, d'Arzignano and Vivaro families.[1] Despite these difficult circumstances, a commune dominated by a popular *comunanza* and nominally independent of the noble factions, made its appearance. Its organisation, as revealed by the statutes of 1264, was very similar to the Paduan constitution of twelve years later. Laws against private jurisdictions, private castles and injuries caused by *potentiores* were included, though it is doubtful if the commune was ever strong enough to put them into effect.[2]

The independence of the Vicentine commune was precarious from the start. There was, perhaps, some hope of stability so long as there was a chance that the *pars Marchionis et Comitis* might establish itself in Verona, but in September 1260, Count Simone da San Bonifacio and his followers were driven out of the city, and Vicentine territory became the buffer state between potentially hostile powers. Thereafter, the young commune was in constant difficulties. The exceptional preservation of the Bassanese archives helps to illustrate one of the problems which was probably not untypical. In September 1260 the commune of Bassano, which had placed itself under the protection of the Paduan commune when it emerged from the power of the Da Romano, was transferred to the jurisdiction of Vicenza through a decision of the Paduan *podestà* Marco Quirino. If the aim of this generous award was

---

[1] The chief narrative source for events in Vicenza is Smereglo, *Annales Vincentinae*, pp. 8–12. Although the author was born about 1240 and was a native of Vicenza, his account of this period is not necessarily free from errors of detail, since he appears to have written it largely from memory after 1311.

[2] Lampertico, *Statuti del Comune di Vicenza*; V. Bortolaso, 'Vicenza dopo la morte di Ezzelino', *NAV* XXIV (1912), pp. 23–46.

to strengthen the commune of Vicenza, it was not achieved, as within two years, the Bassanese had begun a series of disputes over tolls, taxation and military service which the Vicentines were not strong enough to settle, so that an appeal had to be made to the Paduan commune and *podestà*.[1] For a few years, the Vicentine commune leant heavily on the moral support of the bishop Bartolomeo da Breganze, who tried to keep the peace by appointing only moderate Guelphs as *podestà*. But in 1262 the Imperialists began a revolt in the contado which the forces of the commune were unable to subdue. Such a situation could only lead to intervention on the part of Vicenza's stronger neighbours.

Paduan influence in the Vicentino had been strong since the expulsion of the Da Romano, and the first *podestà* of the liberated commune was Aicardino de Litolfo of Padua. The next *podestà* of Paduan origin, Rolando Engleschi, took office in 1264, and though the chronicler Smereglo is wrong in placing the beginning of the Paduan domination in this year, it is probably true that Paduan influence increased; a version of the Paduan annals contains a report, which is probably independent of Smereglo, that Paduan troops assisted at the siege of the rebels in Arzignano at the request of the Vicentines.[2] The next *podestà* of Vicenza was also a Paduan, but in 1266 Count Guido appointed Marco Quirino, a Venetian whose close relations with the *pars Marchionis* are shown by his previous tenure of office in Padua in 1259–60. Smereglo has the unlikely story that the previous *podestà* and a number of other Paduans immediately stirred up a new revolt in the Vicentine contado, but it is much more probable that the immediate cause of the Paduan occupation was the intervention of the Veronese, who occupied a number of frontier fortresses, including the town of Lonigo, during the summer of 1266. On 9 September, a Paduan force led by the *podestà* was met by Count Guido of Vicenza at Grisignano, just within Vicentine territory. Guido, as leader of the local *pars Marchionis* appealed for help 'as already many castles of the Vicentine district are in the hands of the men of

[1] Verci, *Marca Trivigiana*, docs. nn. 105–6, 113–15, 125, 136–8, 146, 149–50.

[2] 'Hoc anno fuit exercitus Paduanus circa Arzignanum, resistente Egano de Arzignano cive Vicentiae contra suam civitatem, et hoc fecerunt Paduani ad petitionem Vicentinorum', *Chronicon de Potestatibus Padue et Carrariensibus*, MS BP 757, f. 6.

Verona, the enemies of the men of Padua, Vicenza and Treviso'. The Paduans refused to move unless they were given the keys of Vicenza, and this was at last conceded.[1]

The Paduan domination of Vicenza began as a temporary military occupation at the request and in support of the local *pars Marchionis*. In the course of time it led to the political subjugation of the smaller city and the dismemberment of its contado, but it is typical of the ways of the Paduan commune that theory and fact were never made to coincide. The *custodia* of the gates and fortifications of Vicenza, unwillingly conceded at Grisignano, was ratified by the commune's council of four hundred on 20 September 1266.[2] The Paduan statutes providing for the election of the *podestà* of Vicenza by the Paduan council was passed before June 1267.[3] In June 1267, the men of Bassano were instructed to obey the Paduan commune in all respects as they had formerly obeyed the commune of Vicenza. At the same time, a committee set up by the Paduan Consiglio Maggiore recommended that the commune take possession of the property of the Vicentine commune in Bassano and Fontaniva, in satisfaction of a debt of £11,000 owed to the Paduans for services rendered, presumably in driving out the Veronese.[4] The repayment of this debt was made as difficult as possible, and the property in question was duly seized in September 1269. The formal annexation of Bassano and its territory took place in 1272, and in 1281 Lonigo was referred to as within the Paduan district.[5] Vicenza and its immediate contado retained its nominal independence and the Vicentine commune was separately represented in treaties in 1267 and 1279.[6] There was no constitutional change; the Paduan *podestà* and his officials and the Paduan garrisons in the city fortresses were sufficient to ensure the effective control of the subject commune until 1311.

The Paduan occupation of Vicenza began with the acquiescence not only of the *pars Marchesana* under Count Guido but also with the support of representatives of all

[1] G. Maccà, *Codice Diplomatico Vicentino* (MS Bertoliana G. 7–8–15), I, *sub anno*.
[2] Verci, *Marca Trivigiana*, docs. nn. 159–60.
[3] *Stat. Com.* 333, 335–6, 339–44, 347–9.
[4] Verci, *Marca Trivigiana*, docs. nn. 178–80.
[5] *Stat. Com.* 351–3, 1220; Gennari, *CDP* VI, f. 217.
[6] Verci, *Marca Trivigiana*, docs. nn. 170, 243–4.

sections of the Vicentine commune. The resolution to ratify the cession of the fortresses in 1266 was proposed by the *anziani* on behalf of the *comunanza* and supported by a *gastaldione* of the guild of notaries on behalf of the guilds, and by a judge speaking for the commune. The Vicentine Guelphs obtained the security they desired. The Veronese were driven out and the *pars Imperialis* brought under control, so that even the visit of the Hohenstaufen Conradin to Verona in 1269 produced no new disturbance. But the Paduan occupation had been accepted only under duress, and the popularity of Paduan rule soon waned. At first, opposition was confined to Imperialist families like the De Vivaro, but in 1290 the arrest and death of Count Beroaldo showed that members of the Vicentine *pars Marchionis* were now under suspicion. The threat of revolt became ever-present for, as Machiavelli noticed some two centuries later, 'nelle repubbliche è maggior vita, maggior odio, più desiderio di vendetta; nè gli lascia nè può lasciare riposare la memoria dell'antica libertà'.[1] The city-republics were totally unable to solve the problems of representation for a community larger than one which lived within earshot of a single council bell. Without the customary checks on their activities, the Paduan officials in Vicenza abused their powers, so that even the Paduan patriot Mussato admitted the injustice of Paduan rule in Vicenza.[2]

The acquisition of political control over the Vicentine state had the effect of opening up Vicentine territory for exploitation by Paduan citizens. Many Paduan magnates had long-standing interests in the Vicentino and these were joined by the newly enriched citizens seeking outlets for their capital. One way of acquiring land was by marriage. Aicardino de Litolfo, the *podestà* in 1259, had himself excepted from the statute forbidding the marriage of heiresses to non-citizens so that he could marry Odilia da Breganze 'who was very rich and succeeded to half the inheritance of the lords of Breganze'.[3] Pierconte da Carrara married a daughter of Pietro de Guizzardo of Vicenza with a dowry of £2,000 which may have been paid

---

[1] *Il Principe*, ed. Burd, p. 205.
[2] 'Vicencia ... Paduanae plebis insolentes dominatus abhorrens, quibus saepe veris plerumque et falsis criminationibus ex factionum suspicionibus nunc regelati cives, nunc securi percussi occubuerat', *Historia Augusta*, col. 360.
[3] Lampertico, *Statuti del Comune di Vicenza*, p. 140; Smereglo, p. 9.

in land. Antonio Bibi increased his estates at Montegalda by marrying a local heiress. Other lands passed into Paduan hands by simple inheritance, like the possessions of Pietro, Count of Montebello, which were divided among his kinsmen the Da Lozzo and Da Carturo.[1] The Vicentine authorities were powerless to protect the interests of their own citizens, as they undoubtedly would have done had they been free to do so.

In 1284, the Paduan Consiglio Maggiore passed a resolution allowing Paduans to buy land in the Vicentino without restriction, and this may have facilitated many purchases of which no record has survived.[2] The revolts against the Paduans, especially that of 1290 in which Count Beroaldo and his son-in-law Giordano de Seratico were killed, brought important estates into the market. A substantial part of Beroaldo's property, including the village of Malò, passed into the hands of Enrico Scrovegni who sold it to Vitaliano Lemici. The estate of Beroaldo's mother Ziborga came into the possession of the Paduan Franciscans as 'the poor of Christ' and after her death was sold, against her express prohibition, to Ubertino and Giacomino da Carrara and Bonaccorso Schinelli for a sum of over £5,800.[3]

Another means by which Paduans acquired influence over the Vicentine commune was through moneylending. The Vicentine records show the commune borrowing considerable sums, sometimes from Florentines resident in Vicenza or Padua but mainly from the leading Paduan moneylenders. Of these, the Scrovegni were the most prominent in the years 1282-9 and the Dalesmanini after 1302. It may be no coincidence that in 1297, when Frassalasta Capodivacca was *podestà* of Vicenza, his kinsman Tavanello lent the commune £1,500, or that Vitaliano Lemici should appear among the creditors of the commune in 1296, three years before he bought Malò.[4]

As in most of the smaller Italian cities, the bishop of Vicenza still exerted a considerable influence over temporal affairs, and the Paduans made repeated efforts to ensure that

[1] G. Mantese, *Memorie Storiche della Chiesa Vicentina* (1954), II, p. 353.
[2] Verci, *Marca Trivigiana*, doc. n. 281.
[3] Arch. Vescovile, Vicenza, Feudorum XXV, f. 287v; Da Nono, *De Generatione*, f. 41v; AS Padua, Corp.Sopp., S. Antonio 150, ff. 81-92.
[4] See above, pp. 185, 187.

the Vicentine church was ruled by a bishop favourable to themselves. Bartolomeo da Breganze was a moderate supporter of the *pars Marchionis;* on his death in 1269, the Paduan candidate was Gomberto Cattanei da Limena, abbot of the Vicentine house of S. Felice and brother of the abbot of S. Giustina in Padua, but he was unsuccessful and an unpopular Papal nominee was appointed. Ten years later, the *podestà* Bellebono Guarnerini tried to intrude his brother Antonio, a canon of Padua cathedral, into the Vicentine see. His claim was supported by the *pars Marchesana,* but the reigning bishop was able to maintain his position with the help of the local *pars Imperialis.*[1] It was not until 1303 that the Paduans secured the appointment of a bishop of Vicenza who had close ties with the *pars Marchionis* and the Paduan commune. In that year, the Trevisan Pope, Benedict XI, who had many Paduan friends, nominated Altegrado Cattanei da Lendenara, a member of a family long allied to the Estensi, who had been archpriest and a professor of law at Padua for many years.[2] Altegrado's identification with Paduan interests was such that when Vicenza threw off Paduan rule in 1311, he escaped to Padua and was never able to return.

The power of the bishop of Vicenza was not restricted to the influence which he might wield over the citizens and commune, which in the case of Bartolomeo da Breganze was considerable, but included the right to grant vast fiefs in the contado which carried with them considerable territorial power. Both Paduan and Veronese families held ecclesiastical fiefs in the diocese of Vicenza. In 1260, Bartolomeo granted the tithes and *comitatus* of Bassano, Angarano and Castigliano to Beroaldo, count of Vicenza, and the Paduan Marco da Montemerlo.[3] In 1280, Bishop Bernardo, who had just weathered a Paduan-inspired effort to supplant him, granted Marco da Montemerlo's share of the fief to Marco's son-in-law Giovanni Forzatè, nephew of the bishop of Padua.[4] The Forzatè were magnates and *male ablati* whose relations with the Paduan commune were not good, so the citizens must have

---

[1] Smereglo, pp. 12–14; Mantese, op. cit. II, pp. 300–5.
[2] See above, p. 146; *Reg. Benedict XI,* n. 1127; for privileges of this pope in favour of Paduans, see nn. 155, 303, 337, 648, 719, 905.
[3] Verci, *Storia degli Eccelini,* III, doc. n. 254.
[4] Dondi dall'Orologio, *Istoria Ecclesiastica Padovana,* VII, doc. n. 153. For the relations of the Forzatè with the commune, see below, pp. 257–8.

been relieved when the Forzatè interest in the tithes of Bassano was finally bought out by the commune of Bassano in 1306.[1] On the other hand, Paduan interests were well served by some of Bishop Altegrado's enfeoffments, such as the grant of extensive tithes in Schio and Santorso to Vitaliano Lemici in 1309, and the *districtus* and *comitatus* of Selvazzano to Gonfredo Scrovegni in 1310.[2]

The full extent of Paduan infiltration into the Vicentino can never be known, but the evidence is sufficient to show how closely the various means of exploitation were interlocked. The *podestà*, the financiers and those with property interests were often the same individuals. The Vicentino played an important part in the rise of the new Paduan families of the communal period, giving them administrative experience as *podestà* and estates with territorial power on a scale scarcely to be found in the Paduan contado. However, if the new magnatial families are more prominent in the records than the older aristocracy, it must not be forgotten that many Paduan nobles, especially those descended from the former counts of Padua-Vicenza, already had considerable property within the borders of the Vicentino before 1266. The new acquisitions must have aroused much hostility among the Vicentines, at the same time providing a means by which this enmity could be held in check. Da Nono says of Vitaliano Lemici, that while he lived the Vicentines were powerless to plot against the Paduans, and the local strength of the Da Lozzo was probably no less; when Nicolò da Lozzo went as *podestà* to Vicenza in 1299, he seems to have held court almost as an independent *signore*.[3] The old families of the *pars Marchionis* and the newer families of the commune had a common interest in the Vicentino.

The occupation of Vicenza in 1266 brought the Paduan commune into closer contact with the rival city of Verona. There, Mastino della Scala, head of the *societas mercatorum,* was gradually building up the power of his family, and had abandoned his earlier policy of conciliation with the *pars Marchionis* for a positive alignment with the Ghibellines.

---

[1] Arch. Vescovile, Vicenza, Feudorum IV, f. 182; Tua, *Reg. Arch. Bassanesi*, nn. 808–9, 824–5.
[2] Arch. Vescovile, Vicenza, Feudorum IV, ff. 145, 169.
[3] *De Generatione*, f. 38v; Smereglo, p. 17.

Forestalled in Vicenza and driven out of the Vicentino, the Veronese did not take up the challenge, for the times were not good for the Imperialists. In 1277, Mastino della Scala was murdered, and the Paduan Guelph leader Guido da Lozzo was believed in some quarters to be responsible.[1] Then in 1278, Enrico, bishop of Trento, seized the opportunity to throw off Veronese tutelage, and asked for Paduan help. The commune sent Marsiglio Partinopei, a *popolano* knighted two years before, as *podestà* with a body of troops, and war with Verona followed [2] In a short time, the Paduans were able to create a formidable alliance against the Imperialist city, and much of the support came from the *pars Marchionis*. In November 1278, the communes of Cremona, Brescia, Parma, Modena and Ferrara and Gerardo da Camino, joined the Paduans against the Veronese. Though not personally a party to the treaty, being represented by the commune of Ferrara, which he controlled, Obizzo d'Este was present as a witness, as were the Paduan magnates Giacomino Papafava da Carrara and Engolfo Conti.[3] The *Chronicon Estense* notes that Obizzo served with the Paduans at the siege of Cologna for forty-two days. The war went on for two years and apart from the reoccupation of the Trentino by the Veronese, was without decisive results, being brought to an end by a compromise peace in 1280.[4] As a reward for his services, Gerardo da Camino was awarded Paduan citizenship.

The war of 1278–80 proved the security of the western frontier of the Paduan state; a chance to strengthen the vulnerable north-eastern border came in 1283. Here the territory of the weak commune of Treviso was all that lay between Padua and the backward frontier province of Friuli, where wars between the communes and the nobility, headed by the patriarchs of Aquileia and the counts of Goriza, were endemic. The traditional Paduan policy in this area was based

---

[1] This is shown by the destruction of Guido's tomb by Veronese troops in revenge in 1313 (Mussato, *Historia Augusta*, col. 515); the appearance of two of the alleged assassins in Guido's house is also highly suspicious (*Liber Regiminum*, p. 335). On the other hand, the local *Cronaca de Romano* (Mon.RDVSP ser. III, II, p. 419) accuses certain Veronese only.

[2] The narrative sources for this war are *Liber Regiminum*, pp. 332–4, and *Chronicon Estense*, p. 43.

[3] Verci, *Marca Trivigiana*, docs. nn. 229, 231.

[4] Ibid. n. 243.

on alliances with the patriarchs, the bishops of Feltre and Belluno, and the Da Camino family. Many of the patriarchs both before and after the fall of the Da Romano, were supporters of the *pars Marchionis*.[1] Gregorio da Montelongo, the patriarch from 1251 to 1269, assisted at the capture of Ferrara in 1240 and the defence of Padua against Ezzelino in 1256. Raimondo della Torre (1274–99) went to take up his high office, escorted by his nephew Goffredo, who was *podestà* of Padua that year, and 'almost all the Paduan nobility'.[2] From 1302 to 1315, the patriarch was Ottobuono de Razzi, previously bishop of Padua, and he was succeeded by two more of the Milanese Guelph Della Torre, Gastone (1316–18) and Pagano (1318–1331), the latter having been bishop of Padua since 1302. All of these maintained friendly relations with the Paduan commune. Relations with the bishops of Feltre and Belluno were defined by a treaty made in 1260, by which the bishop became a Paduan citizen with a tax assessment of £70,000, undertaking to build a *palazzo* worth £1,500 in the city by way of security. He was bound to give the commune military aid, Paduans were to be exempt from tolls, and none but Paduans might be appointed *podestà* in the two cities controlled by the bishop.[3] The last provision, at least, was observed almost without exception until the early fourteenth century.

The weak link in the Paduan chain of alliances in this quarter was the one nearest home with the commune of Treviso. The Trevisan fortress of Noale was only fifteen miles from Padua, and relations between the two communes had not always been friendly in the past, so it was a matter of some significance when a close alliance was established soon after the fall of the Da Romano. At first, Padua and Treviso appear to have been linked only by the general league of all the four cities of the March, concluded in 1262, but in 1267 this was superseded by a closer defensive alliance between Padua, Vicenza and Treviso, excluding Verona, which was expressly directed against Conradin and his allies, and this was revived

---

[1] The classic history of the Patriarchate of Aquileia is B. M. de Rubeis, *Monumenta Ecclesiae Aquiliensis* (1740); a recent general history of Friuli, P. Paschini, *La Storia del Friuli* (1953).
[2] *Liber Regiminum*, pp. 331–2.
[3] *Statuti Carraresi*, f. 299r; Verci, *Marca Trivigiana*, doc. n. 97.

in 1279.¹ A more technical treaty between the two communes, designed to facilitate the settlement of disputes between their citizens without recourse to reprisals, was concluded in 1266.² But the stability of all these arrangements must have been constantly threatened by the existence of a hostile party led by the Castelli family within the Trevisan state. The Paduans had much to gain by a suppression of the Castelli and their party.

There is some evidence which suggests that the seizure of power in Treviso by Gerardo da Camino in 1283 was neither unwelcome to, nor unexpected by, some of the leading elements in the Paduan *pars Marchionis* and commune. Gerardo had served with the Paduans in the war of 1278–80 and had become a Paduan citizen; his last recorded act before he carried through his coup was to intercede for the Paduans with Obizzo d'Este in the dispute concerning the frontier village of Lendenara.³ This cannot have been earlier than August 1283, and on 15 November the city of Treviso was in his hands. The Castelli and their followers put up some resistance in the contado, and in the brief campaign, Gerardo had the support of Tiso Camposanpiero and a number of Paduan soldiers.⁴ The negotiated peace which provided that Gerardo should buy the Castelli out of their Trevisan possessions left him in urgent need of help of another kind, and this too he found in Padua. On 29 December 1283 Guglielmo Lemici made Gerardo a loan of £302. 7s. gross (about £9,675. 4s. petty), for which twenty-one leading Paduans stood surety. The list of *fideiussores* which included Tiso and Guglielmo Camposanpiero, Manfredo and Engolfo Conti and Guido da Lozzo among the magnates, and Guerico da Vigodarzere, Fulcone Buzzaccarini and Rolando Engleschi among the leading citizens, shows the wide measure of support which Gerardo enjoyed, while the speed with which the loan was arranged suggests the possibility of prior knowledge of Gerardo's intentions.⁵

¹ Verci, *Storia degli Eccelini*, III, n. 266; *Marca Trivigiana* docs. nn. 170, 243–4. ² *Stat. Com.* 1367–81.
³ *Liber Regiminum*, p. 337. For the beginning of the Da Camino *signoria*, see Picotti, *I Caminesi*, pp. 86–105.
⁴ Verci, *Marca Trivigiana*, doc. n. 273
⁵ Picotti, doc. n. ix, pp. 254–6. Here and on p. 106, Picotti dates this document a year too late by overlooking the fact that the year began at Christmas.

Co-operation between the Da Camino and the Paduans did not cease with the passing of the crisis which inevitably attended the establishment of the *signoria*. In June 1284, Gerardo raised two more large loans in Padua, one from Guglielmo Lemici and the other from Renaldo Scrovegni. The numerous Paduan *fideiussores* included, in addition to those named in the first loan, Marsiglio I da Carrara, Zilio Maccaruffi and Manfredo and Guecillo Dalesmanini.[1] These loans were soon repaid, but others were raised later as need arose, as there is record of the repayment of £12,000 to Renaldo Scrovegni in 1288 and £8,600 to Artusio Dalesmanini in 1299.[2] The Da Camino remained on good terms with the Paduan magnates of the *pars Marchionis*. Tiso Camposanpiero married Gerardo's sister and served as *podestà* in Treviso in 1286–7, and Nicolò da Lozzo, who celebrated his wedding to Gerardo's daughter Agnese in Padua in 1286, held the same office in 1303–4. The Trevisan records are in this respect far from complete, but other Paduans who served as *podestà* during the Da Camino *signoria*, included Guido Negri, Giordano da Vigonza and Albertino da Castelnovo.[3]

From every point of view, the Da Camino *signoria* made an inestimable contribution to the security and prosperity of Padua. Paduan magnates and moneylenders alike profited from the friendship between the two cities, as did the merchants of both communes. In particular, the Paduan state was shielded from the turbulence of Friuli and the Alpine regions, and was able to remain at peace with Venice, the patriarch and the Da Camino, in spite of disputes between these three. As a common friend, the commune was able to arbitrate between the competing powers in the Friulan hinterland in 1291.[4] The link between Padua and Treviso survived the fall of the Da Camino in 1312 and, although the material aid given was small, the Trevisans remained the constant allies of the Paduan commune in its last fatal struggle with the Della Scala.

In its relations with its neighbours to the west and north-east, the Paduan commune was generally successful in securing

---

[1] Picotti, op. cit. pp. 250–4; repayment, ibid. p. 106 n. 6.
[2] AS Venice, *Codex Tarvisinus*, ff. 331r, 333.
[3] Picotti, pp. 335–6.
[4] A.S. Minotto, *Acta et Diplomata e R. Tabulario Veneto* (1870–4), I, p. 40.

MAP 11. North-East Italy

its interests, largely through the support of the *pars Marchionis*. To the south, where the commune had the river Adige, which was both a natural frontier and an important trade route, almost within its grasp, the situation was radically different. The territories in question were not threatened by an Imperialist party but were held, for the most part, by members of the *pars Marchionis* and the whole came within the sphere of influence of the state of Ferrara which was controlled by the Marchesi d'Este themselves. Consequently, an aggressive policy in this quarter did not command the same wide measure of support among the Paduans as when the enemy was the Ghibellines. Most of the Paduan nobles looked upon the Marchesi as the natural social and political leaders of the region and a collision between the commune and the Estensi presented them and their clients with a serious conflict of loyalties. Such traditional ties carried less weight with the poorer members of the Paduan *popolo*, most of whom were only enfranchised between 1256 and 1277; their natural policy, which they expressed through the *comunanza* organised on a guild basis, was equally anti-magnatial and anti-Estensi. For this reason, hostility towards the Estensi is closely linked to other signs of militancy on the part of the lesser *popolani*, and the two lines of development must be followed together.

The alliance between the Paduan commune and the Marchesi d'Este was never closer than in the first years after 1256 when the existence of the restored commune was still menaced by the Da Romano. The Marchese Azzo was the natural leader of the local forces against Ezzelino, and his influence over the commune must have been great; nevertheless, Rolandino, writing very soon after the event, makes it clear that this never amounted to a virtual *signoria*. For example, Azzo appointed the *podestà* of Padua in July 1258, but only as a special privilege granted him by a resolution of the Consiglio Maggiore.[1] Similarly, he was given authority to negotiate the alliance against Ezzelino in 1259 in the name of the commune only because the urgency of the crisis overcame the misgivings of those of the Paduan councillors who had been at first unwilling to bind the commune to unknown conditions.[2]

---

[1] *Cronica*, p. 148.
[2] 'Set primo visum est populo Paduano durissimum consentire seque astringere ignotis ordinamentis vel consiliis, que non noscunt'. ibid. p. 155.

The same historian who recorded these points, also reflects a considerable admiration for the Estensi as the symbols of the regional *pars Ecclesiae,* a sentiment which was probably typical of the Paduans of his class, since the statute which provided for the thanksgiving procession on the anniversary of the capture of the city gave to the Marchese, if present, the place of honour with the bishop and the *podestà*.[1]

The final defeat of the Da Romano in the summer of 1260, though it reduced the commune's dependence on the military aid of the nobility, did not produce any immediate change of policy. Indeed, in the important matter of the appointment of *podestà*, the commune showed a remarkable stability in the early years after 1256. In June 1260, Marco Quirini, the first *podestà* of the restored commune, was elected for another term, and in 1261 and 1263 the supreme magistrature went to Giovanni Badoer and Lorenzo Tiepolo, both Venetian supporters of the *pars Marchionis*. In 1263 and 1269, Matteo Correggio of Parma, Azzo's nominee in 1258, was re-elected by the commune. By this time, it was the Estensi who were drawing on Paduan help. In 1264, Azzo d'Este died, commending his grandson and heir to the protection of Cardinal Ottobuono Fieschi and the communes of Ferrara, Mantua and Padua. The young Obizzo II and his advisers decided to put through his election as *signore* of Ferrara. At this critical moment, Paduans were prominent among his supporters: the key office of *podestà* was held by Pierconte da Carrara, and three Paduans, Tiso Camposanpiero, Giacomino Papafava da Carrara and Antonio Crosna, were among the witnesses of the election.[2] Like Gerardo da Camino some twenty years later, the new Guelph *signore* received early financial assistance from Paduan circles. In 1267 and 1269, Obizzo is recorded repaying

---

The words of the treaty, 'Et intellegatur commune Cremone pars Barbarasorum, quae est in civitate modo, et regit ipsam civitatem et nunc est commune, et eodem modo intellegatur civitate Mantue et Ferrarie et Padue, pars dominorum Marchionis Estensis et Comitis Verone, quae nunc regunt ipsas civitates et sunt communia' (Cipolla, *Relazioni Verona—Mantova Sec. XIII*, p. 78), are therefore misleading, as *de facto* Azzo did not enjoy the same powers in Padua as he did in Ferrara.

[1] *Stat. Com.* 559.

[2] L. Simeoni, 'L'Elezione di Obizzo d'Este a Signore di Ferrara', *ASI* XCIII, i (1935), pp. 165–88. For the document recording the election, see Muratori, *Antichità Estensi*, II, pp. 25–7.

a loan of £15,000 from Marco Badoer, who was acting on behalf of Obizzo's sister Costanza d'Este, the wife of Guido da Lozzo. The *fideiussores* were Venetian and Paduan, and among them appear Giacomino Papafava, Pierconte da Carrara, Guerico da Vigodarzere, Antonio Crosna and Renaldo Scrovegni.[1]

For the first sixteen of Obizzo II's twenty-nine-year rule in Ferrara, reciprocal aid continued to pass between him and the Paduan commune. About 1277, Paduan soldiers were serving with the Marchese, presumably in his war against Verona, Mantua and the Archbishop of Ravenna;[2] then, in 1279–80, Obizzo fought with the Paduans against the Veronese at Cologna. By the terms of the peace, Obizzo was to have his jurisdiction over Cologna and other frontier villages, which had been seized by the Veronese, restored to him, and the Paduan commune protested strongly when this was not done.[3] Similarly, the commune supported the Estensi in a dispute with the Venetians in 1279, sending ambassadors to Venice to urge that 'the Lord Doge and the commune of Venice should not oppress or molest the Lord Marchese and the commune of Ferrara', and to explain 'that the Lord Marchese is a Paduan citizen, and that the city of Ferrara is so bound to the city of Padua that in no way can the city of Padua abandon the said Marchese and the commune of Ferrara'.[4]

Like the Da Camino in Treviso, the Estensi in Ferrara constituted the Paduans' first line of defence, not only against the Veronese but also *vis à vis* the warlike regions of Romagna and the March of Ancona. Nevertheless, the persistence of the alliance was remarkable, in view of the potential source of discord represented by the overlapping claims of the Estensi and the commune in the southern part of the Paduan contado. Este, Montagnana and the surrounding region, known as the Scodosia, was the original home of the Este family, and they continued to have extensive possessions there over which they claimed jurisdiction. In 1213, the Paduan army had captured the town of Este and, in Rolandino's view, the whole area

---

[1] AS Modena, AMS III, nn. 21, 31.
[2] *Stat. Com.* 118.I; *Annales Mantuani*, p. 27.
[3] AS Modena, AMS III, n. 54
[4] AMS III, n. 45.

pertained *de jure* to the Paduan commune, but in fact the situation was probably far from clear in 1256, when Ezzelino's castellans in the area surrendered not to the commune but to Azzo d'Este, thus immeasurably strengthening his hand in the negotiations which followed.[1] By an agreement concluded in August 1260, the commune recognised Azzo's jurisdiction over Este, Montagnana and their dependent villages, while reserving the right to direct taxation, military service and jurisdiction in cases involving its own citizens. At the same time, Azzo surrendered his property in the fortified town of Monselice, a valuable base for future Paduan expansion.[2] There is no positive evidence to show how long this compromise lasted; there are occasional references to an Estense viscount in Este and Montagnana, but on the other hand the statutes of 1276 show the commune appointing *podestà* and castellans throughout the area. As there is no trace in the chronicles of any dispute, it seems likely that Obizzo surrendered his jurisdiction, though not his property and fortresses in the area, as a part of the price of Paduan support in the early days of his *signoria*. The first sign of a break in the friendly relations between the Paduans and the Marchese appears only in February 1282, when Obizzo had a deed drawn up giving all his possessions in the Padovano to his son Francesco. Revoking this gift in 1289, Obizzo declared it to have been made for fear of the Paduans.[3]

In tracing the faint trail of evidence left by the changes in the government of the commune leading up to this radical change of policy, it is necessary to go back to the year 1279, when the war with Verona was at its height. War always constituted a severe test for any communal regime, and in that year cracks began to appear in the façade of Paduan unity. In August, a plot was discovered in Vicenza, in which the Paduan nobles Bartolomeo and Ansedisio Schinelli were implicated and they were consequently exiled. In Padua, there was some dissatisfaction with the way that the *podestà* had imposed

---

[1] *Cronica*, pp. 23-4, 127. Rolandino's remark, 'et erat tunc (1213) Este et Montagnana totaque Scodesia *more debito* sub iurisdictione Paduani communis', was therefore, in the years 1260-2 when it was written, highly topical and tendentious.
[2] AMS III, nn. 1-4; Verci, *Marca Trivigiana*, doc. n. 102.
[3] AMS III, n 69: V.n. 30.

military service, and in November the *anziani* decided on the appointment of a *capitano del popolo*, as provided for at their discretion by the statutes. The nomination of Matteo da Correggio as *capitano* is a sufficient indication that no change of policy was intended, as Matteo was a professional *podestà* of Guelph sympathies who had already served three terms in Padua. A month later, the *pars Ecclesiae*, dissatisfied with the *podestà's* lack of zeal in punishing the Vicentine conspirators, and with his failure to send troops on some obscure enterprise in Treviso and Bellunese territory, expelled him and substituted the *capitano*, Matteo da Correggio thus becoming *podestà* of Padua for the fourth time. This change would seem to indicate that the *pars Ecclesiae*, under the local leadership of Guido da Lozzo and Martino de Guidoto, which was also the war party, was in a position to direct the policies of the commune. Probably the influence of the magnates increased also, for they would mostly have adhered to the *pars Ecclesiae* and their service in the field must have been invaluable to the commune in time of war.[1]

The war having been brought to a fairly successful conclusion in September 1280, there was no visible change in the policies of the commune until the end of May 1281. Early in the month, the *podestà* was writing to the Veronese in support of Obizzo d'Este's claim to Cologna; though the news of a defeat suffered by the Milanese Guelphs may have had some influence, the reaction in Padua seems to have been touched off on 29 May by the murder of some of the reputed assassins of Mastino della Scala in the courtyard of Guido da Lozzo's house in Padua. The *Liber Regiminum*, which is the chief source for these events, is brief to the point of obscurity, but it would seem that, in demanding justice, Guido da Lozzo's *pars Ecclesiae* overreached itself. One of the murderers implicated Guecillo Dalesmanini and Giovanni Forzatè, two of the magnates not closely related to the *pars Ecclesiae*, but later withdrew his accusations with the result that not only they, but also Guido da Lozzo and Nicolò da Castelnovo, as leaders of the opposing faction, having paid £1,000 security for their good conduct, were banished to their villages. The exile of these four leading magnates cleared the

[1] For this and the following paragraph, see chiefly *Liber Regiminum*, pp. 333–5.

way, in September 1281, for the passing of the most severe anti-magnatial legislation ever put through by the commune.

Special measures against the magnates, that is, those whose wealth, in money and followers made them a potential danger to the security of the state, were an essential part of the legal structure of any commune where the rule of the *popolo* was a reality. On the one hand, the central government had to be protected from the pressure exerted by the magnates from without, or from infiltration by their clients from within; then, since the main strength of the magnates tended to be concentrated in the remoter areas of the contado, special protection had to be given to the rural communes and the free tenants of these regions against the *potentiores* who might otherwise oppress or overawe them. An aspect of these latter measures was the assertion of the commune's exclusive right of jurisdiction in all matters, except those pertaining to fiefs and the rights of a landlord over his own tenants: a claim which was in the interests of the peasants, the *popolani*, the majority of whom owned or leased land in the contado, and the administrative class alike.[1]

The basic Paduan anti-magnatial legislation belongs to the early thirteenth century, when the *popolo* was first consolidating its control over the commune. The date of the revival of these measures after 1256 is not known, but additional statutes on the subject were passed in 1266,[2] and others followed from time to time, notably a group in 1270 and another in 1277–8.[3] None involved any new principle, and their effect on friendly magnates cannot have been unduly oppressive, since they were willing to serve with the commune in the war of 1278–80. But the laws of 1281 introduced a new procedure by which the *podestà* was bound to act against any magnate disturbing any citizen in his property or rights on the oath of a single plaintiff, without any further proof and not admitting any proof to the

---

[1] G. Fasoli, 'Richerche sulla legislazione antimagnatizia nei comuni dell'alta e media Italia', *RSDI* XII (1939), pp. 86–133, 240–309. Paduan anti-magnatial legislation is discussed at length in M. A. Zorzi, *L'ordinamento comunale*, pp. 55–102.

[2] *Stat. Com.* 85, also the list of magnates attached to *Stat. Com.* 635 must date from before the end of 1266 (see above, p. 63).

[3] *Stat. Com.* 461, 595, 637–8, 640 (1270); 85.I, 457–8, and statute of 1278, Appendix II.

contrary.¹ This so weighted the scales of justice against the *potentiores* that it was abused; many magnates were condemned, and in the following year disorders broke out. Without doubt, Obizzo d'Este was among the aggrieved magnates.

The situation was aggravated by a simultaneous attack by the commune on the clergy, who were the only other powerful class which could not be absorbed into the *comunanza*. Conflicts of this kind were nothing new. A dispute over taxation for the upkeep of the roads seems to have been dragging on since 1266; in 1274 the commune tried to put pressure on the clergy by forbidding their tenants the use of the public roads.² The issue in 1282 was the laxity of the bishop in punishing criminous clerks, and the tactics adopted by the commune were similar; by a notorious statute, the commune virtually excluded the clergy from the protection of the civil law. A common element with the struggle with the magnates was provided by the person of the bishop, Giovanni Forzatè, who, since he entered the city with the victorious Guelphs in 1256, seems to have become progressively less and less in harmony with the religious and secular aspirations of the citizens. But the obvious parallel between the two conflicts does not mean that they followed the same course. The death of Bishop Giovanni in 1283 and the long vacancy occasioned by the disputed election which followed, seem to have taken the edge off the struggle with the clergy for a time, but it flared up again with the appointment of a new bishop in 1287 and a settlement was not reached until 1290, long after the battle with the magnates had died down.³

Having broken with the Estensi and the magnates early in 1282, the group in control of the commune took a new step in August 1283, when a resolution was passed by the Consiglio Maggiore ordering the acquisition by every means possible of the jurisdiction and fortifications of Lendenara.⁴ The village on which the commune now cast its eyes stands south of the main stream of the Adige, on a branch leading to Rovigo

¹ AD 2902, Zorzi, pp. 201-3.
² *Stat. Com.* 979, 459.
³ *Liber Regiminum*, pp. 336-9; Dondi dall'Orologio, *Istoria Ecclesiastica Padovana*, VIII, pp. 12-15, 40-7. There is no satisfactory modern treatment of Church-State relations in Padua.
⁴ AMS IV, n. 8.

which, with its county, was controlled by the Estensi. Lendenara itself constituted an enclave not yet absorbed by any of the larger communes, and the jurisdiction, which included the right to levy tolls on the river traffic, was mostly divided among the members of the Cattanei family of Lendenara, other shares being held by the counts of San Bonifacio, Badoer Badoer and Obizzo d'Este. All were noble members of the *pars Marchionis* but most of them had interests in the Padovano or the Vicentino through which the commune could exert pressure. At first, the new policy was very successful; within a few months a total of 1/3 and 3/60 of the jurisdiction was purchased for £22,500 from the Cattanei and Badoer.[1] But the move threatened the territories of Rovigo and Ferrara, and Obizzo refused to sell his share, even though Gerardo da Camino came to plead with him on behalf of the commune.[2] Doubtless, Obizzo had his own ways of exerting pressure in return, and by April 1284, the commune had capitulated. An attorney was appointed to sell the shares already acquired to Obizzo; in exchange, Paduan merchants were granted freedom from tolls in Ferrara and its district, a similar privilege in Lendenara being granted by Obizzo and the remaining lords of Lendenara.[3]

While the external policies of the commune are fairly clear, the corresponding changes within the ruling groups in the city in the early 1280s are very obscure. The statute ordering the purchase of Lendenara was drawn up by seven *statutarii*, five of whom were judges of undistinguished *popolani* families. The *anziani* in office are also named, and their personal responsibility is implied by a clause ordering the *podestà* to protect them from possible reprisals and another prolonging their term of office for a further two months. Their leader was Paduano Gambarini, an experienced judge who had helped to draw up the anti-magnatial statute of 1278. There is nothing here to suggest a socially radical movement within the *comunanza* and no evidence for any change in the constitutional balance of the commune. The absence of the names of the leading Paduan families, such as those supporting Gerardo da

---

[1] AMS IV, nn. 5-7, 9-17. A. Medin, 'I documenti originali dei primi acquisti di Padova nel Polesine', *MRIV* XXVII (1907), n. 10, prints parallel documents from the Badoer archives, but his account as a whole is distorted through his not having seen the documents at Modena.

[2] *Liber Regiminum*, p. 337.

[3] AMS IV, nn. 22-4.

Camino at the time, from all the documents relating to the purchase of Lendenara may not in itself be significant, but it is remarkable that the agreement with Ferrara which followed the abandonment of that policy was witnessed in the Consiglio Minore by Guido da Lozzo and Giovanni Forzatè, two of the magnates exiled in 1281, and by Zilio Maccaruffi and Renaldo Scrovegni. In 1286, the Palazzo Comunale was the scene of the sumptuous wedding festivities of Guido da Lozzo's son Nicolò and Agnese, daughter of Gerardo da Camino, at which Obizzo d'Este presided; Padua had returned to the bosom of the *pars Marchionis*.

The first crisis in Padua's relations with the Estensi caused little change either within the commune or outside; the second crisis which lasted from 1289 to 1294, was much more important in all respects. In the interval, the direction of the commune's ambitions had shifted away from Lendenara, where Obizzo had strengthened his position by further purchases in 1285 and 1287,[1] to another enclave formed by the lands of the monastery Vangadizza, which lay on the Adige immediately above Lendenara. Obizzo was the *advocatus* of the house, but his chief interests in these years were elsewhere. In 1288, Modena submitted to him, and in 1290 he occupied Reggio; probably with a view to securing these acquisitions, Obizzo sought an agreement with Alberto della Scala, the ruler of Verona, whose daughter he married in July 1289.[2] By this date, the Paduans had so disturbed the lands of Vangadizza that Pope Nicholas IV tried to enlist the strength of Verona by appointing Alberto della Scala the special protector of the house.[3] For some reason, neither Obizzo nor Alberto intervened effectively on behalf of the monastery, and in 1292 the commune extorted an advantageous agreement from Abbot Bernardo, by which the abbey and its lands were declared to be a part of the Paduan district and subject to the commune. Besides the right to appoint *podestà* in all the villages under his jurisdiction, the abbot ceded land at Castelbaldo on both banks of the Adige for a nominal rent and the commune began at once to build a castle and fortified bridge to command the river and its traffic.

[1] AMS IV, nn. 33-5, 40, 43-5; V, n. 21. The shares purchased ranged from 1/9 to 1/192.
[2] *Chronicon Estense*, pp. 47-9.
[3] *Registres de Nicholas IV*, ed. Langlois, n. 7500.

The only resistance to this move seems to have come from the General of the Camaldolese order, to which the house belonged, who placed the commune under an interdict in January 1293.[1]

At this point, in February 1293, Obizzo d'Este died, and his death revealed a recurring weakness of the Estense state, the ancient family tradition that the *signoria* should be treated like the estates and the title, and be divided equally among the heirs. On this occasion, the elder brother Azzo VIII succeeded in persuading his brother Francesco to accept him as sole ruler of the state, but the third brother, Aldovrandino, felt himself unjustly treated and after failing to find support in Bologna came to Padua where he agreed, after some negotiations, to hand over to the commune his third share in the family estates in the Padovano, the territory of Castelbaldo, the jurisdiction of Lendenara and the patronage of the monastery of Vangadizza.[2] This his brothers refused to accept, and a short war followed. In an autumn campaign, the Paduans took the fortresses of Este, Cero and Calaone; in the following spring Alberto della Scala changed sides, and the Paduans, in co-operation with a Veronese force, laid siege to the castle of Venezze in the lands of Vangadizza. Faced by this combination, Azzo accepted the arbitration of Patriarch Raimondo della Torre of Aquileia, and agreed to a peace by which the Paduans attained most of their objectives. In return for the restoration of their lands in the Padovano, less the castles of Este, Cero and Calaone, which were destroyed, the Estensi recognised Paduan control over Vangadizza and ceded a third part of the jurisdiction of Lendenara.[3]

---

[1] J. B. Mittarelli and A. Costadoni, *Annales Camaldulenses* (1755–64), pp. 197 et seq. corrected in detail by A. Medin, MRIV XXVII, 10, pp. 5–9.

[2] AMS VI, nn. 29–32, 40.

[3] The best account is *Liber Regiminum*, pp. 341–2, but it is to be noted that the entry under the rubric '1294' refers to events taking place between July 1293 and June 1294. See also *Annales Patavini*, p. 188 and *Chronicon Estense*, p. 51. Two documents throw interesting sidelights on the policy of the commune at this time. Biblioteca Estense MS 1271 (Lat.) is an inventory of all the possessions of Azzo and Francesco d'Este in Paduan territory, compiled by order of the commune between May and August 1293. AD 3667 is a sentence of the *podestà* in favour of the convent of S. Maria de Festomba in a case brought under the statutes *de maleablatis*, concerning some property of the convent in Baone, illegally occupied by the Estensi for many years. Only in September 1293, just after the beginning of hostilities, was the convent able to get redress.

With this reversal of traditional alliances, which saw the Paduans and the Veronese co-operating in a war against the head of the *pars Marchionis,* was associated the emergence of a new political force within the city, the Union of the Guilds. While an earlier statute speaks of the *congregatio* of the guilds recognised by the commune,[1] which in 1287 numbered thirty-six, the earliest reference to the Union is a statute of the period July to December 1293. This provided that:

> all and each of the guilds of the city of Padua, both those which appoint *anziani* as well as all the other mechanical guilds, may be understood to be and are from henceforth a single body, society, brotherhood or league to maintain and conserve the city of Padua and its district in a peaceful state as a commune, free from the domination of any tyrant or any other single person.

To this end, the guilds took on the supervision of the arms of their members, while a chronicle speaks of a ceremony at which the incoming *podestà* presented standards bearing the arms of the guild and the *comunanza* to each of the *gastaldiones,* while the standard of the *comunanza* was given to the *iudex ancianorum*.[2]

Both the words of the statute and the situation at the time make it sufficiently clear what the 'military' union of 1293 was intended to accomplish. As always, war was exerting a disturbing effect on Paduan society and the government of the commune. At the beginning of hostilities, the Consiglio Maggiore delegated dictatorial powers to a *credenza* of twelve.[3] Though this committee had to be confirmed in office every fifteen days, it represented a dangerous concentration of power in the hands of a few who might be corrupted or overawed. There were two dangers, either or both of which may have been facing the commune at this time. On the one hand, the magnates of the *pars Marchionis* may have been threatening to exert pressure to make the commune reverse its policy, as in 1284, and make peace with the Estensi; or a magnate faction may have been seeking to take advantage of the war to install

---

[1] 'Fratalea quilibet que sit in congregatione aliarum frataliarum', *Stat. Com.* 405.
[2] *Liber Regiminum,* p. 342; *Stat. Not.,* f. 27v, Zorzi doc. v, pp. 205–6. Dr Zorzi's interpretation of the 'military' union as having no political significance (p. 142) seems to me unsound.
[3] *Annales Patavini,* p. 206.

its leader as *capitano*, as the first step towards a *signoria*. Although writing over twenty years after the event, Da Nono may have recorded a reliable tradition when he said of Guecillo Dalesmanini that, 'at the time when the Paduans had the war with Marchese Azzo d'Este, he could if he had wished, by the voice of the *popolo* have been made its *capitano*'.[1] The reference in the statute to 'the domination of any tyrant or any other single person' which echoes the words of the alliances with Vicenza and Treviso of 1262, 1267 and 1279, shows that it was an internal menace which the legislators had in mind in creating a militia organised on a guild basis. The only reference to the guilds' bands in action belongs to a chronicler's account of the civil war between the Carrara and Lemici factions in 1325.[2]

The Union of the Paduan guilds did not die with the crisis which had created it, but gradually developed a series of institutions with political functions which established themselves as features of the Paduan constitution right up to the last days of the free commune. In 1295, an already existing council of *gastaldiones* passed a resolution, which was duly ratified in the chapters of all the guilds, constituting themselves 'one body and one union, united according to the provisions of the statutes of the Paduan commune'. There were to be monthly meetings of the *gastaldiones* supported by additional councillors, to consider proposals 'for the honour and utility and peaceful state of the city of Padua and its district, and of the *comunanza* and all the guilds of the Paduan *popolo*'.[3] The successful launching of this council and its recognition by the commune are proved by the wording of statutes of 1297 and 1299 which add the *gastaldiones* and the guilds to the usual formulae used to describe the commune and its officials.[4] Several of the resolutions passed by the council of *gastaldiones* in the early fourteenth century have been preserved. Suppressed by the Guelph oligarchy which gained control of the commune in the first years of the war against Verona, the

[1] *De Generatione*, f. 38r.
[2] 'Et postea . . . campana magna communis sonavit ad martellum, et confalones fratalearum cum suis frataleis et populo iverunt ad plateam propter rixam et praelium, quae erat inter Paulum Dentem ex una parte et Carrarenses cum multis sequacibus ex altera . . .', *Annales Patavini*, p. 246.
[3] Roberti, *Corporazioni*, pp. 69–74.
[4] Zorzi, docs. viii & xi, pp. 209, 213.

Union was revived in 1315 and the new office of *defensor populi* created, to be superseded by the appointment of a *capitano del popolo* in January 1318. The Union and the council of *gastaldiones* survived the *signoria* of Giacomo da Carrara and persisted in some form until the election of Marsiglio da Carrara in 1328.[1]

The development of the Union may be compared to that of the *comunanza* which preceded it. Like the *comunanza*, the Union was primarily concerned with the protection of the lives and interests of its members. A resolution of the council of the Union dated 2 December 1300 set up a committee of *XV gastaldiones* to look into complaints of injury by members, and the office of *defensor populi* was instituted with similar objects in view.[2] The means envisaged were always those of influencing the communal authorities, either by the *gastaldiones* or the *defensor* approaching the *podestà* directly, or through the disciplined action of the Union's members in the various councils of the commune. The pressure which could be exerted by a well-organised body in these ways on the rather diffuse government of the Paduan commune should not be underestimated. Something of the Union's effectiveness can be seen from the reaction which it provoked in the College of Judges. In 1302, the chapter of the College resolved that the College should join the Union; when this came to nothing, the chapter took steps to impose voting discipline on its members who belonged to the Consiglio Maggiore, and later to ensure that the desires and opinions of the College were made known to each incoming *podestà*.[3] But like the *comunanza*, the Union supplemented, but never attempted to substitute its own organisation in the place of the governmental machinery of the commune. Constitutional changes were few. The *podestà's* term of office was shortened to six months in 1293, and about 1300 the number of *anziani* was raised from twelve to eighteen.[4] Unfortunately, there is no evidence as to how this number was made up, but it is likely that the representation of the guilds was increased, since it is clear that Mussato associated the

[1] For references to the council of *XV gastaldiones* during the nominal Hapsburg *signoria*, 1320–8, see AD 5735–6, 5867, 5933, 5938, 6127, 6267; the last of these is dated 19 April 1328.
[2] Roberti, pp. 77–8, 83.
[3] *Stat. Coll. Iud.*, ff. 75r, 79v, 97r; Zorzi, pp. 167–77, 234–5.
[4] *Liber Regiminum*, p. 342; *Annales Patavini*, p. 263.

regime of the *XVIII anziani* with the dominance of the *gastaldiones* of the guilds within the commune.[1]

The most important difference between the Union and the *comunanza* was that while the latter had widened the basis of the city government by enfranchising the *popolo*, the Union restricted the holding of office and most of its privileges to those of its members who were already enrolled in the *comunanza*. It is true that in the 'military' union of 1293, no distinction was made between the major guilds who appointed *anziani* and the minor guilds whose members practised 'mechanical arts', some of whom would not have been members of the *popolo*. However, as the movement developed and became more political, power was increasingly concentrated in the hands of the members of a few of the leading guilds. Though the council of *gastaldiones* included the elected leaders of all the guilds, extraordinary meetings could be called only if the representatives of two or three of the major guilds or groups of minor guilds which banded together to elect *anziani* made a request to one of the *gastaldiones* of the notaries, one of whom presided at all meetings.[2] In the committee of the *XV gastaldiones*, the predominance of the major guilds, and especially of the notaries, was even more pronounced, as four of the fifteen were to be notaries, one of whom was to be president. It was not therefore empty hyperbole, when the preamble to the confirmation of the statutes of the Guild of Notaries in 1325 declared that 'the men of the said guild were and are those who sustain the public burdens and duties of the said city, and by whom almost the whole city is governed'.[3] In

---

[1] 'More primo, quo ante bellum sub antianis XVIII civitas gubernatur, vivendum: Unionem Tribunorum pro ipsorum libitu aggregendam omnesque ius restituendum Tribunancie potestati . . .', *De Gestis*, coll. 613–14. I have found no evidence to support Roberti's statement (p. 61, followed by Zorzi, pp. 166–7) that the XVIII *anziani* were chosen nine from the guilds and nine from the *comunanza*. Apart from the evidence of Mussato, it seems very unlikely that the guilds would have given up the clear majority among the *anziani* which they had enjoyed since at least 1276.

[2] 'Et si videretur duabus vel tribus gastaldiis maiorum fratalearum que faciunt ancianos, intellegendo unam gastaldiam fratalearum prout sunt simul coniuncte ad faciendum ancianos, quod gastaldiones deberent congregari . . .', Roberti, p. 71.

[3] 'Homines dictae fratalee fuisse et esse qui sustinuerunt et sustinent cuncta onera et factiones dictae civitatis, et per quos quasi tota civitas gubernatur', MS BP 339, f. 83r.

1306, the Union resolved that those who were not members both of a guild and the *comunanza* could not sit in its councils as *sapientes* but could attend meetings only to complain or to excuse themselves.[1] These facts explain why the Union never pressed for radical changes in the internal affairs of the commune but remained essentially a pressure group within the *comunanza*. Even the special legal protection which it offered was intended only for those who were full masters of one of the major guilds who had the right to participate in the election of the *anziani*.[2] No doubt the Union by and large represented the political organ of the lesser members of the *comunanza*, among whom urban and mercantile interests were somewhat stronger than in the *comunanza* as a whole. The Union was probably influential in the passing of some of the few statutes which have survived from the period 1295 to 1311, such as those which sought to revive the city's wool market and a group setting up new officials to regulate the supply of foodstuffs.[3] But the nature of the Paduan economy was such that no clear-cut division of interests was possible within the *comunanza*. Most of the enfranchised guildsmen had a personal interest in the prosperity of agriculture, while the non-guildsmen who owned urban property must have favoured the growth of the city. Above all, the professional administrators provided the leadership both in the *comunanza* and among the guildsmen; the common interests of the judges and notaries were a bond which united the leaders of both parts of the *comunanza*.[4]

[1] 'Quod etiam alie persone quam de comunantia et frataleis possit venire in Unione et quando congregabuntur quindecim gastaldiones solummodo ad lementandum se de aliqua iniuria illata et ad se excusandum de eo quod diceretur de ipso per aliquem vel dici velet; et facta sua excusatione vel sua lementatione incontinenti recedere debeat . . .', Roberti, p. 79.

[2] 'Item firmamus et ordinamus quod si alicui fratrum fratalearum populi Paduani et Unionis, intellegendo illos solum esse de frataleis Unionis, qui in arte et officium exercent pro frataleis et cuncta honera sustinent pro frataleis, seu fratalea in qua scriptus est, et vadit ad faciendum ancianos pro frataleis solum, facta fuerit aliqua iniuria vel molestia . . .', Roberti, pp. 77–8.

[3] *Stat. Coll. Iud.*, ff. 8v–9r (May 1301); *Statuti Carraresi*, ff. 192r (August 1308), and 3–5r (April 139, Roberti, pp. 117–18).

[4] It may be no coincidence that positive evidence for the leadership of the *iudex ancianorum* among the *ancani de comunancia* comes only from the period of the Union. While Stat. Com. 442, dated 1262, laid bown that the *vexillum comunancie* should be given to one of the *anciani* to be chosen by his colleagues in office, the statute of the uilitary union of 1293 decreed that it

The main evidence for a distinctive policy pursued by the Union comes from the field of external affairs. The Union made its appearance at a time when the old division between the *pars Ecclesiae* and the *pars Imperialis* was dissolving as the watershed was reached between the violent party conflicts begun in the time of Frederick II, and the equally fierce party warfare touched off by Henry VII's expedition in 1310. Characteristic of this period were a number of unexpected Guelph-Ghibelline alliances, the first of which was Obizzo d'Este's Della Scala marriage in 1289. This was followed by the Padua-Della Scala alliance of 1294 and the Estensi-Visconti treaty of 1295.[1] The most extreme case of the reversal of traditional alliances is to be seen in 1304, which found the Paduan commune, supported by the benevolent neutrality of Verona, at war with the Venetians who had the help of the Estensi, the Da Camino and the patriarch of Aquileia.[2] It is not possible to say how far the Union was responsible for the policies of the commune in these years. Perhaps the classes which it represented were less affected by the traditional loyalties of the past than the nobles and the older families of the *popolo;* but the breaking of old ties seems to have been countenanced by some members of all classes and represented the arrival of a generation for whom the memories of Frederick II and Ezzelino and the Estensi-Da Romano feud had grown dim. All that can be said with certainty is that the Union retained an interest in the policy of southward expansion on the part of the commune which was a characteristic of the period of its birth.

The first evidence connecting the Union with the territory gained in 1294 comes from a statute of 1295 by which the commune sought to exploit its new foothold on the Adige by building a fortified bridge at Castelbaldo. The provision that progress in this work, which was known as the fortress of Pizone, should be reviewed every fifteen days by the *podestà* and the *gastaldiones* takes on a great significance in view of what

---

should be given to the *iudex ancianorum*. In 1321, the council of the Union called on the *XV gastaldiones* to request the *iudex ancianorum* to enforce discipline among the other *anciani de comunancia* (Roberti, p. 85).

[1] AMS VI, n. 54.
[2] *Liber Regiminum*, p. 347. For further details of the 'salt war', see below, p. 272.

followed.¹ By an undated resolution of the council of *gastaldiones* which may be placed before November 1300, the Union sought to press the commune to take action in the matter of the garrisoning and conservation of the fortress of Pizone.² A similar resolution was passed in January 1308, and when the Union was revived after a period of eclipse in 1315, the statutes making the safeguarding of Pizone the responsibility of the *podestà*, the *anziani* and the *XV gastaldiones* were revived at the same time.³ Part of the explanation is to be found in two documents of 1310 and 1312, which show the Union collecting rents from property in Castelbaldo, which it had taken over from the commune in the latter half of 1310.⁴

After 1294, the policy of further southward expansion awaited an opportunity which did not come until 1305. In that year, when Azzo d'Este was faced with a hostile combination which included Verona and Bologna, to which he was about to lose both Modena and Reggio, his brothers Aldovrandino and Francesco quarrelled with him and retired to Lendenara. After a pause which suggests that there was no pre-arranged plan, Francesco agreed to surrender to the commune his share in Lendenara and the family property in the Padovano and it is likely that Aldovrandino, who was not a strong character, did likewise. To this, Azzo reacted energetically, capturing Lendenara and forcing the Paduans to withdraw. A reconciliation between Azzo and the commune seems to have followed quickly, and was certainly complete by the winter of 1307; in January 1308, Azzo died in Paduan territory at Este, in the house of Nicolò da Lozzo, on his way to seek a cure at the baths of Abano.⁵

On his death, another family dispute over the inheritance broke out, with Aldovrandino and Francesco pressing their claims against Azzo's illegitimate son Fresco, who had succeeded him in the *signoria* of Ferrara. Almost at once, the

---

¹ *Stat. Not.*, f. 29v, Roberti, p. 74–6.
² Statuta et Ordinamenta Fratalee Muratoriorum, Gennari *CDP* IX, p. 1380.
³ Verci, *Marca Trivigiana*, doc. n. 492; Stat. Fruttaroli, AS Padua, Fruttaroli I, f. 8, Roberti, p. 81.
⁴ AS Padua, AD 5011 (Zorzi, pp. 236–8), and Corp. Sopp. S. Agostino 168, n. 66.
⁵ *Chronicon Estense*, pp. 61–8; Ferreto Ferreti, *Opere*, ed. C. Cipolla, FSI (1908–20), I, pp. 214–21.

brothers agreed to cede their rights in Rovigo and certain villages of the Polesine to the Paduans in return for help against Fresco; when Aldovrandino seemed unwilling to ratify this agreement, he was placed under the ban of the commune and forced to hand over his rights to his sons Obizzo and Renaldo. But Fresco had obtained the support of the Bolognese and the Venetians, the latter, who had been complaining of the tolls levied by the Paduans at Lendenara, being particularly concerned to prevent any possible extension of Paduan rule to Ferrara.[1] The Paduans, who had been repulsed by the Venetians only four years before, were unwilling to risk another encounter and abandoned Francesco again, and he was forced to withdraw from the Polesine where he had been building up a base. It even appears from a document of 3 March 1308 that the commune had entered into some kind of agreement with Fresco.[2]

At last, in September 1308, the cautious policies of the commune brought their reward. With the Papal forces which had been called in beginning to counter-balance Fresco's Venetian allies in Ferrara, Francesco carried out a successful coup in Rovigo, which he promptly sold, together with its whole district, to the Paduans. Fresco and the Venetians were in no position to retaliate, and reluctantly recognised the new situation. At last, the Paduan commune was firmly astride the Adige and its southern frontier extended almost to the gates of Ferrara.

Little is known of the internal politics of the Paduan commune at the moment of its greatest territorial expansion, but there are some shreds of evidence which suggest that the Union was active, and that it may have been involved in the occupation of Rovigo which marked the culmination of the policy with which it had been particularly associated since its foundation. When the crisis began, in January 1308, the Union urged the repair of the fortress of Pizone; in February, the *podestà*, *X sapientes*, the *anziani* and the *XV gastaldiones* ordered the unfortunate Aldovrandino to complete the cession

---

[1] Predelli, *Libri Commemoriali*, I, nn. 306, 314–15, 327–8, 348. 'Prohibeant nostri Paduanis ne intrent Ferrariam', AS Venice, Misti III, f. 14, cit. Soranzo, *Venezia e la S. Sede*, p. 68, q.v. for a comprehensive treatment of the war of Ferrara and its consequences 1308–13.

[2] Cipolla, *Relazioni Verona-Mantova Sec. XIV*, p. 157, Soranzo, p. 71.

of his goods to the commune.¹ In August, the passing of a statute to encourage the Paduan *Arte della Lana* suggests that guild interests were still active; finally, the Venetian recognition of the annexation of Rovigo in September was made in reply to an embassy sent to Venice by the *podestà, sapientes, anziani* and *XV gastaldiones*.²

It should not be imagined that the policies of the commune in the last two decades before 1310 had created an irreparable breach in the traditional alignment of the city with the *pars Marchionis*. The disputes between the Paduans and the Estensi were in a sense only family quarrels. When, in December 1307, the commune protested to Azzo VIII over some disturbances in the frontier area, he humbly asked forgiveness in the following terms:

Well do the men and commune of Padua know that the house of Este was born and created of Padua, and that the late Marchesi Azzo and Obizzo, for whom indeed Padua was always a father, had and held her as a mother, and she treated them as true sons; and if the present Marchese at any time has erred in any way, with all reverence he is sorrowful towards the commune of Padua and repents.³

The language of this reply was doubtless influenced by Azzo's overriding desire for peace; he was, moreover, a dying man, but he must have calculated that his words would be heard with sympathy by at least some of the city fathers to whom they were addressed. After his death, though the conflict became sharper, there is nothing to show that anything essential had changed in the relations between Padua and the Estensi; even Francesco, after his many betrayals, was willing to fight for the commune in 1312. But, from 1308, the quarrels were no longer confined to the family. The Papal intervention in Ferrara proved to be the prelude to the mounting of Henry of Luxemburg's Italian expedition. As in the time of Frederick II, the March was caught up for a time in the affairs of Europe. Although the direct influence of the Emperor's coming was short-lived, the equilibrium which had existed up to 1308 was never restored.

[1] Verci, *Marca Trivigiana*, doc. n. 492; AS Modena, AMS VIII, n. 20.
[2] *Statuti Carraresi*, f. 192r; AS Venice, *Liber Commemorialis*, I, f. 134, *cit.* Soranzo, pp. 254–6.
[3] AS Modena, AMS VIII, n. 14; Soranzo, p. 243.

CHAPTER IX

The Crisis of the Paduan Commune

ON 9 April 1311, nearly a year after his rising against the Venetian government had ended in fiasco, Baiamonte Tiepolo came to Padua to canvass support among his friends for a second attempt. His visit was reported in detail to the Venetian *signoria* by a spy, who observed him first going in to lunch with Tiso Camposanpiero, and then followed him to the house of the Papafava family in Via S. Martino, where the *parlamenta* of Tiso's *pars* were normally held. The meeting was well attended—the whole street was full of people—and through the heavy rain the spy picked out the leaders whom he knew. The Paduan magnates present included representatives of the Camposanpiero, Carraresi and Maccaruffi, and among the *popolani* were Albertino Mussato, Rolando da Piazzola and Pietro Altichini; from outside Padua came two ambassadors on behalf of Riccardo da Camino, *signore* of Treviso, and two of the Venetian Quirini, a family long associated with Padua and Baiamonte's chief supporters in his coup the previous June. The *pars* of Tiso Camposanpiero was clearly none other than the local segment of the *pars Marchionis;* the only group of families notably absent were the Da Lozzo, Da Castelnovo and Schinelli.

The spy somehow insinuated himself into the meeting and noted what was said. First Baiamonte made a blustering appeal for help; within twenty days, he said, he would return to Venice and make a shambles of his enemies. He then found a pretext to withdraw and it was the turn of Riccardo da Camino's ambassadors, who delivered a message of general encouragement without committing their master to any definite course of action. The Paduan leaders then began to discuss their response. The first two speakers were Enrico Scrovegni and Filippo da Peraga, and they were for offering Baiamonte all possible aid; the Da Peraga had been in arms the previous summer, and Filippo, whose uncle Badoer Badoer had suffered death for his part in the earlier rising, promised to come himself with 800 well-equipped men. A more cautious note was struck by Maccaruffo Maccaruffi, who spoke next. He suggested that if Baiamonte was so certain of success, he should first seize Venice, and then his friends would support him as might be necessary, but to offer help openly at this stage would be imprudent. Maccaruffo's scarcely veiled sarcasm set the tone for the last and most interesting speech recorded by the spy. The speaker was the notary Matteo Filarolo, a man of modest personal standing but of considerable experience, having served Guido da Lozzo, Tiso's predecessor as leader of the *pars*. He said:

Gentlemen, if there was ever a time when our *pars*, which has ruled in this city for the last fifty years, should be of one body and mind to preserve and increase itself and also increase all its friends, now is that time. For we have lost our greatest source of strength, that is the house of Este, and the coming of the Emperor is bad for us, and therefore I would be willing to do much to keep us one together and procure our increase and that of our friends. And so I say that if what Baiamonte says is true, it will be good to support him as he wishes, but I advise Baiamonte to arrange his affair better than he did the last time.[1]

In his analysis of the weakness of the *pars Marchionis* in 1311, Matteo Filarolo placed the uprooting of the Estensi, the *fortitudo maxima* of the *pars* first, and the coming of the Emperor second. The causes of the eclipse of the house of Este from 1308 to 1317 are obscure, and remote from the internal history of the Paduan commune. It had begun when Azzo lost control of Modena and Reggio in 1305, but it became catastrophic only with the intervention of outside powers in the family dispute which followed his death. Fresco's appeal to the Venetians found them willing to abandon their centuries-old policy of isolationism towards the Terrafirma and engage in a disastrous adventure in Ferrara. When the Paduans failed him, Francesco d'Este, or possibly Guido da Montebello, bishop of Ferrara, on his behalf, called in the temporal power of the Papacy, but Clement V, when he intervened, did not do so to support either party but to make good an ancient Papal claim to the direct rule of Ferrara as a part of the Papal State. From that moment, in April 1308, it is true to say that whichever side

[1] AS Venice, *Liber Commemorialis*, I, f. 162v, printed in Picotti, *I Caminesi*, pp. 295-7.

won the war over Ferrara, the Estensi were bound to lose. The victory of the Papal forces in August 1309 was recognised by the Venetians in the following year, and peace was eventually made between the major contestants, but for the Estensi there could be no permanent acquiescence in the loss of the city which had been their home since 1240 and their personal *signoria* since 1264. In exile, they never lost sight of a return to Ferrara, and they were willing to consider help from any quarter in order to accomplish this aim, even if it meant consorting with Imperialists or heretics. The identification of the *pars Marchionis* with the *pars Ecclesiae* was at an end.[1]

For the Paduans, the course taken by the war of Ferrara was profoundly disturbing. The grand alliance between the *pars Marchionis*, the church and the Venetians which had proved decisive against Salinguerra and Ezzelino in the mid-thirteenth century, had fallen apart. At first, the Paduans tried to mediate between Venice and the Pope, but as the war progressed they were forced to make a choice between the contestants. With its usual opportunism, the commune inclined towards the winning side. Pagano della Torre, bishop of Padua, led a force of Paduan volunteers to join the Papa army; the property of the excommunicate Venetians in thel Padovano was confiscated, and in general the conduct of the commune was such as to earn a letter of commendation from Clement V.[2] The Paduans could now expect the friendship and support of the Papacy, but it was worth surprisingly little. The precarious regime of the Papal governors in Ferrara, remotely controlled from Avignon and surrounded by the hostile intrigues of the *pars Marchionis* and the Venetians, proved no substitute for the powerful Estense *signoria*. Perpetually insecure, in 1312, the Papal Vicar in Ferrara resorted to political murder to remove the menace represented by Francesco d'Este. The disturbances which followed this event persuaded Clement V to buttress his hold on Ferrara by confiding the *signoria* to Robert of Naples. The Angevin succeeded in holding the city until 1317, but with his widespread interests he was far inferior to the

---

[1] Soranzo, *Venezia e la S. Sede, passim*. Most authorities say that Francesco invited Papal intervention, but the Vicentine historian Ferreto Ferreti (*Opere*, I, p. 243) attributes the initiative to the bishop, who was a Vicentine by birth.

[2] Ferreti, *Opere*, I, p. 256; Verci, *Marca Trivigiana*, doc. n. 507.

Estensi as a leader of the local Guelph parties. Nor did the Guelph cause receive any clear direction from above, since Clement was committed to support Henry of Luxemburg's expedition to Italy for the Imperial crown.

When Matteo Filarolo described the coming of Henry VII as bad for the *pars Marchionis*, he was speaking from a narrowly Paduan point of view. While it would be true to consider the *pars Marchionis* as traditionally Guelph rather than Ghibelline, this was not an essential characteristic; moreover Henry came not as a Ghibelline but with the blessing of the Pope as the mediator between all parties. What his arrival threatened was change: a source of fear to all parties in possession and of hope to all exiles. Thus the leaders of the Veronese segment of the *pars Marchionis*, in exile in Vicenza, sent to Henry recognising him and requesting the return of all their rights and possessions in Verona.[1] Riccardo da Camino, the Guelph *signore* of Treviso, angled for the appointment as Imperial Vicar no less than the Ghibelline Della Scala of Verona. The Paduans had nothing to gain from the Emperor and much to lose. There was no place in the Paduan constitution for an Imperial Vicar with any independent power and the Paduans had a deep-seated fear of the title and the interference which it represented. But there was no desire to reject the nominal authority of the Emperor as such, and Paduan representatives attended Henry's coronation as King of Italy in Milan in January 1311, and during the spring negotiations went on to find some compromise by which Padua could show herself 'faithful to the Empire' without any real loss of independence.

Padua was fortunate in having no exiles at her gates clamouring to return; her Achilles' heel was the subject city of Vicenza which was always seeking an opportunity to regain its independence. On 15 April 1311, less than a week after Matteo Filarolo had uttered his warning, the blow fell. The citizens of Vicenza, aided by a force of Veronese and Imperial troops under Aimo, bishop of Geneva, rose against the Paduan garrison and drove it out, bringing to an end the Paduan domination which had begun in 1266.

The loss of Vicenza had the effect of transforming the Paduans' attitude to Henry of Luxemburg. Rather surprisingly,

---

[1] F. Bonaini, *Acta Henrici Romanorum Imperatoris*, I, n. xc. For a recent account of Henry VII's expedition, see W. Bowsky, *Henry VII in Italy* (1960).

the commune seems to have accepted the loss of political control as inevitable, at least for the time being; what those who governed the commune could not tolerate was the confiscation of Paduan property in the Vicentino which the Vicentines, following the Paduan example set in 1266, carried through under the pretext of an indemnity. As an additional refinement, the Vicentines cut off an important part of Padua's water supply by closing the dam across the Bacchiglione at Longare. To obtain redress, the Paduans turned to the Emperor-elect, showing themselves prepared to make substantial concessions, even receiving Henry's nominee as Imperial Vicar, so long as it seemed possible that he would use his authority to secure an equitable settlement with the Vicentines. In February 1312, after prolonged negotiations at Henry's court in Genoa, a Paduan legation in which the leading spirit was Albertino Mussato, returned to Padua with an Imperial letter appointing two judges to hear the Paduan complaints. Mussato's eloquence would probably have succeeded in persuading the Consiglio Maggiore to accept the Imperial arbitration, had not news been received on the second day of the debate, that Henry had appointed Cangrande della Scala, already Imperial Vicar of Verona, to be Imperial Vicar of Vicenza also. Rolando da Piazzola used this information to raise the spectre of Frederick II and Ezzelino which had haunted the Paduans for a generation, and carried the majority of the assembly with him. The council voted to throw off the Imperial authority, and join Florence, Bologna and the other cities in rebellion against the Empire.[1]

The Paduan commune's rejection of the Empire was, in effect, a declaration of war against Cangrande della Scala and Verona. The Emperor, fully occupied with his march to Rome and later in Tuscany, was in no position to intervene, except through the Imperial Vicar of Verona and Vicenza. Though posing as the Emperor's servant, Cangrande, like Ezzelino, was really intent on building up a new state which would embrace the whole of the March. The Paduan commune was the rallying point of the opposition to this design. The Guelph league, led by Florence and Bologna, gave the Paduans moral support, but each of the members was too occupied in its own region to do more. The contest was between the Paduan

[1] Mussato, *Historia Augusta*, coll. 411–20.

republic and the Veronese *signoria* for the domination of the March.

The Paduan prospects at the onset of the war were not unfavourable. The city was apparently at the height of its mediaeval prosperity; in total resources there was probably not much difference between the Paduans and the Veronese. But whereas the Paduans had the support of a body of Veronese exiles led by Count Vicinguerra da San Bonifacio, the number of Paduan Ghibellines was at first negligible. Almost the only family with a continuous tradition of Ghibellinism going back to the time of Frederick II was the Paltinerii of Monselice. The head of the family, Guglielmo Novello, had a personal history of bad relations with the commune. In 1277, he had been involved in a violent dispute with the Dalesmanini over the annulment of his sister Zilia's marriage to Giacomo Dalesmanini; in 1288 he was condemned to death for murder, but was pardoned after a year in exile in 1289.[1] In 1312, he was described by Villani as 'il gran capo di parte Ghibellina in Padova' and as such, when the commune broke with the Empire, Guglielmo came under immediate suspicion. It was deemed safer to allow him no opportunity for treason; while the forces of law and order turned a blind eye, he was assassinated.[2]

For fifty years and more, Guelphism in Padua had been synonymous with political orthodoxy, so that all dissident elements of whatever character tended to be branded as Ghibelline. Thus those who fled or were driven into exile as friends of Guglielmo Paltinerii had no traceable connection with the Empire but were in bad odour with the dominant party in the city for a wide variety of reasons. Marco Forzatè, for example, was the son of the Giovanni Forzatè who had been confined to his villages by the *podestà* in 1281. He and other members of his family had been under the ban of the commune between 1297 and 1303 for reasons which are now obscure, but which were probably connected with their position as powerful magnates in the important region of

---

[1] *Stat. Com.* 85.I, Corona 2206, ff. 107–13; L. A. Botteghi, 'Iacopo Dalesmanini e le fazioni di Padova nel 1277', *ARAP* XX (1904), pp. 139–54; *Annales Patavini*, p. 230, *Liber Regiminum*, p. 340.

[2] Villani, *Cronica*, IV, p. 31; Cortusi, p. 14. For the Paltinerii, see above, p. 77.

Bassano.¹ Da Nono mentions that they waged a series of private battles with the Lemici.² Renaldo II and Gaboardo Scrovegni, also exiled in 1312, were closely related to the Paltinerii and Forzatè by blood and marriage. Their mother was Giacomina Paltinerii, a noble but worthless woman according to Da Nono, who had persuaded Gaboardo to renounce his wife, a daughter of Zilio Maccaruffi, in favour of a sister of Marco Forzatè, thus opening a feud between her sons and the Maccaruffi. In addition, Renaldo's daughter Alice was married to Marco's kinsman Forzatè Forzatè.³ However, all the Scrovegni did not follow the same lead: Enrico, married to a daughter of Francesco d'Este, remained a constant if rather weak-kneed supporter of the Guelph cause to the end.

Apart from Traverso Dalesmanini, an illegitimate offspring of a declining family, the alleged Ghibellines among the Paduan magnates were confined to the Paltinerii, Forzatè and Scrovegni, none of them families of the first rank in either prestige or power. Evidence for a strong Ghibelline party among the Paduan *popolo* is equally lacking. One or two individuals of the administrative class were known as Ghibellines before 1310; Simone Enghelfredi, the most distinguished of these, died without heirs in 1311, and Giovanni Caligine, who had been *podestà* of Verona in 1305, went into exile in Venice when his term of office as Imperial Vicar of Arezzo expired.⁴ The origins and significance of the Ghibelline associations of these men are obscure, but it is possible that, as trained lawyers, they were influenced by the ideal of the Emperor as the universal guardian of the law, in the same way as Albertino Mussato can be seen to have been deeply influenced by the glamour of the Imperial title and its historical associations. In his letters can be traced some of the stages by which Mussato's earlier misgivings were overcome, largely, one suspects, because of the friendship and personal favours bestowed on him by Henry.⁵ In the crucial debate, Mussato

---

¹ Verci, *Marca Trivigiana*, doc. nn. 398, 410; Tua, *Reg. Arch. Bassanesi*, nn. 790–2, 804, *etc*.
² *De Generatione*, f. 35.
³ Ibid. f. 44r; AD 6038. See Genealogical Table 16, p. 189.
⁴ See above, pp. 113–18.
⁵ Compare the misgivings expressed in Ep. V with the praise of Henry in Ep. II; Graevius, coll. 36–8, 41–2.

urged the dangers of breaking with the Emperor-elect, yet, after the vote, he immediately fell into line with the majority of the council, and became one of the strongest protagonists of the war with Cangrande.

It is even harder to find evidence of serious Imperialism among the lesser members of the Paduan *popolo*. If, as is possible, a majority of the guildsmen had once supported Ezzelino, there is nothing to suggest that this had given rise to a Ghibelline tradition in this class. Because of their association with anti-Estensi policies, the leaders of the Union laid themselves open to charges of Ghibellinism but there is nothing to show that, for example, they rallied to Mussato's side in February 1312.[1] As for the general populace, their political consciousness must have been overwhelmingly Guelph, having been formed by the stories of Imperialist atrocities enshrined in the Ezzelino legend. Verona was associated with Ezzelino as the traditional enemy, and even the title of Imperial Vicar was regarded with fear. When the commune finally rejected Henry VII, the mob tore down the Imperial insignia on the public buildings, and a year later the guilds organised celebrations when the death of the Emperor became known.[2]

In the war with the Della Scala, the Paduan commune faced all the disadvantages of a democratically controlled regime in competition with a despotism. The nature of the war placed a high premium on unity of purpose and a strong executive, able to make instant decisions for the safety of the state. Castles and walled towns were virtually impregnable except to a long siege or a surprise attack coupled with treason; both placed a maximum strain on the defending population. With the advanced base of the Della Scala at Vicenza only seventeen miles from the gates of Padua, the normal manoeuvre in mounting a surprise attack was to march out the army from the one city at sunset so as to appear before the walls of the other at dawn. Even in times of truce, the danger of treason was ever-present, and the tension, which manifested itself in the hunting down of alleged traitors, must have been extreme. On the other hand, in the first decade of the fourteenth century

---

[1] E.g. the *Chronicon Estense* (p. 60) alleges that Francesco d'Este surrendered Lendenara to the Paduan Ghibellines in 1305 and Mussato accused the *gastaldiones* of being under Ghibelline influence (*De Gestis*, col. 587).

[2] *Historia Augusta*, coll. 391, 421; *Stat. Not.*, ff. 71v–72r.

the Paduan commune had apparently developed a remarkable degree of political stability. The bare chronicles of the period record the unsuccessful war against Venice in 1304, the annexation of the county of Rovigo in 1308, and the Tiepolo conspiracy of 1310, in which members of the *pars Marchionis* with lands in Paduan territory were involved, without mentioning that any of these events and the complicated political manoeuvres which surrounded them were the occasion of any civic disorders of the kind which had broken out from time to time in the later thirteenth century. If, as is probable, the guilds played an important part in the government of the commune during these years, the interests of friendly magnates were not neglected. For example, in 1299 the commune condemned Alberto della Scala, *signore* of Verona, to death for instigating an attempt on the life of Tiso Camposanpiero, and in 1302 reprisals were granted against the Della Torre and the commune of Milan in satisfaction of a claim by Ubertino da Carrara for the dowry of his daughter-in-law, Elena della Torre.[1]

If there was any fatal weakness in the Paduan state in the early fourteenth century, it should be looked for not at the political but at the social level, in the social tension displayed in the writings of the two most important Paduan historians of the period, Mussato and Da Nono. It is not that these two writers directly record the class conflict: they rather reveal it through their prejudices, which lead them to emphasise class issues beyond all reason, contrasting strongly with the stress on social unity to be found in Rolandino. Thus Da Nono, in his summary of Rolandino's account of the fall of the city to Frederick II in 1236, tilts the narrative so as to emphasise the treachery of the *XVI* native *podestà* appointed to deal with the crisis, who are no longer, as with Rolandino, of the *maiores* of the city, but *popolani* who receive Imperial *privilegia* and £1,000 each as their reward for the betrayal of the city.[2] Similarly, Mussato tends to blame every disaster on the guildsmen, whom he calls vile mechanics wrapped up in sordid commerce, corrupt, incompetent and under the influence of Ghibelline demagogues.[3] Both writers inveigh against the Paduan

---

[1] *Annales Patavini*, p. 232; *Statuti Carraresi*, f. 146v.
[2] *De Generatione*, f. 21.
[3] 'Ad Tribunos quidem, quos Gastaldiones vocitabant, omnia publica,

usurers; the whole of the *De Generatione* is built round the contrast between the good old nobility and the ignobility of the newly enriched moneylenders, while Mussato's lurid attack on the vices of the Altichini came strangely from the lips of one who had been their political ally right up to the outbreak of the rising against them.[1] How far one is justified in generalising from the prejudices of two such unusual personalities it is difficult to decide. Mussato's natural talents had raised him from obscurity to a leading position in the commune; in an autobiographical poem, he describes how he consciously attached himself to the nobility and aped their ways.[2] Da Nono, on the other hand, believed that his family had been depressed far below their natural station, and he compensated for his present mediocrity by idealising the good old days when the city could boast two or three hundred noble young men taking knightly exercises on feast days, while any *popolano* who dared to show his face at the noble banquet which followed would have been set upon by the young aristocrats.[3] What Mussato and Da Nono seem to be reflecting from their widely differing points of view, is an uneasiness amid the new-found affluence of Paduan society, and a failure to accept the increased social mobility and new sources of wealth which economic development had brought.

However, the tension within Paduan society might never

---

privataque iudicia transtulere, et hi omnes opifices erant et qui sordidis commerciis vitabundi volutabantur. Hi forenses, publicasque causas sedentes, applaudibus hortantibusque Gibolengorum demagogis audiebant, iudicioque glorientes ad nutum finiebant', *De Gestis*, col. 587.

[1] Cf. 'Verum secunda optimarum rerum felicitas adeo iam ambitiosos illos effecerat, ut abusu, luxuque labefacti, licentiosiores insolescerent paulatim. Unde identidem bonorum horum prodierat immoderata corruptio, iniquorum scilicet testium, omnisque falsi detestanda crimina, ususque voracis foenoris et lasciviens sanies omnis morbosa cupidinis', *De Gestis*, col. 586; 'In hoc tempore, quasi omnes Patavi pecunias fenori mutuabunt, quod mea lege maledictum est . . . Et nisi ab hiis delictis se abstineant Paduani, maius flagellum quam fuerit Ecerini, mandabo super eos . . .', *Visio Egidii*, p. 3. For Mussato on the Altichini, see *De Gestis*, coll. 607–8.

[2]   'Dilixi proceres et eis solertior haesi
       His propior multa sedulitate fui.
       Utque erat urbanus tanto mihi carior usus
       Regnat in his mixta nobilitate vigor?'
                                      Elegia, Graevins, col. 64.

[3] *De Generatione*, ff. 27v–28r.

have come to the surface had it not been for the strain imposed by the long and unsuccessful war against Verona. None of the problems faced by the commune were new, but they were present in an extreme form. It was always necessary in war to concentrate power in the hands of a few; government by committee could quickly degenerate into government by a clique. Simultaneously, war conditions increased the power of the more warlike magnates and their trained followers, at the expense of the less experienced and less easily mobilised citizens. As the war progressed, the problem of leadership became acute; to oppose Cangrande della Scala who, combining the widest civil and military powers, had emerged as one of the great captains of his age, the commune failed to find a general of even moderate abilities. In consequence, the political life of the commune became dominated by rival leaders advocating contradictory policies, prepared in the last resort to threaten their rivals with civil war. In the end, a single faction led by the Carraresi and supported by the Della Scala, prevailed over all its rivals and set up the *signoria*.

It is indicative of the nature of Paduan society that the breakdown, when it came, did not follow the lines of the class divisions, nor did it centre about the institutions within the state, like the *comunanza* or the Union of the Guilds. Long before the end, these had become insignificant beside the rivalry of the nobly led *partes*. The old *pars Marchionis* which had dominated the state for so many years was gradually dissolved into its component parts. In each segment, the nucleus consisted of a magnate family or group of families, supported by its rural tenants and urban clients. To be effective, a magnate leader needed a group of loyal citizens to further his interests within the commune; when it came to civil war, the members of his own family and his more wealthy followers among the *popolo* made up the cavalry, while the peasants of his estates became the infantry, and his castle was converted into a military base. The fractional *partes* therefore represented a cross section of the classes within the Paduan state, with a strong territorial element, but the most striking feature was the dominance of the great families. Years of anti-magnatial legislation had failed to impair the essential bases of their power, land and men. Even before the war, Filippo da Peraga had been able to promise to raise 800 armed men at short notice, and in the first campaign the Paduan army contained 700 knights and 600 squires raised by the nobility, while the conscript knights of the citizen class numbered 1,200.[1] The process of disintegration revealed the *pars Marchionis* for what it had always been, a loose-knit confederation of magnatial families and their adherents of all classes.

The first campaign against the Veronese in the summer of 1312 saw the *pars Marchionis* rally for the last time to the side of the Paduan commune. The Paduan army which took the field at the engagement at Quartesolo included Francesco d'Este, Guecillo da Camino, Tiso Camposanpiero, Giacomo Grande da Carrara and Nicolò da Lozzo.[2] But casualties and defections among the great families of the region began very soon. Francesco d'Este was killed in August, and from that date none of the Estensi are mentioned as serving the commune. Guecillo da Camino, who succeeded his murdered brother Riccardo as *signore* of Treviso in April, led a successful raid into the Vicentino and was rewarded with the honour of nominating the next *podestà* by the Paduans.[3] What he wanted, however, was the office of commander in chief, and when this was not forthcoming he retired and began to treat with the Ghibellines of Friuli and indirectly with Cangrande. In December, a group of Trevisan Guelphs staged a coup and seized the city, which reverted to a communal regime.[4] There is nothing to show that the Paduans were involved in the plot, but its results were on the whole in their interests, since the second generation of the Da Camino had shown themselves very unreliable as allies, with no firm attachment to the Guelph cause. Like most *signori*, they were attracted to the Emperor because he could give their regime what it needed most, an unimpeachable title of legitimacy.

Barely a week after the fall of Guecillo da Camino came the first major defection among the Paduan nobility, the rebellion of Nicolò da Lozzo. Contemporaries explained this disaster in terms of Nicolò's personality; Mussato builds up a striking picture of a brilliant but unreliable man which might be suspect as a literary exaggeration were it not substantially

---

[1] *Historia Augusta*, coll. 429–30.
[2] Ibid. coll. 425–6.
[3] Ibid. col. 446; *Liber Regiminum*, p. 351.
[4] *Historia Augusta*, coll. 481–6.

supported by Da Nono.[1] Although neither writer mentions the fact, the family had a chequered political record. Nicolò's grandfather had been a supporter of the Estensi, but his father Guido had, in his younger days, been one of the last Paduan noblemen to associate himself with Ezzelino's government. In later life, as we have seen, Guido became the leader of the Paduan Guelphs and married a sister of Obizzo d'Este. Despite his parentage, Nicolò's personal career suggests that he was only loosely attached to the party, the leadership of which passed to Tiso Camposanpiero. It is probably significant that the Da Lozzo and their neighbours did not attend the meeting addressed by Baiamonte Tiepolo in 1311. If Nicolò had any consistent policy, it was probably bound up with his territorial interests. His lands were cut off from Padua by the Pedevenda but lay open towards Verona and Vicenza. Perhaps he hoped to acquire the *signoria* of Vicenza or to carve out an independent enclave for himself. His closest personal ties were with the Estensi and the Da Camino; Francesco's death and Guecillo's defection may both have had an influence on him.

Not much is known of the composition of Nicolò da Lozzo's *pars*. Doubtless, its main strength lay in the men of the Pedevenda, his tenants, who could be mobilised about the castle of Lozzo.[2] Nicolò had a bosom companion, a *popolano* called Antonio da Curtarolo, the son of a judge, with whom he had been associated since at least 1302. By chance, it is known that the taverner Brazaro de Iza and his son Domenico were also followers of Da Lozzo. Perhaps they were his tenants in Galzignano. When they joined Nicolò, they left a considerable debt in the city.[3] More important were Nicolò's noble kinsmen and neighbours, the Maltraversi of Castelnovo and the Schinelli of Rovolon, whose lands the war with Verona placed in an equally exposed position. The latter, who had been involved in the Vicentine plot of 1279, were probably the first of the Paduan nobles to defect, Pancetta Schinelli being killed in action on the Veronese side in June 1312.[4] The Castelnovo, on the other hand, seem to have followed Nicolò's lead.

[1] Ibid. col. 486 et seq.; Da Nono, *De Generatione*, ff. 30r, 38r.
[2] In the campaign of 1312 Nicolò captured Noventa Vicentina, not far from Lozzo, 'evocatis Pedevendae colonis'; *Historia Augusta*, col. 425.
[3] AD 5163; see above, p. 141.
[4] *Historia Augusta*, col. 427.

Albertino, who had been Guecillo da Camino's *podestà* in Treviso at the time of his fall, surrendered his castle of Boccon to Cangrande early in 1313, and the family is definitely listed among the rebels in 1319–20.[1]

After the expulsion of the Ghibellines and the defection of the Da Lozzo faction, it was natural that the defenders of Padua should begin to close their ranks. A week after the loss of Vicenza, the commune had set up two committees, of eight and twelve members respectively, for the defence of Padua and the recovery of the subject city.[2] By the beginning of 1313, these had been superseded by a secret council, or *credenza*, of eight, and four *conservatores libertatis, status et partis*.[3] The *pars* to be understood in this title is made clear by a reference, in May of the same year, to the syndic of the commune and the Guelph party of the city of Padua, which is the first specific evidence that a *pars Guelpha* now formed a part of the constitution of the city.[4] About the beginning of November, there was a further change in which a Guelph council was set up to vet the decisions of the Consiglio Maggiore, and from which the *anziani, conservatores* and councillors were to be chosen. It was probably at this time that the council of *gastaldiones* of the guilds was deprived of its powers.[5] The real significance of these developments was that power in Padua was becoming increasingly concentrated in the hands of a small clique of predominantly rich *popolani*, notably the Maccaruffi, Polafrisana, Altichini, Da Terradura and Mussato, whose policy was to pursue the war with the utmost vigour.[6] Except for the Maccaruffi, none of the group were of the magnate class, but they could hardly have remained in power without the support of the remaining great families, especially the Carraresi.

In the early months of 1314, discontent with the government of the city by the *pars Guelpha*, which was ruling 'not in

[1] Ibid. coll. 494–5; Cortusi, p. 33.
[2] Verci, *Marca Trivigiana*, doc. n. 524.
[3] Bonaini, *Acta Henrici VII*, I, n. 292.
[4] AD 5182.
[5] Mussato, *De Gestis*, col. 587. This is the most likely sequence of events; as on other occasions, Mussato groups together developments which took place over a considerable space of time. Cf. Zorzi, *L'ordinamento comunale*, pp. 189–92.
[6] Cortusi, p. 15.

accordance with justice, but in the interests of party' was becoming widespread among the lower classes.[1] Matters were brought to a head in April, when Pietro Altichini proposed in the *credenza* that Nicolò and Obizzo da Carrara should be exiled on suspicion of Ghibelline sympathies. In this, he may have been moved solely by jealousy, or it may have been that some of the Carraresi were beginning to doubt whether the war could be won, and may have been taking soundings for a compromise peace, which would have lent a certain substance to Pietro's accusations. At all events, the younger members of the house of Carrara took up the challenge, and Padua was given over to a day and a night of civil war. The struggle revealed where power in the city really lay. The Carraresi helped by the mob, completely outmanoeuvred the *podestà* and the troops of the *comunanza* and Pietro and his sons, together with the Ronchi, a family closely associated with the Altichini, were put to death, and Albertino Mussato was forced to take refuge in the contado. Eventually, the *anziani* and *gastaldiones* restored order. The innovations introduced by the *pars Guelpha* were abolished, and the constitution in force at the outbreak of war was restored.[2] The Union of the Guilds was revived and showed a spurt of activity during the first six months of 1315 and the new office of Defensor Populi was set up.[3]

Despite this apparent recovery on the part of the commune, the fight of April 1314 marks the first step in the advance of the Carraresi towards the *signoria*. Albertino Mussato and the Maccaruffi had saved themselves by allowing the Altichini to become the scapegoats for the whole of the *pars Guelpha,* but their influence over the commune was now rivalled by that of the Carraresi. While the Maccaruffi advocated an all-out effort in the war with Verona, Giacomo da Carrara emerged as the leader of those who were willing to consider a compromise peace. A series of military disasters eventually made Giacomo's policy the only course open to the Paduans. In September 1314, after a rout at the gates of Vicenza, Giacomo arranged his first

---

[1] 'Regentes civitatem non per iustitiam sed per partem', Cortusi, loc. cit.; cf. 'facta hec tractabantur non per iusticiam set per partem', Rolandino, p. 57.

[2] *De Gestis*, coll. 607–14; Cortusi, pp. 21–2.

[3] Roberti, *Le corporazioni*, pp. 81–3. Cf. *De Gestis*, col. 614; once more, Mussato's chronology is vague.

peace with Cangrande.¹ This was broken in July 1317 when a group of Vicentine exiles led by Vicinguerra da San Bonifacio, with Paduan help, made an unsuccessful surprise attack on Vicenza.² Cangrande retaliated in kind, but his plots were better laid. The town of Monselice fell by treason and in the autumn of 1317 the fortresses of the southern part of the Paduan contado surrendered to him one after another. By the end of the year, the Paduan authorities were proposing to hand back their hard-won territories beyond the Adige to the Estensi, as they were no longer able to defend them.³ Despairing of further resistance, the Paduans had no choice but to accept a second and more humiliating peace.

The second peace negotiated by Giacomo da Carrara and his party provided the essential basis for his election to the *signoria*. By its terms, the Paduan exiles were to be allowed to return, and at Easter 1318 the Ghibellines, among them Marco Forzatè, Gaboardo Scrovegni, Traverso Dalesmanini and Michele Schinelli, though not apparently any of the Da Lozzo or Castelnovo, returned to their native city. For a few months, the various factions co-existed in the city while Giacomo tried to build up his position by a policy of conciliation towards the extremists of both parties. In the case of the Ghibellines, he was successful, and it was the Guelphs, beginning with the Maccaruffi and followed by the Lemici, Camposanpiero and Mussato, who went into exile, clearing the way for Giacomo's election as *capitaneus* and *dominus generalis* on 25 July.

The *signoria* of Giacomo da Carrara proved to be no more than an eighteen-month interlude in the story of the decline of the commune. At home, Giacomo's position was insecure from the start, since it depended chiefly on the support of the Ghibelline magnates and the traditionally Guelph *popolo*, but in any case, his external policy of peace and conciliation was doomed by Cangrande, who seems to have determined upon the immediate conquest of the remaining cities of the March of Treviso. Help was necessary from any quarter where it could be found, and in January 1320, Giacomo surrendered

---

¹ *De Gestis*, coll. 645–60.
² The vicissitudes of the Paduan commune from December 1317 to October 1320 are related at length in Mussato, *De Gestis*, ed. Padrin, pp. 17–90; for a shorter account see Cortusi, pp. 25–37.
³ AS Modena, AMS X, n. 30.

the *signoria* to Frederick of Austria, one of the two contenders for the Imperial title, in return for a promise of assistance against Verona.

In the ensuing war, many of the old *pars Guelpha* responded to Giacomo da Carrara's appeal and returned to make common cause with him against the Della Scala under the Hapsburg *signoria*. But the Maccaruffi, formerly the strongest advocates of the war against Cangrande, did not return; with their supporters they passed finally into the exiles' camp and served with the attacking forces during the great siege of Padua in the summer of 1320. The leaders of this *pars* were the four Maccaruffi brothers, Corrado da Vigonza, Marsiglio Polafrisana and three sons of Ailino da Terradura. Within the city, it is noteworthy that both the Maccaruffi and the Da Terradura had their *palazzi* in the short Via S. Clemente, near the central square; in the contado, the interests of the group were spread over a wide arc to the east and south of Padua.[1] The main stronghold of the Maccaruffi was at Brugine, near Piove di Sacco, while the Polafrisana, coming from Noventa, were close neighbours of the Da Vigonza who seem to have originated as minor feudal nobility in the territory just east of Padua. Corrado da Vigonza was eventually taken by the Carraresi in the tower of Curano on the Venetian border, but he had also held the castle of Vighizzolo south of Este, deep in the homelands of the Estensi.[2] In fact, ties with the Marchesi may have been traditional with other families of the *pars*. According to Da Nono, Marsiglio Polafrisana's grandfather had been a professional knight at the court of Azzo VII and, as we have seen, there is some evidence that Zilio Maccaruffi, the leader of his family in the previous generation, had been on good terms with Obizzo II.[3]

Though the Maccaruffi faction finally left Padua in about March or April 1318, to follow the train of events it is necessary to return to the previous August, when Ferrara was regained by the Estensi. Among those who helped Aldovrandino's sons Renaldo and Obizzo to drive out Robert of Anjou's garrison were 80 Paduan cavalry and 600 infantry; a version of the Paduan annals names Maccaruffo Maccaruffi and Marsiglio

---

[1] For the earlier history of the Da Terradura, see above, pp. 138–9.
[2] Cortusi, pp. 39, 40, 45.
[3] *De Generatione*, f. 45r; above, p. 119.

Polafrisana as among those present.[1] Maccaruffo had been on terms of the greatest confidence with the Estensi for some years, as his selection as arbitrator between Aldovrandino and his brother Francesco's heirs in 1313 shows;[2] his brother Benastrutto's daughter was married to the young Renaldo d'Este. Presumably, the Maccaruffi could now count on the support of the Estensi should they attempt to contest with the Carraresi for the *signoria* of Padua. About this time, Da Nono reckoned their total forces to be superior to those of the Carrara, their supporters being particularly strong in the city, but in the opinion of the historian, their tenants in the contado were somewhat more difficult to mobilise than those of their rivals.[3] In the event, for reasons which will always be obscure, the Maccaruffi never made an independent bid for the control of Padua. The fall of Este and Monselice to Cangrande in the winter of 1317 must have made things difficult for them, since their estates were laid open to Veronese attacks and their communications with Ferrara were threatened; even so, there is something inexplicable in the way they tamely went into exile. Hostility to the Carraresi now predominated over every other motive, and to bring them down the Maccaruffi were willing to plot with Cangrande and the Ghibelline exiles. When they returned to Paduan territory, it was in the train of Cangrande's invading army, and during the siege Maccaruffo himself was captured and executed in the city where he had once had the supreme power almost within his grasp.

The defection of so powerful a family as the Maccaruffi was a serious blow to the declining fortunes of the Paduan commune. It was not only their own dependants and adherents that they carried with them into the camp of Padua's enemies; they were also instrumental in turning the Estensi, the greatest family of all, against the Paduans in their hour of need. At first, the evidence for this is circumstantial. The Maccaruffi must have left Padua for Ferrara soon after the peace with Cangrande, which is dated 14 March 1318, and by 19 May, Cangrande was appointing a representative to conclude an alliance with the Estensi against the Paduans.[4] Nothing is more

[1] *De Gestis*, ed. Padrin, p. 12; *Annales Patavini*, p. 264.
[2] AMS X, n. 6.
[3] *De Generatione*, f. 38v.
[4] *De Gestis*, ed. Padrin, pp. 32–6; AMS X, n. 26.

likely than that the young and inexperienced *signori* of Ferrara should, at this moment, have been influenced by the older Maccaruffi with whom they were so closely related. By the spring of 1319, it is certain that they, with the Maccaruffi and the Ghibellines Marco Forzatè and Traverso Dalesmanini, were involved in a comprehensive plan for the dismemberment of the Paduan state, from which the Estensi were to gain the permanent annexation of the Paduan territories south of the Adige.[1] As it happened, the campaigns of 1319 and 1320 did not go as planned and only the Estensi secured their objectives. The surviving Maccaruffi, who must have hoped to return to Padua under Veroncse and Ferrarese protection, seem to have finally settled to a new life in the Estensi dominions, where they appear from time to time in the service of the Marchesi.

From the point of view of Renaldo and Obizzo d'Este, excommunicated and threatened by the church and the Angevins, the value of the alliance with Verona was chiefly defensive. With the re-establishment of the northern frontier of their state at the Adige, they had no further territorial claims on the Paduan commune and they do not appear to have participated personally in any offensive action on Paduan territory. But their passive hostility may have decided the fate of Padua, since through it the commune was cut off from the assistance of the great Guelph cities of Bologna and Florence, which might otherwise have intervened to save their northern ally, with whom they had co-operated since the days of Henry VII. The moral effect of the new state of affairs was also considerable. The *pars Marchionis et Ecclesiae* which had enveloped the restored commune from its earliest days was shattered. Some idea of the feelings generated in Padua can be seen from the answers of the Paduan witnesses to the Papal inquiry into help given to the Estensi in 1321; a notary Nascimbene de Raivo testified that the Estensi, having once looked on Padua as their mother, had suddenly turned against her and Gualpertino Mussato said that they were more hated

---

[1] *De Gestis*, ed. Padrin, pp. 52–3. The voluntary cession of Rovigo, Lendenara, etc. which had been proposed by the Paduan authorities in December 1317 had not been carried out, as Obizzo da Carrara was still *podestà* of Rovigo on behalf of the Paduan commune in October 1318 (AS Padua, Liber Tabularum f. 163v).

by the citizens than even Cangrande himself because of the memory of their former friendship.[1]

The resounding defeat of Cangrande's besieging army outside Padua in August 1320 won for the Paduans a few more years of comparative independence under the suzerainty of Frederick of Hapsburg. The government of the 'royal city' as Padua was now styled, remained largely in the hands of the citizens and the influence of the German captains, handicapped by the barrier of language, does not seem to have been felt much, except in military affairs. The commune entered a kind of twilight existence; its institutions were still intact, but the life was slowly ebbing from them.

The departure of the Maccaruffi left only one faction standing between the Carraresi and the complete domination of the state. The professional association of the talented notary Albertino Mussato and the rich usurer Vitaliano Lemici can be traced back to the last years of the thirteenth century;[2] their co-operation for political ends must have begun soon after Mussato's entry into the Consiglio Maggiore in 1296. In 1297, a version of the Paduan annals reports that the commune took possession of the island of Calcinara and several other villages on the marshland border with the Venetian town of Chioggia.[3] Presumably, this was against the wishes of the owner, the Paduan Benedictine monastery of S. Giustina, since there is a Papal letter dated 10 May 1298, addressed to the bishop of Padua, ordering him to take action against the commune which had occupied Calcinara, a third of the castle of Concadalbero and other property pertaining to the monastery by violence. The abbot Renaldo died in the following year and, after a disputed election, the Pope wrote on 17 February 1300 appointing Gualpertino Mussato, the brother of Albertino.[4] The election of the obscure son of a court-messenger to be the head of Padua's most wealthy and distinguished religious house was sufficiently extraordinary for even Boniface VIII to feel that it required some explanation. As if to forestall protests, he wrote to Gualpertino giving a brief

[1] Cipolla, *Relazioni Verona-Mantova Sec. XIV*, n. xciii.
[2] See above, pp. 167–8.
[3] *Annales Patavini*, p. 231.
[4] *Les Registres de Boniface VIII*, ed. Digard, Faucon, Thomas & Fawtier, II, nn. 2576, 3422, 3460.

account of how he had absconded from the monastery of Vangadizza to study canon law in Padua, settling near his brother and the Lemici in the small house of S. Polo, of which he was eventually made prior. Da Nono tells substantially the same story of Gualpertino, alleging in addition that he poisoned the prior of S. Polo, had several illegitimate children and, after his appointment to S. Giustina, quarrelled with the monks and murdered two of them.[1] Guizzardo da Bologna, an author favourable to Mussato, writing in 1317, attributed Gualpertino's appointment to Albertino, who almost certainly met the Pope about this time, probably on a mission on behalf of the commune connected with the abuses of the Franciscan Inquisition in Padua.[2] Although Mussato was later to show, with Henry VII, considerable ability in the art of extracting concessions from the great, it is likely that more substantial inducements than the poet's eloquence were involved on this occasion; Da Nono says that Vitaliano Lemici spent £14,000 to secure the election of Gualpertino.

Dubious as it may have been from a moral point of view, Gualpertino's appointment was a political triumph for the commune. Almost at once, the new abbot entered into a real or fictitious exchange by which the city gained possession of Calcinara; a statute of 1301 ruled that the area was to become the inalienable property of the commune.[3] The attempt to exploit the acquisition by the building of salt pans offended the Venetians, who successfully defended their monopoly in a short frontier war in 1304, but the ultimate frustration of their policy did not permanently impair the standing of Mussato and the Lemici in the public life of the city.[4]

The crisis of 1311 came at an unfortunate time for the Lemici. Their power had reached its peak under Vitaliano, reputed the most wealthy of the citizens and, in Da Nono's opinion, it had been inferior only to that of Tiso Camposanpiero, Nicolò da Lozzo and the Carraresi. At his death in 1311

---

[1] *De Generatione*, ff. 45v–46r.
[2] *Ecerinide*, ed. Padrin, pp. 74–5. Mussato mentions his meeting Boniface VIII, *De Gestis*, col. 619.
[3] *Statuti Carraresi*, f. 214v.
[4] There is a good account of this war, which is only briefly mentioned in the Paduan sources, in Ferreto Ferreti, *Opere*, I, pp. 226–34. See also Sambin, 'Le relazioni tra Venezia, Padova e Verona', *AIV* CXI (1952), pp. 205–15.

he left his heir a minor, encumbered with debts and with much property in the Vicentino.[1] The leadership of the family and *pars* at this crucial time fell partly upon Albertino Mussato, who was Guglielmo II's legal guardian, and partly upon Guglielmo's cousin Martino Cane. Both Martino and his father Zamboneto had been *podestà* of Vicenza and had much property in the Vicentino, especially in the village of Camisano.[2] It was therefore natural that the *pars* should join the Maccaruffi in promoting the vigorous prosecution of the war for the recovery of Paduan rights in Vicenza.

During the earlier part of the crisis, the most notable feature of the *pars Lemici* was the way in which Albertino Mussato managed to keep himself close to the centre of power despite several radical changes of regime. From 1312 to 1314, he was a leading member of the *pars Guelpha*. In the rising against their oppressive rule in April 1314, Mussato was in considerable danger, and was forced to take refuge for a time in the village of Vigodarzere. Writing after the event, Mussato represented the quarrel as being essentially between the Carraresi and the Altichini; at the time, however, Giacomo da Carrara sent a messenger to the friendly commune of Treviso, who described the issue as principally between Giacomo and Mussato.[3] If this was so, the reconciliation which allowed Mussato to return almost at once and resume his leading role in the prosecution of the war, suggests considerable moderation on one or both sides. Mussato's second exile began in the spring of 1318, soon after the departure of the Maccaruffi with whom, up to that time, the historian had been very closely associated. Nicolò da Carrara launched a personal attack on Mussato's brother Gualpertino, so that the abbot was forced to take refuge in the Lemici *palazzo;* later, for greater security, the brothers fled to the castle of Treville, which was the property of the Camposanpiero. Eventually the Mussato established themselves at Chioggia, while their house and that of the Lemici was sacked by the mob. While at Chioggia, Mussato was approached by Nicolò Maccaruffi and Galvano

---

[1] See above, pp. 187-8.
[2] Smereglo, pp. 13, 15, 18; Cortusi, p. 13, Mussato, *Historia Augusta*, col. 421. The Cane are the only family of any importance not treated in the *De Generatione*.
[3] Verci, *Marca Trivigiana*, doc. n. 669.

da Terradura, who tried to persuade him to join their treacherous attack on Padua in concert with Cangrande. It was this which precipitated Mussato's decision to return to Padua and serve the commune in its time of greatest need.[1] During the siege, Albertino was in Tuscany seeking help; on his return, he continued to play an active part in Paduan affairs right up to his final expulsion in 1325.[2]

Throughout this period, the *pars Lemici* was precluded from playing a major independent role by the lack of a leader of magnatial standing. Albertino Mussato was clearly a diplomat and politician of considerable skill, but he had not the resources to command a party and his power depended, in the last resort, on his ability to persuade a majority of the Consiglio Maggiore to vote with him. Since he detested the guildsmen and all that they stood for, he must have looked for support mainly to the non-guild members of the *comunanza*, a class whose lasting loyalty it must have been almost impossible to secure. For example, Rolando da Piazzola was a close friend of Mussato, some of whose literary and historical interests he shared, yet on two of the crucial issues of the time, the rejection of the Emperor and the election of Giacomo da Carrara as captain-general, he was one of the leading advocates of the policy opposed by Mussato. Moreover, as the account of the murder of the Altichini shows, the troops of the *comunanza*, some of which were commanded by Mussato on that occasion, could be less effective in a crisis than a rabble led by a few ruthless noblemen. Among Mussato's closest supporters were his brothers Pietrobono, a notary and Gualpertino who, as abbot of S. Giustina, had an income of the order of £1,000 a year.[3] Another powerful helper was the Milanese Pagano della Torre, bishop of Padua from 1302, to whom Mussato dedicated his *De Gestis Italicorum;* not only did he attempt to protect the Altichini in 1314, but on at least two occasions he played an active part, with abbot Gualpertino, in the defence of Padua against the Veronese.[4]

[1] *De Gestis*, ed. Padrin, pp. 39–40, 53.
[2] Grion, *Delle rime volgari*, p. 265; Cortusi, pp. 39, 43.
[3] This emerges from the provision in the will of Marsiglio da Carrara (*Documenti Carraresi*, I, n. 35) that Perenzano da Carrara be given property giving him this income if unable to secure the abbacy of S. Giustina.
[4] *Historia Augusta*, col. 446; *De Gestis*, col. 653.

With the passage of time, the situation of the Lemici was gradually transformed. In 1319, Bishop Pagano was translated to the see of Aquileia and in 1324 death removed the moderating influence of Giacomo da Carrara, on whose understandings with Mussato much of the unity of the *partes* had depended. Inevitably, the Lemici began to fill the gap left by the Maccaruffi as leaders of the opposition to the Carraresi, and the young Guglielmo began to look like a potential rival to Marsiglio da Carrara. In 1325, Ubertino da Carrara and Rizardo da Lendenara decided to take advantage of Mussato's absence on a mission to Germany and forestall future trouble by picking a quarrel with Guglielmo and murdering him. The vendetta was taken up by Guglielmo's illegitimate brother Paolo, but he and his supporters were defeated in a street battle by the concentrated forces of the Carraresi and were driven out of the city.[1] The proscription of the whole party which followed was decisive, for although Albertino Mussato continued to intrigue for his return from Chioggia until his death in 1329, Marsiglio allowed the poet to make only one more brief visit to Padua.

The segment of the *pars Marchionis* which finally remained in control of the city was based on the prolific Carrara-Papafava clan with their large possessions around Carrara and Agna, in the south and south-eastern parts of the Paduan contado, where they were sheltered from the first impact of the Veronese war. Although he put the finishing touches to the *De Generatione* after Giacomo da Carrara's election as *dominus generalis,* Da Nono did not foresee that the Carraresi would become the future rulers of Padua. He clearly expected the new tyrants to come from the Camposanpiero family, and repeats the legends connecting them with the Da Romano. In his opinion, the prestige of the family was second to none, and in 1311 Tiso Camposanpiero was the most powerful man in Padua.[2] The meeting of his *pars* was attended by the Carraresi and representatives of all the leading magnates in the city, except the Da Lozzo and Castelnovo; in addition, he enjoyed close relations with the Da Camino *signori* of Treviso. An important element in his power was the fact that twice in the later thirteenth century the headship of the family had passed from father to only son,

---

[1] Cortusi, pp. 42–4; *Liber Regiminum,* p. 357–8.
[2] *Visio Egidii,* pp. 3–4; *De Generatione,* ff. 17v, 38r.

giving the advantages of undisputed leadership and undivided estates.¹ The luck of the Camposanpiero broke in 1312, when Tiso IV died leaving only an adolescent grandson, Guglielmo II, who for some reason never played a leading part in public affairs, and a posthumous son, Tiso V, who was brought up by his mother, a sister of Marsiglio da Carrara.² Thus, like the Lemici, the Camposanpiero lacked the leadership necessary to make a stand against the Carrara during the decisive years. The nearest that they came to making a challenge was just before the election of Giacomo da Carrara in July 1318, when Cunizza da Carrara called out her forces between Padua and Treviso and they were joined by Onore da Vigodarzere and Marsiglio Polafrisana.³ But this mobilisation came too late to stop the election, and the opportunity was lost. The knight Giovanni, of the illegitimate branch of the family, was persuaded to return to Padua in August 1318, and was active in the defence of the commune until 1325, when he was exiled for his part in the rising of Paolo Lemici and took refuge in Ferrara.⁴ The young Tiso V grew up a supporter of the Carrara, and received his knighthood and the keys of Camposanpiero from the victorious Cangrande in 1328.⁵

By contrast, the Carraresi illustrate both the advantages and disadvantages of numbers. In the crises of 1314, 1318 and 1325, the family could stand together with invincible effect, but in the intervals they often suffered from divided leadership corresponding to their much divided estates. Giacomo Grande must have inherited less than a sixth of the estate of his grandfather and namesake, who died in 1240, and his leadership of the family depended on his personal qualities of seniority and statesmanship. At times, the younger and more violent members of the family, Marsiglio, Ubertino and Nicolò, seized the initiative and Giacomo had little control over them. His death, and that of his brother Pierconte which also seems to have taken place about 1324, had the effect of reconcentrating his

---

¹ Although Tiso II (d. 1235) left three sons, the line of two of these died out; Tiso III (d. 1266) had only one son. See Genealogical Table 4. Da Nono records a popular belief 'In domo de Camposanctipetri non succedit nisi unus', *De Generatione*, f. 17v.
² AD 5108; *Historia Augusta*, col. 430.
³ *De Gestis*, ed. Padrin, p. 44.
⁴ Ibid. pp. 55, 79; *De Traditione*, col. 758; AMS XI, nn. 10, 19.
⁵ Cortusi, pp. 55–6.

paternal inheritance in the hands of his only nephew Marsiglio. Although his inherited wealth must have been much greater, Marsiglio had even less authority over the firebrands of the family than his uncle had had. Unable to settle a serious feud which developed between Ubertino da Carrara and Marsilietto Papafava, Marsiglio pretended to be neutral, while persuading the German *vice-capitano* to secure Marsiglietto's condemnation and exile on a trumped-up charge. As for Nicolò, during the last days of the commune he pursued his own policy of immediate surrender to Cangrande in opposition to Marsiglio, and in 1327 he went into open revolt in the contado with his supporters, who included some of the Paduan Ghibellines, such as Marco Forzatè and his nephew Giordano, and Prosdocimo, the son of Giovanni Caligine.[1]

It was Giacomo da Carrara's achievement to turn the disunity of his family to advantage. His character was something of an enigma to contemporaries; Mussato was unable to decide whether his reticence was a mark of sincerity or a cloak for duplicity.[2] He certainly exploited the opportunities created by the violence of his younger relations while disclaiming responsibility for their lawlessness. But at heart he was a patriot and a man of the commune. His *signoria* was as widely based as possible. He strove to reconcile the factions, and was willing to accept anyone who was willing to serve under him for the good of the city. Although he could never have been elected without the votes of the Ghibellenes and the influence of Cangrande, his aim was to give the Paduans a breathing space and preserve what he could of the independence of the city. Had he been willing to surrender the overlordship to Cangrande, no doubt he could have remained the *signore* to the end of his life; instead, he chose to lay down his office in return for the German assistance which offered some hope of saving the city. At first, Marsiglio tried to follow the same policy and in 1327 he sent a powerful mission to Germany in a desperate attempt to enlist further aid against Cangrande

---

[1] Mussato, *De Traditione*, coll. 732–8, 744–8; Cortusi, pp. 49–51. See Genealogical Tables 5 and 6. The *Gesta Magnifica Domus Carrariensis*, ed. Cessi, RIS XVII, i, vol. II, p. 251, suggests that Nicolò was planning to marry his daughter to Mastino della Scala and presumably displace Marsiglio with the help of Cangrande.

[2] *De Gestis*, ed. Padrin, pp. 44–5.

and the Paduan exiles. But when little headway could be made against Nicolò and the other rebels who had the eastern part of the Paduan contado in their hands, Marsiglio finally accepted the *signoria* on the terms which Giacomo had refused. Before his election, he agreed to become a satellite of Cangrande; within the city, his rule was based not on reconciliation but on the dominance of his own *pars*:[1]

Among the early and constant supporters of the Carrara faction were the noble Rizardo da Lendenara, and Francesco and Aicardino Capodivacca, members of a rich and powerful family with a reputation for usury. The alliance of these families had been cemented by marriage; Francesco was Marsiglio da Carrara's son-in-law; Aicardino was married to a daughter of Fava Papafava.[2] Another adherent of the *pars* was Partinopeo Partinopei, a son of the knight Marsiglio, who had served the commune against Verona in 1278.[3] As the star of the Carraresi was seen to rise, a number of ambitious timeservers among the *popolani* attached themselves to their interest. For example, Pantaleone and Dusio Buzzaccarini had played an important part in public life under the commune, serving as *podestà* and on important embassies, but by 1328 they were safely in the Carrara camp.[4] The change of regime brought no interruption in the succession of offices held by the leading judges Aldovrandino Campanati and Schinella de Doto.[5]

From 1325, Marsiglio da Carrara virtually ruled the city in conjunction with the German *capitani* and was in a position to reward his followers with the property of the numerous exiles. Rizardo da Lendenara received a large share of the estates of the Sanbonifacio and his son married the daughter of Renaldo II Scrovegni with a dowry which, according to

---

[1] *De Traditione*, coll. 733, 746–7, 749–51; Cortusi, pp. 53 et seq.
[2] Da Nono, *De Generatione*, ff. 38r, 43r.
[3] See above, pp. 105, 137.
[4] Pantaleone, a knight and professional *podestà*, was a leader in the armies and councils of the commune from at least 1314 (see e.g. Verci, *Marca Trivigiana*, doc. n. 705; Cortusi interpolation, RIS XII (1728), coll. 806–7; *Annales Patavini*, p. 237); he died in 1333. Dusio was *podestà* of Rovigo in 1310 (AS Padua, Corp. Sopp. S. Agostino 168, n. 61), of Bassano in 1319 (Verci, *Marca Trivigiana*, doc. nn. 924, 927), and as *podestà* of Treviso, in January 1320 he urged the German commander there to march to the relief of Padua (Liberale de Levada, 'De Proditione Tarvisii', *Memorie del B. Enrico*, pp. 199, 209).
[5] See above, pp. 99–100, 136–8.

Mussato, amounted to the fabulous sum of £8,000 *per annum*. Another Scrovegni heiress, the daughter of Gaboardo, was bestowed on a son of Aicardino Capodivacca. Marsiglio used the confiscated goods of, among others, the Lemici, Maccaruffi, Da Terradura and Giovanni Camposanpiero to increase his own resources.[1] In addition, he enjoyed the revenues of the monastery of S. Giustina from the flight of Gualpertino Mussato in 1325 until 1334, though his attempts to install an illegitimate son of Giacomo Grande as abbot were unavailing.[2] In November 1328, after Cangrande had been duly elected Imperial Vicar and *dominus generalis* of Padua, there was a celebration in Verona at which further rewards were distributed. Among those who received their knighthood were Marsiglio and four of the Carrara-Papafava, Rizardo da Lendenara, Aicardino and Francesco Capodivacca and Dusio Buzzaccarini.[3]

It would be unprofitable to pursue very far the question of how far the Carrara *signoria* was legitimate. The legal forms were observed in both elections. Giacomo's appointment was decided upon in the Consiglio Maggiore and then confirmed by acclamation in the general *arengo* of the inhabitants, which was revived for the occasion; Marsiglio was created *capitaneus, protector et defensor generalis* by a resolution of the Consiglio Maggiore.[4] But the electors were hardly free agents. It was not

[1] *De Traditione*, coll. 746-7, 757-8.
[2] Ibid. col. 757. The veracity of Mussato's account of the last days of the commune has been called into question, for example by H. Spangenburg, *Can Grande I von Scala* (1892), pp. 140-8, but in the case of the seizures of monastic property, it is supported by the evidence of a Papal letter of 24 Feb. 1330 attacking Marsiglio and Ubertino, *hostes Dei et Ecclesiae*, for invading the rights not only of S. Giustina but also of S. Maria in Vanzo and S. Stefano di Carrara (Dondi dall'Orologio, *Istoria Ecclesiastica*, VIII, doc. n. lxx). The Carrara 'custodia' of S. Giustina was terminated in Feb. 1334 (Arch. Vescovile, Diversorum, f. 97).
[3] *Annales Patavini*, p. 250.
[4] The document recording the election of Giacomo (Arch. Papafava 39, n. 1) is printed in F. M. Colle, *Storia Scientifico-Letteraria dello Studio di Padova*, I, pp. 29-33. The circumstances are described by Mussato, *De Gestis* ed. Padrin, pp. 42-4, and Cortusi, pp. 26-7. For Marsiglio's election see *Annales Patavini*, p. 249, and Mussato, *De Traditione*, coll. 749-50; the 'official' account is to be found in a letter announcing the election to the *podestà* of Treviso (Verci, *Marca Trivigiana*, doc. n. 1103). The beginnings of the Carrara *signoria* are compared with those of the Della Scala and Da Camino in F. Ercole, *Dal comune al principato* (1929), pp. 53-118.

only a matter of the remote pressure exercised by Cangrande and his armies. In 1318, the commune had been forced to accept the return of the exiles, and Giacomo's election as captain-general was preceded by an outbreak of violence in which the Guelph opposition fled and their houses were sacked. Ten years later, the situation had become much more chaotic. After his defeat in 1320, Cangrande seems to have decided to let the exiles do his work for him, and from 1322 the authority of the Paduan commune in what remained of the contado was progressively reduced to nothing by a series of revolts led by Corrado da Vigonza, Filippo da Peraga and Nicolò da Carrara. Inside the city, life and property were no longer secure. The German garrison were quite ineffective in keeping law and order. If, in 1325, they were unable to prevent the younger Carraresi from attacking and killing the *podestà* and most of his staff, it is easy to believe that they were powerless to protect the private citizens from the numerous outrages reported by Mussato during the last days of the commune. Indeed, Cortusi also accuses the Germans of acts of violence themselves, and mentions that Marsiglio was building up an army of *contadini*, presumably his tenants, just before his appointment. To speak of a free election in these circumstances is clearly unrealistic.[1]

It is, however, worth examining the actions of the *popolo*, and of the guildsmen in particular, during the last days of the commune with a view to discovering their attitude towards the *signoria*. The first act of political self-assertion by the Carraresi in 1314 led, as we have seen, to a revival of the Union of the Guilds, which was particularly active in the years which followed.[2] In 1315, the commune renewed the long-standing alliance with Treviso, once more under communal government after the expulsion of Guecillo da Camino, using the old formula 'for the defence and preservation of the (existing) state of both cities, without any domination or tyrant', suggesting that the *popolo* was, at this stage, still officially opposed to a *signoria*.[3] In January 1318, the commune faced the deteriorating

---

[1] *De Traditione, passim.* Though Mussato, as an embittered exile, may have exaggerated in detail, his account is supported in general terms by Cortusi, pp. 43–51, who was a moderate supporter of the Carraresi.

[2] See above, p. 266.

[3] 'Ad defensionem et conservationem status sine ullo dominio et tyranno utriusque civitatis'; Verci, *Marca Trivigiana*, doc. n. 737; cf. 'Omnes civitates predictas in statu pacifico et tranquillo manutenebunt sine dominio alicuius

situation in the traditional way, by the election of a foreign *capitano del popolo*.[1] The appointment was for a term of six months, and the second holder of the office, Obizzo degli Obizzini of Pisa, a man praised by Mussato, provided the last centre of resistance to the election of Giacomo da Carrara in July 1318. Attacked by Nicolò da Carrara in the name of the nobility, as the holder of an odious and contumacious office, Obizzo tried to rally the *gastaldiones*, but they were overawed and Obizzo finally agreed to leave, making the way clear for the election of Giacomo.[2] From this, it may be concluded that the *gastaldiones* accepted the *signoria* only under duress, for Mussato would have been only too glad to have held them responsible if he could.

Once elected, Giacomo tried to conciliate the guildsmen as a part of his policy of restoring unity to the city. He organised a ceremonial presentation of banners to the guilds and the *gastaldiones* acted as godfathers to his infant son.[3] Symbolically enough, the child soon died. During the rule of Frederick of Austria's agents, the Union continued in being and, in 1321, the council of the Union made one of its most direct interventions in the political life of the commune, ordering, among other measures, the *XV gastaldiones* to see that the *anciani pro frataleis* did not neglect their duties, and urging the *iudex ancianorum* to enforce a similar discipline on the *anciani de comunancia*.[4] The Union was still putting what strength it had behind the institutions of the commune, but in a situation increasingly dominated by the cavalry of the magnates, the forces of the *popolo* were at a great disadvantage. They were unable to intervene effectively in the battle between the Carraresi and Paolo Lemici in 1325 and failed to defend the *podestà* from the violence of the Carraresi immediately afterwards. With this example of ruthlessness before them, and with frequent crimes and outrages going unpunished by the authorities, the guildsmen can hardly be blamed for supporting,

---

persone'; the alliance between Padua, Treviso, Verona and Vicenza, 1262, idem, *Storia degli Eccelini*, III, doc. n. 266.

[1] Bianchi, *Documenti per la storia del Friuli*, I, n. 48.
[2] *De Gestis*, ed. Padrin, pp. 40–2.
[3] *Annales Patavini*, p. 264; the rubric 1321 should be corrected to 1319.
[4] *Stat. Speziali*, MS. BP 940, f. 14v, Roberti, *Le corporazioni*, pp. 84–8.

or at least not opposing, Marsiglio, as the only way out of an intolerable situation.[1]

The election of 1328 marks the end of an era; with it the communal form of government, in which the executive was strictly subordinate to a broadly-based council, disappeared from the major cities of northern Italy. The *pars Marchionis* which had liberated the city from the tyrant Ezzelino in 1256 had disintegrated and itself produced a tyrant. In the course of time, the social order characteristic of the commune was profoundly modified. The ideal of government *ad communem* gave way to the service of the prince. The shortcomings of the Paduan state are so much in evidence during the last days of the commune that its virtues may easily be overlooked. Arbitrary in its treatment of subject cities and sometimes oppressive towards those who did not belong to the *popolo*, the Paduan commune nevertheless represented a noteworthy experiment in responsible government with a franchise which was remarkably wide for the times. It collapsed not through any inherent weakness, but through the tensions created by a long and desperate war. The child of favourable circumstances, the commune could not adapt itself to the harsh conditions of the fourteenth century. Even with all the advantages of despotic rule, the Carrara *signoria* was never more than a buffer-state between the Della Scala and Visconti on the one hand and the Venetians on the other. At great cost, the Carrara princes maintained a precarious and intermittent independence for some seventy-five years, until they finally succumbed to the Venetians in 1405, and Padua relapsed into the more tranquil role of the university city of the Venetian state.

[1] 'Post Pauli Dentis [de Lemicis] commotionem, quae adeo populi Paduani enervatio, exitiumque extremum fuit, ut nec Respublica ulla, seu communitas aliqua dici posset, populus inde ac plebs, Carrariensium uti pecora aut servilia mancipia facti sunt, tantae vitae circumventi formidine, ac dominorum plurimorum perplexitate ut in quem unum dominum intenderent, cuius umbrae aut tutelae se se committerent, ipsi haud scire possent', *De Traditione*, col. 716.

CHAPTER X

Padua and the Dawn of the Renaissance

THE passing of the Paduan commune marked the end not only of a political system but also of an intellectual movement. More than almost any other city of the day, Padua was the home of a distinctive intellectual tradition which was in some ways as precocious as the constitution was archaic. Some of the ideas expressed by Paduan thinkers in the communal period, especially what has been called Paduan civic humanism, seem to foreshadow some characteristics of the Florentine Renaissance of the early fifteenth century, while others anticipate the scientific school for which Padua was subsequently famous; both provide interesting material for comparison with later intellectual developments. Naturally, the city was far from being culturally isolated or self-sufficient and there were many cross-currents produced by outside influences; nevertheless, a central stream of ideas may be traced which were characteristically Paduan, whose development was unmistakably moulded by the local environment. Though the university exerted its influence, the Paduan tradition was above all a civic one, carried on almost exclusively by members of the governing and administrative class, so that the points of contact between the cultural and political life of the city were many and in their rise and fall the two were closely linked.

The immediate background to the distinctive culture of the Paduan commune is to be found in the Italian intellectual climate of the twelfth and early thirteenth centuries. The Italian contribution to the European intellectual revival of this period was, considering the wealth and position of the peninsula, remarkably meagre outside the few specialised fields which the Italians made their own. While cultural phenomena can never be entirely accounted for in material terms, this characteristic is obviously related to the organisation of Italian education which was dominated first by the secular school and then by the nascent universities, so that the intervening period in which, north of the Alps, the cathedral school and the secular courts played a leading part, was largely by-passed. Thus twelfth-century 'humanism' was poorly represented in Italy and Italian culture was the first to show the virtues and defects of the academic specialisation characteristic of the universities. The practical sciences of medicine and law were the bases of the higher faculties in the Italian universities, and in these subjects the Italians were the leaders of Europe. Literature was comparatively neglected; the vitality of the Sicilian school is there to show what might have happened had there been other courts rich and stable enough to provide a home for poets and scholars. The communes, with no tradition to guide them, were slow to develop as centres of culture.

The early cultural history of Padua is dark indeed, but it would appear that law at least was taught there before the thirteenth century and in the university, which took shape about 1222, law was the dominant faculty.[1] Thus, both by the period in which it developed and by its subject matter, with its close bearing on the growth of the commune, the Paduan law school would seem to have been eminently suitable as the centre of a local tradition. That this did not take place may perhaps be attributed to the failure of the city to produce a great jurist during the formative period, so that Padua became a satellite to the parent university of Bologna, largely staffed by visiting teachers of the Bolognese school who struck no roots in Padua. By the later thirteenth century, it is clear that this situation had come to be accepted as normal; the statutes discouraged the appointment of native professors and were designed to keep 'foreign' jurists at arm's length from the commune, with the result that their influence on the life of the city is hard to trace. The gulf could have been bridged only by a great teacher of law who happened to be a Paduan citizen and none appeared during the communal period. As it happens, no Paduan doctor up to the mid-fourteenth century has left any writings, but even if they had, it is unlikely that their works would have shown any local characteristics, for the Italian university lawyers were highly academic. It is significant that a collection of texts and comments on the law, the *Summa*

[1] Gloria, *Università*, pp. 103–26; Roberti, 'Diritto romano e coltura giuridica in Padova sulla fine del secolo XII', *NAV* ns. IV (1902), pp. 162–201.

Commemorialis Utilium Iuris, in which local statutes are cited, was the work of Geremia da Montagnone, a city judge who was not a doctor associated with the university.[1]

The roots of a specifically Paduan culture are to be found not in the higher faculties of the university but in the unpretentious work of obscure local annalists. Simple annals were both the most common and the most basic form of mediaeval historical writing and although usually associated with a major church or monastery, they could be adapted to the needs of almost any institution. Thus the urban revival was followed by the appearance of civic annals. In these, the deviation from the monastic pattern might be slight, amounting to little more than the substitution of the civic year, identified by the names of the consuls or the *podestà*, for the ecclesiastical year, but by their very nature such local annals were ideally suited to become the sounding boards of civic pride and self-consciousness. The possibilities for elaboration were almost boundless, but their realisation was very uneven. The chronicles of the commune of Genoa, for example, begin in the first years of the twelfth century and by 1167 the city had appointed an official chronicler; on the other hand, annals of the most primitive kind continued to be compiled throughout the Middle Ages and beyond.[2]

The Paduan annals which, as at present known, do not go back before the year 1174, are not particularly outstanding examples of their kind. Though only one version is extant in its original manuscript, seven others have been printed from later compilations, excluding fourteenth-century vernacular versions which do not contribute any new material.[3] The complexity of the relationships between the various compilations suggests that they are based on a considerable number of independent annals, exactly how many it would be difficult to determine. Moreover, it is probable that by 1258, Padua had already produced a number of simple descriptive works of a wholly different type, histories of families of the *genre* of Da Nono's *De Generatione*. It is true that the only positive evidence for this

---

[1] See above, p. 131.
[2] There is no satisfactory work on the Italian civic annals as a whole; for north-eastern Italy in the first half of the thirteenth century, see Arnaldi, *Studi sui cronisti della Marca Trevigiana*.
[3] See List of Sources below, p. 324.

is Gianfrancesco Capodilista's description of the mysterious volume containing the 'annalia' of Antonio d'Alessio compiled in 1258, incorporating the work of Giacomo Ardenghi of 1168 and Ziliolo the chancellor of 1196, which he says he saw in Basle in 1434 but which has never been heard of before or since. The inaccuracies of Capodilista's family history show that he is not a man to be trusted implicitly; on the other hand, the excerpt which he gives from Ardenghi verbatim and the summary of Alessio are very plausible and would have required considerable skill to invent. It is also hard to believe that the ground was totally unprepared for the appearance of Zambono d'Andrea's verses and Da Nono's *De Generatione*.[1]

The identity of these early Paduan writers is largely a matter of conjecture, but such indications as there are point unmistakably to the administrative class, particularly the notaries, as the most likely originators of both strains of Paduan historical writing. It is Rolandino who, in the prologue to his history, throws most light on these hidden recorders of Paduan history. He describes how his father, a notary of Padua, used to write not only contracts but also notes of events taking place in the March of Treviso 'after the custom of the good old simple people' and how in 1223 these notes were handed on to Rolandino with the admonition to continue them.[2] The notaries were the most numerous representatives of the new, urban, literate laity, and by their profession were well placed for the collection of news. But in addition to these advantages, which they shared with the judges, the notaries had a further incentive to become annalists. In their registers, they were already bound to keep a record of their own professional activities, and it is possible that some of the annals were actually written in among the copies of contracts. An example of this procedure, which is very primitive despite its late date, has been found in a Paduan notarial register of the mid-fourteenth century.[3] With regard to the non-chronological writings, the

---

[1] See above, p. 68.   [2] *Cronica*, p. 5.

[3] P. Sambin, 'Notizie di una cronaca tra i rogiti di un notaio padovano del secolo XIV', *AIV* CX (1951–2), pp. 99–112. The connection between the notarial profession and the writing of chronicles is a recurring theme in Arnaldi's *Studi sui cronisti della Marca Trevigiana*, see especially pp. 111–33. I am unable to accept the author's assimilation of the *bona fides* of the historian to the *publica fides* of the notary, except in the case of an official history like the Genoese annals.

name of Ziliolo the chancellor is a clear indication of the commune's civil service as the most likely point of origin. In the city chancellery there would almost certainly have been records of the noble families' holdings and *privilegia* for the guidance of the commune in its relations with them, and these could easily have formed the nucleus of family histories of the D'Alessio and Da Nono type. It is extraordinary that there is so little evidence for this natural development taking place at an early date anywhere else but in Padua.

The background to Padua's cultural emergence was therefore a body of writings on current affairs, mainly local in interest, emanating from the milieu not of the schools or university, but of the administrative class of the commune. For this activity to be raised to the level of intellectual significance, an outside influence was necessary, and this came about in the person of Rolandino. Born in 1200, Rolandino was sent to study rhetoric at Bologna under the Florentine master Boncompagno de Siga. There we may assume that he met with the idea of history as a form of literary art, as exemplified by the remarkable *Liber de Obsidione Ancone* which his teacher had completed in 1201–2.[1] In this work, a simple historical event was used as the vehicle for an elaborate exercise in rhetoric, embellished by learned allusions and enlivened by dramatic dialogues put into the mouths of the leading participants. The historical element is small, and Boncompagno's aim seems to have been to use the account of the siege of Ancona by Barbarossa's supporters in 1174 to epitomise the whole struggle of the communes against the Empire. His method was the antithesis of the chronicler's; not the pedestrian recording of events but an imaginative reconstruction.

Although Rolandino had graduated and returned to Padua before 1226, it was not until 1260 that he began to write up his notes and those left to him by his father into a continuous history. During the interval, he had lived through the harrowing experience of Ezzelino's tyranny and it was his determination to expose its evils to future generations which inspired him to write. If this moral purpose sometimes betrayed him into exaggeration, it must also have contributed to his remarkable

[1] Ed. G. C. Zimolo, *RIS* VI, iii (1937). Rolandino's relations with Boncompagno are discussed in Arnaldi, op. cit. pp. 146–54.

single-mindedness in concentrating on his chosen theme. There is hardly a vestige of the rambling annals in Rolandino's history; everything which did not contribute to the understanding of the rise and fall of the Da Romano was either minimised or excluded altogether. Thus the beginnings of the university are not mentioned, and the celebrated S. Antonio is given only one short chapter in which not a single miracle is described, but only the saint's fruitless intercession with Ezzelino on behalf of some political prisoners, which serves to underline the merciless character of the tyrant.[1] Boncompagno, it is true, had set an example in this respect by confining the action of his history to a single city and a single year, but while Boncompagno's work was a literary exercise, Rolandino's has all the force of a deeply felt experience. In the Paduan history, the balance between fact and imagination is redressed. Fictitious embellishments are very few; instead, actual events drawn from annals and from the author's own notes and experience are woven into a coherent pattern. There is no doubt that as a historian, Rolandino was far superior to Boncompagno.

Rolandino's history represents one of the most successful fusions between chronicle material and the mediaeval rhetorical tradition of the schools. In Padua, the *Rolandina* as it came to be called, became a part of the city's political tradition, serving at a more sophisticated level the same function as the songs and verses of the Ezzelino legend among the populace in maintaining the political ethos of the restored commune.[2] But though it was well known, it found no immediate imitators, mainly because the local history of the next fifty years did not offer any of the stirring dramatic themes favoured by mediaeval writers. During this predominantly peaceful period, literary culture in Padua broadened and diversified; some of the annals became more elaborate than before, but the main innovations were in the field of vernacular and Latin verse. The small groups of experimental writers did not produce any major works, but the pre-humanists in particular created a revolution in taste in an erudite minority which ensured that when the

[1] Rolandino, pp. 43-4.
[2] But the evidence adduced by Dr Arnaldi (op. cit. pp. 135-6) to support his view that Rolandino was somehow made the official chronicle of the Paduan commune seems to me insufficient.

time came for learned history to be taken up again, it was written in a style far removed from that of Rolandino. In considering the growing points of the Paduan tradition after 1262, it is convenient to begin with the writers in the vernacular for although their work was less significant for the future, the group offers many interesting parallels with the Latin writers on whom the attention of scholars has generally been concentrated. Time has taken a heavy toll of the writings of the Paduan vernacular poets, but each fragment which remains points beyond itself to a greater corpus which has been lost. The leading figure seems to have been Aldovrandino Mezzabbati who, according to Dante, was outstandingly successful in forging a *volgare illustre*, raising himself above the level of the unpromising local dialect.[1] Andrea da Tribano, Giacomo Flabiano and Albertino Mussato were presumably his followers; a fragment of an exchange of sonnets between them, written between 1318 and 1325, has survived on a single sheet which was once part of a much larger collection, laid out on what was, for the times, a lavish scale.[2] Another writer of the group was Antonio da Tempo, whose chief work, the *Delle rime volgari*, was completed in 1332.[3] Even from this bare and partial record, several facts stand out. Socially, the vernacular writers all belonged to the administrative class. Aldovrandino was a doctor of law, Antonio da Tempo a judge; Mussato and Andrea da Tribano were notaries and Giacomo Flabiano was probably the son of Flabiano *medicus* and a kinsman of Mascara Mascara the judge.[4] Then, while there is nothing to suggest that any member of the group had much poetic talent, they

[1] 'Inter quos omnes unum vidimus nitentem divertere a materno et ad curiale vulgare intendere, videlicet Ildebrandinum Paduanum', *De Vulgari Eloquentia*, I, 14. For verses by Aldovrandino, see M. Barbi, *Studi Danteschi* (1920), I, p. 40 et seq.; for his professional career, see above, p. 150.
[2] Gius. Billanovich, 'Biblioteche di dotti e letteratura italiana tra il trecento e il quattrocento', *Studi e problemi di critica testuale*, Collezione di opere inedite o rare, vol. 123 (1961), pp. 335–48. This important fragment is printed, ed. F. Novati, 'Poeti veneti del trecento', *Archivio Storico per Trieste, l'Istria ed il Trentino*, I (1881), pp. 130–41.
[3] For other verses by Antonio, see S. Morpurgo, 'Rime inedite di Giovanni Quirini e Antonio da Tempo', ibid. pp. 142–66.
[4] For Antonio da Tempo and Andrea da Tribano, see A. Zenatti, 'Antichi rimatori padovani', *Atti dell'Accademia scientifica Veneto-Trentino-Istriana*, I (1904) pp. 5–16; for Giacomo Flabiano, AS Padua, Perg. Div. 3563–4, Corona 1133.

were serious and self-conscious in their poetising; it can hardly be due to chance that Antonio da Tempo's pioneer treatise on the technique of Italian verse should make its appearance in a milieu where the study of Latin verse was being carried on more profoundly than elsewhere.

The Paduan Latin writers were very similar to the vernacularists both in their social origins and in their attitude to poetry. All were lawyers by training, exchanging the same kind of occasional verse among their friends; but while the Italian poets sought to develop a *volgare illustre*, some of the Latin group developed a preference for the literature of antiquity, unearthing forgotten texts, studying the style and metre and imitating them to the best of their ability.[1] In so doing, they necessarily rejected in some degree the post-classical developments of style in Latin prose and verse, so that there is some justification in calling them pre-humanists since they foreshadow some of the attitudes and achievements of later generations. But their distinctiveness should not be exaggerated: their attempts to write in the ancient manner were at first only sporadic, and in the narrow circle of Paduan *litterati* they could never become an entirely exclusive group. Despite occasional protestations of disdain for other schools of literature, most of the pre-humanists are known to have tried their hand in other styles or media. Mussato wrote in the vernacular, and there is no good reason to doubt that Zambono d'Andrea was the author of a thoroughly 'mediaeval' verse chronicle; even Lovato, in many ways the most fastidious of the group, has at least one poem in rhyming Latin verse attributed to him.

In the present state of knowledge, any inquiry into the origins of the Paduan pre-humanist movement must begin with Lovato Lovati who, even when all that is known about him is put together, remains a commanding but inscrutable figure.[2] His professional career was, as we have seen, extra-

---

[1] No comprehensive study of the Paduan pre-humanists has yet appeared; the best introduction is R. Weiss, *The Dawn of Humanism in Italy*, with an extensive bibliography. For a comparison between early humanism in Italy and in other parts of Europe, see B. Smalley, *English Friars and Antiquity in the Early Fourteenth Century* (1960); pp. 281–7 are devoted to the Paduans.

[2] For Lovato, see R. Weiss, 'Lovato Lovati', *Italian Studies*, VI (1951), pp. 2–28. His surviving poems appear in *Lupati de Lupatis, Bovetini de Bovetinis, Albertini Mussati necnon et Jamboni Andreae de Favafuschis Carmina*

ordinary. Born the son of a notary about 1237, he worked his way up from notary to judge, attained a knighthood in 1291 and ended his life in 1309 a leading member of the citizen body.[1] His intellectual development followed a parallel course, but the two sides of his activities never quite seem to make contact. The earliest poem which can be dated belongs to the years 1267-8, but the handwriting in which he drew up a document in 1261 shows that he was already acquainted with Carolingian manuscripts and had therefore probably already begun his researches into classical literature.[2] He was a scholarly rather than an inspired poet. Some of his verses were in the mediaeval tradition, but in others he tried to reproduce what he had found in the manuscripts of Verona and Pomposa and at his best, his technical competence and purity of style placed him in a different class from his contemporaries. Petrarch, who was well placed to judge, rated Lovato easily the first among the poets of his generation. From about 1290, Lovato was clearly the doyen of a small group whom he led both in the writing and the study of poetry. From the testimony of his pupils and some surviving notes which were probably his, it is clear that he studied Seneca's tragedies at first hand and explained the metre, perceiving rhythms to which previous generations had been largely deaf.[3]

In his extant writings, Lovato acknowledges no master, and the names of his early correspondents throw no light on the origin of his interests. Of his Paduan friends, only Zambono d'Andrea belonged to Lovato's generation, but his position within the group was clearly subordinate to Lovato. The existence of Carolingian manuscripts of classical authors readily accessible in the chapter library at Verona and the monastic library at Pomposa was obviously a *sine qua non* of his activities; what needs explanation is why this young man sought out these manuscripts and what it was that enabled

---

Quaedam, ed. L. Padrin (1887), and 'Epistole inedite di Lovato Lovati e d'altri a lui', ed. C. Foligno, *Studi Medievale*, II (1906-7), pp. 37-58, with notes by R. Sabbadini, ibid. pp. 255-62.
    [1] See above, pp. 134-5.
    [2] Guido Billanovich, *Italia medioevale e umanistica*, I (1958), p. 156.
    [3] Gius. Billanovich, *I primi umanisti e le tradizioni dei classici latini* (1953), pp. 18-21.

him to appreciate what he found. All the threads of the inquiry led back to Lovato: beyond him there is only conjecture.

It has been suggested by some scholars that early Italian humanism was imported ready-made, as it were, from France.[1] This theory is based on the similarities of development in the two countries, but there is nothing to support it in the evidence relating to Lovato. French influence was strong in north-east Italy, particularly in Venice, but it was French romances, not classicism, which captured the Italian imagination, and the medium was the vernacular, not Latin. In the early fourteenth century, for example, an anonymous Paduan was responsible for the first part of *La Prise de Pampelune,* a French poem on the Charlemagne legend[2] and Da Nono's dream world was clearly deeply indebted to romances of French origin. We do not need to speculate on Lovato's attitude to this popular cult, since it forms the subject of one of his verse letters. Writing to Bellino Bissolo, a minor Latin poet of Milan, he gives a lively picture of a French poem which he heard recited in Treviso; while deploring the barbarism of the language, the poet defended French epics as a fit subject for Latin verse.[3] This looks like a defence of what may have been Lovato's masterpiece, a Latin epic on Tristan and Isolde, of which only six lines and a partial paraphrase by Giovanni de Virgilio have survived.[4] Nowhere is there any hint that Lovato was knowingly indebted to French humanist influence.

If Lovato's humanism did not come from outside, its genesis must be sought in his Italian and Paduan background. The only thing which is known for certain about Lovato's education is that it must have been mainly in the law, and it has been suggested that it was the Italian humanists' legal training which supplied an essential element in their appreciation of the classics; accustomed to look to antiquity for authority in law, they transferred this attitude to literature.[5] This theory seems to rest on an excessively rosy picture of the ordinary practitioner's experience of the law; rather than an intelligent

[1] P. O. Kristeller, *Studies in Renaissance Thought and Letters* (1956), p. 569 et seq.
[2] Ed. A. Thomas, Anciens Textes Françaises (1913).
[3] Ep. II, Foligno, pp. 49–51.
[4] P. H. Wicksteed and E. G. Gardner, *Dante and Giovanni del Virgilio* (1902), pp. 190, 325.
[5] Weiss, *Dawn of Humanism*, p. 5.

respect for antiquity, the ordinary judge or notary would be more likely to pick up a dead weight of forensic jargon, especially in a period when most of the pleading must have been carried on in the non-literary vernacular. Some of the humanists showed a marked antipathy to legal studies. Mussato advised Marsiglio against them and seems to have abandoned his notarial profession as soon as his circumstances permitted; the fact that Petrarch had thrown up his own legal training adds a special sting to his comment on Lovato that he would have made a better poet if he had not mixed the Twelve Tables with the Nine Muses and diverted his talents to the din of the law courts.[1] The only branch of the legal profession which was directly concerned with the interpretation of ancient texts was the university jurists and the thread connecting them with early humanism is, both in Padua and elsewhere, a very tenuous one.[2]

If the universities contributed anything to early humanism, it is in the faculties of arts rather than the faculties of law that the link should be sought. A legal education presupposed a grounding in grammar and rhetoric which, in Padua, was mainly the responsibility of the masters of arts. Mussato certainly passed through the hands of one of them, for in a verse letter to *magister* Bonencontro he saluted the master of his *prima juventa,* and two other grammarians figure among the recipients of his letters.[3] One of these was Guizzardo da Bologna who was co-author of a learned commentary on Mussato's *Ecerinide;* another admirer was Giovanni de Virgilio, professor of Latin literature at Bologna from 1319. It is true that only one of the Paduan professors of Mussato's day is

[1] Mussato, Ep. XII, Graevius, col. 48; Petrarch, *Rerum memorandarum,* II, lxi, 1, cit. Guis. Billanovich, *Primi umanisti,* pp. 15–16.
[2] There were, it is true, some canonists with humanist interests teaching at Bologna in the early fourteenth century, including Guido de Guisis and Giovanni d'Andrea, later a friend of Petrarch (Smalley, *English Friars and Antiquity,* pp. 95–7). Another canonist, Bovetino da Mantova, may have participated in an exchange of verses between Lovato and Mussato under the nickname Bos, but the evidence on this point is contradictory (F. Novati, 'Nuovi anedotti sul cenacolo letterario padovano del primissimo trecento', *Scritti storici in memoria di G.Monticolo* (1922), pp. 170–7). On the other hand, the examples of Aldovrandino Mezzabbati and Cino da Pistoia could be cited in support of a connection between jurists and vernacular poetry. The whole subject would repay further study.
[3] Epp. IV, XIII–XV, Graevius, coll. 40, 50.

known to have been a serious poet in his own right; this was Pace del Friuli, professor of logic in the early fourteenth century who favoured political subjects and was the author of the earliest surviving poem in praise of the Venetian republic.[1] Although the evidence for a positive link with Mussato is lacking, it is extremely likely that they were acquainted as they both enjoyed the patronage of Pagano della Torre, bishop of Padua and later patriarch of Aquileia. But if the university grammarians did not participate in the experiments themselves, they at least recognised the merits of the *dilettanti*, for it was the College of Artists which gave Mussato his poetic crown in 1315.[2] There are certainly no grounds for projecting the later rivalries of the grammarians and the humanists back to early-fourteenth-century Padua.

Unfortunately, the evidence for contact between the university artists and the early humanists is much weaker in the formative period of the thirteenth century. Lovato's education coincides with the eclipse of the university during the later years of Ezzelino's rule and the predominant influence in the reconstituted College of Artists after 1256 seems to have been that of Rolandino. Two of Rolandino's colleagues at the time of the approbation of his history in 1262 are known to have written verse; of master Montenaro's *De Luna Cleri* only fragments survive, but master Morando's *Vinum Dulce Gloriosum*, a cheerful paean in praise of wine, has been preserved in its entirety as it so appealed to Fra Salimbene that he copied it into his chronicle; it certainly throws no light on the origins of humanism.[3] The influence of his formal education on Lovato must be sought in another quarter, though one which presumably fell within the province of the masters of grammar and rhetoric. An important part of the mediaeval lawyer's training was the *ars dictaminis*, a highly stylised form of rhythmic prose used in the drawing up of letters and legal documents. One of its functions was to make forgery more difficult, as a

---

[1] L. Lazzarini, *Paolo di Bernardo e i primordi dell'umanesimo in Venezia* (1930), p. 15; Gloria, *Università*, p. 369.
[2] *Stat. Coll. Iud.*, f. 176r; Mussato, Ep. I, Graevius, col. 34.
[3] For the College of Artists in 1262, when its members included six professors of grammar and rhetoric and one of logic, see Rolandino, pp. 173–4. Montenaro's poem is known only from some lines quoted by Geremia da Montagnone, *Epytoma Sapientiae*, see Gloria, *Università*, p. 373. For *Vinum Dulce Gloriosum*, see Salimbene, *Cronica*, ed. F. Bernini (1942), I, p. 313.

skilled lawyer could use his knowledge of the various forms to detect a corrupt text. This was a technique analogous to that of the humanist scholar; dictaminal Latin was very unclassical, but its composition and recognition demanded an ear for cadences and could have developed a sense of style.[1] A link through the *ars dictaminis* would help to explain the relative prominence of the notaries among the humanists; inferior to the judges in their strictly legal training, they would have an equal opportunity of becoming practised in the *dictamen*. Lovato's humanist studies go back to the period when he was in practice as a notary and his interest in the *ars dictaminis* is proved by a collection of *formulae dictandi* in a manuscript in Lovato's own hand written in or about 1290.[2]

Two stages are discernible in the development of the early Paduan humanist movement. At first, it was a matter of literary studies and exercises which were the private pastime of a small group of friends; later the subjects and interests become much more public and political. To judge from surviving fragments, Lovato's early verse was chiefly concerned with personal and literary problems, such as complaints of illness and the consolations of literature, while his later poems either relate to particular political events or deal with moral problems which have a distinct bearing upon public life. The change may be placed in the 1290s when Lovato's position was established socially and politically and he had gathered round him a group of friends and pupils of the younger generation. It was in response to the promptings of these younger men that the new orientation seems to have come about. Lovato's lost verses on the Guelphs and the Ghibellines, for example, were dedicated to his nephew Rolando da Piazzola,[3] but the main initiative was undoubtedly that of his most brilliant pupil, Albertino Mussato. Unfortunately the celebrated controversy on whether it is better to have sons or not cannot be dated, but in 1301–2 Mussato was consulting Lovato about the political prospects raised by the expedition of Charles of Valois and the two exchanged further verses on the salt war with Venice in 1303–4. From this point the thread of verses on

---

[1] Smalley, *English Friars and Antiquity*, p. 282.
[2] Gius. Billanovich, *Primi umanisti*, p. 17.
[3] The sole evidence for the existence of this work is a note by Gianfrancesco Capodilista printed by Lazzarini in *Archivio Muratoriano*, I, p. 332.

topical themes can be traced through Mussato's celebration of the acquisition of Rovigo in 1308 and the poems recording the stages in his reactions to Henry of Luxemburg, up to a patriotic defence of Padua which he wrote while a prisoner of war in Vicenza in 1317.[1] Some scholars have regretted this involvement in current affairs which brought the humanists' eloquence back from the romance of Tristan and Isolde to the Paduan market place, yet without it Mussato and his circle might have left no greater literary remains than Lovato and his friends before 1300. The political crisis which broke in 1311 had the opposite effect to that which might have been expected. Mussato's two greatest works, the *Historia Augusta* and the *Ecerinide*, which were the culmination of the whole early humanist movement in Padua, were both the products of the years 1311–15; only after this date is the strain of the times reflected in the deterioration of the *De Gestis Italicorum*. Initially, at any rate, involvement was beneficial to Mussato as a writer; much as he owed to the ancients and Lovato, it was his role as a Paduan citizen which inspired his highest achievements.

There was nothing obvious or inevitable about Mussato's turn to contemporary history after 1311. The *Historia Augusta* represented a completely new departure in humanist circles where nothing on this scale had previously been attempted. The second and third decades of the fourteenth century saw stirring events in many parts of Italy, yet nowhere else did they inspire a major history in the humanist idiom except Vicenza, where Ferreto Ferreti wrote under the direct influence of Mussato. It is true that reasons can be found for this development which lie within the humanist movement itself. In his prose histories Mussato was trying to emulate his revered fellow-citizen Livy, while in his verse tragedy *Ecerinide* his model was Seneca, into the study of whose works he had been initiated by Lovato.[2] But Mussato must also have been aware of the Paduan chronicle tradition going back at least a hundred years, and he must have recognised in Rolandino a historian of real stature whose work, far from being simple and unpolished,

[1] Padrin, *Carmina Quaedam*, nn. I–XII, XXV–XXVI, XXVIII–XXXI, XL, XLII–XLIX; Graevius, Epp. I, V, XVII, coll. 34, 41, 51.

[2] For Mussato and Livy, see R. Sabbadini, *Le scoperte dei codici latini e greci nei secoli XIV–XV* (1905–14), II, pp. 107–8; for Seneca and the *Ecerinide*, W. Cloetta, *Beitrage zur Literaturgeschichte des Mittelalters und der Renaissance* (1890–2), II, pp. 29–34.

had earned its writer honour and the approbation of the university. It was from the Ezzelino legend which had received its classical statement at the hands of Rolandino, that Mussato drew the historical element of the *Ecerinide*, which represented that fusion of poetry and history first canvassed by the rhetoricians; after his coronation by the College of Artists which owed something to the example of Rolandino's approbation, Mussato took the title 'poeta et historiographus'.[1]

For all their differences, Rolandino and Mussato shared the common ideal of history as the fusion of fact and imagination. By this standard, there can be no doubt that Mussato failed to reach the measure of his predecessor. He came nearest to doing so in the *Ecerinide* where the verse has a real eloquence and the whole play has a sustained artistic unity. Yet the drama only triumphs at the expense of history. Rolandino achieved his artistic and didactic aims within the limits of historical reality but Mussato, to heighten the drama, was willing to turn his back on historical probability altogether. Thus he makes great play of Ezzelino's supposed demonic parentage; did he really believe this or was it introduced only for dramatic effect?[2] The prose histories, on the other hand, despite the many vivid passages scattered through them, have very little unity at all. The *Historia Augusta* sets out to be an account of Henry of Luxemburg's Italian expedition, but the Emperor fails to hold the centre of the stage which is increasingly dominated by Paduan affairs as the work proceeds. In the *De Gestis*, there is no discernible theme at all; after an attempt to keep up with events in the whole of northern Italy in the early part, the last three books concentrate on Padua alone. Large tracts are no more than an elaborate and pretentious chronicle. Thus behind their classicising façade, Mussato's histories were substantially mediaeval, while despite its mediaeval appearance Rolandino's history was in fact remarkably modern.

In fairness to Mussato it must be repeated that he worked under great difficulties, so that the *De Gestis* was probably

[1] For the connection between history and rhetoric in the Middle Ages, see Kristeller, *Studies in Renaissance Thought and Letters*, pp. 567, 571, n. 53; for the approbation of Rolandino's *Cronica*, see Arnaldi, *Studi sui cronisti della Marca Trevigiana*, pp. 79–110.

[2] See A. Zardo, 'L'Ecerinis di Albertino Mussato sotto l'aspetto storico', *RSI* VI (1889), pp. 497–512.

never completed. The lack of a modern edition of his works also makes appreciation difficult. To a great extent, the contrast between Rolandino and Mussato is a measure of the difference between the Paduan outlook in 1262 and 1315. The sense of relief and hope in the newly restored commune is reflected in Rolandino's faith in the justice of the Guelph cause and his complete mastery of his material. His local pride and self-confidence are shown most clearly in a passage where he declares that through her Trojan founder Antenor, and by virtue of the recent persecutions which have tried her, Padua is worthy to be called a second Rome.[1] Mussato's world was larger and more complex, but less under control. He had seen his city defeated by the Venetians and the Veronese and his sense of local self-sufficiency had been punctured by his encounters with two claimants to a universal dominion, Boniface VIII and Henry VII. Intellectually, he was aware of the classical writers Livy, Sallust and Seneca, not as equals but as models to be imitated; he sensed that Padua could not compete with Rome.

Rolandino and Mussato were both careful stylists but their canons of taste were poles apart. Mussato's were, of course, far nearer to the classical and in this he looked towards the future. He and his circle revived the elegy, the eclogue and the soliloquy, and in drama his success was outstanding; the *Ecerinide* has been described as 'the first and best play to imitate Seneca; it was so successful that Mussato may be called the father of renaissance tragedy'.[2] Yet this promise for the future was achieved only at the cost of a lessening of the immediate impact. His works can never have made easy reading, for except for a few passages which are on the whole the least classical, Mussato's prose is always stilted and contrived, and only in verse does he achieve real fluency. By attempting to follow the ancients, Mussato cut himself off from the greater part of his natural audience in the lawyer

[1] 'Numquid Padua condam est ab Antenore constituta, egresso civitatem Troianam eadem hora cum Enea, conditore Romano? Numquid passa est multas tribulaciones et werras, ut ipsa Roma? Numquid in suis civibus est offensa crudeliter, turribus et palaciis, domibus et decoribus suis dirutis et prostratis? Nempe, se michi parcat Romana curia, iam Padua dici potest quasi secunda Roma', Rolandino, p. 159.

[2] B. L. Ullman, 'Some Aspects of the Origin of Italian Humanism', *Philological Quarterly*, XX (1941), p. 221.

and administrative class. Thus the Guild of Notaries had to ask him for a work which they could understand, less highbrow than the *Ecerinide;* yet it was precisely for such men that the message of the tragedy concerning the menace of the tyranny arising in Verona was intended.[1] The paradox of Mussato the politician expending immense energy on writings on current affairs whose style would prevent their reaching more than a fraction of the potential audience, points to the problem of what exactly their literary activities meant to the members of the humanist group.

Humanist studies had begun as the private garden of a select few, and in the early works, most of which were in the form of letters, classical allusions and nicknames were developed as a kind of private language, intelligible only to other members of the group. In poems intended only for private circulation among friends, this trait is explicable, though even here the desire to follow a classical form at all costs could lead to absurdities; for all the honoured ancestry of the pastoral idiom, there is something incongruous in Mussato and Giovanni de Virgilio discussing the siege of Padua in 1320 through the metaphor of Old Mother Padua set on by dogs.[2] But even in Mussato's public works, the tragedy and the histories, he clearly wrote for a few friends and for posterity, not for the mass of his contemporaries. This cult of exclusiveness suggests a sense of insecurity, and throughout the verse of the humanist circle there is a recurring preoccupation with the status of humanist studies which is really a defence of the humanist scholar himself. Thus Lovato hotly urged Latin against the vernacular as the only fit medium for epics and Giovanni de Virgilio felt it was unbecoming for Dante to write in Italian.[3] Criticism of the pagan elements in his poems stung Mussato into a sweeping defence of classical mythology as embodying the same immortal truths as Christianity, claiming that the poets of antiquity had performed the same functions as the theologians. The nobility of tragedy extolled in Mussato's letter of thanks to the College

---

[1] 'Non altum, non tragedium, sed molle et vulgi intellectioni propinquum', *De Gestis,* coll. 687–8. Mussato's answer was the epic poem *De Obsidione Paduanae Civitatis,* printed as books IX–XI of the *De Gestis,* which is largely rhetorical and has little value as history.

[2] Wicksteed and Gardner, *Dante and Giovanni del Virgilio,* pp. 184–5.

[3] Above, p. 292; Wicksteed and Gardner, pp. 146–51.

of Artists seems to imply the nobility of the tragedian.[1] A certain amount of this kind of writing ought not to be taken too seriously, but occasionally the poet's personal involvement is fully exposed, as when Lovato compares himself to the great poets of the past in the consolation which he is able to draw from literature in his illness,[2] or when Mussato in the elegy on his birthday describes the struggles of his youth and his admiration for the manners of the nobility and his efforts to assimilate himself into their ways.[3] This may be related to what is known of the social position of the early humanists. Every member of the group had been profoundly affected by the social mobility of the thirteenth century. Unlike the later humanists, almost all were self-made men. Zambono d'Andrea and Lovato belonged to the class of *popolani* who had somehow made good during the years of Ezzelino's tyranny; Rolando da Piazzola's background was apparently similar.[4] Mussato's origins were even more humble and his sense of insecurity was exacerbated by the heights to which he rose and the rumours concerning his illegitimacy.[5] The only exception to this pattern within the group was Geremia da Montagnone, the author of an important *florilegium* showing humanist influences, who belonged to an old feudal family which had descended socially into the administrative class.[6] In this, he may be compared to Da Nono whose preoccupation with class and status had a similar origin.

From this aspect, the problems of the early Paduan humanists represent in an extreme form the predicament of the leaders of the newly maturing urban communities in Italy, who were seeking to make a place for themselves in a world hitherto dominated by the ideals of the clerks and the feudal nobility. In this situation, there was a persistent tendency for the bourgeoisie to take over the ideals of the nobility as they found them or as they imagined them to have been in the past.

---

[1] Ep. XVIII and I; Graevius, coll. 54, 34.
[2] Ep. IV, Foligno, pp. 55–6.
[3] Graevius, col. 64 cit. above, p. 261, n. 2.
[4] For Lovato see above, p. 134; and Zambono, p. 163. Rolando da Piazzola's father, Guido, had been a member of the Consiglio Maggiore in 1254 (AS Cremona, ASC 1794).
[5] See above, pp. 166–7.
[6] See above, p. 131. For the literary significance of Geremia's *Epytoma Sapientiae*, see Weiss, *Il primo secolo dell'umanesimo* (1949), pp. 15–50.

Da Nono, with his constant harking back to the good old days, displayed especially in the fantastic knightly contests which make up the greater part of his *De Hedificatione*, is an eccentric example of this tendency; the considerable Gothic and chivalric element in the culture of the Renaissance proves the continued attraction of these ideals. The humanists too sought their roots in the past, but whereas the devotees of chivalry tried to graft on to their urban culture aristocratic virtues which were essentially alien to it, the humanists brought themselves into contact with the ancient world, with whose urban civilisation they had a real affinity. Slowly and with faltering steps, the humanists of the late fourteenth and early fifteenth centuries moved on from the reconstruction of the style of the classical world to the recovery of something of its civic spirit. It is this which makes the humanists the key figures in the origins of the Renaissance; in the search for historic roots for the urban world in which they found themselves, the enthusiasts for chivalry found silver, but the humanists eventually struck gold.

The Paduan group were remarkably successful in reviving the forms of classical literature, but they were still a long way from taking the next step and recovering something of its spirit. In his histories, Mussato used his favourite classical writers in a typically mediaeval way as models of style and sources of erudite embellishments; for example, he translated Paduan institutions into Roman terms, the Consiglio Maggiore becoming the Senate and the Defensor Populi the Tribune of the Plebs, but without any comment to show that he appreciated what these implied comparisons might mean. Although the humanist attitude to literature implied some kind of historical periodisation—Geremia da Montagnone was one of the first anthologists to distinguish between classical and post-classical authors—the Paduans never extended this idea into other aspects of history. Thus Mussato accepted Henry of Luxemburg quite uncritically as the successor of Augustus, and one may search the whole of the *Historia Augusta* in vain for any serious reflection on the Empire as a historical institution. Like Dante, Mussato fell under the spell of Henry VII and was therefore quite incapable of making the revolutionary reappraisal of Roman history in favour of the republic as against the empire which was eventually achieved by Vergerio and Bruni some sixty years after his death. Only in the *De Traditione* which belongs to the last years of his life, is there evidence that Mussato had realised the parallel between the fate of the Roman republic and the Paduan commune.

Another step which the Paduan humanists failed to take was the revaluation of the active life and the civic virtues which had been eclipsed by the contemplative and ascetic ideals in mediaeval theory. There was, it is true, a difference between the two generations in this respect. In his poems, Lovato takes up a consistently pessimistic pose with regard to the active life, regarding his literary pursuits as a welcome escape from a harsh and unattractive world. Consulted on political problems, he counsels resignation; in the dispute as to whether it was better to have sons or not, he took the negative side.[1] Though this provoked Mussato to a defence of hope and though several of his verses express patriotic sentiments, late in life he could still attack his friend Marsiglio for 'deserting the sacred paths of study for the unspeakable acts of men'.[2] As citizens, the Paduan humanists were deeply involved in politics and the struggle for power must have occupied a considerable proportion of their waking lives, but as *litterati* their ideal was withdrawal and detachment. Mussato was perhaps the first republican philosopher-statesman since Cicero, but if he had had the fortune to discover the letters to Atticus which revealed Cicero's political involvement, one feels that his reaction would have been quite as shocked as Petrarch's.[3]

Mussato's coronation as a poet and historian in December 1315 marks the cultural apogee of the Paduan commune. After many years of slow growth, the Paduan tradition had flowered into what has been called 'the first example of a civic culture fused with classicism'[4] and the Paduan pre-humanists were beginning to exert their influence over like-minded scholars in other cities. The small Vicentine group headed by Benvenuto Campesani and Ferreto Ferreti, however much they might

---

[1] Padrin, *Carmina Quaedam*, nn. I–XII, newly edited by E. Bolisani, 'Un importante saggio padovano di poesia preumanistica latina', *AAP* LXVI (1953–4); also Padrin, n. XXVI. Another poem (n. XXXII) expressing similar sentiments may also be Lovato's.

[2] Ep. XII, Graevius, col. 48.

[3] See H. Baron, 'Cicero and the Roman Civic Spirit in the Middle Ages and Early Renaissance', *BJRL* XX (1938), pp. 72–97.

[4] Baron, *Crisis of the Early Italian Renaissance*, I, p. 102.

differ from the Paduans in politics, were intellectually their satellites. Mussato was in touch with the nascent humanist movement in Venice, and his correspondents included Cangrande's chancellor Benzo d'Alessandria, the commanding figure in early humanist circles in Verona, and Giovanni de Virgilio, the professor of Latin literature at Bologna from 1319, who tried in vain to arrange a meeting between the crowned Paduan and the uncrowned Dante.[1] But very soon the deterioration of conditions in the city following the war with Verona began to have an adverse effect on Paduan culture as the scholars became more and more involved in the struggle for political survival. Foreign students left and native Paduans were sent into exile. But though it broke up the group, exile had its compensations in the shape of leisure for writing and recollection. The last phase in the evolution of the Paduan tradition under the commune was expressed in the work of exiles.

The distinguishing characteristic of this last phase in the culture of the Paduan commune is the injection of a scientific element into a tradition which had been up to that point predominantly literary. Though natural science had not been neglected in Padua during the thirteenth century, for Albert the Great is thought to have studied there and the Polish scientist Witelo refers to experiments carried out in Padua, it did not exert very much influence on the main stream of the Paduan tradition until the very end of the communal period.[2] Though proof is lacking, it is reasonable to attribute this new development to Pietro d'Abano, one of the leading scientists of the day, who settled in Padua about 1306. The son of a Paduan notary, Pietro had had an Italian medical training which he followed up by a visit to Constantinople, where he seems to have learned Greek, bringing himself into direct contact with the main sources of medical knowledge, and about 1292 he was in Paris, the chief source of scholastic Aristotelianism. He had thus been in touch with all the main streams of scientific thought in the period, and his works typify the

[1] L. Lazzarini, *Paolo di Bernardo*, pp. 4–6; G. Biscaro, 'Benzo da Alessandria etc.', *ASL* ser. IV, VII (1907), p. 312; Wicksteed and Gardner, *passim*.

[2] Lynn Thorndike, *A History of Magic and Experimental Science* (1923), II, pp. 454–6, 523; see also R. H. Randall, *The School of Padua and the Emergence of Modern Science* (1961), pp. 15–68.

scientific outlook of the age, in which the natural world was regarded as mechanistically subject to a hierarchy of causes.[1] Pressed to its logical conclusion, this view could lead to the assertion of a complete natural determinism, with the natural world an entirely closed system dependent upon an impersonal First Cause. Doctrines of this kind, known loosely as Averroism, were heretical and rendered their exponents liable to condemnation by the church. Although his modern commentators have acquitted Pietro of the charge of Averroism, he did not escape accusations of heresy in his lifetime and according to a fifteenth-century tradition his body was burned by the Inquisitors after his death. Possibly because of this official discouragement, Pietro did not found a scientific school in Padua and Paduan Averroism as a continuous tradition leading up to Galileo does not begin until the fifteenth century. Instead, his influence was absorbed by the prevailing Paduan ethos with its increasing interest in current history and politics.

The central stand in Pietro d'Abano's thought was astrological, the belief that natural bodies were subject to celestial influences which was an integral part of the medical theory of the day. The idea that astrology might explain historical events had already been mooted in Padua, where the discussion can be traced back to the period of Ezzelino and Frederick II. Both these rulers were notorious for the reliance which they placed on astrologers and the controversies which this aroused are reflected by the various chroniclers in their characteristic ways. The author of the *Chronicon Marchiae Tarvisinae*, a simple man and a fanatical Guelph, roundly condemns the astrologers for the futility of their prognostications in view of the Divine freedom of action.[2] Rolandino's attitude is more cautious. He does not attack the scientific basis of astrology; indeed, he clearly believed there must be something in it, or he would hardly have recorded the detailed horoscope of Ezzelino's last expedition which he uses to account for the tyrant's defeat and

[1] For Pietro's thought, see Thorndike, op. cit. II, pp. 874–947; Randall, op. cit. pp. 28–35; and B. Nardi, *Saggi sull' Aristotelismo padovano dal secolo XIV–XVI*, pp. 1–74.

[2] 'Non enim Omnipotens planetis contulit dietatem, nec eorum motibus suam potentiam alligavit, sed in se retinuit plenitudinem potestatis. Reputandi ergo sunt fatui et infecti, qui totam spem suam in constellationibus posuerunt, et Creatorem non timent quotidie suis sceleribus provocare', *Chronicon*, pp. 32–3.

capture. On another occasion, he wryly points out an influence which the astrologers failed to take into account; the Emperor's new city of Vittoria was bound to canker because of the aspect of Cancer at its foundation. The insecurity of the times was an obvious inducement to prognostications of all kinds and Rolandino mentions six Paduans whom Ezzelino put to death because they had had recourse to lots, astrology and geomancy to try to discover the future fate of the city.[1]

There is evidence to show that interest in astrology was still alive in Padua in the early fourteenth century outside the restricted circle of the university and the medical profession. Da Nono records the exact day and approximate hour of the birth of Nicolò da Lozzo, presumably because the prophecy of the fateful role which he would play in the history of the commune which was attributed to Zambono d'Andrea was based on his horoscope.[2] The civic authorities chose the planets and their influences as the subject for the decorated ceiling of the Palazzo Comunale which, according to tradition, was painted by Giotto under the guidance of Pietro d'Abano.[3] In the humanist circle, the example set by classical authors encouraged an interest in auspices, portents and analogous attempts to foretell the future. In Mussato's histories, the year commonly begins with an account of signs and portents. Throughout his writings, Mussato shows a lively amateur interest in astrology and if, in a late work, he takes the opportunity to condemn the exaggerated claims of the professional astrologers, he is no more inclined to doubt the scientific basis of the art than Rolandino had been.[4]

The years from 1311 to 1325 were for Mussato years of activity; in exile after 1325 he had time for reflection. In his last works, the *De Traditione Patavii ad Canem Grandem* on the fall of the city in 1328 and the *De Lite inter Naturam et Fortunam* which is mainly autobiographical, he was able to develop ideas which had existed in his earlier writings only in embryo. Both works embody the results of his meditations on his political experiences and particularly on the disasters which

[1] *Cronica*, pp. 84, 160–1, 139–40. For Rolandino's attitude to, and knowledge of astrology, see Arnaldi, *Studi sui cronisti della Marca Trevigiana*, pp. 177–87.
[2] *De Generatione*, f. 30r.
[3] *Visio Egidii*, p. 19.
[4] Dazzi, *AV* V, vi (1929), pp. 409–16; Rubenstein, *Saxl Essays*, pp. 179–80.

had overwhelmed the Paduan commune after 1311. Relating these to what he had read of the history of the Roman republic, and making use of some general ideas freely adapted from Aristotle's *Politics,* Mussato postulated a constant tendency in human nature, through which peace and prosperity lead to a growth in cupidity and a decline in public spirit; it is this which has caused the balanced constitution of the commune to decline into oligarchy and finally into tyranny. But beside this psychological explanation of the fall of the commune, based on the common characteristics of human nature and the city-state, Mussato put forward a radically different theory tracing Padua's vicissitudes to something peculiar to herself. In the *Ecerinide,* Mussato had suggested that there might be something in the soil of Verona that tended to produce tyrants; now he proposed that Padua's fluctuations of fortune might be due to some occult influence, emanating perhaps from the site of the city, which caused it to pass through cycles of prosperity and decline of some forty or fifty years duration.[1] This set of ideas clearly belongs to the world of natural science dominated by astrology, whose leading Paduan exponent Pietro d'Abano had already suggested that particular historical periods might owe their characteristics to siderial influences. It is also reminiscent of the horoscope of the city of Vittoria reported by Rolandino. As a theory of historical causation, Mussato's idea was obviously an unprofitable dead end; on the other hand, the underlying assumption, that the city as a human community might be regarded as a natural phenomenon subject to natural laws, was revolutionary and potentially world-shaking. Although Mussato does not seem to have known it, as he wrote, this assumption had just provided the basis for the masterpiece of another exile, the *Defensor Pacis* of Marsiglio.

Marsiglio Mainardini was the last of the great men of the Paduan commune; had events not intervened, he might have succeeded Mussato and Pietro d'Abano and become the leader of the next generation of Paduan thinkers and writers.[2] Born into the Paduan administrative class between 1275 and 1280, he was thus Pietro's junior by thirty years and Mussato's by twenty and his early intellectual development was deeply

[1] Rubenstein, art. cit. pp. 169–83.
[2] For Marsiglio, see Gewirth, *Marsilius of Padua*; the known facts relating to his life are given I, pp. 20–3.

influenced by these two leaders of Paduan science and letters. He must have met Mussato quite early in his academic career, since he consulted the poet as to whether he should study law or medicine; the decision in favour of medicine brought him into the field dominated by Pietro, whose pupil he probably became. Like Pietro, Marsiglio studied in Paris where he absorbed the current Aristotelian philosophy, not without an Averroistic tinge. About 1313 he returned to Padua, where the indications are that he intended to stay, since in 1316 and 1318 he obtained Papal letters reserving for him the first vacant benefice and canonry in the city. Although he seems to have spent an earlier period in the services of Cangrande, his final departure from Padua about 1319 was unforeseen and up to the end of his life Mussato was urging him to return. There is no clue as to Marsiglio's motive in leaving, but it is most unlikely to have been a difference with the ruling group of the city of an ideological kind, as he certainly remained on good terms with Mussato. One possibility is that he had become attached in some way to the Maccaruffi and the Estensi, who also deserted the commune about this time. At all events, the period of war and political upheaval which affected Mussato towards the end of his life, struck the younger man in the middle of his career, so that his genius, which might otherwise have flowered in a Paduan context, became the property of the whole of Europe.

Marsiglio's ideas have been generally viewed and discussed in a European context, yet they were also characteristically Paduan and a natural development of the preceding currents in Paduan intellectual life. It has been shown that the analysis of the state in the *Defensor Pacis* was not only based on general Italian experience but on specifically Paduan ideas and institutions.[1] In what other city was there a tradition of responsible government of some sixty years' standing, with a sovereign body which was so widely representative of the *universitas civium* as the Paduan Consiglio Maggiore? The full discussion of the problems involved in the election of a prince, whether it should be for life only or hereditary and the conclusion in favour of the former, is much more meaningful when applied to an Italian *signoria* than to the Empire; the chapter may well reproduce some of the questions raised in

[1] Above, pp. 210–12.

Padua in the period leading up to the election of Giacomo da Carrara in July 1318.[1] Even the central theme of the book, the attack on the temporal power of the church, which made it so useful to Louis of Bavaria, may have sprung originally from local, though not strictly Paduan experience. The Paduan commune had reached a working compromise with its clergy about the year of Marsiglio's birth, so this conflict, which never really threatened to overthrow the state, is unlikely to have made a deep impression on him. The Papal intervention in Ferrara in 1308, on the other hand, could certainly be regarded as the blow which had destroyed the *tranquillitas* of north-east Italy, especially to someone moving in circles which were in touch with the injured Estensi, as Marsiglio may well have done. It may be significant that among the few specific examples of Papal intervention in secular affairs given by Marsiglio, Ferrara, Bologna and the Romagna are particularly mentioned.[2]

The *Defensor Pacis* is written in the form of a scientific treatise, using the language and methods of scholasticism, in which Marsiglio may have had the help and advice of a collaborator, Jean of Jandun. The author's medical training is apparent in his whole approach to the state as an organism whose health, that is its *tranquillitas*, is to be preserved. This was not just the literary convention to be found in other mediaeval writers, but was part of Marsiglio's fundamental redirection of attention from the supernatural ends of the state to the problems of its immediate practical preservation, which enabled him to draw his revolutionary conclusions. Many of the arguments, it is true, were drawn from Aristotle, who also tended to think of the state in biological terms, but the selection and arrangement was entirely original; as the inheritor of a highly developed civic culture, Marsiglio could approach the *Politics* with an independence which his predecessors did not have.

The scholastic form of the *Defensor Pacis* has obscured the importance of Marsiglio's link with the humanists. Yet there is no warrant for regarding humanism and scholasticism as in any way antagonistic at this period; both were comparatively new to Italy and the later rivalries had not had time to

[1] *Defensor Pacis*, pp. 94–112.
[2] Ibid. p. 481.

develop.¹ Marsiglio's choice of medicine as his main study did not cut him off from the humanist circle; Mussato addressed a study of the metre of Seneca's tragedies to him and remained his friend to the end of his life; the poet's last letter, written after Louis of Bavaria's Roman expedition, urged Marsiglio to return to Padua.² The similarities of approach between Mussato's last writings and the *Defensor* suggest that, since Mussato shows no sign of having seen his friend's work, their ideas had a common origin in discussions in Padua, at which Pietro d'Abano may have been present, sometimes between Marsiglio's return about 1313 and Pietro's death in 1316–18. Like the early humanists, Marsiglio rejected the mediaeval tradition and went back to the original sources, which in his case were Aristotle, the New Testament and St Augustine. These he used to overthrow not just the prevailing canons of taste but the whole theory of the subordination of the state to the church and in so doing he achieved a renaissance of the secular spirit of antiquity more radical than anything yet dreamed of by the students of literature. Yet Marsiglio does not really prefigure the fifteenth-century Renaissance so much as suggest another path which Italian culture might have taken. The Renaissance of the fifteenth century was primarily a moral and aesthetic revolution led by scholars whose interests were mainly literary. The role of science was secondary, yet in the early fourteenth century science was neither negligible nor incapable of growth; Marsiglio suggests how a renaissance might have developed, more scientific in content and scholastic in form. The Renaissance did not produce another Marsiglio, it produced Machiavelli, and the difference between the Renaissance which was and the renaissance which might have been is epitomised in the contrast between the *Defensor* and the *Prince*.

The Paduan intellectual tradition which we have traced, much as it was supported by outside influences such as those associated with the university, was essentially rooted in Paduan society and the Paduan state. It was the tradition not just of Padua, but of the Paduan commune. The administrative class from which all the Paduan thinkers sprang, looked to the

---

¹ Kristeller, *Studies*, p. 575 et seq.
² 'Evidentia Tragediarum Senecae', see Novati, *Scritti storici G. Monticolo*, pp. 187–92; Mussato, Ep. XVI, Graevius, col. 51.

commune for their sustenance. They ran the commune and their experience as citizens was as essential to them as what they learned in books. This is proved by the changes which took place after the establishment of the *signoria* in 1328. Despite the wars and plagues of the later fourteenth century, intellectual activity did not come to an end in Padua but it changed its character.[1] Petrarch and his circle and later Vergerio and Conversino, were dependent upon the favour of the house of Carrara; where Lovato and Mussato had been citizens of a republic, their successors were courtiers. The effect of this change is most clearly seen in the Paduan chronicles, which continued to be produced almost without a break. Guglielmo Cortusi, whose work is a primary source for the period 1311 to 1368, retains something of the outlook of the commune under which he had grown up. For him, the city is still the centre of his interests, but his successors shaped their chronicles not round the commune but the fortunes of the Carrara family. They rewrote the history of the last years of the commune not only so as to show the ruling family in a favourable light, but also exaggerating the part played by individuals. The practice of treating Paduan history, even before the final establishment of the *signoria*, as an aspect of the biographies of the leading Carraresi, was begun by the compilers of the *Gesta Magnifica Domus Carrariensis* and the same episodic pattern was retained by the later historians of the family, Vergerio and Gatari. A naïve emphasis on the role of individuals is a mark of popular history at all times, and none of these writers possessed anything approaching the intellectual capacity of Mussato or Marsiglio, but it may be that they reflected a weakness of the cultural *milieu* in which they lived. A state where so much depended on the will of the ruler was hardly the place to encourage a sensitivity towards the significance of impersonal factors in the rise and fall of political systems which had been tentatively explored by the writers of the communal period.

[1] For Paduan culture in the fourteenth century, see Baron, *Crisis of the Italian Renaissance*, I, pp. 101–20.

APPENDIX I

The Paduan Guilds in 1287

IN 1287, the Paduan commune recognised the following thirty-six guilds, which have been arranged for easy reference according to the kind of occupation involved. (Original MS *Statuti Carraresi*, f. 47r, published by Roberti, *Le corporazioni*, p. 122).

Notaries (notarii)
Physicians (medici)
Barbers (barbitonsores)

Merchants (mainly textile) (mercatores, includes negociatores?)
Woollen workers (lanarii)
Linen workers (linarolli)
Cloth Weavers (tellarolles)
Dyers (pignolati)

Tailors (sartores)
Doublet-makers (zuparii)
Old and re-made clothes merchants (strazarolli)

Tanners (curzarii)
Skinners (peliparii)
Shoemakers (cerdones)
Cobblers (zavaterii)
Saddlers (sellarii)

Carpenters (marangoni)

Masons (muratori) includes brick-makers (fornaxerii)
Coopers (mastellarii)

Goldsmiths (aurifici)
Smiths (fabri)

Spice merchants (speciali)
Millers (monarii)
Bakers (pistores)
Green grocers (fructarolli)
Grocers (caxalini)
Butchers (becarii)
Salt merchants (sallaroles)
Taverners (tabernarii)
Fishmongers (piscatores)

Waggoners (boarii)
Boatmen of S. Giovanni (nautae a S. Johanne)
Boatmen of Ognissanti (nautae ab Omnibus Sanctis)
Wine porters (portatores vini)

Market Gardeners (ortolani)
Reapers? (segatores)

The Paduan statutes of 1420 (*Codice Riformato* f. 31r, Roberti, p. 136) contain substantially the same list, except that the salt merchants and the saddlers are omitted.

APPENDIX II

The Statute of April 1278

THIS statute, which is of fundamental importance for the identification of the Paduan magnates and their territorial power in the communal period, has survived only through late copies preserved in the archives of the various branches of the Papafava family. It was published by M. A. Zorzi, who used an eighteenth-century copy by Brunacci of a document belonging to the S. Francesco branch of the Papafava, which seems to have been subsequently lost.[1] There are, however, two virtually identical copies of the document in the Papafava archives, belonging to the late sixteenth or early seventeenth centuries, and these, though there are some omissions, often show a better reading than the Brunacci transcript. In view of its importance, and because in the existing printed version, many of the place names are so corrupt as to be unrecognisable, a new version is printed here, based mainly on Archivio Papafava Cod. 14, ff. 11–12, except where the Zorzi version is clearly to be preferred. Omissions supplied from Zorzi are in square brackets.

Statutum Patavinum conditum 1278 de mense Aprilis

Nomina statuentium: dominus Patavinus de Gambarinis, d. Bonifacius de Guarnerinis, d. Joannes de Thebaldo, d. Benedictus de Zueca.

Statuimus et ordinamus quod infrascripti nobilies et magnati utriusque sexus quilibet scilicet in villis infrascriptis et earum districtibus sibi subditis, ut inferius designantur, communia et nomina villarum teneantur et debeantur omnes et singulos homicidias et forbannitos pro homicidio probato et pro communi Padue condemnatos ad mortem pro aliquo crimine forbannito pro libris quinquaginta vel ab inde superius si ipsi forbanniti vel aliquis eorum extiterint vel habitaverint seu conservaverint in aliqua infrascriptarum villarum vel eius territorio palam vel occulte, capere quo ad potestatem et commune Padue conducere vivos seu in ipsa hora et loco capiendis occisos ab eis.

Nomina ipsorum nobilium seu magantum qui tenentur et teneri debent, et nomina villarum ipsarum sunt haec:

---

[1] *L'ordinamento comunale*, pp. 199–201, based on Brunacci, *CDP* III, p. 1800.

APPENDIX II 313

D. Marchio Estensis in Este, Cero et Calaone.
D. Guido de Lucio in Lucio, Cortellada, [Valnogaredo], Fontanafrigida, Viminellis et ipsarum villarum districtibus.
D. Honor de Vicoaggeris in Vicoaggeris et eius districtu.
D. Guericus de Vicoaggeris in Rustica et eius districtu.
D. Guericus predictus et d. Henricus Trapola in Vico Alticherio et eius districtu.
D. Nicolaus de Castronovo in [Castronovo], Boccone, Zovone, Covarolo et eius districtu.
D. Thirennus et Ugucio de Lendenaria, et Badoarius filius d. Marci Badoarii de Venetiis in Cinto et eius districtu.
D. Nicolaus de Castronovo et d. Bartolomeus et Ansedisius fratres de Schinellis et d. Margerita filia quondam d. Ugolini de Schinellis in Rebolone et eius districtu.
D. Guido de Lucio, d. Manfredus de Dalesmaninis in Faedo, Galzignano, Turrilia et ipsarum villarum districtibus.
D. Hengulphus Comes et d. Artusius et Jacobus fratres de Dalesmaninis et d. Albertus Tertius et d. Cubitosa eius uxor in Arquade et eius districtu.
[D. Micael de Montagnone et d. Avogarus et d. Oldericus quondam d. Bartholomei filii quondam d. Hangelerii de Montagnone in Montagnone, Montegroto, Villa Vanza, Villa Tora et earum villarum districtibus.]
D. Palma et d. Aledesia et d. Altedisia filie quondam Marci de Montemerlo in Montemerlo et Saccolongo et territoriis.
D. Jacobus de Dalesmaninis in Camponogara et Burgomarzo et districtibus ipsorum.
D. Jacobus predictus et d. Traversus de Saza in Perarolo et eius districtu.
D. Manfredus de Dalesmaninis in Fossato, Paludello, S. Brusono, Portocurano, Strata, Sarmatia et districtibus ipsarum villarum.
D. Artusius de Dalesmaninis in Noventa et eius districtu.
D. Aicardinus Caputnigrum in Savonara et eius districtu.
D. Thedusius de Forzate et Joannes eius nepos in Capitevici, Rosaria, Merlaria, Cambroso, Vallonga et ipsarum villarum districtibus.
D. Papafava de Carraria in Anguillara, Agna, [Cesso, S. Syer] Burgoforte et eius districtu.
D. Marsilius de Carraria et filii quondam Bonifacii in Carraria et eius districtu.
D. Matheus de Flabiano in Pontecasale et eius districtu.
D. Tiso de Camposanctipetri in Comparione, Laurillia, Lauriola, S. Justina in Colle, S. Euphemia quae est inter Cittadellam et Onariam, S. Andrea Musonis, tota curia Camposanctipetri et ipsarum villarum districtibus.
D. Balzanella de Peraga in Perarolo, Murelis, Fiesso, Cadonicis, et ipsarum villarum districtibus.
D. Ungarellus de Ungarellis et d. Nicolaus quondam d. Aldrigetti,

d. Viola cum d. Crescentia eius uxore in Cono et eius districtu.
Item si quis tenuerit in aliqua villa Paduani districtus palam vel occulte in domo vel alibi aliquem de predicti forbannitis pro homicidio vel condemnatis ad mortem, seu forbannitis condemnatis in libris 50 vel supra, si fuerit aliquis vel aliqua de predictis nobilibus superius specificatis, condemnetur communi in libris 500, et si fuerit aliqua persona non specificata superius, condemnetur in libris 200 pro quolibet forbannito et qualibet vice, quibus condemnatis in . . . factis.

APPENDIX III

The Matricula of the Paduan College of Doctors of Law [1]

In nomine domini nostri Jesu Christi et eius matris Mariae virginis et gloriose, beati Prosdocimi episcopi, Danielis martiris, Justinae virginis et Antonii confessoris protectorum civitatis regiae Patavinae,

Haec est matricula doctorum utriusque iuris sacratissimi collegii Paduani, in qua descripti sunt omnes doctores qui in eodem collegio fuerunt ab anno nativitatis domini nostri Jesu Christi 1135 usque ad annum domini 1349, et ad tantorum doctorum memoriam sempiternam dominus Johannes Lodovicus de Lambertaciis utriusque iuris doctor, prior colegii, in scriptis redigi fecit ante matriculam novam collegii supradicti anno domini 1382.

Dominus Joannes de Cacio Ep. Pad. milles et decretorum doctor.
Jacobus Baldoinus de Bononia legum doctor.
Simon Vicentinus legum doctor.
Ugutio Ep. Ferrariensis decretorum doctor.
Guido de Susaria legum doctor.
Tancradus de Bononia decretorum doctor.
Gerardus Ep. Paduanus sacre pagine et decretorum doctor.
Guilielmus domini Acursii legum doctor.
Rodolfus de Brandello legum doctor.
Buzacarenus de Buzacarenis de Padua legum doctor.[2]
Nicolaus de Brantella de Plebe decretorum doctor.
Jacobus de Ardizonis de Verona legum doctor.
Arnaldus de Cataneis de Limena Abbas Sancte Justine decretorum doctor.
Jordanus de Transalgardis de Padua Prior S. Benedicti decretorum doctor.
Albertus domini Odofreddi de Bononia legum doctor.
Johannes Forzate Ep. Paduanus decretorum doctor.
Dinus de Musello legum doctor.
Thomas de Piperata de Bononia legum doctor.
Ugo Denarius de Padua legum doctor.
Fulco fil. dni. Buzzacareni de Buzzacarenis legum doctor.

[1] MS BP 1361 III; Gloria, *Univerità* p. 146 et seq.
[2] Native Paduans who flourished after 1256 are italicised

Salion fil. dni. Buzzacareni legum doctor et milles.
Jacobus de Cupraniis de Limena Abbas S. Justinae decretorum doctor.
Aldovrandinus fil. dni. Ugonis Denarii utriusque iuris doctor.
Gerardus de Vitaliano de Padua legum doctor.
Meliadusius de Buzzacarenis Abbas Prathalee decretorum doctor.
Henricus fil. dni. Lambertacii de Bononia legum doctor.
Thebaldus de Thebaldo de Padua legum doctor.
Jacobus de Arena de Parma legum doctor.
Stephanus Sasso de Padua decretorum doctor.
Odoricus de Cupraniis de Limena Abbas S. Justinae decretorum doctor.
[Federicus de Capitibusliste milles et doctor.]
Nicolaus de Matarellis de Mutina legum doctor.
Joannes Tadus de Rosano de Padua milles et legum doctor.
Pax Tadus de Rosano de Padua milles et legum doctor.
Altegradus de Cupraniis de Lendenaria Ep. Vicentinus decretorum doctor.
Lupus dni. Aleardi Cupranii de Limena legum doctor.
Vitalianus de Vitaliano de Padua legum doctor.
Simon de Hargelfredis [Hengelfredis] de Padua legum doctor et milles.
Princevalus de Comitibus de Padua Paduanus episcopus decretorum doctor.
Aliotus dni. Henrici de Lambertaciis de Bononia legum doctor.
Oldradus de Ponte de Laude legum doctor.
Barotus de Lingua de vacca de Padua legum doctor.
[Rolandus de Capiteliste legum doctor]
Ottobonus Ep. Paduanus decretorum doctor.
Zambonus de Baialardis de Padua legum doctor.
Boatius de Mantua Archieps.[1] Paduanus decretorum doctor.
Simon Botatius canonicus Paduanus decretorum doctor.
Paganus della Turre de Mediolano Ep. Pad. decretorum doctor.
Henricus de Consilve de Padua legum doctor.
Rizardus de Malumbris de Cremona utriusque iuris doctor.
Guido de Leonico de Vincentia decretorum doctor.
Belcharius de Bocone de Padua legum doctor.
Compagnonus dni. Compagnoni de Pontelongo de Padua legum doctor (de illis a Sale).
Buzacarenus dni. Salioni de Buzacarenis legum doctor et milles.
Nicolaus de Malumbris de Cremona utriusque iuris doctor.
Albertus Gaudini de Crema legum doctor.
Honoratus de Brandello canonicus Pad. decretorum doctor.
Henselmus de Barbarano de Vicentia legum doctor.
Manfredus de Manfredis de Padua legum doctor.
Laurentius dni. Henrici de Consilve legum doctor.
Schinella de Docto de Padua milles et legum doctor.
Albrigetus dni. Fulconis de Buzacarenis legum doctor.
Joannes Andree de Bononia decretorum doctor.
Petrus de Sala legum doctor.

[1] Read Archipresbiter.

Carlinus de Cremona de Madelbertis legum doctor.
Tugresolus de Ansaldis legum doctor.
Jacobus de Nuvalento de Brixia decretorum doctor.
Zenobius de Ciprianis de Verona legum doctor.
Beneventutus de Cividada Beluni legum doctor.
Franciscus de Nichisola de Verona legum doctor.
Jacobus de Belebono de Ferraria decretorum doctor.
Petrus de Quartariis de Parma legum doctor.
Pauanus dni. Buzachareni de Buzacarenis legum doctor.
Robertus de Baratis de Parma legum doctor.
Coradus dni. Petri de Sala legum doctor.
Jacobus de Ruffinis de Parma milles et legum doctor.
Ildebrandinus de Comitibus de Urbe Ep. Pad. legum doctor.
Antonius de Reprandis de Marostica legum doctor.
Albrigetus de Montagnana decretorum doctor.
[Carotus Capud liste legum doctor]
Bonsignorius de Bonsignoribus de Bononia legum doctor.
Pinus de Gazadinis de Bononia legum doctor.
Bonincontrus fil. dni. Joannis Andree de Bononia decretorum doctor.
Rainerius de Arsendis de Furlivio legum doctor.
Nicolaus de Verona legum doctor.

List of Sources for the History of the Paduan Commune relating mainly to the Years 1256-1328

PUBLIC RECORDS OF THE PADUAN COMMUNE

Statutes

Liber Statutorum Communis Padue 1276, with additions to 1285, MS BP 1235, published as *Statuti del comune di Padova dal secolo XII all'anno 1285*, ed. A. Gloria, Padua, 1873. (Sometimes referred to as the Codice Repubblicano).

Liber Statutorum Communis Padue 1362, MS BP 1237, known as the Codice Carrarese. Inedited; some excerpts printed in appendices to Botteghi, 'Clero e comune in Padova', *NAV* IX, (1905), Roberti, *Le corporazioni padovane*, and M. A. Zorzi, *L'ordinamento comunale*.

Most of the communal legislation not incorporated into these two codes has been lost, but a few statutes have been preserved through copies in private archives, or in the records of the Paduan guilds; for the latter see Roberti, *Le corporazioni padovane*, and Cessi, *Le corporazioni dei mercanti della lana*, appendix, doc. ii. See also:

'Statuti extravaganti', appendix I, M. A. Zorzi, *L'ordinamento comunale*, pp. 199–223.

'Riforme del Maggior Consiglio del comune di Padova per l'estimo del 1304', A. Medin, *BMCP* ns. I. (1925) pp. 37–42.

Statutum noviter factum super officio iudicis et officio bonorum rebellium civitatis Padue 1320, Arch. Papafava, 31. A sixteenth-century copy, Ambrosiana E. 38 supp. f. 62, is followed by further statutes of the same year.

Diplomatic

There are no manuscript or published collections of the treaties of the Paduan commune or its diplomatic correspondence, which have been preserved almost exclusively in the archives of neighbouring cites. The most important of these are listed below.

Miscellaneous

Descriptio Civium Paduanorum 1320, copy by C. Campagnola, 1547, MS BP 253 II, printed by G. Grion, *Delle rime volgari*, Collezione di opere inedite o rare, Bologna 1869, appendix I, pp. 254–88. Another copy by F. Cesso, 1644, MS BP 1860 IX is more accurate in places.

LIST OF SOURCES

STATUTES OF THE MINOR COMMUNES OF THE PADUAN CONTADO

Statutum Magnificae Communitatis Cittadelle et eius Territorii, undated, but apparently of the Venetian period, late copy in Biblioteca della Corte d'Appello, Venice, MS 2.C.72/15; excerpts published by Gloria, *Dell'agricoltura nel padovano*, 1855, pp. 132-7.

Statuta, Banna et Ordinamenta Communis S. Georgii de Perticis, (thirteenth cent.) MS Marciana XIV (Lat.) 288, published by Checchini, *NAV.* XVIII (1909), pp. 174-84.

Decreta et Privilegia Magnificae Communitatis Este 1318, original MS Archivio Municipale, Este, published Padua, 1629.

Statuta Communis Montagnanae 1366, with additions to 1461; original MS in private hands, copy of 1874 in the *municipio*, Montagnana.

Statuta Communis Pernumiae 1225-1315, Biblioteca Capitolare Padua, MS D.52; part published by Gloria, *Dell'agricolutra*, I, pp. 138-60. See E. Zorzi, *Il territorio padovano*, pp. 232 *et seq*.

SECULAR CORPORATIONS

Paduan Guilds[1]

Statuti della Fraglia dei Fruttaroli 1218-1350, copy of 1463, with additions up to 1574, A. S. Fruttaroli I; excerpts published in Roberti, *Le corporazioni*, pp. 187-203.

Statuti della Fraglia dei Marangoni, 1257-1317; MS of 1317 with additions to *c*.1462, BP 899; ff. 1-15 published by Roberti, pp. 207-20.

Statuta et Ordinamenta Fratalee Muratoriorum Civitatis Padue, fourteenth century, late-eighteenth-century copy by Gennari, *CDP* IX, pp. 1371-90.

Statuti della Fraglia dei Muratori, 1273-1437, with additions to 1609; MS BP 913, ff. 1-21, published ed. G. Lupati, per lauria Co. Camerini, Padua 1891.

Statuti della Fraglia dei Notai *c*.1260-1341; Archivio Notarile, Padua, part published in Roberti, pp. 157-83.

Reformationes Frataleae Notariorum 1334-57, MS BP 825.

Liber Statutorum Frataleae Notariorum 1420, compiled by Sicco Polentone, MS BP 339; the Confirmatio Ordinamentorum Frataleae pro Domino Rege 1325, appears f. 83.

Statuta Frataleae Specialiorum 1260-*c*.1400, MS BP 940, part published in Roberti, pp. 223-44.

Guilds of the Paduan contado

Statuti del Collegio dei Notai di Cittadella, sixteenth-century MS A. S. Padua, with privilege of 1256.

[1] For a full bibliography of material relating to the Paduan guilds, see Roberti, pp. 277-87.

Other secular corporations

Statuta et Matricula Collegii Iudicum, 1273–c.1400, Archivio Antico dell'Università di Padova, MS n. 123; part of statutes published by Roberti in *Ateneo Veneto*, I (1903).

Matricula Doctorum Utriusque Iuris 1135 (?)–1349, sixteenth-century copy, MS BP 1361.III, printed as Appendix III above. The earliest extant statutes of the College of Doctors date from 1349–82, and were published by Gloria, 'Antichi statuti del collegio padovano dei dottori iuristi', *ARIV*. ser. VI, vol. vii (1889).

Statuta Universitatis Paduae 1331, Capitelsbibliotek, Gnesen, MS 180, published by H. Denifle, 'Die Statuten der Juristen-Universität Padua vom Jahre 1331', *ALKM*. VI (1892), pp. 309–544.

RELIGIOUS CORPORATIONS ETC.

Episcopal records

Libri Feudorum I–V; Archivio Vescovile, Padua.

Cathedral Chapter

Archivio Capitolare is rich in documents of the communal period. The material is grouped by subjects and is well indexed.

Rotuli Capituli, sixteenth-century copies of selected documents in the chapter archive, arranged chronologically; vols. XIX–XXIX cover the period 1256–1339.

Miscellaneous documents from the archives of religious houses and corporations

Archivio Diplomatico, Archivio di Stato, Padua; arranged chronologically, Boxes XIV–LVI, nn. 1884–6284, are from the period 1256–1328.

Archivio Corona, Archivio di Stato, Padua; arranged under house of origin but numbered progressively.

Corporazioni Soppresse, (Monasteri Padovani)
Monasteri del Territorio
Monasteri Veneti
Scuole Religiose Soppresse.
} Archivio di Stato, Padua.

Corporazione Religiose, Padua, in Archivio di Stato, Venice.

Catastico di S. Agostino di Padova 1508, containing documents from 1226, Bibl. Civ. (Bertoliana) Vicenza, G.8–9–5.

L'obituario di S. Agostino in Padova, MS Bibl. Civ. (Bertoliana) Vicenza, G.2–9–20, published ed. G. Mazzatinti, *Misc.RDVSP* II, ii (1894), pp. 1–45.

Catastico Verde di S. Giustina, Archivio Papafava 43. Documents from other Paduan religious houses collected by C. Ceoldo about 1800 are in Archivio Papafava, nn. 26, 31, 34, 37.

LIST OF SOURCES

FAMILY ARCHIVES

Archivi Privati } Archivio di Stato, Padua.
Pergamene Diverse}
Documenti Carraresi, 1095–1385, MS BP 990.I. G. Bianchi, Illustrazioni dei documenti Carraresi (notes on the above), MS BP. 990.III.
Documenti per servire la storia dei Carraresi, G. R. Papafava, 5 vols., MS BP 928.
Archivio Famiglia Obizzi, containing documents relating to the Negri and Sala families, Cattaio, Battaglia, near Padua; index in Archivio di Stato, Padua.
Archivio Papafava, Padua.
Documenti della Famiglia Mussato, 4 vols., Seminario, Padua, n. 746.

NOTARIAL

Registers

Archivio Notarile, Archivio di Stato, Padua; relevant vols, nn. 168, 176, 398, 407.
Liber Breviaturarum Galvani Beldomandi 1323–, Archivio Vescovile, Padua, Diversorum.

Formulary

Fragment of a notarial formulary from the Paduan episcopal chancellery, MS BP 2228.XLI; see Roberti, 'Intorno ai frammenti di un formulario notarile del principio del secolo XIV della curia del vescovo di Padova', *ARAP* XXII (1906).

INSCRIPTIONS

Argi Patavini Inscriptiones, J. Salomonio with additions by J. P. Tomasini, Padua 1696.
Urbis Patavinae Inscriptiones Sacrae et Prophanae, J. Salomonio, with additions by J. P. Tomasini, Padua 1701.

MISCELLANEOUS MATERIAL RELATING TO PADUA IN ARCHIVES OTHER THAN PADUAN

Bassano

Archivio Municipale, see P. M. Tua, 'Registro degli archivi Bassanesi', *BMCB* V–XI (1908–14).

Acta ad Patavinos Spectantia ex membranis Tabularii Basaniensis, G. B. Verci, MS BP 818.

Statuti del comune di Bassano dal 1259 *e dal* 1295, ed. G. Fasoli, Mon.RDVSP ns. II (1940).

Cremona

Original documents relating to the alliances between Ezzelino da Romano and Oberto Pelavicino, 1252–4; those giving lists of Paduan citizens, Archivio di Stato, Cremona, ASC 1772–90, 1793–5. See L. Simeoni, 'Nuovi documenti sull'ultimo periodo della signoria di Ezzelino', *Rendiconto della Sessione della R. Accad. di Scienze dell'Istituto Bolognese*, ser. III, vol. IV, 1929–30.

Mantua

Privilegia Communis Mantue, Archivio di Stato, Mantua, containing treaties with the Paduan commune, 1285, 1291, ff. 200–207.

Modena

Archivio Marchionale Segreto, Archivio di Stato.

Liber in quo scripta sunt . . . possessiones Azonis et Francisci Estensis in Padua vel Paduano districtu 1293; Biblioteca Estense, n. 1271 (Lat.).

Treviso

Raccolta Scotti. Only a small part of this important collection is now available in the Biblioteca Comunale. The archives of Treviso, which were among the richest in N.E. Italy, suffered heavily in World War II, and a large part of them is still in disorder and inaccessible.

Udine

Register of Gabriele da Cremona, notary to Pagano della Torre, bishop of Padua and patriarch of Aquileia, believed to be in the Archivio Archivescovile, Udine. Excerpts published by G. Bianchi, *Documenti per la storia del Friuli* (1844–5).

Venice

Important documents relating to Padua appear in the various calendars of the Venetian archives, such as Giomo, *Misti*, Minotto, *Acta et Diplomata*, and Predelli, *Libri Commemoriali*.

Codex Tarvisinus (Trevisaneo), Archivio di Stato, is of exceptional importance for the Venetian hinterland; see Picotti, *I Caminesi*, p. 6.

LIST OF SOURCES 323

Verona
Famiglia Bevilacqua, Antichi Archivi Veronesi, Archivio di Stato, Verona.

Vicenza
(*Original documents*)
Archivio Torre, Archivio di Stato.
Statuti del comune di Vicenza *1264*, MS Bibl. Civ. Vicenza (Bertoliana), G.22-8-2, published by Lampertico, Mon.RDVSP ser. II, vol. 1 (1886).
Statuti del comune di Vicenza 1311. MS Bibl. Civ. Vicenza, (Bertolina), G.22-8-3.
Libri Feudorum I-V, Archivo Vescovile, Vicenza.

(*Collections of documents copied from various archives*)
Zibaldone, F. F. Vigna, 13 vols., Bibl. Bertoliana MS G.5-7-2-15.
Codice Diplomatico Vicentino, G. Maccà, vol. I (753-1407), Bibl. Bertoliana MS G.7-8-15.
Miscellanea I-XIII, G. Maccà, Bertoliana G.7-8-2. Additional volume in folio, Bertoliana G.21-11-20*.
Selva di Memorie Vicentine, P. Borgo, Bertoliana MS G.21-11-1.

(*Archives in the Province of Vicenza*)
Pergamene Antiche, Archivio Municipale, Malò.
Pergamene Antiche, Archivio Municipale, S. Vito di Leguzzano.

COLLECTION OF DOCUMENTS, MAINLY FROM PADUAN ARCHIVES

Gloria's *Codice Diplomatico Padovano* ends in 1183; in the absence of a continuation, the most important collections of documents relating to the March of Treviso available in print are contained in Verci's *Storia degli Eccelini* (1779), III (Codice Diplomatico Ecceliniano), and in the appendices to his *Storia della Marca Trivigiana*. Although the transcription is not very accurate, many of the documents recorded have since been destroyed, lost or have become otherwise not available.
Codice Diplomatico Padovano, I-IV, index vol. V; G. Brunacci, Seminario, Padua, MS n. 581.
Codice Diplomatico Padovano VI-IX; G. Gennari, Seminario, Padua, MS n. 582.
Appendice al Codice Diplomatico Padovano, I-II, G. Brunacci, Seminario, Padua, MS n. 583.[1]

[1] The above collections made by the leading Paduan *eruditi* of the late eighteenth century, contain material of all kinds drawn from a wide range of archives, some of which has since been lost.

Monumenti della Università di Padova 1222–1318, A. Gloria, MRIV XXII, 1884.
Monumenti della Università di Padova, 1318–1420, 2 vols., A. Gloria, 1888.
Notizie per servire alla storia dello studio di Padova, I, 1222–1405, G. Morelli, Bibl. Universitaria, Padua, MS n. 1675.

LITERARY SOURCES

Paduan chronicles and histories

Annales Patavini

Liber Regiminum Padue, ed. A. Bonardi, appendix to Rolandino's *Cronica*, RIS VIII, i (1906), pp. 175–376.

The above constitute the main corpus of the Paduan annals; other versions containing further material are:

Chronicon Paduanum, ed. T. Habinger (1908).
Chronicon de Potestatibus Padue et de Carrariensibus, sixteenth-century MS BP 757; for a vernacular version closely related to the above, see G. Fabris, 'Una redazione volgare inedita degli Annales Patavini', *ARAP* LV (1938–9).
ROLANDINO PATAVINO, *Cronica in factis et circa facta Marchie Trivixane*, ed. A. Bonardi, RIS VIII, i (1906).
Chronicon Marchiae Tarvisinae et Lombardie, ed. L. A. Botteghi, RIS VIII, iii (1916).
ALBERTINO MUSSATO, *Historia Augusta de Gestis Henrici VII Caesaris*, RIS X (1727), coll. 1–568.
— *De Gestis Italicorum post mortem Henrici VII Caesaris*,
 (i) Books I–VIII, ibid. coll. 571–686.
 (ii) Books VIII–XIV, ed. A. Padrin, *Sette libri inediti del De Gestis Italicorum post Henricum VII*, Mon.RDVSP III, iii (1903).
— *De Obsidione Paduanae Civitatis* (in verse), published as Books IX–XI of *De Gestis*, RIS X, coll. 687–714.
— *De Traditione Patavii ad Canem Grandem*, published as Book XII of *De Gestis*, ibid. coll. 715–68.
— *Ludovicus Bavarus*, ibid. coll. 769–84.
GIOVANNI DA NONO, 'De Hedificatione Urbis Patavie'.
— 'De Generatione aliquorum Civium Urbis Padue, tam nobilium quam ignobilium'.[1]
— *Visio Egidii Regis Patavie*, ed. G. Fabris, *BMCP* X–XI (1934–9), pp. 1–20.

---

[1] Both inediti; for a list of MSS, see Fabris, *BMCP* X–XI (1934–9), pp. 21–5. The most important are Seminario Padua, n. 11, and Bibl. Civ. S. Daniele di Fruili, n. 264, pp. 168–268.

LIST OF SOURCES

GUGLIELMO CORTUSI, *Chronica de Novitatibus Padue et Lombardie*, ed. B. Pagnin, RIS XII, v (1941).
Gesta Magnifica Domus Carrariensis, ed. R. Cessi, RIS XVIII, i (1942–8).
GATARI, G., *Cronica Carrarese*, 1318–1407, ed. A. Medin, RIS XVII, i (1909).
VERGERIO, P. P., *De Principibus Carrariensis et gestis eorum*, ed. A. Gnesotto, *ARAP* XLI (1924–5), pp. 327–475.

Miscellaneous writings with some bearing on Paduan history

MARSIGLIO MAINARDINI, *Defensor Pacis*, ed. R. Scholz, MGH Leges VII (1933).
GEREMIA DA MONTAGNONE, *Epytoma Sapientiae* (1505).
— 'Summa Commemorialis Utilium Iuris', Marciana, MS cl. V (Lat.), xv.
ALBERTINO MUSSATO, *Epistolae, Elegia, Soliloquia etc.*, Graevius, Thesaurus Antiquitatum et Historiarum Italiae VI, ii (1722), coll. 00–00.
— *Ecerinide*, ed. L. Padrin (1900).
— 'Contra Casus Fortuitos' MS BP 2531.
— 'De Lite inter Naturam et Fortunam', ibid. and Bibl. Colombina (Seville) MS 5-1-5. Excerpts from the above from the Paduan MS were published by L. A. Moschetti, *Miscellanea di studi critici in onore di V. Crescini* (1927), pp. 567–99.
ALBERTINO MUSSATO, GIOVANNI DEL VIRGILIO AND DANTE, *Eclogae*, see P. H. Wicksteed and E. Gardner, *Dante and Giovanni del Virgilio* (1902), also ed. E. Bolisani and M. Valgimigli (1963).

The minor poems, mainly in the form of verse letters, written in Padua during the communal period, are to be found in the following collections:

BOLISANI, E., 'Un importante saggio padovano di poesia preumanistica latina', *AAP* LXVI (1953–4).
FOLIGNO, C., 'Epistole inedite di Lovato Lovati e d'altri a lui', *Studi Medievale*, II (1906–7), pp. 37–58.
PADRIN, L., *Lupati Lupatis, Bovetini de Bovetinis, Albertini Mussati necnon et Jamboni Andreae de Favafuschis Carmina Quaedam*, per nozze Giusti-Giustiniani (1887).
NOVATI, F., 'Poeti veneti del trecento', *Archivio Storico per Trieste Istria e Trentino*, I (1881), pp. 130–41.

Bibliography

Manuscript (only manuscript works cited in footnotes, or otherwise of particular importance are listed)

Annali di Bassano, Museo Civico, Bassano, 33C.15.

BRUNACCI, G., *Codice Diplomatico Padovano*, 4 vols., Seminario, Padua, n. 581.

— *Appendice al Codice Diplomatico Padovano*, 2 vols., Seminario, Padua, n. 583.

Chronicon de Potestatibus Padue et Carrariensibus, Bibl. Civ. Padua, BP 757.

FABRIS, G., *Serie dei podestà antichi e moderni e dei sindaci di Bassano*, Museo Civico, Bassano, 259D.3.

GENNARI, G., *Codice Diplomatico Padovano*, vols. VI–IX, Seminario, Padua, n. 582.

MACCÀ, G., *Codice Diplomatico Vicentino*, 2 vols., Bibl. Civ. Vicenza (Bertoliana), G.7–8–15.

MONTAGNONE, GEREMIA DA, *Summa Commemorialis Utilium Iuris*, Marciana, Venice, cl. V (Lat.), xv.

MORELLI, G., *Notizie per servire alla storia dello studio di Padova*, vol. I, 1222–1405; Bibl. Universitaria, Padua, n. 1675.

NONO, GIOVANNI DA, *De Hedificatione Urbis Patavii*, Seminario, Padua, n. 11.

— *De Generatione aliquorum civium urbis Padue, tam nobilium quam ignobilium*, Seminario, Padua, n. 11 and Bibl. Civ. S. Daniele di Friuli, 264.

Raccolta Scotti, Bibl. Comunale, Treviso.

Serie dei podestà di Bologna, Archivio di Stato, Bologna.

VERCI, G. B., *Acta ad Patavinos Spectantia ex membranis Tabularii Bassaniensis*, Bibl. Civ. Padua BP 818.

Printed works

AFFÒ, P. I., *Storia della città di Parma*, 4 vols., Parma 1793.

ANGELINI, G., *Catalogo cronologico de' rettori di Bergamo*, Bergamo 1742.

Annales Mantuani, ed. G. H. Pertz, MGH.SS XIX, Hanover 1866, pp. 19–31.

Annales Patavini, ed. A. Bonardi, RIS VIII, i, Città di Castello 1906, pp. 175–265.

ARIAS, G., *Studi e documenti per la storia del diritto*, Florence 1920.

ARNALDI, G., *Studi sui cronisti della Marca Trevigiana nell'età di Ezzelino da Romano*, Instituto Storico Italiano per il Medio Evo, Studi Storici fasc. 48–50, Rome 1963.

BARBI, M., 'La questione di Lisetta', *Studi Danteschi*, I, Florence 1920, pp. 17-63.
BARON, H., 'Cicero and the Roman Civic Spirit in the Middle Ages and Early Renaissance' *BJRL* XX (1938), pp. 72-97.
— *The Crisis of the Early Italian Renaissance*, 2 vols., Princeton 1955.
BARTOLUS (Bartolo da Sassoferrato), *In Duodecim Libros Codicis Commentaria*, Basle 1562.
BENEDICT XI, *Le Registre de Benoit XI*, ed. C. Grandjean, Paris 1905.
BESTA, E., *Riccordo Malombra, professore nello studio di Padova, consultore di stato in Venezia*, Venice 1894.
BIANCHI, G., *Documenti per la storia del Friuli dal 1317-1325*, 2 vols., Udine 1844-5.
BILLANOVICH, GUIDO, ' "Veterum vestigia vatum" nei carmi dei preumanisti padovani', *Italia Medioevale e Umanistica*, I (1958), pp. 155-243.
BILLANOVICH, GUIDO, AND TRAVAGLIA, G., 'Per l'edizione del "De Lite inter Naturam et Fortunam" e il "Contra Casus Fortuitos" di Albertino Mussato', *BMCP* XIV–XXVI (1942-54), pp. 279-96.
BILLANOVICH, GUISEPPE, 'Biblioteche di dotti e letteratura italiana tra il trecento e il quattrocento', *Studi e problemi di critica testuale*, Collezione di opere inedite o rare, vol. 123, Bologna 1961.
— *I primi umanisti e le tradizoini dei classici latini*, Friburg 1953.
BISCARO, G., 'Benzo da Alessandria e i guidizi contro i ribelli dell'impeto a Milano nel 1311', *ASL* ser. IV, vol. VII, pp. 282-316.
BOLISANI, E., 'Un importante saggio padovano di poesia pre-umanistica latina', *AAP* LXVI (1953-4).
BOLISANI, E. AND M. VALGIMIGLI, *La corrispondenza poetica di Dante Alighieri e Giovanni de Virgilio*, Florence 1963
BONARDI, A., 'Le origini del comune di Padova' *ARAP* XIV (1897-8), pp. 209-54 and XV (1898-9), pp. 1-38.
BONCOMPAGNO, *Liber de Obsidione Ancone*, ed. G. C. Zimolo, RIS VI, iii, Bologna 1937.
BONIFACE VIII, *Les Registres de Boniface VIII*, ed. Digard, Faucon, Thomas and Fawtier, 4 vols., Paris 1907-35.
BORTOLASO, V., 'Vicenza dopo la morte di Ezzelino alla signoria scaligera' *NAV* XXIV (1912), pp. 5-53, 336-94.
BOTTEGHI, L. A., 'Clero e comune in Padova nel secolo XIII', *NAV* IX (1905), pp. 215-72.
— 'La fine di Iacopo abbate di S. Guistina di Padova 1271', *Atti dell'Accademia Scientifica Veneto-Trentino-Istriana*, ns. II (1905), pp. 8-23.
— 'Iacopo Dalesmanini e le fazioni di Padova nel 1277', *ARAP* XX (1903-4), pp. 139-54.
BOWSKY, W., *Henry VII in Italy*, Lincoln, Nebraska 1960.
BRESSLAU, H., *Handbuch der Urkundenlehre für Deutschland und Italien*, 2 vols., Leipzig 1889.

CAGGESE, R., *Statuti della Repubblica Fiorentina*, 2 vols., Florence 1910, 1921.
CAVALCABÒ, A., 'I rettori di Cremona', *BSC* 1935-60.
CECI, G., *Todi nel Medio Evo*, Todi 1897.
CERETA, PARISIO DE, *Annales*, ed. G. H. Pertz, MGH.SS XIX, Hanover 1866, pp. 2-18.
CESSI, R., *Le corporazioni dei mercanti di panni e della lana in Padova, fino a tutto il secolo XIV*, MRIV XXVIII, ii, Venice 1908.
— 'La signoria comitale dei Carraresi nel secolo XII', *BMCP* ns. I (1925), pp. 133-48.
CESSOLIS, JACOBO DE, *Liber de Moribus Hominum et Officiis Nobilium*, ed. E. Köpke, Mittheilungen aus den Handschriften der Ritter-Akademie zu Brandenburg, II; Brandenburg 1879.
CHECCHINI, A., 'Comuni rurali padovani', *NAV* XVIII (1909), pp. 131-84.
CHIAPPELLI, L., 'La formazione storica del comune cittadino in Italia. (Territorio Lombardo-Tosco)', *ASI* LXXXIV (1926), pp. 3-59; LXXXV (1927), pp. 177-229; LXXXVI (1928), p. 3-89; LXXXVIII, i, pp. 3-59 and ii, pp. 3-56.
Chronicon Estense, ed. G. Bertoni and E. P. Vicini, RIS XV, iii, Città di Castello, Bologna 1908-37.
Chronicon Marchiae Tarvisinae et Lombardie, ed. L. A. Botteghi, RIS VIII, iii, Città di Castello 1916.
Chronicon Paduanum, ed. T. Habinger, Udine 1908.
Chronicon Parmese, ed. G. Bonazzi, RIS IX, ix, Città di Castello 1902.
CIPOLLA, C., *Antiche cronache veronesi*, Mon.RDVSP ser. III, ii, Venice 1890.
— *Documenti per la storia delle relazioni diplomatiche fra Verona e Mantova nel secolo XIII*, Biblioteca Historica Italica II, i, Milan 1901.
— *Documenti per la storia delle relazioni diplomatiche fra Verona e Mantova nel secolo XIV*, Misc.RDVSP ser. II, vol. XII, i, Venice 1907.
— *La storia scaligera secondo i documenti degli archivi di Modena e Reggio Emilia*, Misc.RDVSP ser. II, vol. IX, Venice 1903.
— 'Il Conte Loisio di San Bonifacio, podestà di Piacenza nel 1277', *ARIV* LXIV (1904), pp. 285-303.
CLOETTA, W., *Beitrage zur Literaturgeschichte des Mittelalters und der Renaissance*, 2 vols., Halle 1890-2.
COLLE, F. M., *Storia scientifico-letteraria dello studio di Padova*, 4 vols., Padua 1824.
CORTUSI, GUGLIELMO, *Chronica de Novitatibus Padue et Lombardie*, ed. B. Pagnin, RIS XII, v, Bologna 1941.
CRISTIANI, E., *Nobiltà e popolo nel comune di Pisa*, Naples 1962.
Cronaca de Romano, ed. C. Cipolla, *Antiche cronache veronesi* QV.
CUSIN, F., 'Per la storia del castello medioevale', *RSI* V, iv (1939), pp. 491-542.
D'ARCO, C., *Studi intorno il municipio di Mantova*, Mantua 1871-4.

DAVIDSOHN, R., *Geschichte von Florenz*, 4 vols., Berlin 1896–1927.
— 'Über die Entstehung des Konsulats in Toskana', *Historische Vierteljahrschrift*, III (1900), pp. 1–26.
DAZZI, M. Q., 'Il Mussato storico', *AV* V, vi (1929), pp. 357–471.
— 'Intorno alla nascità di Albertino Mussato', Pts. I and II, *Archivio Muratoriano*, II (1915), pp. 263–72; Pt. III, Misc.RDVSP ser. IV, vol. IV, pp. 1–105, Venice 1930.
— 'L'Ecerinide di Albertino Mussato', *GSLI* LXXVIII (1921), pp. 241-89.
DENIFLE, H., 'Die Statuten der Juristen-Universität Padua vom Jahr 1331', *ALKM* VI (1892), pp. 309–544.
DE RUBEIS, B. M., *Monumenta Ecclesiae Aquiliensis*, Argentina 1740.
DE VERGOTTINI, G., *Arti e popolo nella prima metà del secolo XIII*, Milan 1943.
— 'Note sulla formazione degli statuti del popolo', *RSDI* XVI (1943), pp. 61–70.
DONDI DALL'OROLOGIO, F. S., *Dissertazioni sopra l'Istoria Ecclesiastica Padovana*, 9 vols., Padua 1802–15.
— *Serie Cronologica-Istorica dei Canonici di Padova*, Padua 1805.
DOREN, A., *Wirtschaftsgeschichte Italiens im Mittelalter*, Jena 1934, Italian trans. G. Luzzatto, Padua 1937.
ERCOLE, F., *Dal comune al principato*, Florence 1929.
FABRIS, G., 'La cronaca di Giovanni da Nono', *BMCP* ns. VIII (1932), pp. 1–33; IX (1933), pp. 167–200; XI (1934–9), pp. 1–30.
— 'Una redazione volgare inedita degli Annales Patavini', *ARAP* LV (1939).
FASOLI, G., 'La legislazione antimagnatizia a Bologna fino al 1292' *RSDI* VI (1933), pp. 351–92.
— 'Richerche sulla legislazione antimagnatizia nei comuni dell'Alta e Media Italia', *RSDI* XII (1939), pp. 86–133, 240–309.
FASOLI, G. AND OTHERS, *Studi Ezzeliniani*, Istituto Storico Italiano per il Medio Evo, Studi Storici fasc. 45–7, Rome 1963.
FEDERICI, F. D., *Storia dei Cavalieri Gaudenti*, Venice 1787.
FERRETI, FERRETO, *Opere*, ed. C. Cipolla, FSI, 3 vols., Rome 1908–20.
FIUMI, E., 'Fioritura e decadenza dell'economia fiorentina', *ASI* CXV (1957), pp. 385–439; CXVI (1958), pp. 443–501; CXVII (1959), pp. 427–502.
— *Storia economica e sociale di San Gemignano*, Florence 1961.
— 'Sui rapporti tra città e contado nell'età comunale', *ASI* CXIV (1956), pp. 18–68.
FOLIGNO, C., 'Epistole inedite di Lovato Lovati e d'altri a lui', *Studi Medievale*, II (1906–7), pp. 37–58.
FRANCHINI, V., *Saggio di ricerche sull'istituto del podestà nei comuni medioevale*, Bologna 1912.
GATARI, G., *Cronaca Carrarese*, ed. A. Medin, RIS XVII, i, Città di Castello 1909.

GAUDENZI, A., 'Gli statuti delle società delle armi del popolo di Bologna', *BISI* VIII (1889), pp. 7-74.
— *Gli statuti delle società del popolo di Bologna*, FSI, 2 vols., Rome 1889, 1896.
— 'Le società delle arti in Bologna nel secolo XIII', *BISI* XXI (1899), pp. 7-126.
GENNARI, G., *Annali di Padova*, Bassano 1804.
Gesta Magnifica Domus Carrariensis, ed. R. Cessi, RIS XVII, i, vol. 2, Bologna 1942-8.
GEWIRTH, A., *Marsilius of Padua*, 2 vols., New York 1951-6.
GIOMO, G., *Lettere di Collegio, rectius Minor Consiglio 1308-10*, Misc.RDVSP ser. II, vol. I, Venice 1910.
— 'Regestro dei "Misti" del senato della repubblica veneta' *AV* XVII (1879) - XXXI (1886).
GLORIA, A., *Codice Diplomatico Padovano, dal secolo sesto a tutto l'undecimo*, Mon.RDVSP ser. I, ii, Venice 1877.
— *Codice Diplomatico Padovano dall'anno 1101 alla pace di Constanza*, 2 vols., Mon.RDVSP ser. I, vols. iv and vi, Venice 1879-81.
— *Dell'agricoltura nel Padovano*, Padua 1855.
— *Il Territorio Padovano Illustrato*, Padua 1862.
— *Monumenti della Università di Padova 1222-1318*, MRIV XXII, Venice 1884.
— *Monumenti della Università di Padova 1318-1420*, 2 vols., Padua 1888.
— *Statuti del Comune di Padova dal secolo XII all'anno 1285*, Padua 1873.
GRION, G., *Delle rime volgari, trattato di Antonio da Tempo*, Collezione di opere inedite o rare, Bologna 1869.
GUALAZZINI, U., *Il 'Populus' di Cremona e l'autonomia del comune*, Bologna 1940.
HANAUER, G., 'Das Berufspodestat in 13 Jahrhunderts', *Mittheilungen des Instituts für Oesterreichische Geschichtsforschung*, XXIII (1902), pp. 378-426.
HAY, D., *The Italian Renaissance in its Historical Background*, Cambridge 1961.
HERLIHY, D., *Pisa in the Early Renaissance*, Yale 1958.
— 'The History of the Rural Seigneury in Italy 751-1200', *Agricultural History*, XXXIII (1959), pp. 56-71.
HONORIUS IV, Les Registres de Honorius IV, ed. J. M. Prou, Paris 1888.
HORTIS, A., *Gli antichi podestà di Trieste*, per nozze Pitteri-Artelli, Trieste 1895.
JONES, P. J., 'Italy' in forthcoming revised edition of *Cambridge Economic History*, vol. I.
KRISTELLER, P. O., *Studies in Renaissance Thought and Letters*, Rome 1956.
LAMPERTICO, F., *Statuti del Commune di Vicenza 1264*, Mon.RDVSP ser. II, vol. I, Venice 1886.

BIBLIOGRAPHY

La Prise de Pampelune, ed. A. Thomas, Anciens Textes Françaises, Paris 1913.
LATINI, BRUNETTO, *Li Livres dou Tresor*, ed. F. J. Carmody, Berkeley 1948.
LAZZARINI, L., *Paolo di Bernardo e i primordi dell'umanesimo in Venezia*, Biblioteca del Archivum Romanicum, Geneva 1930.
LAZZARINI, V., 'Storia di un trattato tra Venezia, Firenze e i Carraresi', *NAV* XVIII (1899), pp. 243-82.
— 'Un antico elenco di fonti storiche padovane', *Archivio Muratoriano*, I (1908), pp. 326-35.
LEVADA, LIBERALE DE, 'De Proditione Tarvisii', ed. R. degli Azzone Avvogari, *Memorie del Beato Enrico*, Venice 1760.
Liber Imbreviaturarum Appuliensis 1221-3, ed. D. Bizzarri, DSSCDCI VI, Turin 1934.
Liber Imbreviaturarum Ildibrandini 1227-9, ed. D. Bizzarri, DSSCDCI IX, Turin 1938.
Liber Regiminum, ed. A. Bonardi, RIS VIII, i, Città di Castello 1906, pp. 268-376.
LOPEZ, R. S., 'The Trade of Mediaeval Europe: the South', *Cambridge Economic History*, II (1952), pp. 257-353.
LOPEZ, R. S. AND RAYMOND, I. W., *Mediaeval Trade in the Mediterranean World*, London 1955.
LUZZATTO, G., *An Economic History of Italy from the Fall of the Roman Empire to the beginning of the Sixteenth Century*, trans. P. J. Jones, London 1961.
— 'La populazione del territorio padovano nel 1281', *NAV* ns. III (1902), pp. 373-84.
MAIN, A., 'Il Cardinale di Monselice, Simone Paltanerii, nella storia del secolo XIII', *NAV* XXXIX (1920), pp. 65-141.
MANSELLI, R., 'Ezzelino da Romano nella politica italiana del sec. XIII', *Studi Ezzeliniani* (see under Fasoli, G.), pp. 35-79.
MANTESE, G., *Memorie Storiche della Chiesa Vicentina*, 3 vols., Vicenza 1954-8.
— *San Vito di Leguzzano dalle origini ai nostri giorni*, San Vito 1959.
MARSIGLIO MAINARDINI, *Defensor Pacis*, ed. R. Scholz, MGH Leges VII, Hanover 1933.
MAURISIO, GERARDO, *Cronica dominorum Ecelini et Alberici de Romano*, ed. G. Soranzo, RIS VIII, iv, Città di Castello 1913.
MCLAUGHLIN, T. P., 'The Teaching of the Canonists on Usury', *Mediaeval Studies*, I (1939), pp. 81-147, II (1940), pp. 1-22.
MEDIN, A., 'I documenti originali dei primi acquisti di Padova nel Polesine', MRIV XXVII (1907), n. 10.
— 'La coltura toscana nel Veneto durante il medio evo', *ARIV* LXXXII (1922-3), pp. 83-154.
— 'Riforme del Maggior Consiglio del comune di Padova per l'estimo del 1304', *BMCP* ns. I (1925), pp. 37-42.

Minotto, A. S., *Acta et Diplomata e R. Tabulario Veneto*, 3 vols., Venice 1870-4.
Mittarelli, G. B. and Costadoni, A., *Annales Camaldulenses*, Venice 1755-64.
Mols, R., *Introduction à la Demographie Historique des Villes d'Europe du XIV au XVIII siècle*, 3 vols., Louvain 1954-6.
Montagnone, Geremia da, *Epytoma Sapientiae*, Venice 1505.
Mor, C. G., *L'età feudale*, Storia Politica d'Italia, ed. F. Vallardi, Milan 1952.
Morpurgo, S., 'Rime inedite di Giovanni Quirini e Antonio da Tempo', *Archivio Storico per Trieste, l'Istria ed il Trentino*, I (1881), pp. 142-66.
Moschetti, A., 'Il "De Lite inter Naturam et Fortunam" e il "Contra Casus Fortuitos" '; *Miscellanea di studi critici in onore di V. Crescini*, Cividale 1927, pp. 567-99.
Muratori, L. A., *Antiquitates Italicae Medii Aevi*, Milan 1738-42.
— *Delle Antichità Estensi ed Italiane*, Modena 1717-40.
Mussato, Albertino, *De Lite inter Naturam et Fortunam* and *Contra Casus Fortuitos*, see Moschetti, A.
— *Ecerinide*, ed. L. Padrin, Bologna 1900.
— *Epistolae, Elegia* etc., Graevius, Thesaurus Antiquitatum et Historiarum Italiae, VI, ii, Leyden 1722.
— *Historia Augusta de Gestis Henrici VII Caesaris, De Gestis Italicorum post Henricum VII Caesarem, Ludovicus Bavarus*, RIS X, Milan 1727.
— *Sette libri inediti del De Gestis Italicorum post Henricum VII*, ed. L. Padrin, Mon.RDVSP ser. III, vol. III, Venice 1904.
Nardi, B., *Saggi sull'Aristotelismo padovano del secolo XIV-XVI*, Florence 1958.
Nelson, B. N., 'The Usurer and the Merchant Prince: Italian Businessmen and the Ecclesisatical Law of Restitution', *JEH* VII Suppl. (1947), pp. 104-22.
Niccolai, F., 'Città e signori', *RSDI* XIV (1941), pp. 168-291.
— 'I consorzi nobiliari ed il comune nell'Alta e Media Italia', *RSDI* XII (1940), pp. 116-47, 292-341, 397-477.
Nicholas IV, *Les Registres de Nicolas IV*, ed. E. Langlois, Paris 1905.
Noonan, J. T., *The Scholastic Analysis of Usury*, Cambridge Mass. 1957.
Novati, F., *Freschi e minii del dugento*, Milan 1908.
— 'Nuovi anedotti sul cenacolo letterario padovano nel primissimo trecento', *Scritti storici in memoria di G. Monticolo*, Venice 1922, pp. 167-92.
— 'Poeti veneti del trecento', *Archivio Storico per Trieste, Istria e il Trentino*, I (1881), pp. 130-41.
Obituario di S. Agostino di Padova, ed. G. Mazzatinti, *Misc.RDVSP* ser. II, ii, Venice 1894.
Ottokar, N., *Il comune di Firenze alla fine del dugento*, Florence 1926.

PADRIN, L., *Lupati de Lupatis, Bovetini de Bovetinis, Albertini Mussati necnon et Jamboni Andreae de Favafuschis Carmina Quaedam*, per nozze Giusti-Giustiniani, Padua 1887.
PARDI, G., 'Serie dei supremi magistrati e reggitori di Orvieto', *BRDSPU* I (1895).
PASCHINI, P., *La storia del Friuli*, Udine 1953.
PELLEGRINI, F., *Serie dei podestà e capitani e dei vicari o giudici di Belluno*, per nozze Miari Fulchis-Migliorini, Belluno 1893.
PEYER, H. C., *Zur Getreidepolitik Oberitalienischer Städte im XIII Jahrhundert*, Vienna 1950.
PICOTTI, G. B., *I Caminesi e la loro signoria in Treviso dal 1283 al 1312*, Leghorn 1905.
PILONI, G., *Historia di Belluno*, ed. L. Alpago Novello, A. Da Borso, and R. Protti, Belluno 1929.
PLESNER, J., *L'Emigration de la Campagne à la Ville Libre de Florence au XIIIe siècle*, Copenhagen 1934.
PORTENARI, A., *La Felicità di Padova*, Padua 1623.
PREDELLI, R., *I libri Commemoriali della Repubblica di Venezia*, Mon.RDVSP ser. I, vol. I, Venice 1876.
RAJNA, P., 'Le origini delle famiglie padovane e gli eroi dei romanzi cavallereschi', *Romania*, IV (1875), pp. 161–83.
RANDALL, J. H., *The School of Padua and the Emergence of Modern Science*, Padua 1961.
RENOUARD, Y., *Les Hommes d'Affaires Italiens au Moyen-Age*, Paris 1949.
RIVA, BONVESIN DELLA, 'De Magnalibus Urbis Mediolani', ed. F. Novati, *BISI* XX (1898), pp. 67–114.
ROBERTI, M., 'Diritto romano e coltura giuridica in Padova sulla fine del secolo XII', *NAV* ns. IV (1902), pp. 162–201.
— 'Intorno ai frammenti di un formulario notarile del principio del secolo XIV della curia del vescovo di Padova', *ARAP* XXII (1906).
— *Le corporazioni padovane d'arti e mestieri*, MRIV XXVI, viii, Venice 1902.
— 'Nuove ricerche sopra l'antica costituzione del comune di Padova', *NAV* ns. III (1902), pp. 77–97.
— *Un formulario padovano di un notaio padovano*, MRIV XXVII, Venice 1906.
RODOLICO, N., 'Di alcuni trattati di arbitraggio nelle questioni commerciali tra Venezia e Padova', *Raccolta di scritti storici in onore di G. Romano*, Pavia 1907, pp. 117–40.
ROLANDINO PATAVINO, *Cronica in factis et circa facta Marchie Trivixane*, ed. A. Bonardi, RIS VIII, i, Città di Castello 1906.
ROMANO, G. AND SOLMI, A., *Le dominazioni barbariche in Italia*, Storia Politica d'Italia (Vallardi), 2 vols., Milan 1940–5.
RONCIONI, R., 'Delle Istorie Pisane', ed. F. Bonaini, *ASI* ser. I, vol. VI, i (1844).
RUBENSTEIN, N., 'Some Ideas on Municipal Progress and Decline in

the Italy of the Communes', *F. Saxl Memorial Essays*, London 1957, pp. 165-83.

Russel, J. C., 'Late Ancient and Mediaeval Population', *Transactions of the America Philosophical Society*, ns. 48, pt. 3 (1958).

— *Mediaeval British Population*, Albuquerque 1948.

Sabbadini, R., *Le scoperte dei codici latini e greci nei secoli XIV e XV*, 2 vols., Florence 1905-14.

— 'Postille alle epistole inedite di Lovato Lovati', *Studi Medievale*, II (1906-7), pp. 255-62.

Salimbene, *Cronica*, ed. F. Bernini, Bari 1942.

Salomonio, J., *Agri Patavini Inscriptiones*, with additions by J. P. Tomasini, Padua 1696.

— *Urbis Patavinae Inscriptiones Sacrae et Prophanae*, with additions by J. P. Tomasini, Padua 1701.

Salvemini, G., *La dignità cavalleresca nel comune di Firenze*, Florence 1896.

— *Magnati e popolani in Firenze à280–à295*, Florence 1899.

Salzer, E., *Über die Anfänge der Signorie in Oberitalien*, Historische Studien XIII, Berlin 1910.

Sambin, P., 'Notizie di una cronaca tra i rogiti di un notaio padovano del secolo XIV', *AIV* CX (1951–2), pp. 99–112.

— 'Le relazioni tra Venezia, Padova e Verona all'inizio del secolo XIV', *AIV* CXI (1952–3), pp. 205–15.

Sapori, A., *Le Marchand Italien au Moyen Age*, Paris 1952.

— *Studi di storia economica medioevale*, 2nd ed., Florence 1946.

Savonarola, M., *Libellus de Magnificae Ornamentis Regiae Civitatis Paduae*, ed. A. Segarizzi, RIS XXIV, xv, Città di Castello 1901.

Scardeoni, B., *De Antiquitate Urbis Patavii et Claris Civibus Patavinis*, Basle 1560.

Sestan, E., 'Le origini delle signorie cittadine: un problema storico esaurito?', *BISI* LXXIII (1962), pp. 41–69.

Simeoni, L., 'La formazione della signoria scaligera', *AAV* ser. V, vol. III (1926), pp. 117-67.

— 'L'elezione di Obizzo d'Este a signore di Ferrara 1264', *ASI* XCIII (1935), pp. 165-88.

— *Le Signorie*, Storia Politica d'Italia (Vallardi) Milan 1950.

— 'Nuovi documenti sull'ultimo periodo della signoria di Ezzelino', *Rendiconto della sessione della R. Accademia di Scienze dell'Istituto Bolognese*, ser. III, vol. IV (1929–30).

Smalley, B., *English Friars and Antiquity in the Early Fourteenth Century*, Oxford 1960.

Smereglo, Nicolò, *Annales Civitatis Vincentiae*, ed. G. Soranzo, RIS VIII, v, Bologna 1921.

Soranzo, G., *La guerra fra Venezia e la S. Sede per il dominio di Ferrara 1308–1313*, Città di Castello 1905.

Spangenburg, H., *Can Grande I von Scala*, Historische Untersuchungen, ed. J. Jastrow, Berlin 1892.

THORNDIKE, L., *A History of Magic and Experimental Science*, New York 1923.
TORELLI, P., 'Capitanato del popolo e vicariato imperiale come elementi costitutivi della signoria bonacolsiana', *Atti della R. Accademia Virgiliana di Mantova*, XIV–XVI (1923), pp. 73-166, reprinted in *Scritti di storia del diritto italiano*, Bologna 1959, pp. 375-480.
— *Un comune cittadino in territorio ad economia agricola*, Miscellanea della R. Accad. Virgiliana, VII, Mantua 1930.
TUA, P. M., 'Regestro degli archivi bassanesi', *BMCP* V–VIII (1908-11), and X–XI (1913-14).
TYLER, J. E., *The Alpine Passes 962–1250*, London 1930.
ULLMANN, B. L., 'Some Aspects of the Origin of Italian Humanism', *Philological Quarterly*, XX (1941), pp. 212-23.
VACCARI, P., *Dall'unità romana al particolarismo giuridico del medio evo*, Pavia 1936.
— *La territorialità come base dell'ordinamento giuridico del contado nell'Italia medioevale*, 2nd ed., Milan 1963.
VALENTINI, A., *Il Liber Poteris della città e del comune di Brescia, e la serie dei suoi console e podestà*, Brescia 1878.
VERCI, G. B., *Storia degli Eccelini*, 3 vols., Bassano 1779.
— *Storia della Marca Trivigiana*, 10 vols., Venice 1786-91.
VICINI, E. P., 'I capitani del popolo di Modena e Reggio', *R. Deputazione di Storia Patria per l'Emilia e Romagna, Sezione di Modena, Studi e Documenti*, III, pp. 189-209; IV, pp. 37-64, 171-88, 235-50.
— 'I podestà di Modena', Pt. 1, 1156-1336; estr. *Giornale Araldico-Storico-Genealogico*, Rome 1913.
VILLANI, G., *Cronica*, ed. I. Moutier, Florence 1823.
VITALE, V., 'Vita e commercio nei notai genovesi dei secoli XII–XIII', *Atti della Società Ligure di Storia Patria*, LXXII (1949).
WEISS, R., *Il primo secolo dell'umanesimo*, Rome 1949.
— 'Lovato Lovati', *Italian Studies* VI (1951), pp. 3-28.
— *The Dawn of Humanism in Italy*, London 1947.
WHITE, L., *Mediaeval Technology and Social Change*, London 1962.
WICKSTEED, P. H. AND GARDNER, E., *Dante and Giovanni del Virgilio*, London 1902.
WINKELMANN, E., *Acta Imperii Inedita Sec.XIII–XIV*, Innsbruck 1885.
ZARDO, A., *Albertino Mussato*, Padua 1884.
— 'L'Ecerinis di Albertino Mussato sotto l'aspetto storico', *RSI* VI (1889), pp. 497-512.
ZENATTI, A., 'Antichi rimatori padovani', *Atti della R. Accademia Scientifica Veneto-Trentino-Istriana*, I (1904), pp. 5-16.
ZORZI, E., *Il territorio padovano nel periodo di trapasso da comitato a comune*, Misc.RDVSP ser. IV, vol. III, Venice 1929.
ZORZI, M. A., *L'ordinamento comunale padovano nella seconda metà del secolo XIII*, Misc.RDVSP ser. IV, vol. V, Venice 1931.

Index

Abano, 48, 249; Cecilia d', 196–7; Manfredo Ricco d', 72, 196–7; Pietro d', 163, 176, 303–4, 309
Administrative Class, Paduan, 1, 49, 108, 216, 247; *see also* Judges, Notaries
Adria, Salione Buzzaccarini, bishop of, 151
Advocatus, office of, 18, 79, 85, 241
Agna, 82, 275
Agostino, S., church of, in Padua, 125, 135–6; Dominicans of, 135, 149
Agriculture, development in mediaeval Italy, 13–16; in Paduan economy, 42–56, 193
Albert the Great, 303
Albignasego, 135
Alessandria, Benzo d', 303
Alessio, Antonio d', 'chronicle' of, 68, 71, 79, 81, 86, 87–8, 286, 287
Alighieri, Dante, 22, 40, 60, 150, 185, 187, 188, 289, 299, 301
Altichini, family, 140–1, 180, 190, 261, 265, 273, 274; Pietro, 140–1, 252, 266
Altinate, Ponte, 31, 37, 46, 86
Ambrosino, Enrighetto d', 165n.
Ancona, March of, 69, 201, 218, 235; siege of, 287
Andrea, Giovanni d', Bolognese jurist, 293n; Zambono d', 68, 163, 290, 291, 300, 305; his 'chronicle', 67–8, 286; Genealogical Table, 164
Andrea, S., church and *via*, 43, 74, 82; family, 89n
Andrew II, king of Hungary, 69
Angarano, 226
Anna, S., convent of, 115
Annals, civic, 285; Paduan (*Annales Patavini*), 5, 47, 285–7, 324
Anselmi, Albertino, 176
Antenor, 31, 69, 298
Antonio, S., 288; basilica of, 2, 31, 34, 74, 181; Franciscans of, 74, 173, 225; *see also* Inquisition

Anziani, 23; Paduan, 237, 240, 249, 250, 251; role in constitution (of 1276), 212–15; reformed, 246, 247n, 265, 281; social origins of, 214–15; individual members, 103, 179n
Judge of the, 114, 137, 215, 240, 243, 247n
Aquileia, Patriarchs of, 195, 228–9, 231, 248, 275
Ardenghi, Antonio, 209; Giacomo, 286
Arena of Padua, 32, 37; chapel, 101, 190
Arena, Giacomo de, jurist of Parma, 84, 141
Arengo, *see* Parlamentum
Arezzo, Imperial Vicar of, 114, 115n, 116, 258; *Podestà*, 125
Argenta, 119–20, 218
Aristotle, Aristotelianism, 303, 306, 307, 308, 309
Arquà, 45, 48, 71, 177
Ars Dictaminis, 294–5
Ars Notaria, 157
Arzignano, 222; family, 221
Astrology, 304–5
Attila, 29, 32, 77
Augustine, St., 309
Austria, Frederick of, 100, 104; his *signoria* in Padua, 3, 136, 245, 268, 271, 277, 281
Averroism, 304, 307
Avvocati of Padua, family, 79, 205, 217; Avezuto, 205; Ugolino, 121, 122, 215

Badoer of Venice, Badoer, 240, 252; Giovanni, 202, 234; Marco Zeno, 58, 79, 202, 235; Stefano, 202
Bagnolo, 143; Pietro da, 176
Bankers, Italian, 16, 41; for Paduan 'bankers', *see* Moneylending, Usury
Baone, Da, family, 72
Barbarano, Enselmo da, of Vicenza, 130

INDEX

Basilii, notarial family, 173
Bassano, 30, 38, 199, 258; *comitatus* of, 226–7; commune of, 221–2, 223, 227; *podestà* of, importance of office, 108; individual office-holders, 72, 98, 117, 134, 139, 140, 278n
Battaglia, 45
Bazalerii, Bonadomane, 169
Beldomandi, Galvano, 172
Bellarini, family, 184
Belluno, bishop of, 169, 195, 229; *podestà* of and treaty with Paduan commune, 106, 229; individual office-holders, 98, 108–9, 111, 112, 113, 142, 169
Benedict XI, Pope, 190, 226
Bentacorde of Florence, family, 183
Bergamo, *podestà* of, 110n, 112, 115n
Berni, Berno, 180; Pietro, 165n; Vendramo, 141
Berti, Domenico and Giacomo, 177, 184
Bibi, Alberto, 116, 169–70, 209; Antonio, 169, 225; Marsiglio, 169–70
Bishops, Italian, temporal powers of, 11–12, 18
Bissolo, Bellino, of Milan, 292
Boatino, Simone, canon of Padua, 146
Bobi, Beldomando, 169
Boccon, 74, 148, 150, 265
Bologna, 69, 101, 249, 250, 256, 270; *capitano del popolo*, 151; *capitani del popolo* and *podestà* appointed concurrently, 24; judicial and notarial professions separated at, 122; notaries created and regulated by commune, 155–7; number of notaries (in 1294), 162; office of *anziani* probably originating at, 24; *podestà*, 111, 115n, 151
university of, canon and civil law, 115, 116, 125, 146, 284, 293n; rhetoric and poetry, 198, 287, 293, 303
Bologna, Guizzardo da, 272, 293
Bonacolsi, Passerino, of Mantua, 114, 200
Bonencontro, *magister*, 293
Boniface VIII, Pope, 271–2, 298
Bonifacio, S. family, counts of Verona, 77–8, 155, 199–200,
240; Lodovico, 155, 203, 204; Riccardo, 202; Simone, 221; Vicinguerra, 155, 257, 267
Bovolenta, 45
Brandello, Onorato de, 146
Breganze, Bartolomeo da, bishop of Vicenza, 205, 222, 225; Odilia da, 224
Brentasicca, 113
Brescia, 203, 228; *podestà* of, 118, 120
Brognacci, Belcaro, 147–50
Brugine, 88, 268; Alberto da, 108
Bruni, Leonardo, 302
Butchers, of Padua, 179–80
Buzzaccarini, family, 58, 150–3; Genealogical table, 152; Buzzaccarino, 58, 148, 150–1, 208, 209; Dusio, 153n, 278, 279; Fulcone, 151, 230; Meliadusio, 146, 151; Pantaleone, 151, 153n, 278; Rolando, 158; Salione the astrologer, 148; Salione, doctor of law, 151

Cacio, Enrico da, 133; Rainerio da, 177
Cagliari, bishop of, 146
Calaone, family, 72; fortress, 242
Calcinara, 79, 271, 272
Caldenacio, Bartolomeo and Tebaldo da, 102–3
Caligine, Giacomo, 113–14; Giovanni, 113–15, 258; Prosdocimo, 277
Camaldolese order, General of, 242; *see also* Vangadizza, monastery of
Camino, family, 195, 196, 200, 205, 229, 275; Agnese da, 76, 231, 241
Gerardo da, 76, 241; borrows money from Paduans, 139, 181n, 185, 187–8, 230–1; serves Paduan commune, 228, 230, 240; his *signoria* in Treviso, 81, 110, 205, 230, 248
Guecillo da, 263, 264, 265; Riccardo da, 252, 255, 263
Camisano, 273
Campagnola, Sachetto da, 165, 171, 174, 178
Campanati, family, 136–8; Genealogical Table, 137; Aldovrandino, 136–8, 278; Giacomo, 108
Campanea Padue, 47, 50, 53

INDEX

Campesani, Benvenuto, of Vicenza, 302
Campolongo Maggiore, Bartolomeo da, 179
Camponogara, 86
Camposanpiero, 276; family, 65, 72, 80–2, 88, 196, 200, 217, 219, 273, 275–6; Genealogical Table, 81; Alessandra, 75
Gerardo, begins feud with Da Romano, 72, 196–7
Giovanni, 104, 276, 279; Guglielmo, (*d.*1251) 206
Guglielmo di Florio, judge, 112, 130, 230
Tiso III (*d.*1266), 81, 198, 206, 218
Tiso IV (*d.*1312), 81, 100, 105, 234, 260, 263, 275–6; *pars* of, 164, 252–3, 264, 275; connection with Da Camino and Treviso, 81, 110, 230, 231
Tiso V (*b.*1312), 276
Campsores, 41–2, 183
Canals, in Padovano, drainage, 48; navigable, 45, 53
Canciano, S., *via*, 177; Agnese da, 142
Candiana, 143; Pietro and Vivarotto da, 185
Cane, Antonio, 218; Martino, 273; Zamboneto, 41n, 273
Caniparii, 175n
Capitano del Popolo, 24, 25, 106; in Padua, 100, 237, 244, 245, 281
Capodilista, family, 68, 72, 102, 115; Caroto, 215; Gianfrancesco, chronicle of, 68, 285–6
Capodivacca, family, 58, 85, 88, 102, 185; Aicardino, 278, 279; Francesco di Frassalasta, 278, 279; Francesco di Marco, 108; Frassalasta, 225; Giovanni, 109; Nicolò, 141; Tavanello, 185, 225; *see also* Paradisi
Carbonara, 178
Carrara, 275; family, 58, 59, 80–3, 88, 188, 205, 217, 218, 252, 273, 275; Genealogical Table, 83; as *podestà*, 110–11; *signoria* of, 3, 49, 100, 111, 244n, 266, 275–82; *see also* Papafava
Carrara, Agnese da, 71; Cunizza da, 276; Giacomino da, 225; Giacomo da (*d.*1240), 205, 276
Giacomo Grande da, 82, 100, 131, 134, 135n, 136; policies under commune, 263, 266–7; relations with Mussato, 273, 275; first steps towards *signoria*, 266–267; elected *dominus generalis*, 274, 275, 276, 279; *sapientes* appointed to fix salary, 100, 136; nature of his *signoria*, 3, 276–7, 279–80; policy towards guilds, 131, 245, 281; character and death, 275–7
Marsiglio di Giacomo da (*d.c.*1292), 111, 181, 231
Marsiglio Grande da, 76, 82, 100, 104, 108, 165, 174, 276n; foundations and nature of his *signoria*, 3, 5, 275–82, 310; ministers and supporters, 165, 174, 178, 278–9; revolts against the Della Scala (in 1337), 137–8
Nicolò da, 111, 266, 273, 276, 277, 278, 280, 281; Obizzo da, 169, 266; Pierconte da, 111, 224, 234, 235; Ubertino di Bonifacio da (*d.*1319), 105, 225, 260, Ubertino di Giacomino da (*d.*1345), 165, 275, 276
Carturo, 67, 107; family, 72–3, 217, 225; Ansedisio da, 73; Traversino da, 73, 131; Uberto da, 73; Ugozono da, 73
Caseta, Martino de, 165n
Castelbaldo, 241–2, 248–9
Castelli, of Treviso, family, 67, 205, 230
Castelnovo, Maltraversi da, family, 74–5, 217, 264–5; Genealogical Table, 74; Albertino da, 137, 231, 265; Beatrice da, 59, 75; Bontraverso da, 206; Nicolò da, 75–6, 110, 237
Castigliano, 226
Cattanei, 77; *see also* Lendenara, Limena
Cavalieri Gaudenti, 102
Censano, Guglielmo da, 169
Census, of city of Padua in 1320, 34–5; of Paduan territory, *see* Hearth Assessment
Centenarii, 33–4, 37
Cero, family, 72; fortress, 242
Cervarese, 74
Cessolis, Giacomo de, 158
Charlemagne, 9; legend of, 292

INDEX 339

Charles II, of Anjou, King of Naples, 69
Chioggia, 31, 45, 271, 273, 275
Chronicles, of March of Treviso, 195–6; Paduan, 5–6, 324–5
Chronicon Marchiae Tarvisinae et Lombardie, 5, 196, 204n, 304
Church, conflict with Paduan commune, 157, 239; temporal power of, attacked by Marsiglio Mainardini, 308; *see also* Bishops, Papacy
Cicero, 302
Cinto, 78
Cittadella, 30, 46, 47, 48, 98; notaries' guild, 161; *podestà*, 94, 161
City-States, ancient and mediaeval compared, 11; role of in Italian history, 6–9, 12–13
Clement V, Pope, 253–5
Clemente, S., *via* 138, 268
Clericelli, Giovanni, 177–8
Codalunga, 30
Collalto, Counts of, 67
Colle, Bonmassario da, of Vicenza 130
Colli Euganei, *see* Pedevenda
Colonga, 228, 235, 237
Comital families, of the Padovano, 70–77
Comital powers, 11, 18; in Padua, 64; to create notaries, 155
Comitatus, 19; of Bassano, 226–7
Commerce, Italian, 8, 13–17; Paduan, 37–9
Communes, Italian, political development of, 12, 17–26; rural, 17, 19
Comunanza, at Mantua, 199; Paduan, 123, 266, 274; organisation of, 93–4, 211–17; development compared with that of Union of Guilds, 245–6
Cona, 85, 168
Concadalbero, 168, 271
Concoreggio, Corrado da, 172
Conselve, 48, 143; Bellengerio da, 170
Conservatores libertatis, status et partis, 265
Consiglio Maggiore, Paduan, compared to Roman senate, 301; corresponds to *universitas civium* of Marsiglio, 210, 307; functions of, 4, 5, 46, 106, 156, 210, 212–14, 216; magnates representation in, 174; meeting place of, 42; membership, changes in, 93, 208, 220; members (in 1254), 32–3, 206, 208, 209, 300n; members, individual, 95, 103, 130, 141–2, 167, 271; powers limited, 265; resolutions and statutes passed by, 94, 157, 223, 225, 233, 239, 243, 256; seats in bequeathed by will, 59, 210n; *signori* elected by, 217, 279; voting discipline imposed, 245; uncertainty of votes in, 274
Consiglio Maggiore, Veronese, 206
Consiglio Minore, Paduan, 210, 213, 241
Constantinople, 303
Consulate, of Italian communes, 23
Consules de Placitis, 23; in Padua, 162
Consuls, of Paduan commune, 18, 71, 85, 86; Prior of, 131
Contado, 'conquest' of by Italian communes, 17, 19–20; alleged exploitation of, 52
Paduan, dependant communes in, 47, 161; economic resources, 43–4; extent of, 30–2, 43; higher jurisdiction reserved to Paduan courts, 47, 49; markets in, 46; *podestà* in, 47, 106–8; population of, 48–9; power of magnates in, 47, 68, 71–88 *passim*, 97–8, 169, 218, 264, 268, 269, 276; taxation of, 52–6
Conti, family, 70–2; Demetrio, 71; Engenolfo, 71, 228, 230; Giacomo, of Arquà, 71, 209; Manfredino, consul, 18, 71; Manfredino II, 72; Manfredo, 72, 230; Percivalle, 125, 146
Correggio, Matteo, of Parma, 234, 237
Cortelà, 74
Cortenovo, battle of, 201
Cortusi, Guglielmo, chronicle of, 5, 111, 310
Costa, 178
Courts, feudal and ecclesiastical, 123–4
Cremona, 32, 111, 203, 228: *podestà* of, 151
Crespo, Francesco de, 174

Croce, S., suburb of, 33, 44, 159
Crosna, Antonio, 99, 234, 235
Cumani, family, 76
Curano, tower of, 268
Curia Militum, bishops', 18, 91
Curia Officialium, 216
Currencies, used in Padua, 42
Curtarolo, Antonio da, 104, 264

Dacia, 54–6
Dalesmanini, family, 58, 71, 85–6, 88, 186–7, 217, 231; Genealogical Table, 186; Artusio, 231; Dalesmanino, 85–6; Dalesmano, 58; Giacomo, 86, 257; Guecillo, 219, 231, 237, 244; Traverso, 103, 258, 267, 270; Uberto, 63
Davidsohn, R., 8, 91n
Defensor Populi, under Paduan commune, 164–5, 245, 266, 301; individual office-holders, 165n
Doctors of law, canon, 146; canon and civil, 147–53
  College of, 100, 124, 145–52; matricula of, 145–6, 315–7
Dominicans, in Padua, 135, 149, 151; *see also* Inquisition
Doto, family, 64, 67, 99–100, 102; Paolo de, 99; Schinella de, 99–100, 147, 278; Zambono I and II de, 99
Dovara, Buoso da, of Cremona, 203
Dowries, examples of, 142, 143, 161, 169, 278–9; social significance of, 59–60; as reserve in case of bankruptcy, 184–5

Ecerinide, tragedy by Mussato, 6, 297–9
Empire, role of in Italian politics, 10–11; Italian intellectuals and, 201–2, 258–9; 301; insecure despots and, 255, 263
Enghelfredi, family, 115–18, 179; Genealogical Table, 117; Enghelfredo, 116–18, 208, 209; Simone, 115–18, 258
Engleschi, Guidota, 54; Rolando, 124, 222, 230
Enselmini, family, 72, 112–13; Anselmino I, 112, 207; Anselmino II, 112–13; Bartolomeo, 103, 112; Giacomo, 112
Enveradi, Gomberto and Ordano, 178

Eremitani, of Padua (Augustinian friars), 101, 190
Este, 31, 45, 46, 47, 48, 68, 76, 235–6, 249, 268, 269; castle of, 244; *podestà* of, 108, 178; Mezzoconte and Tristano d', 185
Este, *Marchesi d'* Genealogical Table, 70; origins, marriages, and social pre-eminence (in March of Treviso), 65, 68–70, 101; political role, 195–7, 199; property and jurisdiction (Padovano), 167, 235–6, 242, 268; raise loans in Padua, 185, 234–5
Aldovrandino d', 242, 249, 269
Azzo VI d' (*d*.1212), and March of Ancona, 69, 203
Azzo VII d' (*d*.1264), captures Ferrara (1240), 199, 202; leads war against Da Romano, 97, 198, 201–3, 205, 218, 268; and Paduan commune (after 1256), 233–4, 236
Azzo VIII d' (*d*.1308), marriage, 69; creates knights, 98, 101; *signore* of Ferrara (1293–1308), 242, 244, 249–51; and Paduan commune, 105, 251
Beatrice d', 69, 101; Costanza d', 69, 75–6, 235
Francesco d', and estates in Padovano, 236; marriage, 70, 258; and family disputes, 242, 249–50; invites Papal intervention in Ferrara, 253; serves commune in war with Verona, 251, 263; his murder, 254, 264
Fresco d', 249–50, 253
Giovanna d', 70
Obizzo II d' (*d*.1293), marriages, 69, 248; relations with individual Paduan magnates, 76, 110, 119, 264; elected *signore* of Ferrara, 69, 110, 234–5; relations with Paduan commune, 228, 230, 234–7, 239, 240, 241–2
Obizzo III d', 120, 250; with Renaldo, *signori* of Ferrara, 103, 104, 268–70
Renaldo d', 70, 119, 269

Felice, S., monastery of, at Vicenza, 226

INDEX 341

Feltre, 134, 186, 195; bishop of Feltre and Belluno, 169, 195, 229
Fermo, S., *centenario* of, 37, 136
Ferrara, commune of, relations with Padua, 119, 195, 228, 233, 240; Paduans resident at, 77, 97, 218; *podestà* of, 110, 111, 234; captured by Estensi (1240), 199, 202, 229; Obizzo d'Este elected *signore* of (1264), 69, 110, 234–5; knightly festival at, 101; lost to Holy See (1308), 250, 253–4, 308; recovered by Obizzo and Renaldo d'Este (1317), 268–70
Ferro, a, family, 180, 184
Fieschi, of Genoa, family, 69, 82; Cardinal Ottobuono, 234
Filarolo, Matteo, 164, 179, 253, 255
Fiumi, E., 52, 91n
Flabiano, Giacomo, 289
Florence, 8, 16, 17, 19, 22, 26, 137, 193; bankers of, 183, 196; *defensor artium et artificium* of, 109, 150, 151; economy and society compared to Paduan, 193; executor of the *ordinamenti di giustizia*, 97n, 106; knighthood at, 92, 96; legal profession at, 122, 156, 157; origin of factions at, 196; *podestà* of, 98, 118, 151
Fontaniva, 98, 223; *vavassores* da, 79
Fonte, castle of, 81
Forzatè, family, 85, 257–8; Giordano, 277
Giovanni, bishop of Padua, 85, 87, 112–13, 124, 146, 190, 239
Giovanni di Forzatè, 226, 237, 241
Marco di Giovanni, 257, 258, 267, 270, 277
Fossato, 150
France, cultural influence of, 292
Franciscans of Padua, *see* Antonio, S., Inquisition
Frederick I, Barbarossa, Emperor, 10, 72, 287
Frederick II, Emperor, 10, 201; ideas on nobility, 60; occupies Padua with Ezzelino da Romano, 1, 73, 260; Paduan attitude to, 6, 197, 202, 248, 304–5

Freising, Otto, bishop of, 60
Friuli, 200, 228, 231, 263; March of, 68; Pace da, 294

Galzignano, 45, 74, 141, 180, 264; Paltinerii, alleged lords of, 77
Gambarini, Paduano, 240
Gastaldiones, of the Paduan guilds, council of, 244–7, 248, 249, 250, 251, 265, 266
Gatari, Galeazzo, chronicle of, 310
Geneva, Aimo, bishop of, 255
Genoa, 69, 256; annals of, 285
Gesta Magnifica Domus Carrariensis, 310
Ghibellines, Paduan, 114–16, 257–9, 267, 270
Ghibellinism, 201–2, 255, 258–9, 263, 301
Giacomo, S., *centenario* of, 30, 37
Gici, Pietro, 107–8
Giotto, 34, 305
Giovanni, S., delle Navi, Porta, 31, 140; port of, 45
Giovanni, S. Evangelista, Venetian monastery, 135
Giulia, S., monastery of Brescia, 97
Giustina, S., Paduan monastery of, 31, 50, 271–2; abbots of, 146, 226, 271–6; so-called annals of, *see Chronicon Marchiae Tarvisinae et Lombardie*; revenues of, seized by Carraresi, 108, 274n, 279
Giustiniano, 179–80; Pietro di, 165n
Godego, castle of, 81
Gorizia, Counts of, 230
Gradenego, of Venice, Elizabetta di Pietro, wife of Giacomo Grande da Carrara, 82, 135
Grain policy, of Paduan commune, 46, 55–6, 247
Grisignano, agreement of, 222–3
Guarnerini, Antonio, 226; Bellebono, 99, 226; Tommaso, 143
Guelph, league, 256, 270; party in Padua and March of Treviso, *see pars Guelpha, pars Marchionis et Ecclesiae*
Guelphs and Ghibellines, lost poem by Lovato on, 295; confusion of parties (*c.*1300), 248; significance of parties in March of Treviso, 201, 202, 255
Guicemanni, Vivarotto, 169

23

Guidoto, Martino de, 164, 237
Guilds, Italian, political role of, 22, 214
Guilds, Paduan, economic aspect of, 44–5; list of those recognised by commune (in 1287), 311; political activities of, 207–8, 213–16, 233, 243–51, 266, 280–2
Guildsmen, Paduan economic and social position of, 132–41, 154–81, 183–5; political attitudes of, 207–8, 233, 259, 280–2
Guisis, Guido de, canonist at Bologna, 293n
Guizzardo, Pietro de, of Vicenza, 224

Hapsburg, Frederick of, 100, 104; his *signoria* in Padua, 3, 136, 245, 268, 271, 277, 281
Hearth-assessment of Paduan territory, 48–9
Henry, VII, of Luxemburg Emperor, 2, 6, 149, 220, 256, 258, 296, 298; Italian expedition, 5, 248, 251, 253, 255–6, 297, 301; coronation at Milan, 105–6, 255; revolt of Paduan commune against, 255, 274
Hohenstaufen, Conradin of, 224, 229; Manfred of, 203; *see also* Frederick I and Frederick II
Humanism, European, 284
Italian, origins of, 290–5, Paduan, 290–303, 305–10

Immigration, *see* Migration
Imperial Vicariate, 25, 255, 256
Industry, Italian, 17; Paduan, 38–40
Innocent III, Pope, 69, 201
Innocent IV, Pope, 201
Inquisition, in Padua, 71, 74, 135, 149, 157, 173–4, 272, 304
Iza, Da, family, 141, 180, 264

Jandun, Jean de, 308
Judges, College of, 49, 113, 126–53, 174, 183, 245
Paduan, defined, 123–6; related to guildsmen, 138–41; moneylending by, 185; from noble families, 130–1; with notarial background, 132–8; number of, 49, 127–30; offices and remuneration, 143–4
Judges of the *podestà* (*iudices potestatis*), 46, 104, 155; in Padua, 125–6, 127

Knighthood, defined, 92; bestowed by communes, 96–7; in Padua, 97–100
Knightly festivals, in March of Treviso, 101, 102, 261
Knights, as ambassadors, 105–6; numbers of, 92–3; as *podestà*, 106–20; as professional soldiers, 104–5

Lainate, Counts of, 155
Lambertazzi, family, of Bologna, 130
Lana, Arte della, Paduan, 39, 251
Lanzaroti, Fruzerino, 180
Latini, Brunetto, 60, 109
Law, Canon, 121; professors of, 146
Feudal, 123
Roman, 10, 58, 61, 121, 123, 127, 258
Law, College of Doctors of, 100, 124, 145–52; matricula of, 145–6, 315–17
Law, doctors of, 145–53, 185; professors of, 125, 147–53
Lazara, Paduano, 159
Lemici, family (*alias* Dente de Lemici), 75, 86, 88, 258, 279; faction of, 186, 244, 271–5; moneylending by, 79, 187–8, 225, 230
Guglielmo I, 86, 103, 167–8, 187, 230–2
Guglielmo II, 168, 187–8, 273, 275; Paolo, 275, 276, 281
Vitaliano, 86, 110, 168, 174, 187, 225, 227, 271, 272, 273
Lendenara, 44, 78; acquired by Paduan commune, 139, 230, 239–41, 242; lost by Paduan commune, 267, 270
Cattanei da, family, 77, 98, 200, 240; Altegrado, 78, 146, 226–7; Anna, 151; Nicolò, 130–1; Rizardo Tartaro, 78, 275, 278–9
Levada, Liberale da, chronicler of Treviso, 93, 278n
Liber Regiminum, 32, 67, 206, 237

INDEX 343

Limena, 38, 45
Cattanei da, family, 78–9; Arnaldo, 78; Giacomo, 78, 146; Gomberto, 226; Luppo, 78, 131, 147; Odorico, 79n, 146
Linen industry, in Padua, 39
Litolfo, Aicardino de, 222, 224
Livellarii, 14, 15, 51, 53
Livy, 296, 298
Lomello, Counts of, 155
Longare, 45, 256
Louis IV, of Bavaria, Emperor, 308, 309
Lovati, Lovato, as judge and politician, 97, 109, 134–6; leader of Paduan humanist group, 290–6, 299, 300, 302, 310
Lovesini, family, 72
Lozzo, castle of, 74, 264
Maltraversi da, family, 74–6, 206, 217, 225; Genealogical Table, 75
Guido I, 69, 75–6, 164, 206, 219, 228, 230, 235, 237, 241, 264; Nicolò, 76, 104–5, 110, 181, 227, 231, 241, 249, 263–4, 305; his faction, 141, 264
Lucca, *podestà* of, 151
Lucia, S., *centenario* and *via*, 37, 43, 116, 117, 159
Da, family, 89n; Tommaso da, 207

Maccaruffi, family, 70, 87–8, 118–120, 252, 265, 266, 279; Genealogical Table, 120; faction of the, 139, 268–70
Maccaruffo, 253, 268; Zilio, 88, 118–19, 215, 231, 241, 258, 268
Macchiavelli, Nicolò, 26, 224, 309
Maggiore, Via, 30, 64, 76
Magnaspissi, Aiperto, 179
Magnati, 21, 25; Paduan, 62–3, 88–89, 217, 226, 262–3; anti-magnatial legislation, 21, 61; in Padua, 63, 217, 218, 226, 238–9, 242n, 312–14; in Vicenza, 221
Mainardini, family, 163–4; Genealogical Table, 165
Marsiglio, 163, 293, 302, 306–9; his *Defensor Pacis*, 210–12, 307–9
Malatesta, of Rimini, family, 77

Maleablati, 63; see also *Magnati* and Usury
Malò, 225
Malombra, of Cremona and Padua, family, 125; Riccardo, jurist, 125
Maltraversi, family, 74–6; see also Castelnovo and Lozzo
Adelmota, 75, 103
Mandugavillano, Guglielmo, 183–4
Manfro, Pietro, 123
Mantova, Bovetino da, 293n
Mantua, 101, 195, 199, 203, 204, 234, 235; *podestà* of, 114, 118; *signoria* of the Sanbonifacio in, 199–200, 202, 204
Manzio, family, 179; Antonio Pellegrino de, 179; Pietro, 184
Margherita, S., *via*, 31, 82
Marini, family, 107
Mariota, De, family, 180
Markets, Paduan, 42, 45, 53; in Paduan territory, 46
Maroni, Marino, 165n
Marostica, Enrico da, 172
Marsiglio of Padua, see Mainardini
Martino, S., chapel of, 43; church and *via*, 43, 82, 252
Mascara, Aicardino, 143; Mascara, 289
Massarii, 175n
Matosavio, Giacomo, 138, Guerico, 123
Maurisio, Gerardo, Vicentine chronicler, 196
Medici, Paduan, 138–9, 176–7
Medicine, professors of, 175–6
Mercatores, guild of, 38; see also *Negociatores*
Mestre, 38
Mezzabbati, family, 147–8; Aldovrandino, 109, 147–8, 150, 279
Migration of population, into Italian cities, 15, 19; into Paduan territory, 44; into Padua, 33–4, 50, 53, 135, 141, 148, 163, 169, 170, 176
Milan, 16, 69, 134, 203, 237, 255, 260; number of notaries at, 162
Miles defined, 91–3
Milites potestatis, 46, 103–4
Milites pro commune, 93–6, 105, 138, 161, 214–15
Milites, rural, 51, 92
Mills, 30, 40, 53, 180–1

Mint, Paduan, 42
Mirabilia Urbis Rome, 30, 42
Mirano, 43
Modena, 101, 104, 228, 241, 249; *capitano del popolo* of, 114, 115n; *podestà* of, 98, 110, 112, 113, 114, 118, 120, 151
Mondino, Giovanni, 176
Moneychangers (*campsores*), 41-2, 183
Moneylending, by Paduans, 64, 86-7, 97, 113, 116-17, 139, 140, 169, 177, 179-90, 225, 227, 230-1, 234-5; place in Paduan economy, 40-2
Monselice, 31, 47, 48, 76-7, 135, 236, 267, 269; counts of, *see* Cumani; *podestà* of, 108
Montagnana, 31, 47, 48, 235-6; notaries of, 161; *podestà* of, 164
Montagnone, Da, family, 82, 131; Enghelerio da, 215; Geremia da, 131, 284-5, 301
Montebello, 72; counts of, 72, 74, 225; Guido da, bishop of Ferrara, 253, 254n
Montecchi, party in Verona, 200
Montecchia, 87
Montegalda, 71, 169, 225; Salamone da, 169
Montegrotto, 45, 53
Montelongo, Gregorio da, Papal legate, 202; patriarch of Aquileia, 229
Montemerlo, Marco da, 226
Montenaro, *magister*, 294
Montenovo, 53
Morando, *magister*, 294
Mota (Vicentino), 71
Murfi, Pietro, 97, 102
Murus Spaldi, 33, 55
Museragli, Guarino, 177: Liberale, 184
Muso, family, 166-7
Mussato, Albertino, family and career, 72, 95, 163, 165-8, 174, 300; as poet and historian, 5, 136, 289, 290, 293, 294, 295-303, 305-6, 307, 309, 310; political activities, 106, 252, 256, 265, 266, 271-5; social and political views, 40, 63, 245, 258-9, 260-1, 263, 301-2; Gualpertino, abbot of S. Giustina, 270, 271-4, 279

Negociatores, 38, 107, 116, 178-9, 183-4
Negri, family, 75; Guido, 231
Nicholas IV, Pope, 241
Noale, 229
Nobles, of Padua and the March of Treviso, 62-90; as judges, 130-1; as *podestà*, 109-11
Nobility, 60-2, 84-5; in Padua, 62-6, 66-90 *passim*
Nogarolo, Baiardino da, 76
Nono, Giovanni da, family background and marriage, 67, 99 views on Paduan magnates (in 1311), 65, 88-90, 269, 275; on nobility, 63-90 *passim*, 131; on notaries, 168-9; on society, as evidence of social tension, 260-1, 300; on usury, 40, 182-4, 186, 190-1
works of, *De Generatione*, 6, 57-8, 65-7, 286; *De Hedificatione*, 65; *Visio Egidii*, 29-32, 39, 42-3
Notarial Archives, 5, 8, 157
Notarial Formularies, 157
Notarial Registers, 156, 171, 172
Notariat, Italian, development of, 122, 154-5; education and cultural importance of, 157; social position of, 158
Notaries, Guild of (Padua), 49, 50, 51, 156, 158, 160, 162, 177, 299 membership of College of Judges and, mutually exclusive, 122, 132-3; numbers, 162; political importance, 246-7
Notaries of Padua, creation of, 154-5; cultural significance of, 164, 286-7, 289, 295, 303, 306; moneylending by, 184-5; numbers of, 161-3; opportunities and remuneration of, 171-5; political importance of, 164-5, 246; profession regulated by commune, 155-7; social position of, 158-61, 165-70
artisan notaries, 159-60; rural notaries, 160-1, 170
Noventa, 86, 268

Obertenghi, family, 68
Obizzini of Pisa, Obizzo degli, 281
Ognissanti, *borgo* and port, 31, 35, 45, 86, 140
Oltrebrenta, 30; *cavalcatores de*, 136

INDEX 345

Onara, 98
Oriago, 43
Orsini of Rome, family, 69
Orsola, S., convent of, 190
Orvieto, *podestà* of, 115n
Otto I, Emperor, 10
Otto IV, Emperor, 86

Padua, bishops of, 55, 234, 271; their administration, 123–4, 147, 156–7, 172; conflict with commune, 157, 239; feudal courts of, 123–4; individual vassals of, 76, 135, 150; *see also* Forzatè, Giovanni, and Torre, Pagano della
Padua cathedral, canons of, 73, 87n, 123, 125, 146, 150, 172, 226, 293n; *custos ecclesiae*, 135
Padua, *podestà* of, the office, 43, 46, 211–12, 238, 245, 248–51; individual office-holders, 96, 202, 221–2, 229, 233, 234, 236–7
Palazzo Comunale, Padua, 1, 2, 34, 43, 175, 181
Paltinerii, of Monselice, family, 77, 257, 258; Cunizza, 108; Giacomina, 258; Guglielmo Novello, 77, 257; Simone, Cardinal of S. Martino, 77
Papacy, occupation of Ferrara by (1308–17), 103, 250, 251, 253–4, 268–70; Paduan embassies to, 113, 272, 298; political role of in March of Treviso (1200–60), 197, 198, 201; power to create notaries, 154–5; temporal power of attacked by Marsiglio Mainardini, 308
Papafava, family, 58, 82, 83, 252; Genealogical Table, 84; Bonifacio, 183; Giacomino, 75, 228, 234, 235; Marsiglietto, 277; Pierconte, 75
Paradisi, family, 58; Enrico, 114; Zamboneto, 185
Paris, university of, 303, 307
Parisio, Pietro di, 133, 140
Parlamentum, 12, 23, 217, 279; of *pars* of Tiso Camposanpiero, 252
Parma, 111, 228; *podestà* of, 120
Pars, political grouping in March of Treviso, 195–9, 220–1, 262–3

Pars Eccelini, 199–205
Pars Guelpha of Padua, 265–6, 273
Pars Marchionis et Ecclesiae, 199–205, 221–4, 232–51 *passim*, 252–5, 262–82 *passim*; in Padua, 218–19, 252–3
Partinopei, Marsiglio, 105, 137, 228; Partinopeo, 278
Patavium, 29, 30, 32, 77
Pauleto, Antonio and Prosdocimo de, 159
Pedevenda, 31, 43–4, 45, 73, 78, 107, 180, 264
Pedites, 21; in Padua, 94, 95
Pelavicino, Oberto, of Cremona, 32, 128, 203, 206
Pepoli of Bologna, family, 69
Peraga, Da, family, 58, 79, 217; Balzanella, 58, 79; Filippo, 252–3; 280
Pernumia, 107, 108
Petrarch, 291, 293, 302, 310
Physicians, Paduan, 138–9, 176–7
Piacenza, 16, 111
Piazzola, Albertino Anselmi da, 176; Rolando da, 108, 252, 256, 274, 295, 300
Pietro, S., convent of, 173; *via*, 73
Piove di Sacco, 31, 39, 45, 48, alleged counts of, 85; Nicolò da, 146
Pipere (*alias* De Vitaclo), Guglielmo, 108; Matteo and Gerardo, 184
Pisa, 16, 55; *capitano del popolo* of, 113
Pistoia, 16; Cino da, 293n
Pizone, fortress of, 248–50
Plumbioli, Paolo, 159
Podestà, in Italian communes, 23–5, 105; Paduans as, 106–51; Paduan professional *podestà*, 111–51
Polafrisana, family, 265, 268; Marsiglio, 268, 269, 276
Polo, S., monastery of, 272; *via*, 168
Polverara Maggiore, convent of S. Maria da, 185
Pomposa, monastery of, 291
Pontecorvo, 31–2, 33
Pontemolino, quarter and *centenario*, 30, 37, 74, 166
Popolo, as political organisation, 20–2, 24, 91–2; competent to create knights, 96; of Padua *see Comunanza*
Popolo, as a social class, 21, 84–5

Population, of mediaeval Europe, rise in, 13–16; of Padua, 32–7; of Paduan territory, 48–9
Potentiores, see Magnati
Praglia, monastery of, 146
Prato, Da, family, 142–3; Genealogical Table, 142
Prato della Valle, 33, 126
Pre-humanists, Paduan, 290–303, 305–10; social origins of, 299–301
Privilegia, Imperial, 64–5, 68, 71, 79, 86, 260

Quarters, administrative divisions of mediaeval Padua, 33, 37; *anziani della comunanza* elected by, 212–13
Quartesolo, engagement at (1312), 263
Quirini, Marco, 202, 221, 222, 234

Raivo, Nascimbene de, 270
Ravenna, Archbishop of, 202, 209, 235
Razzi, Ottobuono de, bishop of Padua and patriarch of Aquileia, 229
Reggio (Emilia), 241, 249
Renaissance, of the twelfth century, 283–4
 Paduan humanists as forerunners of, 290–310
Rio, a, notarial family, 173, 178–9
Riveria, 107
Roads, built by Paduan commune, 38, 45
Robert of Anjou, King of Naples, 254–5, 268
Rolandino, *magister*, life and intellectual significance, 163, 173, 286–9; compared with Mussato, 297–8
 views on astrology, 304–5, 306; Paduan families and society, 59, 63, 66, 77, 93, 119; politics, 94, 196–9, 201, 209, 217, 233, 260
Romano, Da, family, 2, 65, 72, 80, 196, 199, 203, 233–4; Alberico da, 59, 200, 202, 203, 206; Beatrice da, 196; Ezzelino II da, 197
 Ezzelino III da, interest in astrology, 304–5; legend of, 6, 170, 248, 256, 259, 275, 288, 297; marriage and family, 59, 75; party of (*pars Eccelini*), 199–205; *signoria* over Padua and March of Treviso, 1, 2, 32–3, 49, 59, 73, 77, 93, 95, 197–205, 233, 254, 300; supporters and ministers in Padua, 116–17, 148, 150, 169, 205–9, 264; views of Rolandino on, 198, 207, 287–9
Rome, Padua compared with, 298, 301, 306
Roncaglia, Avezzuto da, 176
Roncajette, Matteo da, 176
Ronchi, family, 190, 266
Ronchi di Campanile, family, 64
Rossano, 98, 140; Da, family, *see* Tadi
Rossi, of Padua, family, 139; Alberto, 178; Paduano, 139
Rossi, of Parma, family, 111
Roveda, 178
Rovigo, 119, 239, 240; Paduan occupation of (1308–19); 2, 220, 250, 270n, 296; *podestà* of, 270n, 278n; *visconte* of, 77
Rovolon, 71, 73–4, 79, 140, 178, 180
Rudena, 31–2, 33
Rustega, 98

Sale, Compagnino a, 147
Saletto Scodosia, 85
Salimbene, Fra, 294
Salinguerra, 199, 202, 254
Sallust, 298
Salvemini, G., 52, 96
Sanbonifacio, *see* Bonifacio, S.
Sanguinacci, family, 177; Novello, 99
Santorso, 227
Saonara, 73
Sasso, Stefano, 146n
Sassoferrato, Bartolo da, jurist, 61–2, 64–5, 84, 96, 151
Scala, of Verona, family, 69; Alberto della, 101, 241, 242, 260
 Cangrande della, creates knights, 100, 101; ministers of, 76, 303; influence on Carrara *signoria*, 267, 277, 280; his *signoria* in Padua, 3, 37, 185, 276; his war with the Paduan commune, 3, 71, 98–9, 104, 149, 256, 262, 265, 269, 271, 274
 Mastino della, 203–4, 227–8, 237

INDEX 347

Scarabelli, notarial family, 173
Schalchi, Bernardo, 184, 185; Principe, 139
Schinella, Count, 73
Schinelli, family, 71, 73–4, 114, 206, 217, 264; Ansedisio and Bartolomeo, 73, 236; Bonaccorso, 74, 225; Giacomino, 206; Margherita, 79; Michele, 267
Schio, 227
Science, in university of Padua, 303–5
Scintilla, family, 64, 190
Scodosia, 31, 235
Scrovegni, family, 41, 66, 75, 78, 87, 88; Genealogical Table, 189
  Enrico, builds Arena chapel, 101, 190; character and knighthood, 101–2; economic activities, 38, 188–9, 225; family connections, 70, 76; political activities, 105, 252, 258
  Gaboardo, 258, 267, 279
  Gonfredo, 227; Manfredo, 87, 110, 188; Pietro, 65n, 188
  Renaldo I, 40, 87, 123, 188, 190, 231, 235, 241
  Renaldo II, 258, 278
Selvazzano, 87, 227
Seneca, studied and imitated in Padua, 291, 298, 309
Seratico, Giordano de, of Vicenza, 225
Servi, in Paduan contado, 51–2
Sheep farming in Paduan territory, 44
Siga, Boncompagno de, rhetorician, 198, 287, 288
Signoria, establishment of in Italian city states, 25–6, 214; hereditary versus elective discussed by Marsiglio, 307–8; (for particular *signorie, see* Camino, Gerardo da; Carrara; Este, Azzo VIII d'; Romano, Ezzelino III da; Scala, Cangrande della)
Smereglo, Nicolò, Vicentine chronicler, 109, 204, 221n, 222
Societas, commercial partnership, 143. 179n
Societas Mercatorum of Verona, 203
Societas Militum, 21, 91–2, 103
Societas Populi, see Popolo
Sofia, S., *centenario* of, 32, 33, 37; *magister* Pantaleone di Marchabruni da, 173

Solario, Istriano a, 133
Soldiers, professional, knighthood and, 104–5; social position of, 102–4
Solesino, 135; Egidio da, 135; Giacomina da, 135
Spina, Bonaccorso de, 179
Stefano, S., Porta di, 31

Tadi, family (*alias* Da Rossano), 140, 143, 147; Genealogical Table, 149; Giovanni and Pace, 147, 148
Tailors, of Padua, 116–8, 139, 184
Taverners, of Padua, 44, 140–1, 180, 184
Tax collectors, of Paduan commune, 175, 179n
Taxation in Padua, 52–6
Tebaldi, Tebaldo, 148
Tempo, Antonio da, 289, 290
Teolo, 107; *podestà* of, 107; Paolo da, 135–6
Terradura, 138; family, 265, 268, 279; Andrea da, 133, 139; Ailino da, 139; Galvano da, 273–4; *magister* Giovanni da, 138
Terranigra, 180
Terrarsa, Enrico da, 133
Tiepolo of Venice, Baiamonte, 252–253, 264; Giacomo, Doge, 202; Lorenzo, 202, 234
Todi, *capitano del popolo* of, 115n
Torculi, Giacomo, 97; Perenzano, 180
Torre, Della, of Milan, family, 82, 260; Gastone, patriarch of Aquileia, 229; Pagano, bishop of Padua and patriarch of Aquileia, 125, 229, 254, 274–5, 294; Raimondo, patriarch of Aquileia, 229, 242
Torreglia, 169
Torricelli, *porta* and quarter, 31, 37
Trambacche, 87, 123
Transalgardini, family, 85
Trento, 38, 105, 195; Enrico, bishop of, breaks with Della Scala and accepts Paduan as *podestà*, 105, 228
Treville, castle of, 81, 206, 273
Treviso, 31, 37, 38, 67, 94, 99, 134, commune of, political relations with Padua, 195, 229–31, 244,

348   INDEX

commune of—*contd.*
  273, 280; borrows money from Paduans, 184, 186; guild of notaries of, 162–3; peace of, between Padua and Venice (1304), 114; *podestà* of, 110, 137, 231, 265, 278n
signoria of Alberico da Romano and its aftermath, 200, 205
signoria of Da Camino family, 230–1, 248, 263
Tribano, 107; counts of, 77; Andrea da, 163, 289
Trieste, *podestà* of, 113, 115n
Trissino, of Vicenza, family, 221
Tuscans, 16, 183

Union of Paduan guilds, 220, 243–51, 266, 280–2
Universities, Italian, 145, 175, 283–4; their contribution to early Italian humanism, 292–4
University of Padua, Artists, College of, 175, 294, 297, 299–300; grammar and rhetoric, masters of, 172–3, 198, 293–4
  law, faculty of, 124, 284; doctors of canon law, 146; doctors of canon and civil law, 147–53; College of Doctors of Law, 100, 124, 145–52, 315–17; professors of law, 125, 147–53
  medicine and surgery, professors of, 175–6
  Nova Pacta with Paduan commune (1321), 100, 149, 175; science, 303–5; *stacionarii*, 172
Urbano, S., *via*, 43, 152
Usury, practised by Paduans, 40, 64, 66, 86–7, 97, 113, 116–17, 139, 140, 169, 177, 179–90, 225, 227, 230–1, 234–5; social significance of, 64, 66, 189–90, 260–2

Vaccarino, 168
Valois, Charles of, 295
Valse, Ulric de, 100, 136
Vangadizza, monastery of, 241–2, 267, 270, 272
Vavassores, *see* Fontaniva
Veglo, Giacomo de, 132
Venetians, involved in Paduan politics, 79, 202–3, 221, 234, 240, 252–3; loan to Obizzo II d'Este, 235
Venezze, castle of, 242
Venice, 9, 26, 30, 31, 99, 101
  early humanism at, 294, 303; economic relations with Padua, 38, 40, 45–6, 51; Paduans on diplomatic missions to, 114, 135, 137; Paduans moving to, 101–2, 114, 125, 258; policy towards Terraferma, 195, 202–203, 235; Salt War with Padua (1304), 98, 114, 248, 250, 272, 295; war over Ferrara, 237, 250, 253–4; recognises independence of Carrara *signoria* (1337), 138; absorbs Paduan state (1405), 3, 282
Verarii, family, 139–40
Vergerio, Pier Paolo senior, 301, 310
Vernacular, Paduan writers in, 289–90
Verona, bishop of, 203; chapter library of, 291; counts of, *see* Bonifacio, S.; early humanism at, 303; knightly festivals at, 100, 101; *podestà* of, 114, 115n, 116, 199, 207, 258; trade and wealth of, 37, 38
  pars Eccelini and Da Romano *signoria*, 1, 150, 199–201, 207, 208
  pars Marchionis et Comitis and its expulsion, 77–8, 199–200, 203–204, 255
  Della Scala *signoria*, its establishment, 203–4; intervention in Vicentino (1266), 222–3; murder of Mastino della Scala and war with Padua (1277–80), 183, 227–9, 235, 236–7; external relations (1280–1304), 241, 242, 248, 249, 260; alliance with Paduan commune (1304), 114, 134, 248; Cangrande's war with Padua, 3, 71, 98–9, 104, 149, 256, 262, 265, 269, 271, 274
Vescia, Aldrico, 123
Vicenza, bishop of, 78, 87, 140, 205, 222, 225–7
  commune of, constitution of, 209, 221; loans to, 183, 185, 186, 187, 188, 225

counts of, 72; Count Beroaldo of, 224–5; Count Guido of, 221, 222–3; Countess Ziborga, 74, 225
early humanists at, 296, 302
judges of the *podestà* of, 135, 140, 142
podestà of, office of, 105, 107, 109, 223; individual office-holders, 71, 98, 99, 110, 111, 112, 114, 115, 117, 118, 134, 139, 140, 148, 150, 207, 209, 222, 227
Paduan property in territory of, 71, 73, 187, 223, 225–7, 256, 273
pars Marchionis and *pars Imperialis* at, 78, 200, 204–5, 221–2, 226
Paduan occupation of (1266), 2, 30, 220, 222–7; revolts against Paduans (1279, 1290), 99, 224, 225, 236, 264; expulsion of Paduans (1311), and war, 3, 187, 226, 255–6, 266–7, 296
Vighizzolo, castle of, 268
Vigodarzere, 98, 273; family, 97–9; Gonberto da, 41n, Guerico da, 97–8, 218, 230, 235; Onore da, 98, 276; Simone da, 98, 112; Uberto da, 98–9
Vigonza, Da, family, 104, 268; Corrado, 268, 280; Giordano, 231
Villadelconte, Aicardino da, heirs of, 41n
Villani, Giovanni, 84–5, 92, 257
Villanova, 67
Virgilio, Giovanni de, 292, 293, 299, 303
Visconti of Milan, family, 69, 248, 282; Galeazzo, 101
Visdominus, 18, 87
Vitaliani, Palamede and Vitaliano, 185
Vito, S., di Leguzzano, 188
Vivaro, family of Vicenza, 221, 224
Volta Brusegana, 53

Witelo, Polish scientist, 303
Woollen industry, *see* Lana, Arte della

Zante, Ubertino di, 165n
Ziliolo the Chancellor, 286, 287
Zovon, 74

Towns and Villages in the Paduan Contado

	1	2	3 £
Monselice	1093	—	200 (2)
Piove di Sacco	775	28 + 12*	150 (2)
Este	642	—	100
Montagnana	410	17	70
Pernumia	310	16 + 4	40
Conselve	290	12 + 4	100
Cittadella	225		75 (2)
Tribano	224	12 + 2	40
Legnaro	222	18 + 2	30
Teolo	210	10 + 3	50
Rovolon	175	12 + 1	75
Bovolenta	175	9	—
Abano	175	9 + 3	75
Urbana	131	8 + 2	30
Cervarese	128	10 + 2	25
Polverara Maggiore	127	—	25
Corte	126	7 + 4	30
Arquà	120	7 + 4	100
Galzignano	110	7 + 1	30
Cartura	106	8 + 1	25
Solesino	105	10 + 2	30
Masera	102	10 + 1	25
Campolongo Maggiore	96	6 + 2	30
Camponogara	81	3 + 1	40
Curtarolo	77		30
Campagna	75	6 + 1	20
Carturo			40
S. Angelo di Sala	26		25

1. Hearth assessment of 1281 (*Statuti Carraresi*, ff. 241–94)
2. Assessment of supply waggons + bread waggons for communal militia, (*Stat. Com.* 1010–30, dated 1234)
3. Salary of podesta for half year (*Stat. Com.* 327.1 & 332, dated 1276)

*Estimated figure based on two quarters.